The Complete Homeowner

The COMPLETE HOMEOWNER

Robert Schwartz and Hubbard H. Cobb

THE MACMILLAN COMPANY, NEW YORK

COLLIER-MACMILLAN LIMITED, LONDON

First Printing

Library of Congress catalog card number: 65-18465

The Macmillan Company, New York

Collier-Macmillan Canada, Ltd., Toronto, Ontario

Printed in the United States of America

Contents

Introduction

Shelter is one of mankind's basic needs, but we Americans demand a great deal more than just a roof over our heads. First and foremost, we want a house of our own. We may at certain times prefer to live in apartments or in rental units, but for most families a primary goal in life is homeownership. Not only do Americans want to own their own house, but they also insist that the house contain conveniences that in other countries are almost unheard of, even in the houses of the wealthy. In short, when it comes to shelter, Americans as a whole settle only for the very best.

Homeownership can bring to a family an immeasurable amount of satisfaction and pleasure, but, like all good things in life, it can also bring up special problems—financial problems, legal problems, maintenance and repair problems, and a host of other problems requiring expert assistance.

From the experience of countless homeowners, real-estate brokers, construction experts, and lawyers, we have culled the factual information you will need before you buy a house, as well as the basic knowledge as to how to take care of your acquisition. We have assembled this information to make it easy to read and understand so the house you buy will first of all be the right one to suit both your taste and pocketbook. We have also tried to provide you with full information about construction, proper maintenance, and repairs so that you will be able to avoid many of the headaches so often associated with homeownership.

This book is divided into two separate parts. The first portion of the book concerns itself with the maintenance and repairs likely to be required in the average house. The second part deals with the financial and legal problems that arise in buying as well as in selling a house. One out of every five families move every year, and so selling your house at the best price often goes hand and glove with buying a new one.

Properly used, this book can save the average family thousands of dollars over the course of a few years or even less. Properly, of course, it should be read through from cover to cover so that you will have a thorough grounding in homeownership. Some readers will do this as a matter of course. Others will skim through it for matters immediately pertinent to specific problems and then put it aside as a reference book. If you do decide to use the latter approach, don't skim too lightly. Much of the content of this book is designed to help you avoid problems before they arise; and while it is generally possible to solve problems, it is even better if by advance knowledge you can prevent them from ever occurring. This is just as true with financial and legal matters as it is with repairs and maintenance of the house.

This book can work for you if you give it the opportunity, but as it is a working book it should be kept close at hand and not allowed to drift to the top of a library shelf, where it will no longer be easily accessible. Keep it handy, get acquainted with its contents, and refer to it often, for it can help you and your house to enjoy life together.

ROBERT SCHWARTZ
HUBBARD COBB

The Complete Homeowner

CHAPTER 1

An Outline of Home Maintenance

A favorite topic of conversation among suburban homeowners is the high cost of maintaining a house. Almost every homeowner will have his or her special and horrible example of an outlandishly high bill for what would appear to be a very minor repair.

Sometimes the gripe is against a plumber who charged $15 to run out and change a washer on a leaky faucet that took but a few minutes of his time. Or it may be the carpenter who charged $20 to replace a pane of window glass costing under a dollar. And there are countless examples where, after weeks and weeks of waiting, a workman without the slightest qualifications for the job shows up, and instead of fixing the trouble only makes matters worse.

Often the real cause of complaint is not so much the money as the time, effort, and frustration involved in getting someone to come out and do the work, regardless of price.

There is no doubt about it that hiring workers to keep your home in repair is not only expensive but also can be most irritating because efficient servicemen are hard to find. The old-fashioned handyman who could and would do everything for fifty cents an hour has faded from our scene forever. Now when something around the house gets out of order, you must call in a specialist—a plumber for plumbing, a heating man for the boiler or furnace, a carpenter for a sticky window or warped door, an electrician to change a fuse.

And these specialists cost money. The plumber who comes to fix the leaky faucet is probably also qualified to plan and install a complete plumbing system for a house or commercial plant—and he will charge you accordingly. The same holds true for the carpenter, electrician, or heating expert. When you hire such experts to come to your home to make repairs, you must pay them not only for their own time but also for their general overhead, the cost of operating the office and shop, the truck, insurance, and other factors that combine to make any modern business expensive to operate.

In short, if your are going to hire people to make repairs on your home you are going to have to pay a stiff price, always assuming that you can get them to come to do the work.

The only feasible way to cut down on home-maintenance costs is to do as much of the work yourself as possible. When you must call in a professional, make sure you get a qualified man, and get the maximum use out of him for the money you pay.

You'll be pleasantly surprised to find how many hundreds of dollars you can save each year by making your own home repairs. And by this we don't mean big jobs like installing a new boiler or replacing the roof. Most of the repairs needed around the house are small, and they don't require special skills or special tools. It's the leaky faucets, clogged drains and toilet bowls, stuck windows, loose hinges, and squeaky floors that comprise the vast majority of repair problems; and these can easily be handled by the man or woman who takes a little time to acquire the necessary information.

It is the purpose of this book to supply this type of information. The reader will find that most repair jobs can be done with a minimum number of tools. A hammer, a screwdriver, and a pair of pliers are all you'll need to handle most repairs.

Get to Know Your House

The key to keeping down house-maintenance costs is to learn as much about your house and its equipment as possible. If you have this knowledge, and if you make frequent inspections, you'll be able to avoid many headaches; and even when you can't prevent certain troubles from occurring, you can at least reduce the cost of damage or the amount you spend for repairs.

The parts of a house and the equipment in it seldom fail suddenly. There are usually warning signs; and if you know what to watch for and act the moment you see signs of danger, life will be easier and much less expensive. The smart homeowner is the one who knows his or her home inside and out, and who each month takes the few hours necessary to make inspection and note those areas where trouble seems to be brewing. But to do this with intelligence, you must first get to know your house.

If it's a new house, one of the best ways to learn about it is to ask the builder to go over it with you, carefully explaining not only the construction but the operation of all pieces of equipment. You should learn, for example, what type of paints have been used on the inside and outside, the kind of flooring and its finishes, the materials used for interior walls, the location of the septic tank (assuming there is no street-sewer main). You should obtain from the builder a complete set of blueprints for your house; these will be useful not only when major repairs must be made, but also later on should you get involved in remodeling or expansion.

Most new homes today are sold with a good deal of automatic equipment. You should get from the builder the manufacturers' operating and maintenance literature for all these machines, along with any guarantees or warranties provided by the maker. It is also a good idea to get the names of the firms that sold and installed such large elements in the house as the heating system, the plumbing system, and the kitchen appliances. These firms are familiar with the house, as well as the type of equipment in it, and they may be the logical people to call when and if trouble occurs or if you need information on maintenance or operating instructions.

In the case of an older house, detailed information about it may not be quite so easy to come by. Often the previous owner from whom the house has been purchased can supply a good deal of this, but sometimes he will be hesitant to point out spots where trouble may occur or where it may exist at that very moment. He may fear to lose the sale or, at least, if the papers have been signed, prefer to avoid any possible unpleasantness with you. But he can certainly give you the names of the servicemen who have been taking care of the equipment, and this is most helpful.

Many people buying an older house have found it worth the cost to have specialists in certain fields, such as heating, plumbing, etc., come in and explain the operation of various equipment. Once you have had the heating system explained in detail, it will be much easier for you to keep it in good condition; and you may also be able to make small repairs and adjustments that would otherwise call for an expensive professional visit. While the serviceman is explaining the equipment, he can also give it a complete inspection.

Preventive Maintenance

Once you've learned a good deal about your house, it will be possible for you to practice *preventive maintenance*. This is nothing more than the old theory of a "stitch in time," getting there before trouble occurs or at least holding the damage to a minimum. A good example is the case of the V-belt on the blower of a warm-air furnace. Over a period of years these belts will start to wear and will eventually fail. If you spot a belt that shows wear, it's a simple matter to pick up a new one from a hardware or heating supply store; and it requires only a few minutes to take off the old one and install the new. But if the furnace is ignored, the belt will finally fail—and you may be sure it will pick the coldest night of the year to do so. Probably you'll have a good deal of trouble getting someone to come at once to fix the belt, and until they arrive you'll have a cold house and maybe even some frozen water pipes. What's more, you may have to pay the serviceman overtime for an emergency call.

Many homeowners pay out large sums of money just because they neglect to inspect a certain part of the house at frequent intervals. We know of one family that had to replace almost all the ceilings of the downstairs rooms because of a small leak in the roof. As no one ever bothered to go into the attic crawl space, water coming through a leak in the roof saturated the attic floor insulation. In time, the water seeped into the ceiling plaster; and the damage was so extensive that the plaster, along with the wet insulation, had to be removed and new materials installed. The cost of fixing the small roof leak would have been around $15. The cost of new insulation and re-plastering came to several hundreds of dollars, plus a great deal of mess and annoyance. Few things around a house will fail, like the one-horse shay, all at once. Usually there are warning signals such as strange noises, signs of wear, or imperfect operation. The minute the heating system starts to make peculiar sounds, the minute you see bare wood showing through the exterior paint on the house walls, or an electric appliance doesn't operate as it did in the past, you have been given a warning that you should immediately take action.

Here is a brief checklist of some items and areas about the house that you should cover on your inspection tours.

1. Heating system
2. Hot-water heater
3. Automatic kitchen appliances
4. Plumbing fixture drains
5. Septic tanks (have these inspected by an expert once a year)
6. Exterior paint on outside walls
7. All woodwork 18" or less from the ground or in contact with masonry

8. Roofs (twice a year)
9. Gutters and downspouts
10. Chimney and flues
11. Attic or attic crawl space
12. Crawl space under floors
13. Electric motors
14. Windows and doors
15. Shutters
16. TV antennas
17. Storm windows and screens

How to Find a Competent Serviceman

While the informed homeowner can make a majority of home repairs himself, sooner or later the time will come when he must call in professional help. The trick here is to get the best for the least money and to get the expert when he is needed and not many months after the emergency.

What types of servicemen do you require? First of all, you should have a man who can handle the heating system and central air conditioner (if you have such a unit). Both of these pieces of equipment are complex, and major adjustments and repairs call for a skilled person. What's more, a replacement part for this equipment is usually only available through specialized outlets.

You'll also need a good plumber, not for small fix-it-yourself jobs, but for major problems that may involve installation of new equipment or extensive repairs on the existing system.

Modern automatic appliances, such as washing machines, dryers, and dishwashers, are most complex; and unless you have a complete maintenance manual for your particular model and have access to spare parts, it is doubtful that there is very much you can do yourself on major repairs and overhauls. As a matter of fact, in view of our dependence on appliances, a first-class appliance serviceman may be the most important single expert needed by the homeowner.

You should at least have the names of competent painters, carpenters, and electricians; but these are seldom required on an emergency basis, so there is usually time to shop around when one is needed.

A good way to learn the names of competent servicemen is to ask friends and neighbors to recommend the people they use. Real-estate agents can also offer valuable suggestions, for over the years they have become familiar with most local experts. Once you have a list of those who appear competent, it's worth the time and effort to have them come over and check your house. This gives them the chance to become familiar with your house and its equipment, and also establishes a relationship between you and the men you may have to call on at any moment.

Servicemen are more likely to respond to an emergency call from an old customer than from a complete stranger, so become an "old customer" just as fast as you can, even if it costs a little money. It has been our experience that in most cases wives are better than husbands at developing loyalty on the part of servicemen. A plumber is more apt to answer the tearful wail for help from the lady of the house than the gruff command of her husband. And if the lady of the house can establish contact with the wife of the serviceman, it's almost like money in the bank. A serviceman may be able to turn a deaf ear to a plea for help over the telephone, but it's hard if not impossible for him to resist when his wife takes your side and insists that he pull himself away from the TV set on a Saturday night and go over and "fix that sweet Mrs. Jones's oil burner!"

Besides competent servicemen, every homeowner needs a good local hardware store, lumber yard, and paint store. If these outfits are staffed by qualified persons, they can be a storehouse of information as well as materials.

Saving Money on Service Calls

The largest part of any service bill usually is for labor, so the way to reduce these bills to a minimum is to get the most for the time that you must pay for. And in most cases, the greatest part of time involved is for travel to and from your house. You can therefore save a good deal of money by taking items that need professional attention to the service shop rather than making the serviceman come to your house. This isn't practical with large appliances; but for any portable piece, it's practical and very worthwhile. When it's necessary to have a serviceman call, have him do as many jobs as possible while there. This is where it's important to know your house and the equipment. When you call a plumber to fix a leaky pipe, it will cost little more if at the same time he also checks and even repairs several other items.

You will also save money on service calls if you avoid having to make emergency demands evenings, weekends, and holidays. Most servicemen today get overtime for work after certain hours and on certain days; and if you must have them at these times, you can expect your bill to be a good deal larger than it would otherwise be.

It is also possible to reduce the cost of such calls, when they must be made, by having certain facts at hand when you pick up the telephone. For example, if your heater stops delivering heat and you can tell the serviceman just this and nothing more, he doesn't have much to go on; but if you explain that you have checked the setting of the thermostat, the fuses, and the water level in the boiler, and all appears to be in order, at least he has something to work on and can bring the right tools and perhaps the parts he assumes will be needed to make the necessary repairs.

This approach is even more important when it comes to appliances such as dishwashers, clothes washers and dryers, air conditioners, etc. Try to determine, as far as possible, before you phone, what is wrong; and write down as much information as you can: the name of the appliance, the model and serial number, and other such pertinent details. You'll save time and money if, instead of just saying, "My dishwasher doesn't work," you say, "I have such-and-such brand dishwater, model number so-and-so, serial number so-and-so. It was last serviced by you people six months ago. When I turn on the switch, nothing happens. I've checked to make sure that the door is secure, and also checked the fuse, which has not blown. It's a built-in unit and is permanently wired to a special circuit. I used it yesterday and it was working perfectly." Give your serviceman such information, and he may even be able to tell you over the phone what is wrong and how you can fix it yourself. Even if he can't, he'll have sufficient information to make his call fast and efficient.

How to Avoid Being Cheated

Our experience has been that most servicemen involved in the home repair business are honest. Some are incompetent, and often the homeowner must pay for this. Some servicemen are expensive, but this is usually a case of charging what the traffic will bear rather than dishonesty. It is true that there are many cases on record in which homeowners have been bilked on home repairs and improvements, but these usually involve the out-of-town "suede-shoe boys," as they are called, rather than men from local establishments. The home-improvement industry has been plagued over the years by various rackets. And these racketeers stay in business only because too many homeowners are either gullible or expect to get something for nothing or for a fraction of its real value.

We'll mention a few of these typical swindles. One of the most successful, from the confidence man's viewpoint, has been the furnace-cleaning racket. This has been going on for years, and begins with a house call by a representative of the "firm" who offers to have his outfit clean and adjust the furnace at a very nominal charge. By the time these boys are through, they may have sold the homeowner a new furnace, in spite of the fact it wasn't needed and at a price far above what a local concern would charge.

Termite exterminating sold by door-to-door salesmen is another hazard to the gullible. One even more popular involves the "Model House Promotion," in which a representative of some unknown firm talks a homeowner into having a new roof or siding installed. The homeowner is to get a rebate on every job done on other homes through the block, since his home is being used as a "model." But there are no rebates and the homeowner ends up with a new roof or siding he didn't need, which isn't any good, and which costs far more than one of quality materials would have cost.

Even in these days, when men can calculate how to get us to the Moon, every Spring trucks slowly pass through the quiet suburban and country roads, selling what looks like luscious, rich topsoil. The home gardener, contemplating the damage winter has wrought on his beds, buys a few loads. By the time thousands of noxious weeds spring up and the "topsoil" proves to be worse than useless, the truck and trucker are hundreds of miles away, happily spending the victim's money.

The best way to protect yourself from these "home-improvement" sharks is first of all to remember that no one gets something for nothing, and to beware of strangers with glowing, startling innovations to sell. Trade with local firms that have a reputation to maintain, who are known by the neighborhood banks and real-estate agents. If in doubt, check with your local Better Business Bureau or Chamber of Commerce. These agencies regularly publish warnings in the local newspaper as to this type of swindler in the vicinity, and the reports make interesting reading.

Many homeowners consider they have been cheated, when the real trouble has been lack of a clear understanding in writing between themselves and the service people involved. When extensive repairs and improvements are to be made on the house, it is important that the matter be handled in a businesslike fashion. First you should obtain bids on the work from several contractors. Here, advance planning can work to your advantage. At certain times of the year, some contractors will be rushed, and at other periods business will be slow in their line. If you insist on fast action, or need your work done at the height of the busy season, you'll have trouble getting competitive bids—and those you do get will be on the high side. But if you wait until the slack time of year, you'll not only get plenty of bids but they will be low, simply because the contractor wants to keep his men busy and his overhead paid even if it doesn't mean a large profit to him. House painters, for instance, are usually rushed in the spring and summer but may be readily available in the autumn —an ideal time for outside painting. On the other hand, heating contractors will be on the run in late summer and fall but have an idle period in early spring. When possible, plan your projects far enough ahead to take advantage of these factors.

Once you have selected your contractor, get him to give you a written contract covering exactly what is to be done and what the total cost will be. Do not rely on verbal agreements, for these almost always cause trouble sooner or later. By the same token, once the work gets started, don't ask for changes unless these too are put in writing along with the added cost.

Many homeowners have found that a most satisfactory way to save money on extensive home repairs and improvements is to do the unskilled labor themselves and leave the skilled work to the professional. For instance, if the exterior of the house is to be painted by a contractor, the homeowner does the work of getting the surface prepared for the paint. This involves caulking, puttying, sanding, scraping, and removing dirt. When the painters arrive they can at once start applying the paint and are not forced to take the time to prepare the surface. This is only one instance of how to save money on a major job of repair. If your living rooms are to be wallpapered or painted, take the trouble and time to remove the old wallpaper. This not only saves money; it gives you a pleasant feeling of participation.

CHAPTER 2

Basic House Construction

You really can't expect to keep a house in first-class condition, or to even talk intelligently about it to a workman, unless you have some idea of how it is put together. It is also helpful to know the correct names of the various parts of the structure and their functions. Fortunately, despite the fact that houses come in all shapes and sizes, there are many similarities in construction and terminology. See Figure 1.

Foundations. Every house has a foundation. This usually consists of a footing, which is a large mass of concrete poured into a trench, on which the foundation wall rests. Foundation walls are made of poured concrete or masonry block. In some very old homes, the foundations may be of stone or brick. If the house has a basement, the foundation wall also serves as the basement walls. For a house with a basement, poured concrete foundation walls are best because they are more apt to be watertight than masonry block. Many homes being built today don't have basements. They either have crawl space or a slab floor. In this kind of construction, the foundation walls are low and masonry block is quite adequate. Basement floors are made of poured concrete, usually 4″ thick. If there is crawl space rather than a basement, the ground under the floor may be covered with concrete, but more likely it will be covered with building paper or polyethylene film. This covering prevents ground moisture from reaching the house.

Sills. The house structure is secured to the top of the foundation walls by wood sills. These are usually 2″ x 4″ or 2″ x 6″ stock, bolted to the masonry. In quality construction there will be a strip of copper between the sills and the foundation wall. This is a *termite shield;* it helps to prevent termites reaching the woodwork.

Floor Joists. Houses with basements or crawl space will have floor joists. These are the beams that support the flooring. They are made of 2″-thick lumber and run up to 10 inches in depth. They are

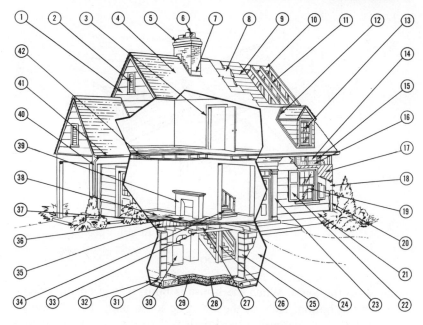

ESSENTIAL PARTS OF A HOUSE

1. Gable end
2. Louver
3. Interior trim
4. Shingles
5. Chimney cap
6. Flue linings
7. Flashing
8. Roofing felt
9. Roof sheathing
10. Ridge board
11. Rafters
12. Roof valley
13. Dormer window
14. Interior wall finish
15. Studs

16. Insulation
17. Diagonal sheathing
18. Sheathing paper
19. Window frame and sash
20. Corner board
21. Siding
22. Shutters
23. Exterior trim
24. Waterproofing
25. Foundation wall
26. Column
27. Joists
28. Basement floor
29. Gravel fill

30. Heating plant
31. Footing
32. Drain tile
33. Girder
34. Stairway
35. Subfloor
36. Hearth
37. Building paper
38. Finish floor
39. Fireplace
40. Downspout
41. Gutter
42. Bridging

usually spaced every 16 inches on center and are supported at the ends by the foundation walls. As a rule, they are given additional support at midpoint, by means of a girder of wood or steel. The girder, in turn, may be given support by posts of wood or metal that rest on the basement floor. You will often find a cross-bracing of wood or metal between the joists. This is called *bridging*, it provides added

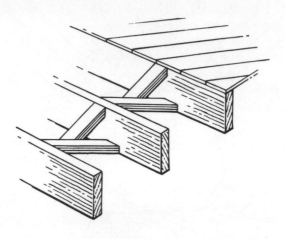

BRIDGING

strength to the joists. When the house is built, it is often the practice to leave the bottom ends of the bridging loose until the flooring has been installed. Sometimes a workman will forget to nail these loose ends into place; and if this is the case, the homeowner should call the builder and have him come back to finish the job.

In some modern construction, you'll find floors framed with very heavy timbers spaced several feet apart. In this type of construction, there are no joists as such, because the timbers plus the subflooring have been designed to carry the necessary load.

Subfloors. This is rough flooring that is nailed directly to the floor joists. Over it may go the finishing flooring, wall to wall carpeting, tile, or a resilient flooring material such as linoleum, vinyl or rubber tile. Subflooring in older homes is made out of tongue-and-groove lumber. In modern construction it is made of plywood. Sometimes subflooring is improperly nailed, and this is a common cause of a squeaking floor.

Concrete Slab. Many houses built in the past fifteen years have slab construction. A concrete slab several inches in thickness is poured over a gravel or shale base. The slab serves as the floor. You will find no crawl space, no joists, girders, posts, or subflooring. There will be a foundation wall, however; and on top of this a wood sill. Except in very warm climates, the edges of the concrete slab must be insulated, or else there will be a lot of heat loss through the edges of the slab. This heat loss can become excessive if heating coils are buried in the concrete slab.

Studding. Most homes built today have a wood-frame construction. With this method, the walls are framed with 2″ x 4″ lumber spaced 16″ or 24″ on center. These pieces are called *studs*. Studding is set in a vertical position and secured at the bottom to the sill and at the top to a plate.

Sheathing. After the studding is in place, it is covered on the outside with sheathing. This may be boards, plywood, insulating board, gypsum board, or one of the other composition materials designed for this purpose. Sheathing helps to stiffen the structure, and also makes the walls tight against water and wind. Many types of sheathing supply a high degree of insulation. Sheathing also serves as a nailing base for many kinds of siding, which is the covering that goes on over the sheathing.

Siding. The final layer on the outside wall is the siding. Its function is to provide a weatherproof covering and to present a pleasing appearance. Siding can be of wood in the form of shingles, clapboards, plywood, or board and batten. Aluminum, asbestos, and hardboard

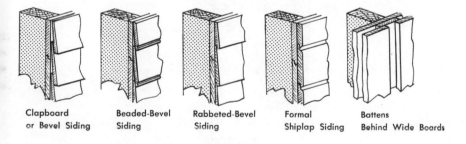

| Clapboard or Bevel Siding | Beaded-Bevel Siding | Rabbeted-Bevel Siding | Formal Shiplap Siding | Battens Behind Wide Boards |

SIDING

are also used as siding. Metal lath is often applied over the sheathing and then covered with cement plaster. This produces stucco siding. Other kinds of masonry siding are stone and brick veneer. When a veneer is to be used as siding, the foundation walls are extended so that they can carry some of the weight of the veneer. After the sheathing is in place, metal clips are nailed to the studding and then a single layer of brick or thin stone is laid up and tied to the house structure by metal clips. A space of about one inch is left between the inside face of the veneer and the sheathing. Because of the high labor costs involved, few homes today are made with solid brick or stone walls. Veneer is just as attractive and just as durable—and costs a good deal less.

Solid Masonry Walls.   In the warmer areas, outside walls of a house are usually made with masonry block. In this kind of construction, there is no studding or sheathing. The masonry wall provides all the necessary support as well as protection from the weather. The masonry block may be coated on the outside with cement plaster to enhance the appearance and improve durability.

Furring.   Furring consists of strips of wood, usually 2″ x 2″, or 1″ x 3″, that are fastened to the inside of a solid masonry wall to provide a nailing base for the interior wall material. Furring also

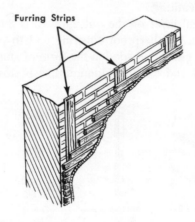

Furring Strips

FURRING

keeps the interior wall material from coming into direct contact with the masonry wall. This is important because, should there be a slight leak in the masonry wall or a tendency toward dampness at certain times, the interior wall material would be damaged if it were in direct contact with the masonry. In cold climates, furring is essential, because if the interior wall material is in contact with the cold masonry wall, it will become cold; and this means that moisture from condensation will appear on the surface. When a basement is turned into a finished room, furring should always be installed over the walls before the finish wall material goes up.

Roof Framework. The pieces of lumber used to frame the roof are called *rafters*. These are usually spaced 16 inches on center; they can be 2" x 6" or larger. Often two opposing rafters will be connected with a piece of wood called a *collar beam*. This helps tie the roof rafters together for added strength. Collar beams also serve as a framework for the ceiling in houses with attics. Today, more and more houses are being built with roof trusses rather than rafters. These trusses are made out of rather lightweight lumber and they are assembled in a factory or at the site and then hoisted into place.

Roof Sheathing. This is the plywood, boards, or insulating boards that are applied over the roof framework. They provide strength as well as a nailing base for the roofing material. In most cases they form a solid deck, but in warm humid climates and when wood shingles are to be used as roofing, the sheathing boards are spaced several inches apart to provide good circulation of air to the underside of the shingles. In some contemporary houses where the roof is almost flat, thick composition insulating-board sheathing is used. This not only provides a base for the composition roof covering, but also insulation and even a finish ceiling for the room below.

Roofing. Many materials are used as roofing over sheathing, the commonest being wood, asbestos, and asphalt shingles. In recent years aluminum has come into use as roofing, and there are older homes with slate or tile roofs. When a roof is quite flat, the only suitable type of roofing is the built-up variety. This consists of several layers of building paper applied with a special compound and then covered with gravel or marble chips.

Windows and Doors. When the outside walls of the house are being framed, openings for the windows and outside doors are framed with 2" x 4" stock. If the opening is very wide, the top of the opening is framed with 2" x 6" or even larger stock. The top of the opening is called the *header,* and the bottom the *sill.* Studding at all points is double to provide adequate support. After the outside sheathing is in place, the frames for windows and doors are set into these openings and secured.

Flashing. This is a sheet of metal used to produce a watertight joint. Flashing is made of copper, aluminum, or galvanized iron. Galvanized iron is the least desirable, because after a time it requires painting to prevent rust and the possibility of leaks. Flashing is usually applied over the tops of window and outside door frames to provide a tight joint, and it is also used about the roof to seal the joint between the roof and the chimney or where two roof angles join. These are called *valleys*.

Interior Partitions. There are two types of interior partitions: load bearing and nonload bearing. Load-bearing interior walls or partitions not only divide the space into rooms but also support the floor above. They usually run at right angles to the ceiling joists above them. Nonload-bearing walls do not provide any support as such to the ceiling above them. They are used only to divide space into rooms, and therefore can be removed without much difficulty. Load-bearing walls cannot be removed unless some means, such as a girder, is provided to furnish the necessary support. Interior partitions are usually made of 2" x 4" studding spaced 16" on center.

Insulation. After the house is weathertight, insulation is applied between the outside wall studs and between the roof rafters or the ceiling joists of the attic floor. The purpose of insulation is to reduce heat loss during the cold weather and heat gain during hot weather. The same kind of insulation used to reduce heat loss and heat gain also helps to reduce sound transfer between walls, and therefore in quality construction it is often applied to interior partitions, especially bathroom walls.

Interior Wall Materials. Interior wall materials are applied to the wall framework after all wiring, plumbing, and other work has been completed. The two most common kinds of wall coverings are plaster and gypsum wallboard, but interior walls are also made of wood, plywood, hardboard, and asbestos board.

Interior Trim. Trim, usually of wood, is used around doors, windows, and other openings. The baseboard or base molding is the trim used to cover the joints where the walls join the floors.

CHAPTER 3

Tools and Materials

Tools

You need some tools to keep a house in good repair. The actual number will depend, of course, on how many different kinds of repairs and improvement jobs you plan to undertake. Those who live in apartments or wish to do only a minimum number of repairs can often get along quite well, as has been said earlier, with a hammer, a screwdriver, and a pair of pliers. If you plan to do a wide variety of jobs, you will need a rather extensive set of tools, but if you buy only the tools that you really need they will soon pay for themselves.

The best way to build up a useful tool kit is to start off with a few basic tools and add to them as the need arises. This is a far safer approach than going out and buying a complete set. Occasionally, jobs come up that require rather expensive or specialized tools. It is usually better in these instances to rent the tool for a day or two than to buy something expensive that you may use only once or twice. Basements and home workshops are full of such tools, used once and now collecting dust and rust. Good hardware stores will rent almost every kind of tool for a small charge per day. In larger communities, there are tool-rental services under this heading in the classified telephone directory; through such dealers you can get almost every conceivable kind of tool.

While it is an extravagance to buy tools that you are not going to have much use for, it is also equally extravagant to buy cheap tools. In the first place, the difference in price between good tools and poor ones is not very great. More important is the fact that cheap tools, especially those with cutting edges such as saws, planes, and chisels, just don't do the job. So buy the best tools you can afford— but buy only the ones that you will really get a lot of use from.

Here are some of the tools that we have found most useful for the more common repair and improvement jobs. The prices given are average for good quality.

Hammers.   This is one tool you can't get along without. The best type for general work is the claw hammer. Hammer heads come in different weights, and handles come in different lengths. Select the one that feels right for you. The ease of hammering depends on the weight of the hammer head rather than the muscle power in the arm delivering the force to drive a nail. If the head is too light, it will mean a lot of effort to drive the nail; if the head is too heavy, hammering for any length of time will become tiring. There are two kinds of hammer head faces, or striking surfaces: smooth or bell. The bell face is better because it can drive a nail into the wood so that the head will be set flush with the wood surface without denting the wood, but it's harder to use than the smooth face job. They cost around $3.50.

Using the Hammer.   Keep the face of the hammer clean. If it's dirty it will slip off the head of the nail. When pulling a nail with the hammer, put a piece of scrap wood between the wood surface and the hammer head. This will increase the leverage and also help to prevent the head from denting the wood. On finish woodwork, stop hammering when the nail is about ¼ inch above the wood surface; and finish off with a nail set. This will keep a slip of the hammer from denting the wood. If a nail starts to bend, pull it out and start with a fresh one. Don't use a hammer to drive metal tools, such as cold chisels, for this will damage the hammer face. Don't use the claws on very heavy work, for they may break. Should the hammer head become loose, get some metal wedges from your hardware store and drive them into the top of the handle. Don't use a claw hammer to drive wood-handled chisels. The correct tool to use here is a wooden mallet.

Nail Set.   This little steel tool is used to set the heads of nails below the wood surface or to drive the nail the last fraction of an inch. They cost around 25¢. We've found it worthwhile to have several about, for they have a habit of becoming misplaced. To use

NAIL SET

them, simply set the point on the head of the nail and top the opposite end with the hammer.

Screwdriver. You'll need several screwdrivers, even in a basic tool kit, because screws come in a wide range of sizes; and unless you have a screwdriver that is more or less sized to the screw, you'll be in trouble. Screwdrivers are not expensive; you can get very fine ones for under a dollar. A good basic set will consists of a 4″, 6″, 8″, and 10″ length blade.

The size of the slot on the head of the screw determines what size screwdriver should be used. The idea is that the end of the screwdriver blade should fit snugly into the slot. If the end is too thick you won't even be able to turn the screw, and if it's too thin it will slip out and damage the head of the screw or the adjoining work. It's quite easy to install and remove wood screws if you have the right size screwdriver; trying to do the job with the wrong size is something else again.

By the way, don't use screwdrivers for anything but turning screws and bolts. If you use one as a pry bar or chisel it will soon be useless.

Some screws have a cross slot on the head rather than a single slot found on the common screw. These cross-slot jobs are called Phillips head screws and require a special Phillips screwdriver. You'll frequently find Phillips head screws on appliances and cars.

One kind of common screwdriver that we have found very handy is the screw-holding type. This has a little metal clip on the side that holds the screw in place. It is especially useful when you have to install a screw in a hard-to-reach spot.

If you plan to do a lot of woodwork that will require the installation of many screws, you might consider the purchase of a ratchet screwdriver. These sell for around $6.50 and have interchangeable blades. They operate on the push-pull method and are easy and fast. If you have a ¼″ electric drill you can get a screwdriver attachment that allows the drill to drive or remove screws.

Saws. If you plan to do any work involving cutting wood, you'll need two saws: a ripsaw for cutting *with* the grain of the wood and a crosscut for cutting *across* the grain. Get a ripsaw with 5 or 6 teeth to the inch and a crosscut with 8 to 10 teeth per inch. A good quality saw will run around $5. If you don't feel you can afford two saws, get the crosscut because it can be used for ripping in a pinch. If you want only a minimum tool kit you may be able to get along with a compass or keyhole saw rather than the rip and crosscut. These saws

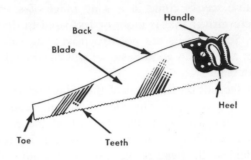

HANDSAW

are designed to cut curves. They cost around $1.25 each. Combination compass saws come with interchangeable blades, which makes them very handy; these cost around $3.

Coping saws, often called *jig saws,* are used to make fine cuts in thin materials. They sell for around 75¢. Back and miter saws are fine-toothed saws, with up to 16 teeth to the inch. These saws are used to make very accurate cuts and are excellent for trim, molding, and cabinetwork. They cost about $3.50. It is best to use them with a miter box, which costs from $1.50 to $35 or more.

Hacksaws are used for cutting metal and they are handy tools to have around the house. They cost around $2.25, but you can get a keyhole hacksaw for 75¢ that is fine for small jobs such as cutting metal curtain rod.

Planes.   Planes are used for smoothing wood and also to remove excess wood. There are a vast number of types and sizes of planes, but for most work around the house the 14″ jack plane and a block plane will be quite adequate. A jack plane will cost around $7.50, and a good block plane will run around $4. If you can afford only one, get the block plane.

Wood-Boring Tools.   You will have to have some tool designed for making holes in wood. The simplest and least expensive is the awl, which is simply a piece of steel with a point at one end and a handle at the other. This is quite adequate for making holes in softwood for screws. It costs $1 or less. Automatic push drills cost around $4 and the handle contains several size bits which can be slipped into the chuck of the drill as required. Most of these drills take bits up to 11/64″ in diameter, and they will make a hole about one inch deep. These drills are good for most work about the house except on masonry and metal. If you need to drill holes in masonry and metal as well as wood, then the hand drill is a good bet. This costs around $3 and will take bits up to ¼ ″ in diameter. When holes larger than ¼ ″ are required, use a brace and bit. This is the standard carpentry tool for large holes. It is a very useful item to have in the tool kit. The brace costs around $6.25 and a set of bits will come to around $5.50.

Chisels. These are used to shape wood or to remove excess wood when it is not possible to do the job with a saw or a plane. A good one for the home workshop is the socket chisel with a "firmer" blade. Chisels cost around $1 apiece. We have found that a ¾ ″ blade chisel is good for most general repair work about the house.

Cold Chisels. Wood chisels should be used only on woodwork. When it's necessary to cut masonry or metal, use a cold chisel. One with a ½ ″ blade will cost less than 50¢, and it is good for general work.

Files and Rasps. These are used for shaping wood and metal. Files have rather small teeth and are designed primarily for metal; rasps have coarse teeth and are used on wood. A shoe rasp with four different cutting surfaces is handy for woodworking and costs around $1. A small triangular file is handy for nicking metal before cutting it with a hacksaw; it sells for about 40¢. A relatively new tool—a sort of combination of a plane and rasp—called "Surform" is a very handy item to have; it can be used in place of a plane or rasp.

Measuring Tools. Every home should have a good measuring tape. An excellent one for general work is the flexible steel tape in a case with a rewind mechanism. These cost around $1.50 for a 72″ long tape. A good basic measuring tool for anyone doing woodworking is the combination square which consists of a 12″ metal rule, plus a small level and a device for marking 90° and 45° angles. These cost about $1.50. If you plan to do any sort of heavy construction, inside or outside, then you'll need a level; one of these will cost around $2.

Miscellaneous Tools. Every home repair tool kit should contain a pair of pliers, a good all-purpose type is the combination slip joint, which sells for around $1. You may also need an adjustable wrench; or you can get the combination pliers and wrench. A putty knife is an essential tool, and it only costs about 75¢.

Power Tools. Whether or not to purchase power tools, and which kind and how many to purchase, depends pretty much on the state of one's bank account and how much shopwork one plans to do. Any job that can be done with power tools can also be done with hand tools, but doing the work by hand usually requires more skill and a good deal more time and effort. The homeowner who plans to do a considerable amount of woodworking and home improvements will often find that the investment of several hundred dollars in power tools is worth every penny; but in many cases, power tools are purchased that have limited use and are a waste of money. We suggest that before you buy a particular power tool you rent one for a week or a month and see just how much use you will get out of it. If, at the end of that time, the tool has proved really useful and functional, chances are that it will be a worthwhile investment.

Electric Drills. One of the least expensive and probably the most useful of all power tools is the ¼ " electric drill. The drill itself costs around $15; a complete kit, consisting of the drill and a wide assortment of attachments, can be had for around $35. These drills can be used for drilling in wood, masonry, and metal, as well as for sanding and polishing if provided with the proper attachments. They can be used for installing screws, and can be equipped with a saw attachment for cutting light stock. In the past year or so, cordless drills have become available (at a somewhat higher price than the ordinary drill). These cordless units have a rechargeable power cell; they are very handy when there is work to be done where there is no handy source of electric power.

Power Sanders. While the ¼ " drill can be used for sanding, when large amounts are involved you'll do better with a tool designed especially for this work. Power sanders start in price at around $15.

Table Saws. These are primarily designed for woodworking jobs such as building furniture, etc. They cost around $75 and up for the table, motor, and 8" saw. Some of them are designed to do a large variety of woodworking jobs. For someone who plans to take up woodworking as a hobby, these combination power tools are excellent.

Materials

It is going to require materials, as well as tools and effort, to keep a house in good repair and to make required improvements. The most basic building material, of course, is lumber; but such products as plywood and hardboard can often be used as a substitute for lumber, and they may cost less and even do a better job. Before attempting any extensive repair or improvement project, you should carefully consider which of the several materials that could be used on the job will produce the best results for the least amount of effort and money. You might also consider which material requires the least amount of skill to use. It seems that almost every week some new building product comes on the market; and while many of these are excellent, some just don't pan out. This is another reason why it's so necessary to have a good lumber yard and hardware store on your side. They can advise you which material will do the job and which will not; and if they are progressive, they will be able to keep you posted on new products that are superior to the old.

Lumber. Wood used for lumber is divided into two groups: hardwood and softwood. Hardwoods come from deciduous trees; softwoods come from evergreens. Hardwoods are used primarily for furniture and flooring; softwoods are used for framing and the vast majority of other work around the house. Most lumber yards don't carry too much hardwood except flooring. Hardwoods, as a rule, are more expensive than softwoods, and more difficult to work with.

Most lumber used about the house will be either boards or dimension lumber. A board is any piece of wood less than 2″ thick, and dimension lumber is 2″ thick or over. Boards are used for light construction, such as cabinets, bookshelves, etc. Dimension lumber is used for framing walls, roofs, and ceilings.

It has come as a rude shock to many homeowners to learn that boards and dimension lumber are given their size when they are rough-sawed. After grading for size, they are put through a planer; and this gives them a smooth surface, but it also cuts down their size by a fraction of an inch. This means that a piece of lumber with a nominal size of 2″ x 4″ will actually only measure 1⅝″ x 3⅝″. This is a very important point when planning a job or when ordering lumber. If, for instance, you decide that a shelf should be exactly 10 inches wide you'll have to take a piece of 1″ x 12″ lumber and rip it down, because a piece of 1″ x 10″ lumber will only be about 9⅝″ in width.

Boards and dimension lumber are usually priced at so much per board foot. A board foot is a piece of lumber 1″ thick, 12″ wide, and 12″ long. When the price of lumber is quoted by the board foot, it is possible to find out how many board feet a particular piece of lumber contains by multiplying the thickness in inches by the width and length in feet. A board 1″ thick, 4″ wide, and 10′ long would contain 3⅓ board feet (1″ x ⅓′ x 10′). If the lumber is priced at 20¢ a board foot, the cost of that particular piece would be 66⅔¢. Fortunately for all of us, more and more lumber yards are giving prices to buyers in linear feet. This means that to find the price of a particular piece of wood you simply multiply the price per linear foot by the length. A piece of 2″ x 4″ that is 8′ long and costs 10¢ per linear foot will cost 80¢.

There are a lot of traditions in the lumber business. One is that when you order you give the thickness first, then the width, and finally the length. If you don't, and the clerk is of the old school, you may be surprised at the size lumber you get.

Lumber comes in certain standard sizes; and it is always best to plan a project to take advantage of these sizes. If you don't do this, it will mean a lot of time spent in cutting boards down to size and also a lot of waste.

Sizes of Boards. The chart below shows the standard size boards that are available at almost every lumber yard. The figure at the left is the nominal size; the figure on the right is the actual size of the board. Boards are available in lengths from 4′ to 16′, at 2′ intervals.

Nominal (inches)	Actual (inches)
1 x 2	¾ x 1⅝
1 x 3	¾ x 2⅝
1 x 4	¾ x 3⅝
1 x 5	¾ x 4⅝
1 x 6	¾ x 5⅝
1 x 8	¾ x 7⅝
1 x 10	¾ x 9⅝
1 x 12	¾ x 11½

When you need a board that is thicker than ¾″, you must order a "five quarter" board. This board has a nominal thickness of 1¼″ but its actual width is 1 1/16″. It is available in the same widths as ordinary boards, and in the same lengths. It is a useful size for certain jobs, such as shelving, where an ordinary ¾″-thick board might sag because of a heavy load.

Grades of Boards. Boards are divided into two basic grades: select and common. The select grades are used where appearance is of primary importance. These boards have few if any knots in them.

There are several different classifications in the select grade. The best and most expensive is "B or better." These boards should only be used when appearance is of vital importance and the work is to be given a natural or clear finish. Boards classified as "C" have a few minor imperfections, but they can also be used where appearance is fairly important. "D" grade boards are excellent for finish work that is to be painted.

The other basic grade is common board; this grade is good for any rough work about the house. A common board, for example, will cost around 12¢ a board foot, and a "B or better" board will cost around 50¢ a board foot. If you are appalled at the cost of lumber, it may well be that what you have purchased is top grade. One of the best ways to save on lumber is to first decide which grade of lumber will be adequate for the job, and then deal with a yard that allows you to look over the stock in that grade and pick out the most desirable pieces.

Boards come with flat or straight edges and also with tongue-and-groove edges. Tongue-and-groove boards are used where a tight fit is necessary, such as for sheathing and flooring.

Dimension Lumber.   Structural lumber used for framing comes in the following sizes (in inches):

$$2 \times 2$$
$$2 \times 4$$
$$2 \times 6$$
$$2 \times 8$$
$$2 \times 10$$
$$2 \times 12$$
$$4 \times 4$$

To find the actual size of any of these pieces, deduct ⅜″ from the thickness and the width. Dimension lumber is available in 2′ intervals up to 24′.

Molding.   These are thin strips of wood, available in a variety of sizes and shapes. They are used to cover joints and seams and for decorative purposes. Most yards carry a wide selection of stock moldings. They are sold by the linear foot, and are relatively inexpensive.

Wood Flooring.   Softwood flooring is made from pine or fir, which are the least expensive kinds of wood flooring available. The cheap-grade softwood flooring will sell for around $20 per 100 board feet. The more durable vertical-grain flooring costs around $30 per 100 board feet. Softwood flooring is good for jobs such as attics and summer homes, where appearance is not vital and where the floor isn't going to receive very heavy wear. On other floors, where appearance and durability are important, hardwood is more desirable. Unfinished oak flooring is available from about $30 per 100 board feet up.

After the flooring has been installed, it must, of course, be sanded and then given a protective finish. Somewhat more expensive, but a great time and work saver, is the factory-finished hardwood flooring that sells for about $10 more per 100 board feet than the unfinished flooring. These boards are given a durable finish at the factory, and once they have been nailed in place they are ready for use. The standard thickness for hardwood flooring is $2\frac{5}{32}''$. An excellent type of flooring for remodeling is the thin $\frac{3}{8}''$ factory-finished hardwood flooring. This can be applied directly over a badly-worn existing floor.

Hardwood flooring is also available in blocks 9" square. These blocks are sold unfinished or with a factory-applied finish. They can be applied with a mastic rather than with nails. They sell for around 50¢ per square foot.

Paneling. Boards suitable for wood paneling are usually $\frac{3}{4}''$ thick and 6", 8", or 10" wide. They come with tongue-and-groove

TONGUE-AND-GROOVE BOARD

edges and with a pattern cut along the edge to produce a decorative joint between boards. Paneling is made from cypress, redwood, and pine. Prices range from around 20¢ a board foot up.

Plywood. It is hard to understand how we got along before plywood was invented, for it is a most useful building material. Plywood is made by cutting thin wood veneers from a log and then gluing the veneers together so that the grain of each veneer runs at right angles to the grain of the adjoining veneer. This method of construction produces a very strong piece of material in relationship to the thickness. One great advantage that plywood has over lumber is that it comes in large sheets, the standard size being 4' x 8'. The inner core of plywood is usually made out of softwoods, and the outside veneer can be of either softwood or hardwood.

Fir Plywood. This is the most common and useful of all plywoods. It is stocked by almost every lumber yard, and it comes in thicknesses of ¼", ⅜", ½", ⅝", ¾", and 1". The standard size sheet is 4' x 8'; but many yards stock certain grades in 3' widths, and it is often possible to buy 4' x 4' and 2' x 4' sheets which are easier to handle than the large-size sheets.

There are two major types of fir plywood: exterior grade and interior grade. Exterior plywood is made with waterproof glues, and this is the only kind of plywood suitable for outside work. Interior plywood is made with moisture-resistant glue; and although it will not be harmed by the amount of moisture ordinarily found in the home, it should not be used outside where it will be exposed to the weather.

Both exterior and interior plywood is graded according to the condition of the outside veneer. If only one side of the plywood is going to be exposed to view, plywood "good one side" (G1S) can be used. If both sides will be exposed, the more expensive "good two sides" (G2S) will be required. In wood paneling, for instance, only one side of the plywood will be exposed; therefore, it would be foolish to spend extra money to get the plywood with two good faces.

A 4' x 8' sheet of exterior plywood ¾" thick will cost around $10.

Hardwood Plywoods. These usually have a core of fir plywood and outside veneers cut from expensive and attractive hardwoods. Hardwood plywood is excellent for furniture, fine cabinetwork, and wood paneling. The sheets come in basically the same sizes and thickness as fir plywood. The cost depends not only on the thickness but also on the kind of wood used as the outer veneer. A 4' x 8' sheet of birch plywood, ¾" thick, will cost about $20; the same size sheet of Philippine mahogany, ¼" thick, will be only around $10.

Plywood Paneling. This is an excellent material for paneling walls. The standard 4' x 8' sheet can be attached directly to the wall studding, or applied over an existing wall after furring strips have been installed. On most work, the ¼" sheets will be adequate.

An excellent type of plywood paneling is called "Plankweld." This is prefinished and comes in a package. Each piece of paneling is 16¼" wide and 96" long. The paneling is fastened in place with special little metal clips which are included in the package. Standard 4' x 8' sheets with vertical V-joint grooves spaced at random intervals are also available.

Working with Plywood. Plywood can be worked with ordinary tools and in the same manner as an ordinary piece of wood. As the large sheets are difficult to handle for cutting, it is usually wise to ask the lumber yard where the plywood is purchased to make some of the cuts before delivering. Most yards will do this at no additional charge. When plywood is cut with a hand saw or with a table power saw, the good side should face up. When cut with a portable electric saw, the good side should face down. The surface of plywood is sanded smooth at the factory, and it does not require additional sanding unless it has been damaged in handling. Be careful when you sand plywood, especially fir plywood. If you sand too hard or too long you'll cut right through the outside veneer and really be in trouble.

Because of the method of construction, the edges of plywood present something of a problem if they are to be left exposed. One way to handle these edges is to cover them with special wood-veneer tape made for this very purpose. These tapes are designed to match the common kinds of hardwood plywoods. The edges can also be covered with wood or metal molding. In the case of fir plywood that is to be painted, the edges can be coated with a wood filler; and after this has become hard, it can be sanded smooth. Fir plywood also presents something of a problem when it is to be painted, for the grain is very wild and must be sealed with either shellac or a special fir-plywood primer before painting.

Asbestos Board. These sheets are made of asbestos fibers and cement. They are highly resistant to fire and moisture and can be used for interior or exterior work. They come plain or in colors, and require no maintenance. The standard sheet is 4' x 8' and comes in thicknesses up to 1/4". A standard sheet 1/4" thick will cost around $9.

Asbestos board is very durable, but it is rather brittle and must be handled with care to avoid cracking. It's wise to drill holes in it before nailing, and avoid striking the surface with a hammer. It can be cut with an ordinary handsaw, but the work will go faster if you keep the saw blade wet.

Gypsum Wallboard. This material is used extensively today for interior walls and ceilings. It is made with a core of gypsum plaster covered with heavy paper. It is also available with a surface covering of vinyl fabric or paper printed to resemble wood paneling.

The standard sheet of gypsum board is made with recessed edges

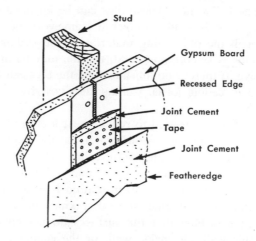

so that after the boards have been nailed to the studding or ceiling joists, the joints between the boards can be filled with special gypsum board joint cement and then reinforced by setting a special tape into the cement. Additional thin coats of cement are applied over the tape until a perfectly smooth and inconspicuous joint has been obtained. After any roughness on the cement has been sanded off, the surface is then suitable for either paint or paper. The standard size sheet of gypsum board is 4' x 8' and it comes ⅜" or ½" thick. The cost of a standard size board ½ inch thick is around $2.50.

Gypsum board (or plaster board, as it is sometimes called) is used extensively today in place of plaster, because it is easier to apply and there is much less fuss and mess than with plaster.

Gypsum board can be cut with a saw or by first scoring with a linoleum knife and then breaking along the scored line. It should be fastened with special gypsum board nails, and the heads of the nails should be driven so that they just dent but do not break the paper covering. The heads are then concealed with joint cement or spackling compound.

Insulating Board. You'll find a wide selection of this material for use as a wall covering. Some brands are prefinished, and all can be installed without much work. Joints are either covered with molding, or, if they are the decorative type, are left exposed. Insulating board can be painted, but it is not suitable for wallpapering.

Ceiling and Acoustical Tile. These tiles are made of wood fibers or fiber glass. They come in a wide range of patterns and colors. The standard size is 12″ x 12″. These tiles can be installed directly over an old ceiling, if it is solid, or over a framework of furring strips fastened through the old ceiling material to the ceiling framework. If the old ceiling is smooth and solid, the tile may be applied with a special adhesive. If there is no finish ceiling, the tiles can be applied to furring nailed to ceiling joists. Ceiling tiles cost from about 17¢ a square foot up.

Insulation. Insulation used to reduce heat loss in winter and heat gain in summer is made of various materials; the most common are glass fibers, mineral wool, and vermiculite. All of these are good insulating materials, and they are fire- and decay-resistant and will not attract vermin. Aluminum foil insulation is also excellent, but it is more difficult to install than the other kinds because it must be placed in such a fashion that the surfaces do not come in contact with the outside wall, the inside wall, or the ceiling coverings. This calls for professional help. Other kinds of insulation come with foil backing, which is also beneficial.

The nonmetallic insulations come in several forms. There are the roll or blanket insulations, batts, and loose pouring insulation. The blanket insulation is encased in a paper covering. The cover has a flange on one side so that the insulation can be nailed or stapled in place. The batt insulation is somewhat similar to the roll or blanket, but it comes in lengths of 48″; the roll comes in lengths up to 80′. Batts are usually used in tight spots where it would be difficult to handle the large rolls. One brand of insulation does not require any fastening; it is simply slipped between the studdings and it holds there by itself.

Loose pouring insulation comes in a bag and is poured into place. It is fine for horizontal jobs such as the floor of an attic.

Rigid insulation is made of wood or vegetable fibers, fiber glass, or foam plastic. The fiber type is often used as wall sheathing. The foam plastic insulation is ideal for insulating around the edges of concrete slabs.

Notes on Use of Materials

The vast majority of building materials today are made by concerns who have spent a considerable amount of time and money developing literature to insure the proper application of the material, and this literature is available at the source of supply. When you purchase building materials, be sure to get these application directions; they are the key to satisfactory work.

Nails. The most useful fastener about the house is the nail. You'll require a rather large assortment to handle repairs and improvements. Nails are made of steel or aluminum. Aluminum nails are the more

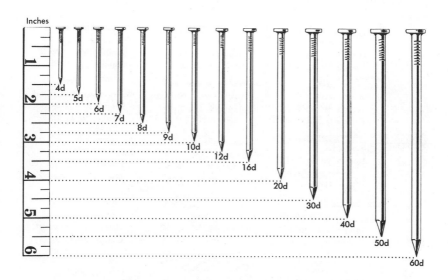

SIZES OF COMMON WIRE NAILS

expensive, but they will not rust and therefore are best for outside work.

The size and weight of most nails is expressed by the term *penny* and this is expressed as *d*. The following table shows the more common size nails expressed in penny size and the actual length in inches.

2 d (penny)	1″ long
3 d	1¼″
4 d	1½″
5 d	1¾″
6 d	2″
8 d	2½″
10 d	3″
12 d	3¼″
16 d	3½″
20 d	4″

Nails are sold by the pound, by the package, or by the keg. A keg contains 100 pounds of nails, so most homeowners buy by the pound or package. There are many different nails designed for all manner of jobs, but most work about the house will involve only a few of the more basic types.

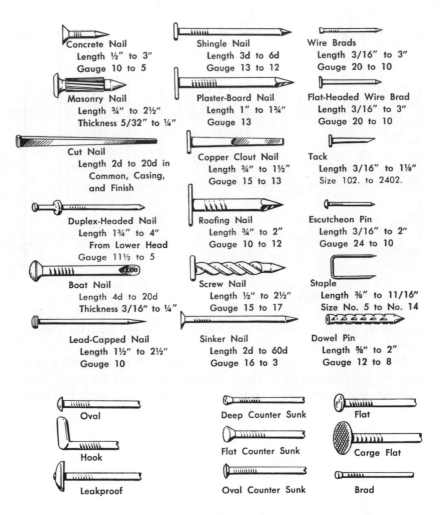

Concrete Nail
Length ½" to 3"
Gauge 10 to 5

Masonry Nail
Length ¾" to 2½"
Thickness 5/32" to ¼"

Cut Nail
Length 2d to 20d in
Common, Casing,
and Finish

Duplex-Headed Nail
Length 1¾" to 4"
From Lower Head
Gauge 11½ to 5

Boat Nail
Length 4d to 20d
Thickness 3/16" to ¼"

Lead-Capped Nail
Length 1½" to 2½"
Gauge 10

Shingle Nail
Length 3d to 6d
Gauge 13 to 12

Plaster-Board Nail
Length 1" to 1¾"
Gauge 13

Copper Clout Nail
Length ¾" to 1½"
Gauge 15 to 13

Roofing Nail
Length ¾" to 2"
Gauge 10 to 12

Screw Nail
Length ½" to 2½"
Gauge 15 to 17

Sinker Nail
Length 2d to 60d
Gauge 16 to 3

Wire Brads
Length 3/16" to 3"
Gauge 20 to 10

Flat-Headed Wire Brad
Length 3/16" to 3"
Gauge 20 to 10

Tack
Length 3/16" to 1⅛"
Size 102. to 2402.

Escutcheon Pin
Length 3/16" to 2"
Gauge 24 to 10

Staple
Length ⅜" to 11/16"
Size No. 5 to No. 14

Dowel Pin
Length ⅝" to 2"
Gauge 12 to 8

Oval

Hook

Leakproof

Deep Counter Sunk

Flat Counter Sunk

Oval Counter Sunk

Flat

Carge Flat

Brad

NAILS

Common Nails.   In sizes from 2 *d* to 60 *d*. Use these for all sorts of rough and unfinished work when appearance is not important. They have large heads that make them easy to hammer and easy to remove, and they are inexpensive.

Box Nails.   Similar to common nails except that they are thinner and weigh less and cost less. Good for light work where the heavier common nail might split the wood.

Casing Nails.   These are much the same as common nails except that they have small heads, and this allows the head to be driven below the surface of the wood. They are more difficult to install and to remove than the common nail, but they should be used on finish work where you do not wish the nail head to be exposed.

Finishing Nails.   These have even smaller heads than casing nails; they are a little thinner and therefore not quite so strong. They can be used for the same type of work as the casing nail.

Brads.   These are small finishing nails which are sold by the length rather than by the penny size. They run from ½″ to 1½″ and are used for all manner of light work.

Miscellaneous Nails.   Among the other types of nails that you may have occasion to use are the steel cut nails used for installing hardwood floors. These have an oblong head and a rather blunt tip that tears rather than cuts the wood fibers, thereby reducing the chance of splitting the wood. Cut nails can also be used for nailing into masonry if the masonry is not too dense. Gypsum wallboard is installed with a special nail, and so are shingles.

Nails are sometimes coated with cement or rosin to give them greater holding power and to prevent them from rusting. In the past few years many new types of nails have been developed to provide greater holding power than the ordinary nail. Screw nails and ringed-shank nails both have very high holding power and should be used when maximum strength is required. Some screw-type nails are designed to be driven into place with an electric drill with a special attachment.

Nails for use in masonry are made out of very hard steel; and these, like the cut nails, can be driven into many forms of masonry without the need for first drilling a hole.

Every home should have a handful or so of tacks, pins, and some of the small special nails that can be so handy from time to time.

Nails should be stored where they will not become damp and rusty, for a rusty nail will not have the holding power of a clean nail. Nails are not expensive, so when one starts to bend while it is being driven in, pull it out and start with a fresh one. Don't waste time trying to straighten a bent nail for reuse—it's not worth the effort.

Selecting the Correct Size Nail. As we mentioned earlier, the manufacturers of most building materials will provide the necessary information of the type, size, and number of nails to use with their product; but for many jobs about the house involving wood there will be no guide, and you'll be more or less on your own. To select the correct size nail, the rule of thumb is to use a nail that is long enough so that two-thirds of its length will penetrate into the piece of wood to which the first piece of wood is being fastened. In other words, use a nail about three times as long as the thickness of the board that is being nailed. If a 1″-thick board is to be nailed, the correct size nail would be three inches long—a 10 *d* nail.

It is very difficult to figure how many nails to use on a job. Amateur carpenters, as a rule, use too many rather than too few nails. When too many nails are used, they may split the wood. Splitting will also occur if the nails are driven too close to the edge of the board, or if they are set in a straight line; stagger the nails, and keep them as far away from the edge as possible.

Wood Screws. Screws are superior to nails for fastening because they have greater holding power and because they can be installed and removed, if necessary, without damage to the wood surface. Always use screws on building projects where appearance counts and where maximum strength is required.

Screws are made of steel or brass. The steel screws are the least expensive and the strongest, but they rust. Use brass screws on work that will be exposed to the weather, such as summer furniture or exterior hardware.

The common wood screw has a single-slot on the head. There are several shapes of heads. The flat-head screw is used when the head is to be set flush with the wood surface. Most hardware is designed to take a flat-head screw. Round-head and oval-head screws are used when the hole is to be counter-bored.

Screws are sold by the box, which contains one gross, but you can usually buy them in smaller quantities at hardware stores.

The proper way to install a wood screw is to first drill a hole in the wood at the point where the screw is to fit. This is called a *pilot hole.* If you are setting short screws into softwoods, you can make this hole with an awl or even with a nail. For larger screws, or when working with hardwood, it is better to use a drill to make the hole. The diameter of the hole should be slightly smaller than the diameter of the threaded portion of the screw. In hardwood, the depth of the hole should be almost equal to the length of the screw.

When a screw is to join two pieces of wood, drill holes in both pieces. Clamp the two pieces of wood together and drill a hole through both pieces. Then enlarge the hole in the top piece so that it is the same diameter as the unthreaded portion of the screw.

If flat-head screws are to be used, there is an additional drilling operation to be done with a countersink. The countersink point is inserted into the hole in the top piece of wood and a recess is made slightly below the wood surface, deep enough to allow the head of the screw to be made flush with the wood surface.

To completely conceal the screw head, first drill a hole with an auger bit slightly larger than the diameter of the screw head and deep enough so that the head will fit well below the wood surface, allowing space above it for plastic wood filler or a wood plug. Then drill the pilot holes.

Lag Screws. These are very heavy screws, with square heads; they can be installed with a wrench rather than a screwdriver. Lag screws are used on heavy work where nails would not provide enough holding power and ordinary screws would be too short.

Sheet-Metal Screws. These come with flat oval heads and are self-tapping. This means that all you have to do is punch the correct size hole into the metal, and the screw can then be inserted. Sheet-metal screws can be used only on thin metal.

Nuts and Bolts. You can buy an assorted package of these at most hardware stores. They are handy to have around as replacement items.

CHAPTER 4

Interior Repairs

Walls and Ceilings

The interior walls and ceilings in most homes are surfaced with plaster or gypsum wallboard often called "sheet rock" or "plaster board." Other materials used are hardboard, plywood, asbestos board, insulating board, and tile.

Gypsum Wallboard Repairs. This material, as we explained in an earlier chapter, is made with a core of gypsum plaster covered with paper. It is applied to the walls in sheets measuring 4' x 8' and the thickness will be ⅜" or ½". In very fine quality construction, two ⅜" sheets will be used.

Small holes in gypsum wallboard can be repaired simply by filling with spackling compound or gypsum wallboard joint cement. When the filler is dry, sand lightly until smooth. For large holes, it is best to use a piece of metal wire lath or heavy insect screening larger than the opening to be patched. Tie a string to the center of this patch and slip the patch through the hole. Pull the string to bring the patch against the rear of the wallboard, centered so it completely covers the opening. Secure the string to hold the patch in place, and then apply patching plaster or plaster of Paris (see "Plaster Repairs," page 38) over the wire lath or screening. When the patching material is dry, cut off the string flush with the patch.

For extensive holes it is best to remove the damaged section of the wallboard. With a large square or straightedge, draw two horizontal parallel lines, one over the damaged space, the second under it. Cut or saw along the lines until you reach the wall studding or ceiling joist on the other side of the opening.

Draw a vertical line down the wallboard over the approximate center of each stud or joist and cut the board on this line with a knife. When the damaged section is removed, a portion of each stud or joist on both sides of the opening will be exposed. This serves

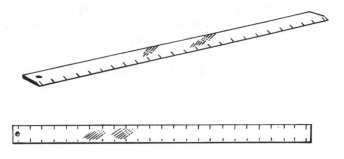

STRAIGHTEDGE

as a nailing base for the patch. It is also advisable to have horizontal nailing bases. For this, cut two pieces of 2″ x 4″ so they will just fit between the exposed pieces of studding or joists. Slip them into place so one-half of their thickness is visible. Toe-nail them to the existing framing. There should now be a wood framework to serve as a nailing base for the patch.

Cut a piece of gypsum wallboard to fit and nail it to the framework with gypsum wallboard nails. Drive the heads so they dent but do not break the paper. Cover the nail heads with joint cement and cover the seams around the patch with masking tape. Paint or paper to match the wall.

Nail Popping.   The nails used to secure gypsum wallboard to the framework will sometimes pull loose and the heads become exposed. This can be due to improper installation or because the wood framing was very green at the time the wallboard was installed. The best remedy is to drive in a new nail close to the existing one. Use a screw-type gypsum wallboard nail and force the wallboard tightly against the framework as you drive in the nail. Remove the old nail and fill the hole and the depression over the new nail with spackling compound or joint cement.

Plaster.   In plaster construction the wall and ceiling framework is first covered with lath to serve as a base for the plaster. Some years ago, wood lath was in use; but today the most common is a gypsum wallboard lath. In some houses the plaster is applied to metal lath; this is perforated, and plaster is forced through the lath holes, where it hardens, making a sturdy mechanical bond.

There is a tendency for plaster in a new house to crack, for there is bound to be some movement as the framework shrinks and the building settles. This is nothing to worry about, and it is best to ignore it until the house is a year or so old. If the cracks are patched sooner, the chances are they will continue to open until the movement in the structure ceases.

Plaster Repairs.   Small holes left in plaster by nails, fasteners, etc., as well as cracks in the surface coat, may be repaired with a patching product such as spackling compound. This material is sold at most hardware and paint stores and is mixed with water into a thick paste. Dampen the edges of the hole or crack and force the compound in with a putty knife. When dry, sand lightly, and prime with shellac or paint.

With large cracks and holes, the edges of the plaster around them should be cut back to form an inverted wedge to hold the patch. This can be done with an old chisel or a sharp putty knife. As with gypsum wallboard, a small piece of metal lath nailed into the hole to the framework or lath will help retain the patch.

You'll need patching plaster or plaster of Paris for large holes, and two coats are better than one. Both of these materials come in powder form, and water must be added; but if too much water is used, it will be difficult to make the patch stay in place. Ceiling patches especially must be mixed as dry as possible. You'll probably find that the prepared patching plasters are easier to use than plaster of Paris, because they don't harden quite so rapidly and therefore allow more time for correct application. Both are sold at paint and hardware stores.

Before applying the patching compound, dust the opening clean and wet down the edges of the plaster. A toy water pistol is fine for this job and is especially handy when patching a ceiling. For large holes, apply the first coat of patching compound so that it comes to within about ⅛" of the surface. Allow it to dry and then apply the final coat, which can be worked smooth with a broad putty knife or a straightedge.

Recurring Cracks.   Certain cracks are difficult to repair, for even after being properly filled they shortly reappear. They usually show at joints in a room where wall and ceiling or adjacent wall meet, and sometimes around windows and door openings.

The best way to deal with this type of crack is to remove about four inches of plaster from each side, then nail a strip of metal lath

5/16"

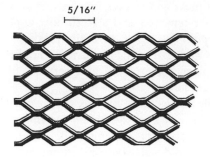

METAL LATH

through the existing lath into the wall or ceiling framework. The metal lath must be secured to the framework, not to the lath. Once the metal lath is in place, a patch can be applied; it should hold with such added reinforcement.

Water-damaged Plaster. If plaster is repeatedly soaked by water it will fail and start to peel and flake. This condition often occurs in the bathroom, where the plaster wall joins the bathtub, or if there is a leak in the plumbing or the roof. The only correct remedy here is to remove all the damaged plaster and patch, after first finding the cause of the leak and correcting it.

Plaster in Generally Poor Condition. In some instances plaster walls and ceilings will be so covered with cracks and poorly installed patches that to attempt to repair them would involve hours and hours of work. The best solution here is to apply some other covering directly over the old plaster. If the plaster is solidly attached to the lath, this can be accomplished without any difficulty. If the plaster is loose or falling away from the lath, then it will have to be removed, but this is a condition that seldom occurs.

The easiest and least expensive way to conceal unsightly plaster is to cover it with a textured paint. These are very thick paints, and they will fill in cracks and other irregularities and produce a relatively smooth surface.

If you prefer something more extensive and expensive in the way of repairs, you can resurface the wall or ceiling with materials such as gypsum wallboard, hardboard, plywood, or ceiling tile. 1" x 3" furring strips are first fastened through the old plaster and lath into the wall or ceiling framework to serve as a nailing base for the new material and also to produce a level surface.

Because of the mess and bother involved, it is seldom practical to have the old plaster removed and a fresh coat applied.

Tile Walls, Repairing. Clay, ceramic, plastic, and metal wall tile found in kitchens and bathroom are usually applied these days with an adhesive. In older homes, clay and ceramic tile are fastened to the wall with cement mortar.

When a wall tile comes loose or falls out, it can be cemented back into place with a special adhesive made for this purpose. These adhesives are also suitable for fastening tile originally set in cement mortar. Remove the old adhesive or cement mortar from the back of the tile and the wall and apply the new adhesive according to directions on the container. Fit the tile into place and use strips of masking tape to hold it until the adhesive is dry. A special white adhesive is used to fill in around the edge of the tile after it is in place. If a tile should become damaged, it can usually be removed by prying it loose with an old screwdriver or cold chisel. Be careful not to damage the adjoining tile. A replacement can then be installed with tile adhesive.

Tiles, Cleaning. Use warm water and a detergent to clean wall and floor tile. Do not use soap for cleaning, because this will leave a deposit that is unsightly. Never use a harsh abrasive cleaning compound or steel wool on any tile, for these can damage the finish. Never use a solvent on plastic tile, for this can ruin it. If the joints between floor tile become badly soiled, you can often improve matters by wiping with a household bleach. The only other solution is to scrape away some of the filler and replace with a mixture of white cement and water. Low quality tile may discolor in time, and there is no remedy for this. If clay or ceramic tile becomes covered with fine cracks, there is usually no cure.

Tile walls that are in poor condition can be painted with enamel or with a special epoxy paint. This is the only type of paint that is satisfactory if the tile is going to be exposed to water, such as on the walls around a recessed bathtub. Even the best enamel will not last here, but the epoxy paint, if applied according to directions, will hold.

Tile, Shrinkage Cracks. Cracks often appear between tile and bathtub, sink, etc. These cracks, while not serious in themselves, may allow water to get into the wall cavity and cause serious damage to the wall and to the ceiling below. A simple way to fill these cracks is with white caulking compound. This is waterproof, and easy to apply. There are also several compounds made for this job and sold under various trade names at hardware stores. Triangular plastic and metal strips are also available for filling around the bathtub. They are cemented into place, and make a durable and attractive finish.

Doors

The most familiar door is the hinged type hung on two or more hinges, for both interior and exterior work. Sliding doors, especially for closets, are popular, for they provide easy access to all closet space and don't take up valuable room by swinging out. Folding and accordion wood and plastic panels are liked for the same reason. Sliding metal doors with large glass panels are used extensively to reach outdoor areas and for natural light.

Hinged Doors. Hinged doors are still the most common type in use, and have been with us long enough for us to learn how to deal with the many things that can go wrong with them. Other types are relatively new, and it will take time to amass a complete file on their shortcomings.

Settling of the building, faulty hanging, or poor maintenance can cause trouble. Wood doors may shrink, expand, or warp due to uneven absorption of moisture. Sometimes trouble may be prevented by adding a third hinge midway between top and bottom hinges. This, of course, must be the same size and style as the others, and should be secured in the same proportion to door edge and door jamb.

It is important that outside doors be kept painted. The edges should receive particular attention, for here the door most readily absorbs moisture. To paint a door, it is wise to take it down. This not only makes it easier to paint but insures that all edges can be properly coated.

Removing a Door. The first step in taking down a door is to open it and push a wedge under the outside bottom corner so the hinges no longer carry the entire weight.

Most doors have loose pin hinges and are simple to take down. The two halves of the hinge are held together by a pin which can be pulled out with pliers or pushed up with a steel punch and hammer. Once the pin is out, the two parts of the hinge will separate. One half is fastened to the door while the other is on the door jamb.

Remove the bottom pin and then the top hinge pin. (When replacing the door, put in the top pin first and then the lower. The lower hinge should never have to support the entire weight of the door.)

If the door doesn't have loose pin hinges or if they are frozen with rust or paint, remove the screws from one half of each hinge.

Failure to Latch. Most doors are fitted with a spring latch that, when the door is closed, engages a hole in a metal plate fastened to

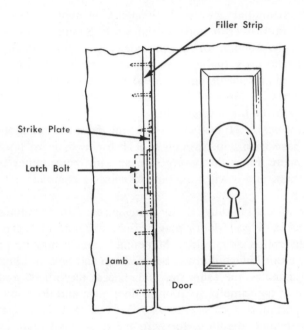

DOOR JAMB SECTION SHOWING FILLER STRIPS

the door jamb. This is called the "strike plate." It sometimes has two holes, one for the latch and one for the lock. When the door fails to stay shut it is usually because the latch is not fitting into the hole in the strike plate. This may be caused by the frame of the door having moved slightly or by shrinkage.

Rub chalk or crayon on the latch and shut the door. When it is opened, some of the marker will show on the metal plate and indicate which way the plate must be moved so the latch will line up. Sometimes all that is needed is to make the hole slightly larger, and this can be done by removing the two screws holding the strike plate and enlarging the hole with a small file. If this is impractical, the strike plate will have to be moved and adjusted. Take off the plate and enlarge the recess in the jamb with a chisel so that the plate can be repositioned. Fasten the strike plate to the jamb and see if the door latches properly. If it does, fill around the plate with plastic wood; and when this is dry, touch up with paint.

If the door has shrunk considerably, the latch may fail to engage because it no longer reaches the strike plate. Then the easiest thing to do here is to shim out the strike plate by slipping thin slivers of wood or pieces of cardboard under it to force it away from the jamb. A more professional approach is to take down the door, remove the hinges, and glue a strip of wood along the hinge edge of the door. The strip should be as wide as the door is thick, and thick enough to allow the latch to engage the strike plate. It is easier to fasten the wood strip to the hinge side than to the latch side of the door.

Rattling Doors. When a door is properly hung, the latch will hold it tight against the stops and prevent rattling. The stops are the thin strips of wood that fit around three sides of the frame and against which the door rests when closed. If there is rattle, repositioning the strike plate so the door, when latched, is firm against the stops, will eliminate it.

Sticking Doors. If a door sticks, first check the hinge screws. Loose screws may be tightened; but if the holes in the wood are enlarged, they won't hold. Removing the old screws and substituting longer ones may help. The holes may also be packed with plastic wood to provide a solid bite for the screws. Another remedy is to

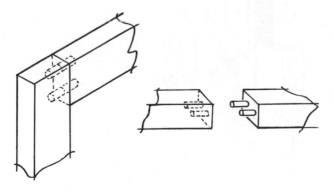

DOWEL JOINT

drill out the holes so that a half-inch wood dowel may be glued in and the screws set in the dowels.

When a door sticks during warm, humid weather, it usually means it has absorbed moisture and the wood has expanded. It's best not to do anything at this time if it can be avoided, for when the weather turns dry, the door will shrink to its original state. Then it can be taken down and painted. This may prevent future trouble; if the

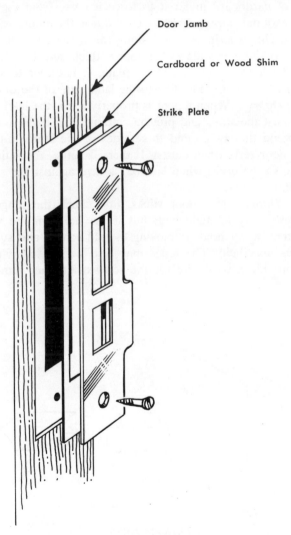

Door Jamb

Cardboard or Wood Shim

Strike Plate

edges are planed off when the door is expanded, there will be gaps when it has shrunk back to size.

Sticking is also caused by movement of the door frame when a house settles. This can be corrected by adjusting the door to fit the new frame position. It is done by changing the hinges slightly. If sticking occurs between the bottom corner and floor or threshold, loosen the bottom hinge on the jamb and slip a piece of cardboard between the hinge and the jamb. This will tilt the door upward. The thickness of the shim needed will depend on how much the door has to be tilted to prevent sticking.

If the shim is very thick, it may be necessary to use longer screws to hold the hinge securely.

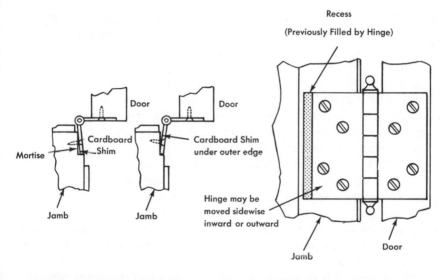

HINGE READJUSTMENTS TO CORRECT ILL-FITTING DOORS

When sticking is at the top corner of the door, place the shim under the top hinge. If the whole edge of the door sticks at the jamb, set the hinges deeper into the wood. This will pull the door away from the latch jamb toward the hinge jamb. To set hinges deeper, remove them and deepen the recess with a chisel.

Sliding Doors. Sliding doors for interior use are often made of ¾" plywood without any frame, and these may warp. There is no effective way to remove the warp; the best policy is to replace the doors with units made of wood-chip composition board, which is more stable than plywood and doesn't warp so easily.

When sliding doors are difficult to operate it usually means that the tracks on which the doors move are dirty or need lubrication. Clean them with a vacuum cleaner and then wipe with a cloth. Finally, lubricate the moving parts with graphite or silicone.

Windows

Most modern windows are made of wood or aluminum, though some are made of steel. Wood windows must be given a protective finish. Paint is generally used as a finish for the outside; paint or a clear trim sealer should be used on the interior surfaces. Most quality wood windows today are treated with a wood preservative that not only protects from decay but also stabilizes the wood to reduce expansion and contraction to a minimum.

Aluminum windows don't require a protective finish, but they can be painted for decorative purposes. Aluminum windows and doors will, after a period of exposure, turn slightly gray; they can be made bright again by rubbing with fine steel wool. You can retard this graying process by coating the metal, after it has been made bright again, with wax or clear exterior lacquer.

Steel windows must be painted to prevent rust.

Older wood windows are subject to the same reactions as wood itself when exposed to varying temperatures and moisture conditions. Moving parts may expand or shrink, making the sash hard to work or allowing rain or cold air to enter. Screws come loose and cracks appear between various parts of the frame. These faults are not true of the modern quality wood window but can be expected on older units or ones of poor quality. However, if sash and frame are properly protected, and repairs made promptly, wood windows will give excellent service.

Aluminum and steel windows are not subject to the same ailments as wooden ones, but they do have their share of troubles. Chief among these is that in winter, condensation may occur on the frame; and if this moisture freezes, the sash will be iced to the frame and cannot be moved. Forcing the sash may bend it or the frame so that the unit will never again work quite the way it should. The correct way to free a frozen metal sash is to apply heat until the ice has melted and the sash can be easily moved.

Double-Hung Windows. This is the kind of window in which the sashes move up and down in the frame. Unless the frame or sash has been bent, the only sort of trouble encountered with metal double-hung windows is that the sash is hard to move; and this can be corrected by applying wax, paraffin, powdered graphite, or a silicone spray along the edge of the sash and in the groove in the frame in which the sash moves.

Problems encountered with double-hung wood windows will depend on whether they are new-style units or the old-fashioned type employing sash cords and weights to hold the sash at the desired point.

Modern double-hung wood windows utilize spring or tension bars along the frame sides of the sash to hold the sash in place. These sashes are usually easy to remove from the frame. Simply push on one side of the sash; this will compress the tension bar on the opposite side so that the sash can be taken from the frame for cleaning or painting. To replace the sash, put one edge against the tension bar and push until the other end of the sash can be slipped into place. If there is too much or too little tension on the bar or spring so that the sash is hard to move or keeps slipping down, it can be adjusted by the screws set into the bar. To provide more tension, loosen the screws, and to get less tension, tighten them.

When the window is painted, be sure to keep paint off this metal tension bar, or the window will be more difficult to operate.

Sticking. Old-fashioned double-hung windows of wood, as has been mentioned, can develop ailments, the most common of which is sticking.

The chief reason for sticking is that paint has worked into the space between sash and window frame. It is often possible to free a paint-stuck sash by running a knife down the seam between sash and frame, or putting a few drops of liquid paint remover into the seam. Paint and hardware stores sell special little cutters for freeing paint-stuck sashes and they work quite well. Another way to free the sash is to take a small block of wood, hold it against the side of the sash, and strike the block with a hammer, moving the block up and down along the side of the sash.

If the sash is badly stuck by paint or has absorbed moisture and expanded, the only way to free it is to take it out of the frame. The lower sash is held in by two small strips of wood called *stop beads* that run along the inside of the frame. These are held in place by screws or finishing nails, and may be removed by taking out the screws or nails. It is usually easier to pry off the piece if it's held by nails than to try to pull out the nails, because the heads are usually small and set below the wood surface. Once one of the strips has been removed, the sash can be taken out of the frame. Usually it is only necessary to remove one of the stop beads, but if the sash is very badly stuck you may have to take them both off. By the way, you can only remove the sash from the inside; it can't be done from the outside.

Should it be necessary to remove the upper sash, the lower sash must come out first. The upper sash is separated from the lower by two pieces of wood called parting strips that run on each side of the frame between upper and lower sash. These are held in place in the same way as the stop beads. Usually, with one removed, the upper sash can be pulled out.

Use sandpaper to remove excess paint from the edges of the sash and from the groove in the frame in which the sash travels. If this is not enough to allow the sash to move easily, plane or sandpaper the sash edges until it does work smoothly. Coat the exposed wood with linseed oil or a wood preservative. Do not use paint, because this will build up a film that might cause sticking again. Be sure to rub the edges of the sash with wax or paraffin before replacing it in the frame.

Replacing a Sash Cord.   Consider yourself lucky if the windows in your house don't have sash cords, because replacing them is a dull and tedious chore. The whole trouble is that when a cord does break, the sash must be taken out of the frame before a new cord can be attached. This job was explained in the previous paragraphs on freeing a sticking window sash. The sash weight, to which one end of the cord is secured, fits into a space inside the window frame. This is called the *pocket*. It can be reached by removing the small wood or metal pocket cover at the bottom of the frame. Once the cover is off, the weight can be taken out. Feed a new cord over the pulley and through the pocket until it can be pulled out through the opening at the pocket's base. Tie this end to the sash weight, replace the weight in the pocket, and put back the cover. Hold the sash up to the frame and pull on the cord so that the weight is just off the bottom of the pocket. Cut the cord, leaving enough to allow a knot to be tied, which fits into a recess made for it in the side of the sash. Replace the sash and test the operation. When the sash is lowered, the weight should not strike the pulley at the top and when the sash is up, the weight should not touch the bottom of the pocket.

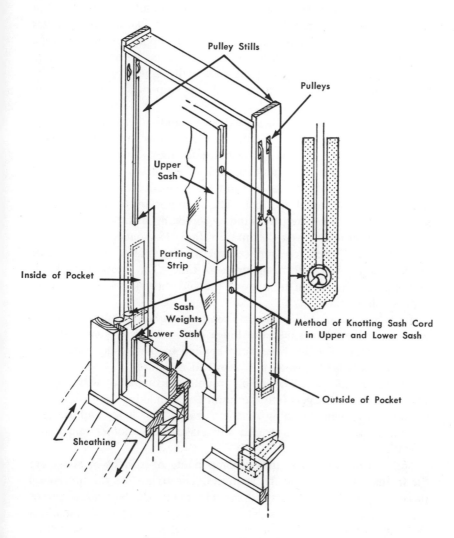

Pulley Stills

Pulleys

Upper Sash

Parting Strip

Inside of Pocket

Sash Weights

Lower Sash

Method of Knotting Sash Cord in Upper and Lower Sash

Outside of Pocket

Sheathing

REPLACING A SASH CORD

When it's necessary to replace a sash cord, it's often advisable to use a sash chain in place of a cord, for a chain will last indefinitely and won't stretch. Even better is to install one of the several brands of sash balances designed for sashes that were originally made for use with weights and cords.

Rattling Windows. Double-hung windows may rattle during heavy winds, and this can be annoying. More important, it indicates that the sash is so loose that it allows a lot of air as well as rain to enter the house. You can correct this situation by applying caulking tape around the edges of the sash or even installing weather stripping, which, if nailed tightly against the sash, will prevent movement. The best remedy, however, is to take off the stop beads and set them closer to the sash.

Casement Windows. These windows, and other types that are hinged, are usually equipped with a sash adjuster. This unit consists of a crank handle, gear box, pivot bar, and track. These adjusters are designed so that they will hold the sash in any desired position. They also make it possible for the window to be opened or closed without having to actually touch the sash. This is important for any sash that swings out, for if covered by window screening or a storm sash, the screen or sash must fit on the inside rather than outside of the sash.

As these adjusters contain several moving parts, they must be cleaned and lubricated from time to time. The best lubricant is graphite. Use a solvent to remove the old dirty lubricant and then apply fresh graphite.

Sticking Casement Windows. Casement and other kinds of hinged windows will stick because the hinge screws have become loose or excessive coats of paint have been applied to the edges. Older units may stick because the wood has absorbed moisture.

Sliding Windows. The chief trouble encountered with sliding windows is that dirt gets into the lower track, making the sashes hard to move. Frequent cleaning of these tracks will help, and rubbing paraffin or wax along the tracks will make for smoother and easier operation.

Stairs, Squeaky. The major components of a flight of stairs are the treads, the risers, and the stringers. The treads are the horizontal pieces that are actually stepped on. The risers are the vertical pieces that run between the treads. The stringers are the two side members that support the treads and risers. In modern stair construction, grooves are cut into the stringers, in which the ends of the treads and risers fit; and a groove is cut along the underside of each tread to accommodate the top edge of the riser. These joints are made tight by wood wedges coated with glue and driven in place. If these wedges become loose, squeaks will occur in the treads. If it is possible to get at the underside of the stairs, squeaks can be eliminated by

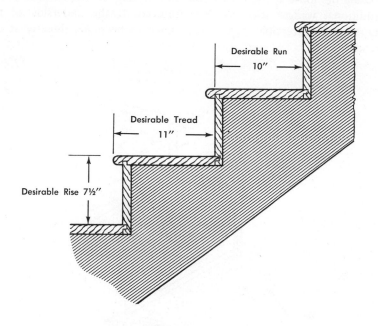

Desirable Run
10"

Desirable Tread
11"

Desirable Rise 7½"

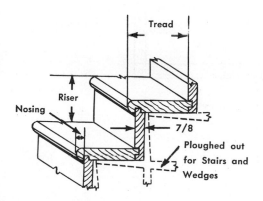

Tread

Riser

Nosing

7/8

Ploughed out
for Stairs and
Wedges

coating the loose wedges with glue and driving them back into place. Additional wedges may also be required. If the underside of the stairs is not accessible, repairs will have to be made directly at the treads.

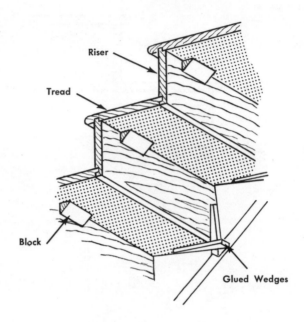

Riser

Tread

Block

Glued Wedges

HOUSED STAIR

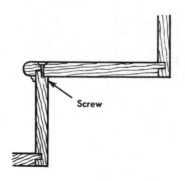

Screw

To do this, have someone stand on the squeaky tread while nails are driven along the front edge of the tread into the riser. The riser is usually set back a short distance from the edge of the tread, so the nails should be spaced so as to reach the center of the edge of the riser. Use a screw or ringed nail for this job. Set the nail heads below the surface, and then fill in over them with plastic wood. Wood screws can be used in place of the nails, but they take more time to install. If wood screws are used, a shallow round hole should be made before the screw is installed, so that the screw head can be set below the wood surface and covered with plastic wood or a wood plug.

Open-Riser Stairs. Basement and attic stairs are frequently made without risers and this can be dangerous for it is very easy to catch one's foot under the tread and take a nasty fall. It's a simple matter to install risers using either plywood, hardboard, or wide boards. Simply nail the riser to the tread and sides of the stringers.

CHAPTER 5

Floors

Floors are made of wood or concrete, and either one can be covered with a wide variety of materials. Both kinds of floors can cause problems, so let's first take up some of the headaches you may encounter with a wood floor.

Cracks between Floor Boards.   If a wood-finish floor is improperly laid, cracks may appear between the boards. While the best procedure is to take up the floor and relay it, cracks can be filled with a wood filler stained to more or less match the rest of the flooring.

There are prepared fillers for this, or one may be made by mixing sawdust and wood glue to a paste. The cracks should be cleaned out before this is applied. When the filler is dry, the whole floor should be sanded and refinished.

Another remedy is to cut wedges from hardboard and drive them into the cracks. The wedge top is then planed down flush with the surface, and the floor refinished. Use wood glue on the wedges to hold them secure. For our money, if there are many cracks to fill, ripping up the floor will probably take less time and effort in the long run than this method, which is arduous and painstaking.

While most cracks between floor boards are due to improper installation, cracks can also be caused by washing the floor with water. Water gets into the wood and causes it to swell. If the boards are tightly fitted together, there will be no room for expansion; and so the wood fibers become dented. When the floor shrinks back to size, areas where the fibers were dented show up as cracks. Never wash a wood floor if you want to keep it free of cracks.

Creaking and Squeaking.   The method used to rid a floor of squeaks and creaks depends on whether it is possible to get at the underside from a basement or crawl space. If so, there are several remedies.

A most effective cure is to take small wood wedges, such as pieces of wood shingles, and drive them between the joists and the subflooring at points where squeaks are found. Many squeaking floors are caused by subfloor boards riding up and down on the nails holding them to the floor joists. Use wedges to stop this movement.

When a squeak occurs between joists, and the wedges are not effective, wood screws can be used. Screws about one inch long are run up through the subflooring into the underside of the finish flooring at the squeak point. Someone should stand on the floor in the room above to force the finish boards down tight against the subfloor, so the screws can penetrate into the finish flooring and hold finish and subflooring tightly together. Another trick is to take a length of 2″ x 6″, toenail it between the joists where squeaks occur and then drive a wood wedge between the top of this piece and the subflooring.

If it is impossible to reach the underside of the floor, squeaks can often be silenced by working talcum powder into the cracks between the squeak board. Better still, renail the squeak board. Use screw nails or ringed nails for this job. Nails should be about 2½″ long and have small heads. Force the squeaky board down and then drive in the nails. These should be set in pairs and at angles so that, if they were long enough, the points would meet below the subflooring. Use a nail-set to finish driving in the nails and to sink the heads below the wood surface. Fill over the heads with one of the colored wax canyons sold at hardware stores for furniture and paneling repairs.

It is best if the nails can be driven through the subflooring into the joists.

When squeaks occur in a floor that has been covered with some material other than wood, such as linoleum or asphalt tile, you should do everything possible to eliminate the squeaks by working from the underside of the floor. If this is out of the question, the nails will have to be driven through the floor covering. Set the nails below the surface and fill in the hole left in the covering with a wax crayon of the correct color.

Floors, Sagging and Weak. Fortunately, most troubles of this nature occur on the first floor of the house, because it supports the most weight. If it is possible to get at the underside of the floor, the homeowner can usually make the repairs himself.

In standard house construction, the floors are supported by wood joists spaced 16″ from center to center. The joist ends rest on the foundation walls, but there is usually a wood or steel girder running at right angles to the joists at their midpoint to give additional

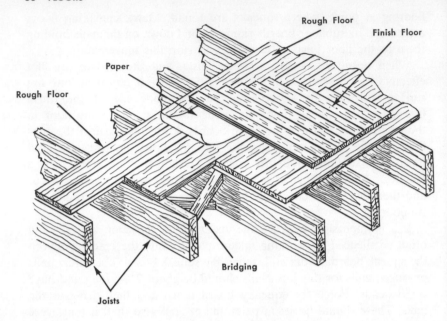

Rough Floor

Finish Floor

Paper

Rough Floor

Bridging

Joists

FLOOR-FRAMING DETAILS

strength. Often this girder holds the ends of the joists, its other end resting on the foundation wall. The girder, in turn, is held up by one or more wood or steel posts resting on the crawl space or basement floor.

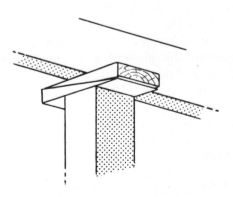

PROPPING UP A JOIST

In spite of all these, a floor may sag or vibrate when it is walked over because the girder has sagged and is no longer providing adequate support to the joists. This can be caused by a wood girder shrinking, or because the posts holding the girder have shrunk, sunk into the base, or been damaged by decay or insects.

The first point to check is at the girder top to see if it is in contact with all the joists. If not, drive small wood wedges, such as shingles, between joists and the girder top. If the posts have pulled away from the girder, drive wedges between the post top and girder. If the posts have cracked the floor and are sinking into the ground, or if they are resting on soil, they must be provided with a solid footing of concrete.

In many cases, the floor is weak or sagging because there aren't enough posts to support the girder, or there are no girders or posts. If the trouble is lack of posts, these are not hard to install. The best kind is the metal adjustable jack post. This comes with a built-in jack at the top. The post is first adjusted to the proper height, and, after it is in place, the jack is turned to bring the girder and floor to the proper position.

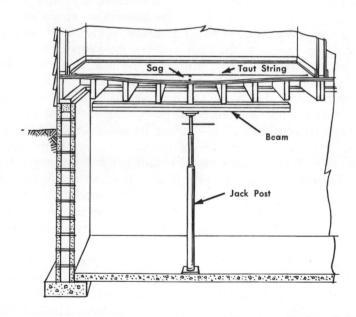

If the floor has sagged, do not try to level it in one operation, for this may crack walls and ceilings above. Turn the jack up about one-half inch each week. If this is done, the house structure will have a chance to adjust without damage. 4" x 4" wood posts are less expensive than metal, but they are more difficult to install. The girder must first be jacked to the correct height with a post and jack, and the new post carefully cut to the correct size and set into place.

It is essential that the girder support post rest on a solid concrete footing. One-foot square and about one-foot deep is a good size. If there is a concrete floor, it is necessary to break through so the hole for the footing may be dug.

If wood posts are used, the footing should be sunk about eight inches below the floor level, with approximately four inches above the floor to protect the post end from dampness and termites. It is wise to use a post that has been treated with a wood preservative. If the basement floor becomes wet at certain times of the year, coat the end of the post with asphalt before setting onto the footing. Footings for metal posts may come flush with the floor.

Installing a Girder and Posts. In the event no girder was provided (and you'll find this condition in older houses), one must be installed. A steel one is best; but if the homeowner means to do the job himself, 4" x 4" wood girder is easier to handle. It should be placed at right angles to the joists at about the midpoint span.

Reinforcing Joists. Where it is not convenient to use a girder or posts, sometimes the floor may be strengthened by reinforcing the joists with lengths of 2" x 4". The floor should be jacked to the right height with a temporary girder and posts, then each joist should be reinforced by running a 2" x 4" along its entire length. A 2" x 4" should be placed on each side of the joist, coming flush with the bottom of it. They must rest on the foundation wall that supports the joists. Spike these to the joist with 16 *d* nails set sixteen inches apart.

It will sometimes happen that a floor on the second or third story of a house will sag. In this event, it is best to rip up the flooring to find out exactly what is causing the trouble. Often you will find that the joists have been notched so deeply, to allow for pipes, that they have cracked and no longer provide adequate support.

Refinishing Wood Floors. After a period of years, or because of neglect, hardwood floors may require refinishing. This is not a very difficult job, but it does require a good deal of time. The first step is to remove the old finish and get the wood nice and smooth. This can be done by hand, first with a paint and varnish remover, and then with sandpaper or a scraper; but the best and fastest way is with an electric floor sander. These units can be rented by the day from hardware, paint, and flooring stores. You will actually need two sanders, the large unit and the small one (called an *edger*). This little unit is for getting close against the walls and in other spots too small for the larger sander to reach. You will also need sandpaper to catch any spots that the edger isn't able to reach. You will need three grades of sandpaper—coarse, medium, and fine—and these can be purchased at the store where the sander is rented.

Before starting the sanding operation, go over the floor carefully. Drive any exposed nail heads below the wood surface, and fill over them with plastic wood or a similar wood filler. If any boards squeak, now is the time to fix them.

There is no great trick to operating a floor sander. The main thing to remember is never to allow the rotating drum to remain stationary while in contact with the floor. If it does, it will make a depression. Most sanders are made so that the sanding drum can be easily pulled off the floor when necessary. When the drum is rotating and is in contact with the floor, keep the sander moving.

The first cut with the coarse paper on the sanding drum can be made across the wood grain. Then make another pass in the direction of the wood grain. All the rest of the sanding should be done in the direction of the wood grain. After you have made the first sanding with the large sander with coarse paper, go to work with the edger and pick up any areas that the large sander couldn't reach.

The coarse sanding operation should remove all traces of the old finish, as well as any stains or very rough spots. If there are discolored areas in the wood after this sanding, the chances are that they are so deep in the wood that sanding will never take them out. They can, however, often be removed with a wood bleach. This operation should be done before the final sanding, because the bleaching operation will leave the wood rough.

The next sanding operation is with the medium-grade paper; and then the fine grade is used for the final sanding. Before doing these last operations, either take off your shoes or pull old socks over them so that you won't soil the freshly sanded floor.

Modern floor sanders have built-in vacuum cleaners and these will remove most of the dust produced by sanding but not all. After the final sanding, go over the floor with the household vacuum cleaner to remove all traces of dust.

Wood Floor Finishes

As finish on a floor you may use shellac, varnish, a floor sealer, or one of the new plastic floor finishes.

Shellac. This is a popular finish because it dries in a few hours. It is not, however, as durable as some other finishes. For best results, apply three thin coats of shellac. A 3-pound cut is most satisfactory. Give the first coat three hours to dry before putting on the second, and let the second coat dry overnight, if possible, before the third.

Shellac may also be used as a base for a wax finish. If wax is rubbed directly on wood it will darken it as it absorbs dirt. A coat or two of shellac under the wax will prevent this. Brush on one or two thin coats of shellac, and then apply the wax. Shellac is often used as a base coat for a varnish finish because it dries quickly and so saves time. You must be sure to use the type of floor varnish that will be compatible with the shellac, for some varnishes do not react well with shellac.

Varnish makes a durable finish; but it takes time and effort to apply, so it's not as popular as it once was. Before it can be put on an oak or similar open-grain floor, a filler must be used. This should be let dry overnight and then sanded lightly. For the most durable job, you should use three coats of varnish; and each coat should have at least 24 hours to dry.

Floor Sealers. These differ from most finishes in that they sink into the wood pores rather than remain on the surface. This makes them most durable; and they are probably the best to use on floors that take hard wear.

Sealers are applied with a brush or roller. The sealer is spread generously over the floor and the surplus wiped away. Before the coat has dried, it should be rubbed down with steel wool. Floor waxing machines can be fitted with steel wool pads to make this easy. Let the first coat dry overnight; then apply the second. Do not be quite so generous with the sealer on this coat; put only as much as the floor will absorb. The final coat is polished with steel wool and given 12 hours in which to dry, after which it should be waxed.

Plastic Floor Finishes. These are as durable as sealers, and they can be applied directly to all wood floors except pine (for which a special primer is needed). Usually three coats of finish are needed; but because this material dries rapidly, it's possible to put on all three coats within 24 hours. Allow about one hour for the first coat to dry, and about four for the second. Give the third coat 12 hours to dry before using the floor.

Preparing Wood Floors for Resilient Floorings. Wood floors make a satisfactory base for resilient floorings such as linoleum, vinyl, etc.; but they must meet certain specifications. First, there should be a double thickness of wood flooring. Resilient flooring should never be applied to a single thickness of wood unless it is the extra-thick plywood designed for this purpose. Most houses today are built with double floors—a subfloor covered with a finish floor—and this make a perfectly good base for resilient coverings. If there is only a single thickness of flooring—and this may occur in the attic or on a porch—then it must be covered with hardboard or plywood before installing the new covering. Lumber yards and flooring stores usually stock hardboard and plywood suitable for this purpose, and there are also special products made just for underlayment. Be sure to install these materials in accordance with the directions, and use the correct size and number of nails specified.

If the resilient flooring is to be applied over a double-thickness wood floor, check the floor and punch down any exposed nail heads. Eliminate any squeaks now, for they will be difficult to deal with after the covering is in place. If the floor is very uneven and sanding won't correct matters, cover it with hardboard or plywood sheets to produce a smooth surface.

The manufacturers of resilient flooring publish complete booklets on exactly how their product should be installed. Be sure to get this literature, and follow the directions carefully. If you do this, you will be almost certain of being satisfied with the product and with your own work.

Concrete Slab Floors. Many homes built since 1946 do not have wood floors, but are built on a concrete slab. This is poured over a bed of gravel; and the surface is usually covered with some type of resilient flooring.

If the concrete slab was not properly installed, cracks may occur. These are not serious, but they are unsightly; they should be repaired by filling with patching cement.

Should damp spots occur on the concrete, it may only be condensation; but it may indicate a leak in the plumbing or heating lines set into the concrete at the time of construction. This is a real headache, for to fix the leak the concrete will have to be broken up to expose the pipes.

Resilient Floor Repairs and Maintenance

Repairs. Damaged floor tiles can be removed by placing a piece of dry ice on the tile for a few minutes. This will chill the tile cement and make it brittle, and the tile can then be lifted out with the help of a putty knife. Asphalt tile can also be removed by heating the tile with a hot iron or blowtorch. Scrape off the old cement from the base. Then replace with new tile, using linoleum cement or a similar mastic. Drop, not slide, the new tile into place. Force it down, and wipe away any excess cement that may come up around the edges.

If tiles are not properly installed, the cement used to set them in place will work up around the edges; this can go on for weeks and even months. The cement can be removed by scraping off as much of the cement as possible with a putty knife, and then wiping the tiles with water and steel wool.

Linoleum and vinyl sheets will sometimes come loose at the seams because of improper cementing or because water used in washing has seeped through to soften the cement. These loose edges can be fastened back by working flooring cement under them with a putty knife.

After the cement is in, force the sheeting down and put on weights to hold it until the cement has dried. If the cement fails in the center of a sheet, there will be a bulge. Split the bulge with a sharp knife or razor; if possible, cut along the pattern so that the cut won't be too conspicuous. Coat a flexible knife blade with cement and slip it through the cut so that the cement can be applied to the underside of the sheet. Force the sheet back into place and weight it down until the cement is dry.

Removing Varnish from Linoleum. Many homeowners make the mistake of coating linoleum with varnish in the belief that this will make the linoleum easier to keep clean. This is not the case; and, to make matters worse, the varnish gives the linoleum a slightly yellowish appearance. After a period of time, the varnish on the heavy-traffic areas will be worn away; and the net result will not be pleasing. The old remaining varnish can be removed but it is something of a chore. Use a remover made by adding three pounds of trisodium phosphate to a gallon of warm water. Apply this to a small area, and wait until the varnish becomes soft; then rub with fine steel wool. As soon as one area is clean, rinse with fresh water and wipe dry. Continue in this way until all the varnish has been removed. Keep off the linoleum until it is both dry and hard, and then coat with wax. Sometimes other finishes are used on linoleum and other resilient floorings, and these cannot be removed without damage to the floor covering. The only suitable protective coating for any sort of flooring is the correct type of wax.

Cleaning and Waxing Floors

To repeat, the key to keeping floors attractive and easy to clean depends on using the correct cleaner and wax. A coating of wax is important for it not only protects the flooring or the finish but also makes daily cleaning easy.

Asphalt Tile. Before waxing, the surface should be cleaned with warm water and a mild household detergent or commercial asphalt-floor cleaner. Apply this solution with a damp mop. Do not flood the floor with water, because this may loosen some of the tiles. Stubborn stains can be removed by rubbing with fine steel wool. After washing, rinse the floor with clean water and allow it to dry. The only type of wax suitable for asphalt floors is a water-base or water-thinned wax. Wax containing a solvent can damage the tile. Also, never use an oil mop for daily cleaning or wiping up dirt. A mop dampened with water is best.

Cork Tile. Wax cleaner is used on cork tile. Avoid water on these floors, because it can damage them. If wax cleaner doesn't do an adequate color-restoration job, buff with fine steel wool and a liquid floor or solvent paste wax, never a water-base wax. A damp mop is good for daily wiping.

Linoleum. Too much water is harmful to linoleum, because it dries it out; so it is best to use a wax cleaner. The best kinds are the solvent-base paste or liquid waxes. A dry mop may be used regularly.

Rubber Tile. Clean rubber tiles with water and a mild detergent. Don't use solvent-type cleaners; they can damage some types of rubber tiles. Rinse after washing, and allow the floor to dry thoroughly before waxing. A water-base wax is best. Run over daily with a damp mop.

Stone, Brick, and Concrete. Such surfaces are difficult to maintain unless sealed with a special masonry floor sealer. This seals the pores in the masonry so that dirt and liquids cannot be easily absorbed. Once the sealer has been applied, detergent and water make a good cleaner. If you wish to apply wax, use a paste wax.

Vinyl. Clean with detergent and water, followed by a rinse of floor cleaner. Use self-polishing or paste wax, and a damp mop for daily wiping of vinyl floors.

General Floor Maintenance. A good floor finish or floor covering will give many years of attractive service if it is given proper care and cleaning. One reason why many floors look dingy is that they are never thoroughly cleaned before a fresh coat of wax is applied. If you want a floor to look bright, then all the old dirty wax must be removed before fresh wax is applied. One of the best ways to do this is with an electric floor waxer fitted with cleaning brushes. These are not expensive, but if you do not wish to purchase one you can rent a machine by the day from most hardware and flooring supply stores. After the floor has been well scrubbed, rinse and dry it; and then it will be ready for a fresh coating of wax.

Many persons prefer not to use wax on floors because they believe it produces a slippery surface. This is true only if the wax is not properly applied. Several thin coats of wax buffed by machine will produce a hard glasslike surface that will not be slippery. Too much wax that has not been buffed will often be slippery, but this is not the fault of the wax but rather of the application.

The protective wax coating on any floor will first show signs of wear at heavy traffic points, such as around doors and near the fireplace. Unless these spots are touched up, dirt may be ground into the flooring; and a good deal of time and effort will have to be spent in getting it out.

Keep an eye on the main traffic lanes in each room and treat these areas when they show signs of wear. Usually it is a simple matter to wipe the area clean with water and a detergent, or with a commercial floor cleaner, and then wax it. Liquid wax will clean as well as renew, and it is effective unless the dirt has been ground into the flooring.

The legs of heavy pieces of furniture can dent many kinds of flooring—even wood. It is wise to equip the legs of heavy pieces with castor cups. Use as large diameter cups as practical so that the weight of the piece will be distributed over several square inches of the floor. It is also wise to move heavy pieces a few inches every few weeks so that the load will not always rest on the same portions of the floor.

Cleaning Hardwood Floors. Water can damage a hardwood floor as well as its finish, so never use it here. For the same reason, never use a water-base wax. Clean with a commercial floor cleaner, and wax with a paste or liquid wax. Run over daily with a dry mop.

Patching Wood Floors. The protective finish on wood flooring will wear off more rapidly on those areas where traffic is heaviest. Keep these traffic areas well protected by wax; and when you note that the floor finish shows signs of wear, renew it at once. If you leave matters too long, the finish will become so worn as to allow dirt to be ground into the wood. This ground-in dirt will not always respond to washing, or wiping with turpentine, and you may have to sand or bleach the area to get it clean again. Thin coats of finish, shellac, varnish or floor seal should be applied to the area after the wax and dirt are removed. If the area is rough, sand lightly with steel wool or fine sandpaper before patching. Apply as many thin coats of finish to the area as are necessary to build up a patch equal to the finish on the surrounding surfaces.

CHAPTER **6**

Paints and Finishes

We use paints and allied finishes around the house for a variety of reasons. Outside walls are painted to protect them from weather and to make them attractive. Paint is used on interior walls and ceilings for decorative purposes and to make cleaning easier. Paints or finishes are applied to floors for appearance and to protect them from wear. Certain metals are painted to protect them from corrosion or discoloration.

Paints contain pigments that make them opaque; so when they are spread on a surface, they conceal what is underneath. Other finishes, such as stains, varnish, and shellac, do not have as much pigment as paint; so they allow some or all the natural color and grain of the material to show through. When it is desirable to hide a surface or completely change its color, use paint. When some natural color, grain, or texture is to show, use a slightly pigmented or transparent finish.

It is important that every surface inside and outside the house be given some protective coating. If this is not done, they will absorb dirt, fade, or deteriorate.

Paints

Paint consists of three ingredients: the pigment which gives color and body; the vehicle in which the pigment is suspended so that it may be applied with brush, roller, or spray gun; and the thinner which reduces the paint to the proper consistency for application.

Paints and allied finishes can be divided roughly into two categories: exterior paints, for outside surfaces exposed to sun and weather; and interior paints, for inside use.

Exterior Paints. Exterior paints are of two types: those designed for house walls and usually referred to as "house paints," and those for trim around doors, windows, shutters, etc.

Pigments for Exterior Paint. House paints are made with one or a combination of several pigments. Before purchasing a house paint it's best to consult with a local paint dealer as to which type of pigment is most suitable for the job and the location. For example, white lead is an excellent material; but it should not be used in areas where there is a high concentration of industrial fumes, for these will react with the lead and discolor the paint. In these locations, a titanium-zinc pigment is best. Other pigments in common use are titanium and titanium-lead-zinc. These pigments are used with a variety of vehicles. The most common types follow:

Oil-Base Paints. These can be applied with a minimum of surface preparation. They cover well, come in a wide range of colors, and clean themselves through a chalking process. They are most suitable for wood exterior walls. Linseed-oil paints are thinned with turpentine or some similar solvent. Oil paints, when properly applied, should last up to six years before requiring a fresh coat.

Alkyd Resin Paints. Alkyd is a synthetic resin. These paints are good for masonry siding, such as stucco and brick, as well as wood. They are somewhat more expensive than oil paints, but they are more resistant to mildew and to discoloration. They do not have quite so objectionable an odor as oil paints, and they can be thinned with an odorless solvent. They will last up to six years.

Latex Paints (Exterior). These are often incorrectly called "rubber-base paints." They are a mixture of latex resins and water; the latex resins may be from either a vinyl or a acrylic system. These paints are more expensive than either oil or alkyd, but they have certain qualities that to many will more than justify the increase in cost. They dry in half an hour and have no objectionable odors. They fade less than other paints and, when properly applied, will outlast other paints. Because they are relatively new, however, there is no definite information on just how long they will last; so don't be taken in by extravagant claims. There do appear to be sound reasons for believing that they will definitely outlast either oil or alkyd paints. Because they are water-emulsion paints, the brushes and rollers used can be washed clean in water. Latex paints are suitable for both wood and masonry.

Another advantage of these paints is that they will permit moisture vapor in back of them to pass through the paint film without causing blistering and peeling. This can only occur, however, when the latex paint is applied to a surface that is completely free of any other finish. In other words, if the wall has previously been painted with an oil or alkyd paint, and there is a problem with blistering and peeling, applying a coat of latex will not do any good. The subject of blistering and peeling paint will be discussed in detail later in this chapter.

Latex paint may be applied over oil or alkyd paint, but only after a special primer has been applied. On new work, a special oil primer must first be applied. You can get most of the advantages of latex paint when it is used on new work, for the costs will not be too much greater than if one of the other types of paint were used. There are fewer advantages on old work, because an oil primer must be applied before the latex; and this means two coats of paint rather than one.

Among the other paints used for exterior work are:

Trim Enamel.   These paints do not chalk, but they can be washed clean with water. They dry to a hard smooth surface and are very durable.

Porch and Deck Paints.   Use these on the floors of porches and outside wood steps. They will stand up well to both wear and weather.

Portland Cement Paints.   These are a mixture of portland cement and an alkali-resistant pigment, mixed with water. These are useful on masonry, because they won't peel or blister or be harmed if the masonry become damp.

Two-Coat House Paint.   The best exterior paint job consists of three coats of paint, for this produces the most durable and attractive finish. There are, however, two-coat house paints that give satisfactory results. These call for a primer, followed by a single finish coat. It is best if the primer and paint are of the same brand, and you must be certain that the paint you use is one intended for two-coat application. Ordinary paints do not have sufficient body and hiding power to do the job.

One-Coat House Paints.   These are designed for use over a previously painted surface that is in good condition, with no peeling or blistering. They should not be used on bare wood.

Interior Paints

Paints formulated for interior work are not suitable for outside work. They should only be used indoors, where they will not be exposed to the weather.

Oil Paint (*Flat*).   This is easy to apply, and it dries in about a day. It is not very resistant to moisture, and therefore it should not be used on bathroom or kitchen walls and ceilings. It doesn't wash well, so don't use it on trim around doors and windows or on walls that require frequent cleaning.

Oil Paint (*Semi-Gloss*).   This is a slow-drying paint resistant to moisture. Because it cleans well, it is good for bathrooms, kitchens, and children's room. It is not quite so easy to apply as flat paint.

Wall Enamel.   This is a slow-drying paint, but it is extremely resistant to moisture and it washes well. It is seldom used except for bathrooms and kitchens.

Alkyd (*Flat and Semi-Gloss*).   These are more resistant to moisture than the flat oil or semi-gloss, and somewhat easier to put on. These paints have less odor than oil paints; but they must be thinned with an odorless thinner if this feature is to be preserved.

Latex.   This is excellent for walls and ceilings, both old and new. It is one of the few that can be applied to new plaster without neutralizing the alkali present. It is easy to apply. Thinned with water, it dries in one-half hour or less, and it is practically odorless. It is washable after it has cured.

Dripless Paints.   These have a semisolid rather than liquid consistency. They do not require stirring, and they can be applied by brush or roller. They are usually somewhat more expensive than other interior paints, but they can be a great convenience because they can be applied with a minimum amount of mess.

Failures in Paint

There are several reasons for paint failures. The most common are improper preparation of the surface and use of the wrong type of paint. For example, if you use an interior paint on an outdoor surface, you can expect a paint failure within a short time. Failures in paint are commoner with exterior paints, because these are subjected to intense sunlight, changes in temperature, and moisture. Low-quality paints are more likely to fail than high-quality paints. Therefore buy the best grade you can afford.

Checking.   When cracks appear in the paint finish coat, but do not penetrate through all the coats, it is termed *checking*. It often happens because the finish coat was applied before the undercoat was hard and dry. The soft undercoat moves, and this cracks the finish coat. Checking also occurs when a non-elastic paint is applied over an elastic undercoat. For instance, ordinary paint will check if applied over enamel, since the enamel is more flexible. Checking can be prevented by making sure the undercoat is dry and hard before putting on the next coat, and by being certain the same type of paint is applied over the old paint. When checking does exist, it is usually unnecessary to remove all the paint; simply sand the wall until the roughness has disappeared, and then repaint.

Alligatoring. When cracks in the painted surface go through all coats, it is called *alligatoring.* This, like checking, can be caused by soft undercoats or poor quality paint. A surface that has alligatored should not simply be repainted. All the old paint must be removed and fresh paint applied.

Blistering and Peeling. These common failures are usually found on exterior surfaces or on interior walls subjected to moisture. Blistering and peeling are caused by moitsure getting behind the paint film. Sometimes this occurs because the wood was damp when the paint went on, but more often it is because water has somehow reached the wood after the paint has dried. Before you repaint an area where paint has blistered or peeled, it is important to find the cause of the moisture and eliminate it. The trouble may be a crack or open seam, somewhere on the sidewall, that lets rain reach the woodwork.

Inspect the exterior wall carefully for loose, warped, or improperly nailed siding, cracks in the wood, and uncaulked joints between windows and doors. Pay particular attention to the wall top where it joins the roof. Open seams here can allow water to flow down into the wall cavity. Check for a leaky gutter or downspout or one set too close to the wall. Even plants and shrubs too near the house can give off enough moisture to make paint peel.

Another common cause for dampness under the paint film is humid air from inside the house passing into the wall cavity and condensing into moisture when it strikes the cold sheathing or siding. This often happens in houses that have been insulated but not provided with a vapor barrier or sufficient vents. However, even when insulation is equipped with a vapor barrier, some moisture may pass into the wall. After condensing on the sheathing it is absorbed by the siding, and eventually it forces the paint film loose. Two things can be done to eliminate this; and sometimes both are necessary if the condition is severe. First, reduce the moisture in the air inside the house as suggested in the chapter on heating. Second, apply a vapor barrier to the room side of the exterior wall. An excellent vapor barrier is vinyl plastic wall covering. Two coats of enamel paint or latex paint are also good or, if you prefer, two coats of aluminum paint as a base for flat paint.

Some exterior paints, such as latex, breathe and allow the moisture trapped in back of them to escape. This reduces the possibility of blistering and peeling.

Non-Drying Paint. Paint will not dry if it is applied to a damp, dirty, or greasy surface and a poor quality or incorrect solvent or thinner is used or if the paint itself is inferior. When a painted area remains "tacky" for more than normal drying time, it sometimes helps to wipe it first with a clean, lintless cloth and then the thinner recommended for use with the paint. If this fails, remove all the paint, either with a remover or steel wool, then sandpaper, and start off fresh.

Paints dry through evaporation of the thinner and other liquids in the vehicle. If the air-moisture content is high, evaporation of the liquids will be slower than on a dry day. It's advisable to paint only when the humidity is relatively low if you are anxious for the paint to dry as quickly as possible. If you must paint indoors during humid weather, you may find it helpful, after all the paint has been applied, to use an electric fan to increase air movement over the freshly painted surface to speed drying. Using a dehumidifier also accelerates the drying process.

Bleeding. Bleeding can be local or widespread. This failure takes the form of a discolored and usually gummy condition in the paint. It can be caused by painting over knots or areas in unseasoned wood that contain a good deal of wood sap and resins. It can also be caused by painting over a stain such as creosote. There is no way to remedy a bleeding condition short of removing the paint, and then either cleaning off the cause of the trouble with a solvent or sealing it off from the finish with several coats of orange shellac or aluminum paint. Before painting new wood, always seal knots and sappy areas with orange shellac or aluminum paint. Before sealing, wipe away surface saps and resins with turpentine or benzine.

Mildew. Mildew is a type of fungus that causes paint discoloration. It attaches itself to the paint and spreads rapidly. It is commonest in warm, humid climates or where a surface gets little sunshine and fresh air, either because of location or nearby plants and shrubs. Unlike dirt, mildew cannot be simply washed off, for the mildew actually damages the paint film.

In sections where mildew can be a serious problem, it's best to use paints for both indoor and outside work that have been made mildew-resistant by addition of a fungicide. Paints can be purchased with the fungicide already added, or ordinary paint can be made more resistant to mildew by the addition of paint fungicides (these are sold at paint and hardware stores).

Mildew should be removed before repainting. This cannot be done with plain water, because that simply spreads the mildew over a larger area. Make a solution of three tablespoons of trisodium phosphate in a gallon of water, and add a pint of household ammonia. Scrub this over the mildew-stained paint, then rinse with fresh water. When the surface has dried, repaint.

Some mildew trouble can be avoided by trimming plants and shrubs near the house so that the painted areas get some sun and fresh air. In some places, mildew is so hard to control that it may be better to use a pigmented exterior stain rather than ordinary house paint. The former is less likely to be damaged by mildew.

Excessive Chalking. After house paint has been exposed to the sun and weather for a period of time, you can run your finger over it and some of the pigments will come off on your finger in the form of a dry chalk. This is quite normal; it allows the paint to more or less clean itself, and it also reduces the thickness of the paint film so that it will be ready for repainting when the time comes. If, however, the paint should begin to chalk excessively after a short time, it means that the previous paint was too thin, or thinned too much, or that an inferior paint was used. Remove the chalk by brushing; then apply two coats of good-quality paint. Permit the first coat to dry for at least three days before applying the second coat.

Paint, Mixing

Pigments in most paints settle to the container bottom; so before the paint is used, it must be thoroughly mixed. The easiest way is with a mechanical agitator that paint dealers usually have in their shops. These will mix the paint without removal of the container top. Once the paint has been mixed with this machine it should be used fairly soon, before the pigments can settle, and it should be given a good stir or two just before use.

To mix paint by hand, remove the container lid and pour off most of the liquid into a clean vessel. With a clean paint paddle, stir the pigment and remaining liquid until it has an even, creamy consistency.

Slowly return the poured-off liquid to this, stirring all the time. When all the liquid has been returned, pour the entire mixture into the second container and repeat the process several times. This is termed *boxing* and insures thorough mixing. As it is used, paint should be stirred from time to time, for pigments soon settle out.

Varnish and latex paints should not be mechanically agitated, because this produces air bubbles that can spoil the finish. They should not be boxed for the same reason. Mix by stirring gently.

Paint, Removing

Old accumulations of paint can be removed by sanding, scraping, or heating so that the paint becomes soft, or by using a liquid or paste paint remover. Which method is better depends pretty much on how much paint must come off, how thick the coats are, and where the painted surface is located.

Small amounts of paint can be taken off with a scraper, coarse sandpaper, or steel wool. An electric sander will speed the process. Paint scrapers with a sharp blade are good; but it's best not to use them on fine work until you've had some practice, because unless properly handled they can gouge the wood or take some wood off along with the paint.

When large areas of paint must come off, melting the paint so that it can be easily scraped away with a putty knife or similar tool is a good method. This is the usual way paint is removed from outside walls. You can use a blowtorch for this, with the flame adjusted so that it is wide and not very hot, or an electrical remover—which is much safer. The electric remover is plugged into an outlet. It develops sufficient heat to melt the paint so that the scraper, often part of the unit, can easily scrape off the softened residue. A blowtorch works in much the same way, but it is not so safe because of its flame. The flame is played over an area until the paint starts to blister, when it can be taken off with the putty knife or scraper. The torch is never used to burn off the paint, only to melt it.

If you use a torch, observe all fire precautions. Make sure no combustible debris is near, and hold the torch so the flame points down to prevent it from getting up under loose shingles or siding. It is best to check with your local fire department before using a torch to be sure that there are no regulations against its use. Also check with your local fire insurance agent.

Except for large areas, such as the outside of a house, a liquid or paste paint remover is the best way to get rid of old paint. There are numerous brands and types on the market. The best kind of remover for use around the home is the nonflammable, no rinse type. Nonflammable, water rinse removers are also good but there will be a delay in refinishing while you wait for the wood dampened by the water rinse to dry.

Some brands of paint removers contain flammable materials, and this fact is indicated on the container. Use these removers indoors with extreme care, and be certain that there are no open flames in the area where you are working.

Any substance that can soften paint is obviously pretty strong; therefore, wear rubber gloves when working with any type of remover. Also be sure that the room in which you are using the remover is well ventilated.

Liquid removers are fine for flat surfaces, but you'll find that the paste or semi-paste removers are best on vertical surfaces.

Using Removers. The remover is spread on the surface with an old paint brush and allowed to remain for several minutes. By this time the paint should be soft enough so that it can be removed with a broad putty knife, scraper, or coarse steel wool. After the paint is off, the wood may require a light sanding. If you use a rinse-type remover, you'll have to rinse either with water (if it is a water-rinse remover) or with a solvent (if it is a solvent rinse).

To get the most benefit from a remover, allow it to do the work. Once applied, let it remain until the finish is so soft it can be easily stripped off with a putty knife or steel wool. It shouldn't require much elbow grease if the remover has had time to do its job. If the paint doesn't come off easily, give the remover more time. Always take off one coat of paint or finish at a time; don't try to do them all with one remover application, for this won't work. Use a fresh application of the remover for each coat of paint or finish. Removing the finish from carvings and scrollwork will be more difficult than flat surfaces, but it can be done. You'll find an old toothbrush and toothpicks very handy for removing the finish from these areas.

Working with a paint remover can be a messy job, so be sure there are ample old rags on hand to clean up with and that floors and nearby surfaces are protected with paper or dropcloths. Old rags and waste used in conjunction with a remover should be considered flammable, and burned or disposed of where they can do no harm.

Most removers will work on all paints, varnish, and shellac; but shellac can also be removed by wiping with denatured alcohol.

Paints, Storing

Paints must be properly stored or they may deteriorate until they are useless. Paints and finishes should be stored where they will not constitute a fire hazard. Water-thinned paints must be kept where they will not freeze since this will ruin them.

No air should get at stored paints, because this will evaporate both thinner and vehicle. One way to make sure the container is tight is to wipe off all excess paint from the rim and set the lid down tight. Then turn the container upside down and store it just as it is. Skin can be prevented from forming on oil paint if a small amount of thinner is poured over the remaining paint and the container is then sealed tight. An excellent way to store paint is to pour the remaining paint out of its original container into a smaller one just big enough to hold the amount left. If the paint fills the container, there will be little air inside to allow evaporation.

As has been said, if air reaches paint in a container, a skin or thick film forms on the surface. Before the paint can be used again, this skin must be carefully removed. Cut around the skin edges with a knife, then lift the skin in one piece if possible. If the film is broken into small sections, these will mix with the paint and you must strain the paint through cheesecloth or an old nylon stocking.

Paint Application

Paints and finishes can be applied by brush, roller, spray gun, or spray bomb. For work about the house, you'll usually find the brush or roller more satisfactory. A spray gun is fine on large jobs; but good spray equipment is expensive, and cheaper instruments seldom produce good results. The exceptions are some water-thinned paints that are especially formulated for spray application. Some can be used with success even with the spray attachment of a household vacuum cleaner. Paint spray bombs are good for small jobs and touch-up work, but they are expensive when a large amount of painting must be done.

Paint Brushes. It pays to buy good-quality brushes and take care of them. A fine brush, given proper care, will last many years and actually improve with use. A cheap brush, on the other hand, doesn't cost much less and won't last. What's worse, it produces poor results.

Usually a brush's quality is reflected in its price, but there are several easy ways to judge quality. When the bristles of a good brush are worked back and forth in the hand, they have a substantial "body" and don't feel skimpy. Don't be upset if a few come loose, for this is to be expected in a new brush. It's not natural, however, after you have worked out the few loose ones, for this to continue. Examine the bristles to see if they are of unequal length, for this is necessary if the brush is to have a good taper.

There are many sizes and styles of brushes, but for most jobs about the home you'll need a 4″ wall brush and a 2″ or 3″ trim brush for woodwork and for reaching into corners.

An oval sash brush about 2″ wide is fine for painting windows. If you plan to work with enamel, you'll want an enamel brush; this has a more pointed tip than an ordinary brush.

If you work with varnish, get a varnish brush—and keep it just for that. Never apply varnish with a brush that has been used with paint or enamel; for no matter how well it has been cleaned, there are sure to be tiny bits of paint in the bristles that will discolor the varnish.

It's a good idea to hang a new brush in linseed oil for about 24 hours. Then take it out and work the oil from the bristles by brushing over old newspapers. This will make the bristles more flexible and allow the brush to do smoother, faster work. Also, the bristles will carry more paint.

Brushes, How to Use.   For easiest brushing, it's best to work with a container about half-full of paint. Dip the brush half the length of its bristles into the paint. If you dip much deeper the paint will get up into the base of the bristles where it will be hard to remove. As the brush is taken out, tap the bristles on the side to remove excess paint. Don't get rid of excess paint by drawing the bristles across the container rim, for this makes a mess and wastes paint.

The most comfortable way to hold a brush is by its metal ferrule, with the handle passing between thumb and forefinger. When possible, hold the brush with bristles pointing down and work with it this way. If bristles are held up, paint may drain down into the base and even onto the brush handle. It shouldn't be necessary to grip the brush too tightly, for this makes work tiring. Also, use your arm rather than just your wrist to move the brush.

Never force a brush so that almost the entire length of the bristles come in contact with the surface. This won't produce a good job, and it is hard on the brush. Start a stroke with about one-third of the bristles' length on the surface; and as the stroke continues, lift up so that less and less of the brush is on the surface. At the end of the stroke only the tip of the bristles should be touching.

How much paint you need on a brush depends on the type of paint you are using and on the surface you are painting. For example, enamels are flowed on with a full brush, but ordinary wall paints call for a drier brush. When painting a ceiling, always work with a rather dry brush so that the paint won't run down the brush handle.

Care and Cleaning of Brushes. It's not an extravagance to buy a good brush, but it *is* an extravagance to buy one and not take proper care of it. First, while using a brush, don't wield it so the bristles will be bent or separated. Don't jab a wide brush into a corner— use a small trim brush for those hard-to-reach spots. Don't use a wide brush to paint a pipe, or chair or table rungs, if it means the bristles will be separated in the middle. Never use a good brush on a rough surface such as masonry. Save old brushes for such work or buy an inexpensive one, for rough surfaces will wear down the bristles rapidly. Old brushes can be used on metal and for applying paint removers.

Most brushes are ruined because of improper cleaning or no cleaning at all. The first rule is not to soak a brush in water. Brushes used with certain water-thinned paints, however, may be washed in water. In any case, after all traces of paint have been removed, the bristles should be worked over paper until free of liquid.

A good rule is always to stop painting about one-half hour before you must quit. This extra half-hour gives you time to clean your brushes properly and store them so they'll be ready for use the next time you need them.

If you plan to use a brush again in the same paint within a few hours, it isn't necessary to clean it. Simply remove the excess paint by brushing the bristles on the surface you are working or on paper; and then, with all the bristles in place, wrap them in wax paper or aluminum foil. This keeps the bristles pliable until you're ready to return to work. If you're quitting for the day but plan to resume work the following day or within a few days, remove the excess paint from the bristles by brushing and then suspend the brush in a thinner or solvent. This is done by drilling a hole through the top of the brush handle and inserting a piece of stiff wire to form a cross-bar so that the brush can be hung without having the bristles touch the container bottom. This is important, for if you simply set a brush in the container, the bristles will be bent; and you may never get them in proper shape again. An excellent investment is a brush-storing unit containing solvents and brush-hanging devices. These do an excellent job of insuring that your brushes are kept in good condition. Solvents suitable for suspension of brushes are mineral spirits, kerosene, and turpentine. Benzine is not recommended, because it is flammable. Kerosene is good; it is inexpensive, and pigments dissolved out of the brush will settle at the bottom of the container. Turpentine is satisfactory for short-term storage; but if a brush is left in it too long, the bristles become coated with a rubbery substance. This can be removed, but it means added work.

Paint and hardware stores usually stock a variety of special products designed to ease the job of cleaning and storing paint brushes. One that we have found to be excellent is "Stat," a jellylike substance that is both easy and safe to use.

There is no problem in connection with brushes used on water-thinned paints; these can be cleaned in a matter of seconds by holding under a faucet and then set out to dry.

When a brush used with a non-water-thinned paint is not to be used again for some time, it should be thoroughly cleaned. Work out as much paint as possible, and then dip the brush in the solvent for a few minutes. This makes it possible to work out more paint. Use a comb or dull knife to scrape away paint that has collected at the base or heel of the bristles. Last, wash the brush carefully in warm water and detergent, then rinse the bristles and lay out the brush with the bristles flat for drying. When dry, wrap the bristles with wax paper or aluminum foil and store in a cool, dry place.

Solvents for Cleaning.   Brushes, rollers, and other painting equipment used in oil paint may be cleaned with turpentine, kerosene, mineral spirits, or linseed oil. With other solvent-thinned paints, use the same material as suggested on the label for thinning. Water is satisfactory for water-thinned paints. Brushes used in varnish are cleaned with the same solvents used on oil paints. Shellac brushes are cleaned with denatured alcohol; and lacquer brushes should be cleaned with lacquer thinner.

Reconditioning Brushes.   Failure to clean a brush properly, or letting paint harden in the bristles, makes reconditioning a real chore. If it's a good quality brush, however, it's worth the effort.

The first thing is to soften the hardened paint. This can be done with one of the many available brush-cleaning compounds. When the old paint is soft, it can be worked off the bristles with a knife, comb, or blunt putty knife. Once the bristles are soft, use more compound to work out all the paint. Now wash the bristles thoroughly in warm water and detergent, and, after rinsing, allow the brush to dry.

Paint Rollers. For large surfaces, such as interior walls and ceilings, most amateurs prefer a paint roller to a brush, because a roller does the job faster. It's unusual, however, that an entire job can be done with a roller alone. Usually a small brush or two should be used to get into spots that can't be reached by the roller. Rollers are good for ordinary paints, but they don't work well with fast-drying finishes such as shellac, lacquer, etc.

There are two basic types of rollers: one has a short nap of mohair, and the other has a wool nap for rough surfaces such as brick or concrete. They come in a variety of sizes and shapes. Some rollers have a hollow cylinder into which paint is poured, but the most popular home type is the pan-fed roller which is inexpensive and easy to use. Professionals use a roller into which paint is fed through a hose from a large reservoir.

Using a Roller. Before starting work, make sure that the roller and pan are clean. You can save time later if the pan bottom is lined with aluminum foil. This will eliminate the chore of cleaning the pan when you have finished. You simply throw away the aluminum foil liner. The pan should be set on a flat surface where there is no chance of spilling. If a ladder is being used, special brackets are available to fasten the pan to the ladder, where it will be handy and won't tip.

Mix the paint, and pour in enough so that half the pan bottom is covered. Run the roller back and forth over the bottom until it is filled with paint. Remove excess paint by rolling it over the part of the pan not filled with paint, and start painting with an upward stroke. The rest can be done by working the roller up and down with diagonal strokes to insure good coverage; but the final roller strokes should be straight up and down.

When the roller begins to dry, reload it; and start the first strokes on an unpainted area, rolling toward the freshly painted surface. Allow the roller to overlap the painted area by about half the roller's width. This will avoid seams appearing when the paint dries. Rollers are cleaned with the same materials used to clean paint brushes.

Spray Bombs. Aerosol spray bombs are available with many kinds of paints and enamels as well as shellac. They cost a good deal more than paint in bulk, so they are generally used only on small work such as furniture or for touch-up jobs.

Directions for the proper use of paint spray bombs are printed on the container, and these should be followed carefully to insure satisfaction. When you have finished using the bomb, turn it upside down and spray against an old newspaper or dropcloth until only gas escapes through the nozzle. This clears the nozzle opening and prevents paint from clogging it.

Spray Guns. Any finish that can be applied with a brush or roller can also be applied with a spray gun. In fact, a spray gun is far superior to a brush or roller for fast-drying finishes, such as lacquer, or on uneven surfaces, such as masonry, where it is difficult to cover the texture with a brush or even a roller. A spray gun is also best for picket or woven-steel fences and for wicker and rattan furniture. As a general rule, the paint or finish for a spray gun must be thinned more than for brush or roller application. Usually directions for thinning for use with a spray gun are printed on the paint container.

One disadvantage of spray equipment is that adjoining surfaces not being painted must be protected with masking tape or paper. Often the job could be done with a brush or roller in the time it takes to mask off these areas. For the average homeowner, spray equipment is best used for large surfaces such as walls and for items such as furniture that can be taken outdoors. It's always best to spray outdoors, for the paint particles produced are easily inhaled. If you must spray indoors, wear a respirator, which can be bought at most hardware and paint stores. Avoid spraying outdoors when there is a strong breeze, for this will blow paint all over the place.

There are a wide range of spray guns on the market. The least expensive kinds are attachments that fit on the household vacuum cleaner. Inexpensive electric vibrator guns are good for small jobs. If you wish to do much spraying, it will pay to buy or rent an "external mix" gun. These are best, and, properly used, will produce professional results.

Much of the trouble with a spray gun comes from improper mixing of the paints and improper cleaning of the nozzle and related parts. The paint must be carefully and thoroughly mixed, because even one small, solid particle will clog the gun nozzle. The nozzle must be carefully cleaned after each use.

Using the Gun. No serious painting should be attempted with a spray gun without practice. The gun should be held about 6″ to 10″ from the surface. If it is stopped even for a second, release the trigger so the flow of paint will cease. If the trigger isn't released, a heavy accumulation of paint will build up and cause the paint to run and sag. At the end of a stroke, let go the trigger. Be sure to hold the gun upright at all times while painting, and do not tilt it either up or down.

Enamels

There are wide selections of enamels for both interior and exterior work. The outstanding characteristic of enamel is that it dries to a hard, smooth finish, usually free of brush marks. It has a varnish base rather than an oil base. Most enamels today have an alkyd varnish base, which makes them most durable. Enamels are slower drying and somewhat harder to apply than ordinary paints.

For best results, enamels should be put on with a special enamel brush, which has a chisel tip rather than the blunt, ordinary brush end. Enamel should never be applied directly to bare wood or an unprimed surface, for a lot will be wasted; it's also difficult to obtain a smooth surface. The best procedure in dealing with a fresh surface is to sand it until it is smooth, and then use a special enamel undercoater. On very porous wood it's often wise to apply a wood filler before the undercoater. When the undercoater is dry, sand lightly with fine sandpaper, dust, and apply the enamel. Enamel is flowed on, not brushed into a surface. Work with a full brush in long smooth strokes in the direction of the grain. Be careful on vertical surfaces and at the end of strokes not to leave heavy accumulations of enamel, for these will spoil the job if not picked up immediately with the brush. Don't go back over an area that has been coated, for enamel is formulated so it will flow together and eliminate brush marks. If you go back over a coated area with the brush, you will leave fresh marks which may not flow out. Allow ample time for the first coat to dry, then sand lightly and dust thoroughly before applying the next coat.

Enamel is more elastic than ordinary paints, so it is best not to use it as a base for paint; a movement of the enamel may cause the finish coat of paint to crack. Enamel may, however, be applied over oil and alkyd paints that are in good condition.

Because it produces a finish that is smooth and durable, and one that is easily cleaned, enamel is excellent for woodwork inside and outside the house, for kitchen cabinets, and for furniture and floors.

Clear and Semitransparent Finishes

Clear and semitransparent finishes are used on woodwork when you do not wish to hide the natural color and wood grain. These finishes can be used in conjunction with a wood stain, or they may be applied directly to the wood. They are used primarily on furniture, interior woodwork, and floors.

Lacquer. This is a very fast-drying finish that comes either clear or in a wide range of colors. Because it dries so rapidly, it is hard to apply by brush; the best results are obtained by using a spray gun. Lacquer must be thinned with a special thinner, which is also suitable for cleaning the equipment used with it. There are slower-drying lacquers called "brushing lacquers"; these can be applied more successfully by brush than standard-type lacquer. Clear lacquer is used on floor finishes and for metal objects of copper or brass when you wish to preserve the natural color. Pigmented lacquers are used extensively for furniture, but the amateur will find that slower-drying enamels produce better results. Other finishes can be applied over lacquer, but lacquer should never be put on over old paint, varnish, shellac, or enamel, because it will act as a solvent and soften the undercoat.

Shellac. This finish comes either clear or orange. It is made by reducing the natural resin secretion of a small insect in denatured alcohol. Shellac is thinned with denatured alcohol; and alcohol is also used to remove old shellac. Shellac is very fast drying. It can be applied either by brush or by spray bomb. It should not be used for outside work or where it will be subject to moisture. It is extensively used on floors, furniture, and wood trim. It can also be used as a sealer. Orange shellac is used as a rule over dark stains. White or clear shellac is used for light-colored woods.

Shellac is usually sold in a container as a 4-pound or 5-pound cut, meaning four or five pounds of shellac gum are dissolved in one gallon of denatured alcohol. This mixture is usually too thick for most house jobs. It can be reduced to a 2-pound cut by adding denatured alcohol. To reduce a 5-pound cut, add an equal amount of alcohol. For a 4-pound cut, add three-quarters of a gallon of denatured alcohol to each gallon of shellac. Shellac should always be applied in thin coats. It dries so rapidly that it's often possible to apply three coats within a 24-hour period. Shellac is best put on with a rather wide brush.

Sealers. These finishes differ from most in that they are designed to penetrate the wood pores, where they harden. Ordinary paints and finishes remain, for the most part, on the surface. Sealers are more durable than other finishes; they are particularly good on floors, because they wear away only as the wood itself is worn. They are easy to apply by brush and can be touched up when worn. Usually two coats of a sealer is sufficient. Besides being used on floors, they are excellent for furniture and interior woodwork such as trim and paneling.

Varnish. Varnish is made with an oil or alkyd resin base. It can be used on floors, furniture, or woodwork inside the house. Exterior or spar varnish is suitable for outside work. There are many varnishes, each designed for a particular job: floor varnishes, furniture varnishes, heat-proof varnishes, etc. Be sure you use the right varnish for your job. An exterior varnish, for example, won't last long if it is used on a floor. A furniture varnish, on the other hand, will not stand exposure to the weather.

Applying Varnish. Varnish should be applied only over a smooth, clean, dry surface. It should not be put on when the varnish is cold or the temperature below 65°, for chilled varnish will not flow properly. Cold varnish can be warmed by placing the container in a pan of hot water. Varnish should be applied with a chisel-tip varnish brush; and it's best to set one brush aside for varnish and nothing else. The surface should be dust-free, for dust will stick to the fresh varnish and ruin the appearance. The surface must be perfectly smooth for varnish, and it's usually necessary to first use a filler on the wood for best results. Apply varnish in the same fashion as enamel, flowing it on rather than brushing it out.

Stains. Unlike paints, which are opaque, stains are more or less transparent; they are used to change or accentuate the color of wood without concealing the grain. Stains come in natural wood colors such as mahogany, walnut, and maple, as well as ordinary hues such as green, blue, yellow, etc. Stains must be applied directly to bare wood. They cannot be used over paints, shellac, or varnish, but they may be brushed over a surface that has already been stained.

There are many different types of stains; but the one best suited for nonprofessional use is the oil stain.

Stains are applied by brush or with a clean, lintless cloth. Allow the stain to remain on the wood for about 15 minutes; and then wipe it off with a clean, lintless cloth in the direction of the wood grain. The longer the stain stays on before wiping, the deeper it will penetrate the wood and the darker will be the effect. If the first coat doesn't seem to produce the desired result, a second and even a third coat can be used, allowing time for drying between coats. Because the end grain of wood is more porous than the rest, it will absorb stain faster and often come out darker than the rest of the work. This can be avoided if you coat the end grain with linseed oil thinned lightly with turpentine a few minutes before applying the stain.

While providing tone and color, stains do not offer any protective coating; and so, after they dry, a coat of shellac, varnish, seal, etc., must be applied. The exception here is the pigmented exterior stain used for outside work; this will be discussed later in this chapter.

Bleaching. Bleaching is required when you wish to make wood lighter than its natural color or to remove discolorations left by dirt or stain. Bleaching must be done on bare wood. Commercial wood bleaches may be bought at paint or hardware stores, or made at home by dissolving half a pound of oxalic acid crystals (sold at paint and hardware stores) in a half-gallon of warm water. The solution is worked liberally over the wood and allowed to dry, when a white powder will show on the surface. Wipe this off; and if the wood is the desired hue or the stain has gone, rinse with denatured alcohol. If another application is required, repeat the process; and when finished, neutralize with washing soda in warm water and let the wood dry.

Fillers. The surface of wood is made up of minute pores, most pronounced in open-grain woods such as oak, mahogany, and walnut. Unless these pores are filled before a finish such as varnish goes on, the liquid will sink into the pores and you'll end up with a rough finish. You can keep applying coats of varnish, sanding between coats, until you build up a smooth, level surface; but it's much easier to level the pores with a filler before varnishing.

Fillers are applied *after* the stain, but *before* the varnish. There are two kinds: paste fillers for open-grain wood, and liquid fillers for closely grained wood such as maple, birch, cherry, and redwood.

Paste Filler. Before use, paste fillers are thinned with turpentine according to the manufacturer's directions. They are put on with a stiff brush. Brush across and then with the grain. Allow the filler a few minutes to set, then wipe off excess with burlap or coarse cloth.

The filler is ready for rubbing when it becomes dull and no longer looks wet. Do not rub before the filler has set or you'll pull it out of the pores. But if you let it set hard, you can't remove it by rubbing and will have to sand. After the surface filler has been rubbed off and the remaining filler is hard and dry, sand the surface lightly before applying the finish.

Liquid Fillers. Special liquid fillers are available, but a thin coat of white shellac makes an excellent filler. Brush it over the surface, let it dry, sand lightly, and dust.

Exterior Painting

In most sections of the country the best time for outside painting is late summer or early fall. In these periods, woodwork and other surfaces are usually thoroughly dry due to warm, dry weather, and there is less chance of a sudden shower to spoil the paint job. Temperatures aren't high, and there are fewer insects to get stuck in the fresh paint and annoy the painter. Late spring is the next best time. Midsummer, late fall, and midwinter are least desirable.

Never paint if there is the slightest chance that the wood is damp or if rain may come before the paint dries. Nor should paint be applied during extreme temperatures, either hot or cold, or when exposed to the direct rays of a summer sun.

It's best to start painting in the morning, after the dew has dried, and to stop early enough in the afternoon so that the fresh paint can set before dew falls. Try to arrange your schedule while painting a house so that you always work in the shade. Start on the west side in the morning, and work around so you'll be painting the east, south, or north exposures in the afternoon with the sun in the west.

If there are insect swarms about, getting into the paint, add an insecticide sold for this purpose at paint and hardware stores.

Be sure to allow plenty of drying time between each coat.

How Often to Paint. As a rule, it shouldn't be necessary to repaint a house oftener than every four or five years; and in the event that alkyd or latex paints are used, this period may be considerably longer. The important point is not to put off painting too long, for if the old paint film becomes too worn and thin, it may crack and peel, requiring the removal of all the old paint. This means starting off fresh with bare wood and applying three coats. On the other hand, If painting is done too often, such a thick coating will build up that it, too, may crack and, in some cases, peel from the weight of the paint film.

Most house paints are formulated so that as they weather their thickness is reduced. This process is often accompanied by chalking. After the paint has weathered for a few years, the binder at the surface breaks down and allows the surface pigments to be washed away by rain. This not only reduces the paint film's thickness, but also keeps the paint clean, because the dirt on the surface is washed off with the pigments. This chalking is normal and is to be expected with paints that have been on for a period of several years.

Miscellaneous Equipment. Besides the paint, brushes, rollers, or spray guns needed, several other pieces of equipment are required. For exterior work, a strong ladder is a must (unless you rent paint scaffolding, which is better because it permits you to work more freely and over a larger expanse than you can reach from a single ladder). You'll want clean metal or pasteboard containers and stirring paddles for mixing paint. A dust brush helps for cleaning surfaces before painting. Putty and caulking compound are used to fill seams and joints. Steel wool, several grades of sandpaper, and a scraper will help smooth rough spots and remove failing paint. Have ample solvent on hand for cleaning equipment and washing up after work. Thin plastic gloves are excellent for keeping paint off your hands.

Dropcloths—canvas, paper, or plastic—are essential for covering plants and shrubs below your work area. Orange shellac or knot sealer should be ready for sealing knots and sappy spots on the wood. Masking tape is used to seal off window glass.

Painting the House

For a first-rate paint job, the outside surfaces to be painted must be carefully prepared. Detailed instruction as to preparation of various materials is given starting on the next page, with the suitable paints for them; but there are some general preparations applying to any house, regardless of materials.

Washing the House. It's always advisable to wash a house before painting to remove dirt and soot. If the house is exposed to salt air or industrial fumes, these can damage fresh paint. Often a good washing will restore bright color to old paint, making it unnecessary to repaint until the paint itself requires renewing.

The house can be easily washed with a garden hose and special brush attachment that also serves as a nozzle. If plain water won't remove the dirt, use a mild household detergent and warm water, with a scrubbing brush. Start at the bottom of the wall and work up, as this will prevent dirt streaks which can be hard to remove. After scrubbing, rinse thoroughly with the garden hose.

Loose siding or shingles should be renailed with rust-resistant nails, such as aluminum. Rust from exposed nail heads should be taken off with sandpaper or steel wool, and the nail heads set below the wood surface and covered with putty.

Clean out gutters, and make sure they are free of leaks. Cracks in stucco, poured concrete, and other masonry surfaces should be repaired (see "Masonry, Repairs," page 197). All joints between siding and window and doorframes should be filled with caulking compound. Check all windows, and remove and replace old failing putty around the glass.

Such items as shutters and window sashes are much easier to paint if taken down and painted in comfort on the ground.

Work Schedule. In painting the outside of a house, the best rule is to start work at the top and work down. This means that work should begin at the highest point on the walls, such as the roof gutters and cornices. On high houses where the wall tops can be reached only from a ladder, paint a strip as wide as you can reach in comfort, and apply the paint *across* the siding rather than vertically. This will prevent lap marks showing when the paint dries. Continue this strip until the wall bottom is reached, then reset the ladder and start painting the adjoining strips, again starting at the highest point of the wall.

If scaffolding is used, or on a one-story house where the highest wall points can be reached without too much difficulty, paint a strip about four feet wide. Don't paint a much wider strip, because by the time the wall bottom is reached, the paint along the strip edges will have set and a seam will show when the next strip is joined to it.

It's best to paint the walls first and then come back to windows and trim.

Aluminum. Even when exposed to weather, aluminum doesn't require a protective finish; the natural oxidation of this metal produces a gray film that serves as a protective coating. Aluminum left unfinished won't stain adjacent painted surfaces. It may be painted for decorative purposes by first wiping down with a phosphoric acid solution, and when dry, applying a coat of zinc chromate primer. Do not use a primer containing lead, for there will be a reaction between the two metals harmful to the paint. When the zinc chromate primer is dry, paint either with an exterior trim paint or standard house paint, depending on whether you're dealing with aluminum windows and trim or with aluminum siding.

If you wish to preserve the natural color of aluminum but prevent the gray film from developing, coat with clear lacquer after first rubbing with fine steel wool.

Asbestos-Cement Shingles and Siding. These do not require a finish for protective purposes, but they are often painted when a change of color is desired or when the shingles are badly soiled or stained. They can be painted with latex exterior paints, special solvent-thinned paints, or oil-vehicle masonry paints. Before painting, the shingles should be brushed clean.

Copper. When exposed to weather doesn't rust or corrode, but it can leave stains on adjoining painted surfaces which are difficult and sometimes impossible to remove. Clean the metal with one pound of copper sulphate to one gallon of water, and then rinse with clear water. The copper then can be painted with an outside trim paint or, if you wish to retain its color, with exterior or spar varnish. Copper is usually found around a house's exterior in the form of flashing over doors and windows, gutters and down spouts, wire insect screening, and electric light fixtures.

Galvanized Metal. Items such as garbage cans, roof gutters, and downspouts should be painted to prevent rusting of the steel. When new, the zinc coating will protect the steel; but the thin coating wears off when exposed to weather and use. New and old galvanized metal can be painted by applying a prime coat of metallic zinc paint. Remove grease and dirt by wiping with a solvent before putting on the primer. The finish coat can be ordinary exterior house paint or trim paint. Spots in old metal should be cleaned of rust and coated with two layers of metal primer, such as zinc dust or red lead.

Iron and Steel. New iron and steel often has a light oil film which must be removed by wiping with a solvent before painting. Rust spots should be taken off with emery cloth or sandpaper. Apply a prime coat of red lead or zinc chromate, and then apply two finish coats of oil or alkyd base paints. On previously painted work, remove loose paint and rust, prime these spots with a metal primer, then apply one coat of finish paint.

Masonry. Brick, poured concrete, stucco, masonry block, and other materials for exterior walls and foundations contain alkali which comes to the surface when the masonry is relatively new or when it grows damp. Since alkali is incompatible with oil-base paints, it's not advisable to use these on masonry surfaces. But there are certain paints and finishes that are immune to the action of alkali. Among these are solvent-thinned resin paints, exterior latex paints, portland-cement paints, and transparent silicone sealers.

Dirt and dust should be removed from the masonry by scrubbing with water. Grease and oil stains can be taken off by scrubbing with a solvent such as benzine. New concrete should be washed with a dilute solution of muriatic acid or a mix consisting of three pounds of zinc-sulphate crystals dissolved in a gallon of water. These are necessary to neutralize the surface alkali.

If the surface has been previously painted and is in good condition, remove dirt and grease and apply fresh paint directly over the old. Loose paint must be taken off by wire brushing or paint remover. Chalk should be removed by wire brushing.

Solvent-thinned paints must be applied to a dry surface. Exterior latex paints can be applied to a dry or wet surface. Portland-cement paints must be applied only to a wet surface.

Portland-cement paints, which come in a variety of colors, are the least expensive finishes for masonry. Dampen the walls with a fine spray from a garden hose, then mix the cement paint with water according to the directions on the package. Don't mix more than can be used in four hours. The paint must be scrubbed into the surface with a stiff fiber brush. These paints become an integral part of the masonry and therefore cannot peel or blister even if the wall gets damp or wet. (But they will lose some opaqueness when wet.)

Silicone finishes are often used on brick when a waterproofing compound that won't change the brick color is desired. These finishes should not be used on masonry less than 30 days old, and they should be applied liberally so that they can be obsorbed by the tiny pores in the masonry.

Plywood, Fir. This material can be either painted or stained. To paint unfinished plywood, the grain must first be sealed; this is done by applying a prime coat of flat oil or alkyd paint, enamel undercoat, or a special penetrating resin sealer. Don't use a water-thinned paint for this prime coat; it will raise the grain. If you wish to paint with a latex paint, use a clear resin sealer or flat white oil paint as the primer. When the primer is dry, the wood can be given two coats of house paint.

For a natural finish, apply a pigmented exterior stain or the Forest Products Laboratory's natural finish.

Roof Shingles (Asphalt). These can be painted with water-emulsion paints. A latex exterior paint is excellent. Tinted aluminum paints are available, and they may give up to five years additional use to a worn asphalt roof. In painting an asphalt roof, it's wise to remember that a light color reflects heat and so makes the house interior more comfortable in warm weather.

Roof Shingles (Wood). These should not be painted, because this encourages warping and decay; but they can be stained with a wood shingle stain, applied with a brush or with a roller having a long nap.

Trim, Doors, Windows, etc. These should be painted with trim paint or trim enamel. If they are to be a different color than the house sidewalls, it's important not to use a paint that chalks, for this will stain the sidewalls.

Window Screens. Screens with plastic or aluminum screening do not require protective coating. Copper screening doesn't either, but it's wise to give it a finish of spar varnish or paint to prevent staining of adjoining painted surfaces. Iron screening needs painting to inhibit rust. The paint to use is a screen enamel, but ordinary trim and sash enamel may be used. Paint, enamel, or spar varnish can be applied to screening with a piece of old carpeting, which is more satisfactory than a brush.

Wood, Paint. If the surface has not been previously painted, it should be thoroughly dusted. Cracks between siding and trim should be filled with caulking compound. Sappy spots and knots should be wiped down with turpentine and sealed with orange shellac or a commercial knot sealer. If the knots aren't sealed off, the resins in them will bleed through the paint.

Some woods contain a good deal of resin and gum, which can prevent penetration of the prime paint coat into the wood pores. Better penetration is obtained if the wood is wiped down with turpentine to remove resins from the pores just before the primer is applied.

The prime or first coat on wood must be brushed in with enough force so it actually gets into the wood pores and doesn't simply form a film on the surface. On previously painted work, sand rough spots smooth; and if there are areas where paint has blistered and peeled, remove loose paint and then prime the exposed wood with a coat of paint. Just before painting, wipe or brush the surface to remove dirt or dust that may be present.

Wood Floors, Decks, Steps and Stoops. These should be painted with a special porch floor enamel, or latex porch enamel, both tough and water-resistant. On new work, apply a primer and two finish coats. On old work, it's essential that the floor be smooth and free of cracks. If the old paint is in poor shape, it's best to strip it off with an electric floor sander. When this is done and the wood is smooth, fill any cracks between boards with white lead thinned to a paste with turpentine and work this into the seams.

All porch floors and decks should be pitched slightly so that water on them will flow off rapidly. If the floor doesn't have sufficient pitch, locate the low spots where water usually collects and drill several half-inch holes through the flooring so the water can flow off. Coat the exposed wood in the holes with paint so it won't absorb moisture.

Wood siding should be given three coats of paint for new work, or if you wish to give the wood a natural finish, use one suggested under "Natural Finish," below.

Wood Siding and Shingles. Shingles can be painted in the same manner as ordinary wood siding; but because they have a rough texture, it is easier to coat them with a roller than with a brush. If the shingles have never been painted, it's better to use a pigmented stain because this is easier to apply than paint and won't blister or peel should dampness get under it. But if the shingles have been painted, you can't use a stain unless you first remove all the old paint.

Wood shingles are sometimes coated with a creosote stain, which presents a problem if you wish to paint them because the creosote will bleed through the paint. Try putting a little paint on an inconspicuous area and leave it for a few weeks to see if the creosote is still active enough to damage the paint. If nothing happens, it's probably safe to paint. If the creosote does bleed through, either give up the idea of painting or seal it off by applying two coats of aluminum paint.

Wood, Natural Finish. All woodwork exposed to weather should be given some type of protective finish. If this isn't done, the wood will fade unevenly and become rough. What's more important, it's more likely to be damaged by moisture.

It should be pointed out that a clear or natural finish will not last as long as paint containing a large amount of pigment. The pigment protects the vehicle in the finish from the damaging rays of the sun. The finish areas receiving the most intense sunlight will be first to go; shaded surfaces will last longer.

A natural finish can be applied only over unpainted wood; it cannot be used on a painted surface until all the old paint has been removed.

One of the best natural finishes was recently developed by the Forest Products Laboratory. It can undergo four years of southern exposure, and lasts even longer in northern latitudes. For 5 gallons of this, you'll need 3 gallons of linseed oil, 1 gallon of pure turpentine, 1 pint of burnt sienna oil color, 1 pint raw umber oil color, 1 pound paraffin wax, 1 half-gallon pentrachlorophenol (10:1 solution), and 2 ounces of zinc citrate. Mix by pouring the gallon of mineral spirits into a 5-gallon container. Place the paraffin and zinc citrate in a separate container and heat over a flame, stirring until the mixture is of uniform consistency. Pour this into the mineral spirits, stirring vigorously. (Keep flame away from mineral spirits!) When the solution has cooled, add the pentrachlorophenol concentrate and then the linseed oil. Stir in colors until the mixture is uniform. Only a single application of this finish is needed, and 5 gallons will cover about 400 square feet. The wood must be dry before application.

Exterior pigmented stains and wood tints are available in various colors. They are easy to put on and will last a year or two. When they begin to fade it's a simple matter to touch up the faded spots with more stain. The only surface preparation needed is to brush dust and dirt away.

Spar or exterior varnish is often used on outside woodwork, but is not the best finish because it has few pigments and so it doesn't last long. Before fresh varnish can be applied, the old varnish should be removed or sanded down, which on a large area such as a house wall means a tremendous amount of work. A pigmented stain or the Forest Products Laboratory finish are more suitable than varnish; but before either can be applied, the old varnish must be completely removed.

Linseed oil is sometimes used as a finish for exterior woodwork; but it is not recommended because it fades, is easily attacked by mildew, and is easily soiled.

Interior Painting

Though most interior wall paints dry in a few hours, several days should be allowed in which to do a room. This gives time to repair walls and ceilings and otherwise make ready so that the actual painting may be done with a minimum of mess and fuss.

Before starting the job, it's wise to take out all furniture, carpets and rugs, and objects hung on the walls. Heavy pieces that cannot be easily shifted should be pushed to the center of the room and covered with dropcloths. It's easier to remove hardware from doors and windows than to paint around them. Take off electrical switch and outlet plates and drop wall and ceiling fixtures. Even if a professional painter is to do the work, you'll save him time and yourself money if the room is prepared before he arrives.

If you're doing the work yourself, besides paint, brushes, rollers, and other painting equipment, you'll need a stepladder high enough to help you to reach the top of the walls. If the ceiling is to be painted, you'll need some form of scaffolding. A single stepladder isn't adequate, for it will have to be moved at frequent intervals. A better method is to use two stepladders with connecting planks. These can be rented at paint and hardware stores. A large, old-fashioned kitchen table makes a satisfactory platform to work from if the ceiling isn't too high.

In painting an entire room, do the ceiling first. After this, paint the walls, and then the woodwork, starting at the highest point and leaving the baseboard for the last. This will prevent the brush picking up small dust particles and dirt and spreading them on other parts of the woodwork. If the floors are to be refinished, they should be done after all other decorating has been completed and has dried.

Preparing for Paint

Plaster Walls and Ceilings. The success of any painting operation depends a good deal on how well the surfaces are prepared. All cracks and holes in plaster walls should be filled with patching plaster or a similar patching compound (see "Interior Repairs, **Plaster** Repairs," page 38). Loose and blistered paint should be taken off and the exposed plaster coated with a wall primer and sealer or a coat of paint. Water-stained areas should have special treatment. First, remove the loose scaling paint and coat the area with zinc oxide. When this is dry, wipe it off and prime with aluminum paint.

It's wise to wash down walls and even ceilings before painting. This is essential for kitchens and bathrooms, for painted surfaces in those places become coated with grease which can ruin a paint job. Clean by wiping with turpentine or with a solution of one cupful of trisodium phosphate to a gallon of warm water. Sponge this over walls and ceilings as well as the woodwork, then rinse with a clean sponge and fresh water.

Wallboard.   Many homes today have walls and ceilings of wallboard, usually gypsum wallboard. Small holes in this can be repaired with patching plaster. In a poor installation, cracks may occur between sections of the board. These can be covered with strips of wide masking tape. Thin coats of joint cement are applied over the tape to form a smooth surface.

Wallpapered Walls.   As a rule it's safe to paint over wallpaper if it is solidly attached, and if the dye used for the pattern does not become soluble when paint is applied and bleed through. This can be tested by putting a little paint on an inconspicuous spot. If the paint dries with no ill effects, it can be assumed that the paper is suitable.

Before painting, it may be necessary to make minor repairs. Any loose edges of paper should be pasted to the wall. If the paper was applied with overlap edges, these should be sanded smooth. If there are spots where paper is missing, patch them with scrap wallpaper. Grease stains in the paper should be sealed with aluminum paint.

There are several disadvantages to painting over wallpaper. If the pattern is strong, it may take several coats to cover it. More important, should the paper come loose later or you should decide to remove it for one reason or another, you will have to sand through the paint film before the paper can be taken off. Many papers are put up with paste that does not contain a fungicide; and when these papers are painted, the paste may mildew, giving off an unpleasant odor. But removing wallpaper is never fun at best; and so most of us take a chance and paint over paper, hoping for the best.

When there are more than two layers of paper on a wall it is never safe to paint, for the weight of the paint may be enough to pull the paper off the wall.

If wallpaper has blistered in many spots and is not solidly attached, it shouldn't be painted. Stay on the safe side and strip it off so you can start your painting with a clean wall surface. For information on removing wallpaper and making repairs, see Chapter 7, pages 100-2.

Rough-Textured Walls, To Smooth.   It is virtually impossible to make a rough-textured plaster surface as smooth as a standard plaster wall, but it is possible to smooth it enough to make it passable. One way to eliminate the roughness is to work a portable electric sander over the surface; remaining spots can be smoothed by an application of plastic paint or spackling compound. These substances have considerable body and will fill in depressions in the surface. The final smoothing can be done with a rubber squeegee of the type used for washing windows. Another way to smooth a wall after sanding is to cover it with canvas or wallpaper liner. These are pasted to the wall in the same fashion as wallpaper and are thick enough to conceal irregularities in the plaster. The canvas covering makes a good base for either paint or wallpaper.

Acoustical Ceiling Tile.   These can be painted with an interior flat paint, either oil or alkyd.

Floors, Concrete.   Concrete floors in direct contact with the earth should not be painted unless free from moisture. To find out, place a piece of tar paper or building paper on the floor and let it stay there for a few days. If there is no sign of moisture when the paper is removed, it's probably safe to paint. If there is moisture, do not paint. Instead of paint, use a concrete hardener or sealer to seal the concrete, making it easier to clean and preventing absorption of dirt. There are also concrete stains that will not be harmed by moisture in the concrete.

Concrete floors must be thoroughly cleaned before painting. If the floor is very dirty, wash with a solution of three ounces of trisodium phosphate to a gallon of warm water. Scrub this over the floor with a stiff fiber brush, and then rinse thoroughly. Don't use carbon tetrachloride to clean a concrete floor, for the fumes from this solvent can be deadly.

Paint will adhere better to a smooth floor if the floor is first etched. This is done by scrubbing with a solution of one part muriatic acid to 10 parts water. Wear goggles, rubber gloves, and old clothes, and keep the acid off your skin. Scrub the solution over the floor with a long-handled brush, and then rinse with plenty of fresh water.

Allow the floor to dry before painting. The best paint to use on a concrete floor is chlorinated-base floor paint. Thin the first coat for easy brushing consistency. The following two coats can be applied as they come from the container. When the final coat is thoroughly dry, apply a coat of paste wax to make it more durable.

Interior Woodwork.   The trim around doors and windows can be finished with enamel, varnish, or a trim seal. If the woodwork has been painted and you wish to repaint, clean the surface and patch any chipped spots in the old enamel with an enamel undercoater, followed by enough coats of enamel to bring the surface flush with the rest of the finish. Apply a coat of enamel to the entire surface.

Flat wall paint isn't satisfactory for wood trim for it is too easily soiled and doesn't wash well.

If you wish to change painted woodwork to a natural finish, all the old paint must be taken off with a paint and varnish remover. After the wood has been sanded smooth, it may be stained and coated with a clear finish such as trim seal.

Woodwork is often given a finish of varnish. When this needs freshening, and the varnish is in good condition, the simplest thing to do is wipe down with a solvent, sand lightly with fine sandpaper, dust, and apply fresh varnish. If you wish to apply paint, it is not necessary or desirable to remove the old varnish. Sand it smooth and apply the paint. Much of the woodwork found in older houses was stained and then finished with a dark varnish. To make this wood light and still have a natural finish, the old varnish will have to be removed and, in many cases, the wood then bleached. It can then be finished with a light varnish, trim seal, or shellac.

To renew the finish on woodwork on which a trim seal has been used, just give the surface a light sanding with fine steel wool and apply a fresh coat of trim seal.

Windows. Areas around windows that are to be painted should first be cleaned. If the windows are of steel, remove any rust and prime the metal with a metal primer. Aluminum windows don't need paint for protection, but they may be painted for decorative purposes. Wood windows require a protective finish of paint or trim seal.

The best paint to use on the inside of windows is a water-resistant gloss enamel. On the outside, use an exterior trim enamel. The best tool for painting windows is a 1½″ sash brush.

The great problem in painting windows is to keep the paint off the glass. One way to do this is to use a thin metal shield called a "painter's time saver," which is held against the edge of the small divider strips as they are painted. Another way to protect the glass is to cover the edges with masking tape or with liquid masking that can be easily stripped off after the window has been painted.

To paint the sashes on a double-hung window, raise the bottom sash so there are a few inches of clearance at both ends. Begin on the bottom sash and paint the top horizontal member. Next paint the muntins or divider strips between the panes of glass, and finally do the vertical members. Now move to the upper sash and paint the exposed muntins and then paint the bottom horizontal member. Lower the bottom sash to its normal position and raise the upper sash to its normal position, leaving a slight gap between it and the top of the window frame.

Paint the upper horizontal member of the top sash and those parts of the muntins that could not be painted before. Then paint the vertical strips in the upper sash and, last of all, the bottom horizontal member of the lower sash.

Painting New Walls and Ceilings

Plaster. It was the custom some years ago never to paint new plaster until it was several months old. This was necessary because the lime in the new plaster would damage ordinary oil paints. Today, if a new plaster wall is to be painted with oil paint, the lime can be neutralized by coating the plaster with a solution made by dissolving four pounds of zinc sulphate crystals in a gallon of water. Brush this over the entire area and allow it to dry. When dry, the zinc sulphate crystals will show on the surface and should then be brushed off. After this treatment, a primer sealer coat, tinted the same color as the finish coat, is put on and allowed to dry. Then the surface is ready for an oil base paint.

Fresh plaster can be painted without the bother of neutralizing the lime in it if a latex paint is used. These paints will not be affected by the active lime in the plaster.

Gypsum Plaster Board. A wall made of this material is ready for painting as soon as it has been installed. This also applies to other types of wallboard such as hardboard, plywood, and insulating board.

It is always desirable, however, to use a sealer on unpainted wall and ceiling surfaces, especially if they are somewhat porous. If a sealer is not used as the first coat, much more paint will have to be used for the job; and it may be difficult to get an even coating because of uneven absorption of the paint.

Linoleum. Linoleum that has faded but is otherwise sound can be given a few added years of life by a coat of paint. The floor should be washed with a detergent to remove all old wax and dirt. The proper kind of paint for linoleum is a floor or deck enamel. A solid color will show dirt more readily than a pattern. To produce a pattern, cover the floor with an application of paint; and when this has dried, take a pan containing a contrasting color and dip a natural sponge into it. Then pat the sponge over the floor. Another way to produce a pattern is to load a brush with a different color paint and tap the bristles across a round stick as you walk around the floor. This will spatter the paint onto the floor in a random pattern.

Radiators. Radiators should never be painted when they are hot. Paint them when they are warm or cool. All old loose paint, dirt, and rust scales should first be removed with a wire brush. If the old paint film is in very poor condition it may be necessary to strip it off entirely. This can be done with a paint remover. It will be much easier to remove the old paint and apply the new if the radiators are disconnected and moved away from the wall.

The most satisfactory paints for radiators are flat wall paints or special radiator enamels. Metallic paints, such as aluminum and bronze, should never be used; contrary to popular belief, these will reduce the heat output of the radiator considerably. If the radiator is already finished with a metallic paint and the paint is in good condition, it's not necessary to remove it. Simply apply flat wall paint or radiator enamel over the old paint. The insulating effect of the metallic paint will be cancelled.

Radiators will be much less conspicuous if they are painted the same color as the walls of the room. This is also true of exposed pipes.

Metal Cabinets. Kitchen cabinets and similar items can be repainted by first removing all grease and dirt from the surface and then rubbing with fine sandpaper or steel wool to cut the gloss on the old finish. Dust carefully, and then apply one or two coats of enamel.

Kitchen Appliances. Kitchen appliances may be treated in the same fashion as metal cabinets. Ranges and units close to the stove should be coated with a special heat-resistant enamel which will not be damaged by temperatures up to 400° F.

Stairs. Stair treads and risers can be painted with a floor enamel. It is impractical to paint the risers, which are the vertical pieces running between the horizontal treads, with a light-colored paint, for they are often scuffed as people go up and down the stairs. Instead, paint them the same color as the treads.

Several methods have been worked out so that the stairs, in homes having only a single flight, can be painted with a minimum amount of inconvenience to members of the household.

One way is to paint the stairs late at night, assuming your bedroom is on the upper floor. Paint the risers and trim first, starting at the top and working down. When you reach the bottom, work up, painting the treads. Be careful not to kick the freshly painted risers. Wipe each tread clean before painting and use a fast-drying enamel to ensure that the stairs are dry in the morning.

Another trick is to paint alternate treads; and when they have dried, paint the ones in between. It is also possible to use stairs on which the paint is not thoroughly dry by covering the treads with pieces of wax paper. These will not stick to the paint, and they will protect it from damage.

Stair treads are sometimes given a natural finish with a floor seal or trim seal. Varnish and shellac are also satisfactory.

CHAPTER 7

Wallpaper and Wallpapering

Cleaning. The safest way to clean soiled wallpaper is with a commercial wallpaper cleaner that can be purchased at hardware, paint, and department stores. This is usually a dough-like substance which, when rubbed over the paper, picks up the dirt. These cleaners can be used on washable as well as most nonwashable papers. The dough from the inside of a loaf of rye bread also makes a good cleaner, and an artgum eraser can be used for removing spots of dirt. Modern washable wallpaper, of course, can be cleaned simply by wiping with a cloth dampened in warm water and a mild detergent.

A nonwashable wallpaper can be made easier to clean by coating it with white shellac, lacquer, or clear varnish when it is first put up; but this will change the color somewhat. These coatings will also make the removal of the paper more difficult, for they will prevent water from penetrating through the paper to the paste. If a papered wall is going to be subject to more than normal soiling, use a washable paper or a vinyl fabric wall covering.

Grease Stains. These can generally be removed by a paste made of Fuller's earth and a nonflammable cleaning fluid. Apply this paste over the stain; and, when it is dry, brush it off. Several applications may be required if the stain is very deep. Grease can often be removed by covering the stain with a clean blotting paper and running a warm iron over the blotting paper.

Ink Stains. Ink eradicators sold at stationery stores will usually remove these stains from wallpaper, but they may also remove portions of the pattern. These can sometimes be renewed with water colors.

Stains that cannot be removed by ordinary methods may be concealed by applying a patch over them.

Loose Wallpaper. When a section of wallpaper starts peeling off the wall, it should be pasted back at once. If this is not done, the paper soon becomes brittle and may crack when pushed back into

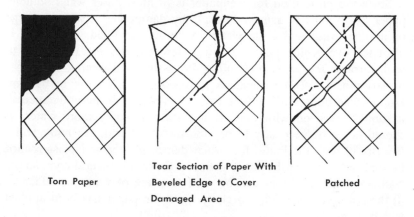

	Tear Section of Paper With	
Torn Paper	Beveled Edge to Cover	Patched
	Damaged Area	

Loose Wallpaper

place. It may also fade somewhat. Either wallpaper paste or a good library paste will do as an adhesive for repasting. Coat the back of the paper with paste and, after allowing a few minutes for the paper to become pliable, smooth it back against the wall. Run a clean cloth over the surface of the paper to remove any excess paste.

Sometimes the paper comes loose in the center of a section, causing a bulge. Split the bulge with a razor blade so that paste can be worked under the paper, and then press the paper firmly back into place. Wipe off the excess paste that oozes out of the joint.

Patching Wallpaper. When a section of wallpaper has become badly damaged or stained, the best thing to do is apply a patch over the damaged section. Take a piece of wallpaper with the same pattern, and considerably larger than the area to be covered; holding it so that the pattern side faces you, tear gently so the edges are "feathered." Coat the patch with paste, and apply to the area so that the pattern on the patch will match the pattern on the wall. The feathered edge of the patch will generally blend with the pattern of the paper and make the patch inconspicuous.

Removing Wallpaper.   It will be necessary to remove wallpaper when the paper is in generally poor condition or when you wish to paint over the paper and the pattern bleeds through the paint, or when there are so many coats of paper on the surface that there is danger in applying another coat of paper or even paint.

Since the paste used for wallpaper is in most cases water soluble, paper can usually be removed simply by dampening it with a sponge or a wide brush and clean water. A spray gun filled with water is ideal for dampening paper. Allow a few minutes for the water to soak through the paper and soften the paste; then remove the paper by stripping it off in vertical sections working from top to bottom. Use a broad putty knife to help free the paper. If properly dampened, it should come off with ease. If it does not, apply more water. It should never be necessary to pry the paper off with the putty knife. Be careful with the knife, for, when damp, plaster and plasterboard become soft and can be easily gouged. There are several commercial wallpaper removers that can be used in place of water or added to it; these are very helpful, especially when the paper has been applied with a water-resistant paste.

One of the best ways to remove wallpaper is with a wallpaper steamer. This device can be rented from a paint or hardware store. This equipment includes a tank in which water is heated to form steam. In the modern units, heat is supplied by electricity. The steam runs through a flexible tube to a wide nozzle, which is moved across the paper, allowing the steam to pass through the paper into the paste.

If there is more than one coat of paper on the wall, you will find it a good deal easier to take off one layer at a time rather than all at once.

Paper that has been painted, varnished, or otherwise waterproofed is harder to remove, for the outer coating prevents the water from reaching the paste. Cut through the coating with coarse sandpaper before attempting to remove the paper.

Removing Paper from Gypsum Wallboard Walls.   As this material is made with a core of plaster covered with kraft paper, incorrect removal of wallpaper can seriously damage the wallboard. Wallpaper can be taken off by sponging with water, but use only as much water as is needed to soften the paste. Strip off the paper carefully and allow the wall to dry. When dry, coat with a varnish size, and when this is dry, sand lightly to remove any roughness. Before wallpapering

a new gypsum wallboard wall, coat the surface with varnish size—
never glue size. The varnish size makes it relatively easy to remove
the paper at some future date.

Wallpapering

While not as easy as painting, papering is a project that can be
satisfactorily handled by the amateur. In addition to the required
amount of paper, the following tools are needed:

1. Smoothing brush for smoothing the paper on the wall
2. Plumb line and chalk
3. Large shears for cutting the paper
4. Seam roller for pressing seams
5. Clean sponge and bowl for wiping down strips
6. Wheel knife or razor blade for cutting and trimming paper
   around trim
7. Prepared wallpaper paste (This comes in package form and is
   far superior to the homemade variety.)
8. Wall size (This is applied to the surface before papering.)
9. Paste bucket and brush
10. Yardstick or measuring tape
11. Straightedge for trimming the selvage on the paper

You will also probably need some patching plaster, spackling compound, sandpaper, and a putty knife to make necessary repairs in
the wall surface before hanging the paper. A good stepladder and a
large, clean surface for trimming, folding, and pasting the paper are
also required. A kitchen table covered with heavy brown wrapping
paper is satisfactory, or you can rent a professional folding table.

Estimating Number of Rolls. The standard roll of wallpaper contains 35 square feet of wallpaper. Of this, about 5 feet will be wasted
one way or another, so it is best to figure 30 square feet to each roll.
Measure the height and length of the walls, and multiply these figures. The result will be the square footage of the wall. Do this with
all the walls that are to be papered. Add them together to get the
total number of square feet to be covered. Then divide this figure
by 30. The result will be the number of rolls of wallpaper required.
(Deduct one single roll of paper for every two doors or two windows
of average size in the walls.)

It is important that all paper of the same pattern have exactly the
same shade of color; this can be determined by checking to see if

the run numbers of each roll are identical. Check the uncoated edge of the paper, which is called the *selvage;* on this is the run number, and it should be the same on each roll. During the printing process, it is necessary to mix fresh colors for the pattern; and each time new colors are mixed, the paper being printed is given a new run number so that the rolls will be identical in hue. There can be enough difference between shades in different runs to spoil the appearance of a room, so be sure that each roll is from the same run.

Method of Hanging.   There are three standard ways to hang wallpaper. The easiest is the lap method, in which one strip of paper is lapped over the selvage edge of the adjoining strip. This is not ideal, because there will be a bulge at each point of overlapping. Far superior to this is the butt joint, in which the selvage is trimmed from both sides of the paper and the two strips are butted at the seams

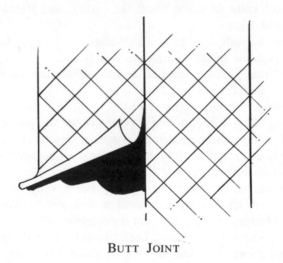

BUTT JOINT

with no overlap. The third method is the "wire edge," in which one strip is lapped over the other by about $\frac{1}{16}''$. With this method like the butt joint, the selvage is trimmed off both edges of the paper.

Preparing the Surface.   Wallpaper may be applied over plaster, gypsum wallboard, and plywood. Before attempting to hang the paper, make sure that the surfaces have been carefully prepared.

New Plaster. This should be treated before hanging wallpaper so that the active alkali in the plaster is neutralized. This is done by coating the plaster with a solution of two pounds of zinc sulphate crystals dissolved in a gallon of water. When this solution is dry, brush off the crystals; and then coat the wall with a glue size.

Old Plaster. Cracks and holes in old plaster should be filled, and, when the patch is dry, sanded smooth. If the surfaces are coated with calcimine or a similar water paint, this should be washed off. If the surface is painted with an oil paint, wash this down with a prepared wall cleaner to cut the gloss; then, when the wall is dry, coat it with a glue size.

Papered Walls. New wallpaper can be applied over old wallpaper if the old paper is in good condition and is tight on the wall. Loose pieces of the old paper should be torn off and the edges sanded so that they are feathered. If the paper is applied with a lap joint, sand these laps to remove bulges. Coat the areas not covered by the old paper with a glue size. If the paper is not tight on the wall, or if there are more than two layers, take off all the old paper. After the paper is off and the wall is dry, coat with a glue size.

Gypsum Wallboard. Patch any holes and open joints with spackling compound or wallboard joint cement. If the wall is new, coat with a varnish size or wall-primer-sealer. Do not use a glue size on gypsum wallboard. If the wall has been previously painted, treat the same as for a painted plaster wall.

Plywood. This material must be covered with a three-quarter pound lining felt to serve as a base for paper. The felt is applied with a special paste, and the strips are joined with a butt joint.

Applying the Wallpaper. Remove furniture from the room as well as any objects hanging or attached to the walls. It will save time to take off the plates from electric wall switches and outlets. Also, drop all electric wall fixtures, or, better still, disconnect and remove them. It will save time if radiators are disconnected so that they can be moved away from the wall to be papered.

Uncurling. Wallpaper will curl when it is unrolled, which makes it almost impossible to work with. The first step is to remove the curl from the paper. This is done by unrolling two or three feet at a time with the pattern side up, dragging it firmly over the edge of the table and smoothing with the other hand. This may have to be done two or three times before all the curl is out.

Measuring. Measure the distance from the molding at the ceiling to the base molding at the bottom of the wall. Hold up a strip of paper on the wall to decide where the pattern is to start at the ceiling line. Mark this point lightly on the paper. Cut off the first strip of paper, using scissors or tearing the paper with a straightedge. Allow about 4″ extra at both top and bottom. Use this first strip as a guide for cutting additional lengths of paper, making sure that the patterns on each strip can be matched up with those on the adjoining strips. Untrimmed paper will have "join here" printed on the selvage. It is best to cut or tear only four or five strips of paper at the start of the operation. This will prevent wasting paper should some of your measurements be incorrect.

Pasting. Stack the sheets that have been cut to size and turn the stack over on the table with the pattern side down. Pull the first sheet off the pile and bring the edge flush with the edge of the table. The point to all this is to keep the paste from getting on the surface of the table. Apply paste with the brush, using long, sweeping strokes. (Be sure that the paste has been properly mixed so that it is free from lumps.) Apply the paste to about two-thirds of the strip, leaving an inch or so unpasted at the end.

Folding. When two-thirds of the strip of paper has been pasted, fold the section in on itself so that one pasted surface comes against the other pasted surface. Line up the edges carefully so they can be trimmed together. Be careful not to crease the paper. Then shift the paper to bring the other section onto the table so that it can be pasted. Then repeat the folding operation at the other end. The paper in this folded state is moderately easy to handle.

Trimming. Assuming that the paper is being hung with a butt joint, the selvage must be trimmed on each side. This can be done with a razor blade trimmer or the special tool made for this purpose. Be sure that the edges are aligned; and using a straightedge as a guide, trim off the selvage, cutting about $\frac{1}{16}''$ inside the selvage. This will insure that none of the selvage remains.

Plumbing the Wall. The best spot to start hanging paper is near a window or door. Often these may not be absolutely vertical, so it is necessary to establish a plumb line. Measure off from a window or door frame a distance of one-inch less than the width of the paper to be applied and mark this location with a thumbtack. Take the plumb line and run chalk on it. Fasten the line to the tack or nail driven into the wall and fasten a plumb bob or weight to the other end so that the weight just clears the floor. When the weight stops swinging, hold it in this exact position and then draw the string tight. Snap the string and it will leave a line for the first strip of wallpaper.

Open the longer section of the first strip of paper by holding it by the unpasted end. Set this portion into position with the edge coming along the guide line and the top overlapping the ceiling molding by a few inches. When the paper is in position, stroke it with the smoothing brush to secure it to the wall. The lower section can now be unfolded and smoothed to the wall. Brush from center to the edges to remove bubbles. If the paper is not positioned quite right, it can be taken down and rehung as long as the paste is still soft. Once the paper is in place, trim off excess paper at top and bottom with the cutter used for trimming the selvage. Because the guide line was established a distance of 1″ less than the width of the paper from the window or door frame, there will be paper overlapping the frame. Brush the paper into this joint and then trim off excess.

The same general procedure is used to hang the succeeding strips. To obtain a tight butt joint, slide the edge of one strip against the edge of the other, rather than try to drop the paper into place. Be careful to properly match the pattern, and do not try to work too fast. When necessary to turn corners, it is best to trim a strip of paper so that only about one-half inch will actually turn the corner. After strips have been on for fifteen minutes, run over them lightly with the seam roller to insure that the edges are on tightly.

It is virtually impossible to hang wallpaper without getting some paste on the paper. This should be removed promptly with a clean, damp sponge or cloth.

The chance of air bubbles appearing under the paper after it is in place can be eliminated if right after a section of paper is in place, the entire area is thoroughly moistened with water.

CHAPTER 8

Care and Repair of Furniture

Good-quality furniture will last for years, or even generations, and requires few, if any, repairs if given proper care. Furniture that has been neglected or improperly treated can sometimes be restored, but this is an expensive and time-consuming operation. The average family has considerable money invested in furniture, and it seems reasonable to give these pieces at least the same care and attention bestowed on the family car.

One of furniture's worst enemies is excessively dry air in the house during the winter months. Even seasoned hardwood, from which fine furniture is made, contains a certain amount of moisture which should remain in the wood. Should the house air be so dry that this moisture is driven out, cracks may appear and glued joints may loosen and come apart. New furniture as well as old will be damaged by very low humidity. For the proper maintenance of furniture (as well as healthful living), the moisture content of the house air should be about 40 per cent during winter. Means of measuring humidity, and increasing it if necessary, are given in the chapter devoted to heating (pages 164-65).

Too much heat is equally bad for furniture, for this also dries out the wood. A piece of furniture should never be placed near a radiator or warm-air register, where it will be subject to high temperatures.

Sunlight, too, can damage furniture, because the ultraviolet light can break down the elements in a transparent finish and also darken the wood. This doesn't mean that furniture should never be placed where it will get sunlight, but it is wise not to allow a good piece of furniture to get a steady dose of sunshine for long periods every day of the year. When closing a house for an extended time, pull the curtains or shades to keep sunlight from injuring furniture and to prevent the upholstery from fading.

Furniture shouldn't be placed where it can be struck by an opening door; and care should be exercised when vacuuming not to hit the furniture.

The finish on most furniture, although fairly durable, can be rather easily scratched and can be damaged by heat and water, alcohol, and other liquids. Many scratches can be prevented if lamps, candlesticks, vases, etc., have felt pads glued to their bases so that no roughness comes in contact with the finish. Dining-room table tops should always be protected from hot plates by cork, fiber, or asbestos mats thick enough to keep heat from reaching the finish. Many appliances, such as toasters, are equipped with insulating legs; but nevertheless, they often produce so much heat underneath that the table-top finish is damaged. Any heating appliance on a table top should have a thick insulating pad under it.

The amount of abuse a piece of furniture can take depends on the type of finish. Shellac and most varnish finishes will be marred by moisture; therefore, pieces with these finishes shouldn't be used where liquids may be spilled on them. Wood sealers and oil finishes are quite resistant to liquids; and when they are damaged they are easily restored. This makes them ideal for children's rooms, recreation rooms, and other places where wear-and-tear is a factor.

Maintenance. Any piece of good furniture should be dusted often, preferably once a day. Allowing dust to accumulate will dull the finish and even seriously damage it. One way to maintain furniture in good condition and protect the finish is to keep it well coated with wax. Wax not only gives an attractive luster, but it also protects the finish from damage by water or alcohol (assuming that the liquid is removed before it has time to penetrate the wax coating to the finish underneath). Wax will also help to prevent loss of moisture from the wood.

The best type of wax to use on furniture is carnauba wax, a paste wax made from the Brazilian wax palm. A water-emulsion wax should never be used on furniture or wood floors, because the water may damage the wood. Many liquid furniture waxes and creams are good, but most experts prefer paste wax.

Applying Wax. It is best to remove the hardware from a piece of furniture before waxing, for this makes it easier to apply and polish. But it isn't worth doing unless the hardware can be removed easily by taking out only a few screws. Wax should never be applied over a dusty or dirty surface. If there's an old coating of wax, or the finish has become dulled from dirt, it should be thoroughly cleaned.

Instructions on how this is done are given under "Washing Furniture," below.

The wax should be applied in a thin coat with a soft, lintless cloth. Get the coat on as evenly as possible; and, after giving it about 15 or 20 minutes to dry, polish with a soft cloth. Assuming that only a thin coat was applied and that it has been properly polished, the result should be a hard glasslike surface that won't attract or hold dirt and which provides considerable protection to the finish. Many people have tried wax on furniture and given it up because the wax produced a soft, dull coating that easily showed dirt, dust, and even fingermarks. This is usually not the wax's fault, but is due to improper application. Either the wax was applied too thickly or not polished enough.

Brown-tinted waxes are usually best on dark furniture, and light wax is used for light-colored pieces. Wax makes a good coating for painted or enameled furniture, as well as furniture finished with shellac, varnish, or lacquer.

Once a piece has been waxed, it should not need another waxing until the existing coat has become worn or soiled. If it is dusted daily, the wax will not become embedded with dirt and dust, and should last many months. It's a good idea to give the wax a light polishing each month after a thorough dusting.

Polishes and furniture creams are used by many because they are easier to apply than wax. The main drawback is that they cannot be rubbed out to a hard, glass-like finish. Some tend to remain slightly sticky, which means they catch and hold dust and dirt.

Washing Furniture.   In time, a piece of furniture, especially if it hasn't been properly maintained by frequent dusting, will become dingy looking because of an accumulation of dirt, grease, and grime. In most cases, the finish can be restored to its original brilliance by washing.

A good cleaning solution can be made by dissolving a mild soap in warm water to produce a batch of suds. Dip a soft cloth into this solution, wring it out so it is just damp and rub over a small area of the piece. As soon as the dirt has been removed from this section, take a second soft cloth, dampen it with fresh, warm water and rinse the area clean. Immediately after rinsing, dry with a dry cloth. It is essential not to use more water than necessary to remove the dirt, for water can be harmful to glued joints as well as to certain finishes. As soon as one section has been washed, rinsed, and dried, move on to another; and continue the process until the entire surface has been done. After this, it should be waxed.

Another excellent cleaning preparation, and one that works well when there is a coating of old wax to be removed, is made by adding three tablespoons of raw or boiled linseed oil and two tablespoons of turpentine to one quart of hot water. Stir these ingredients, then dampen a soft cloth in the solution and apply to a small section. A rinse is not necessary, but the area should be wiped dry after cleaning, before the next section is done. A cloth dampened in turpentine is also good for removing wax and dirt.

Repairing Finishes. Furniture that is in daily use is almost sure to take a certain amount of abuse which will eventually damage the finish. If not too severe, it usually can be restored without a complete refinishing operation. As a matter of fact, it's always advisable to try to repair a finish, even a badly damaged one, rather than attempt a complete refinishing job. Certain finishes, such as those applied to pianos, are very involved and require not only a good deal of special knowledge but also skill. To duplicate the original finish on a piano is virtually impossible. If patching won't do, call in a professional.

Alcohol Stains. This liquid acts as a solvent on certain finishes, such as shellac, and will leave white marks on shellac and varnish. The alcohol should be removed immediately with a soft, lintless cloth. Dab or blot up the liquid rather than wipe it off, for if the alcohol has softened the finish, wiping will make matters much worse. After the alcohol has evaporated, if the finish is rough, try polishing out the roughness with powdered rottenstone and linseed oil. (Directions for this are given in the section dealing with the removal of white marks.)

Burns. Small burns left by cigarettes and cigars can frequently be removed by dampening a finger, dipping it into some cigarette or cigar ashes, and rubbing over the damaged finish. The ashes act as a very fine abrasive and will remove the damaged portion of finish. After a spot has been removed, apply a touch of wax. If the burns are deep, try the powdered rottenstone and linseed oil treatment. If the burn has gone through the finish into the wood, more drastic action is called for. Use fine sandpaper to take off the damaged finish and charred wood, then fill in the spot with the proper color stick shellac. Instructions for application of this are given under "Deep Scratches," page 112.

Heat Stains. White marks left by hot dishes can often be eradicated by wiping with a cloth dampened in camphor oil or turpentine.

If the marks do not respond to this, rub with linseed oil and powdered pumice or rottenstone.

Ink.   Blot up as much of the ink as possible while it is still wet. Do not rub, because this will force the ink deeper into the finish. When the ink is dry, polish the spot with oil and powdered rottenstone. If this does not eliminate the spot, try bleaching out the stain with a solution of oxalic acid crystals and water. The finish will have to be removed from the area before the bleach can take effect. If the bleach doesn't remove the stain, the wood will have to be sanded or scraped until all discoloration has been removed; then apply a new finish.

Nail Polish.   The lacquer in nail polish acts as a solvent on many finishes and softens them. The best procedure is to quickly wipe off the polish before it has a chance to soften the finish. If this can't be done, let the polish dry, scrape it off, and renew the damaged finish.

Paint.   Fresh paint can usually be wiped off, without damage to a finish, with a soft cloth dampened in turpentine. Water-thinned paints can be removed with a cloth dampened in water. Once paint has hardened, it can sometimes be softened by soaking with linseed oil or turpentine. Saturate a piece of felt with the oil or turpentine and place it over the paint. Do not try to soften hardened paint with a paint remover, because this will damage the furniture finish. Once the hardened paint has been softened by the oil or turpentine, it can be carefully scraped off with a razor blade.

Scratches.   Light scratches on a finish can be covered up by simply rubbing furniture wax into them. If the scratch exposes a lighter shade than the original, use a brown or dark wax. Another trick that often works is to rub the meat from a walnut or pecan into the scratch. Scratches can be hidden by rubbing wood stain the same color as the finish into the scratch. Use a toothpick or very fine brush to work in the stain. When the stain is dry, apply several very thin coats of varnish or shellac. Hardware and furniture stores sell special wax crayons in a variety of wood colors; these are useful for concealing scratches.

Deep Scratches.   These, along with nicks and holes in the wood, can be repaired with a material called *stick shellac*. This is somewhat similar to sealing wax. It is sold at better hardware, paint, and furniture stores, in many colors and shades. Select the one that most closely matches the piece to be repaired.

To use stick shellac, remove the particles of damaged finish and wood with very fine sandpaper or a razor blade. Heat the blade of a flexible knife or a small spatula so that it is warm enough to melt the stick shellac when held against it. The blade mustn't be too hot, for this can burn the stick shellac and discolor it. Also, don't heat the blade over a flame that will produce soot, for this will also discolor the shellac. Heat the blade over a gas or alcohol burner, or hold it against a soldering iron until it is hot. Melt off enough stick shellac on the blade to more than fill the cavity in the finish. While the shellac is still soft, force it into the hole, allowing it to come a little above the surface of the finish. Smooth out the shellac, but keep it well above the finish surface. When hard, shave off the excess with a razor blade, being careful not to let the corners of the blade gouge into the adjoining finish. Finally, polish the patch with powdered pumice or rottenstone and linseed oil.

White Marks.   These are caused by water, alcohol, or heat. Sometimes a large area of the finish will take on a white discoloration during very humid weather, but this will usually disappear when the air dries. White marks, on the other hand, can often be removed simply by rubbing with a moist finger and cigar or cigarette ashes. If this fails, the marks may be polished out with a piece of felt or flannel, linseed or machine oil, and either powdered pumice or rottenstone. All of these can be purchased at paint and hardware stores. Special polishing and rubbing pads are also available, but a clean piece of felt or flannel is entirely adequate. The felt or flannel should be folded into a small pad and dipped first into a saucer containing the linseed or machine oil, then into a second saucer holding the powdered pumice or rottenstone. The pad is then rubbed over the discolored part of the finish. Always rub in the direction of the wood grain, and do not apply too much pressure. From time to time, wipe the oil away with a finger to see how the work is progressing. As soon as the white marks are gone, stop; and after wiping the surface clean, coat it with wax. If too much pressure is applied to the pad while rubbing, or if the rubbing continues too long, it will eventually cut through the finish. Rubbing with a felt pad, pumice or rottenstone, and oil can also remove minor flaws such as rough spots, and smooth out stick shellac patches.

Determining the Type of Finish.   A piece of furniture may be finished with one of several finishes. The most popular are lacquer, oil, seals, shellac, and varnish. Before repairs can be made, the type of finish must be determined. This is best done by testing in an inconspicuous spot, for it is virtually impossible to distinguish some finishes simply from their appearance. Shellac is easily identified, because it will soften if a small amount of denatured alcohol is applied to it. Denatured alcohol, however, won't easily soften lacquer or varnish. Lacquer will soften if lacquer thinner is applied. Shellac, lacquer, and varnish all have a rather high gloss. Oil and wood-seal finishes will not have a gloss, but will be somewhat dull; they do not coat the surface of the wood, but flow into its pores.

Patching Finishes.   When a certain portion of the finish becomes worn or must be taken off for repairs, the finish may often be successfully patched. The surrounding edges of the old finish, if it is shellac, varnish, or lacquer, should be lightly sanded so that the edges are tapered. After dusting, several thin coats of the same finish should be applied to build up a patch equal in thickness to the original finish.

If the old finish is an oil or wood-seal, a patch is very easy to make. Simply apply coats of oil or sealer to the area until it is the same color as the rest of the wood.

Bruises and Dents.   When a piece of wood is bruised or dented, the wood fibers are compressed; and they will remain so unless something is done to bring them back to their original condition. This can usually be achieved by a combination of heat and water, which makes the wood fibers expand and resume their former shape. To allow the water to reach the wood fibers, it's usually necessary to remove the finish around the bruise or dent. Do not take off any more finish than is absolutely necessary; and do not scrape or sand the wood under the finish, for this will change the color if stain has been used.

There are several ways to get the heat and water to the damaged fibers. One method is to cover the damaged area with a piece of damp cloth and then run a warm iron over the cloth. The steam generated by the iron and damp cloth will flow into the fibers and bring them back to their original position. An even more effective trick is to place a marble or ball-bearing over the damp cloth directly above the dent or bruise and hold the iron on the mable or ball bearing. Heat from the iron is transferred to the portion of the damp cloth directly over the marred section. If the wood has not been finished, or if a refinishing project is to be done, the wood can be pricked with a needle or fine awl to speed the absorption of water. In any event, after the wood fibers have come back into shape, the area should be sanded very lightly and refinished.

Not all dents and bruises can be removed by these methods. If they fail, fill in the damaged spot with stick shellac.

Veneer Repairs. Much furniture is made with wood veneer, a very thin layer of wood glued to a wood or composition wood base. Veneers are usually made of rare and expensive woods, but the bases are made of common but stable woods that do not expand and contract to any great degree. The art of veneering is an old one. Many pieces of antique furniture are made with a veneered surface. Since veneers are extremely thin, great care must be taken in working with them, because they can easily be broken or cracked. Sanding veneers must be done with utmost caution, for it is possible, especially with coarse sandpaper or a power sander, to cut through the veneer before realizing it.

Loose Veneer. Veneers will come loose, usually at the edges, because of failure of glue or because moisture has worked under the veneer and softened the glue. To repair, the first step is to remove the old glue from the base and from the underside of the veneer. This can be done with an emery manicure board or with a piece of sandpaper folded over so there are two sanding surfaces. Insert the board or sandpaper under the veneer and work it gently back and forth until most or all of the old, hard glue has been removed. If possible, do not loosen more of the veneer; and be careful not to put much strain on it, because it is brittle and will crack easily.

Blow the dust out from underneath the veneer and apply a thin coat of glue to the underside of the veneer and to the base. This can be done with a flexible knife or a hacksaw blade. After the glue is on, gently press the veneer back into place. If it does not go down easily, place a damp cloth over it until it becomes pliable. Once the veneer is down it will have to be held with clamps or with a weight until the glue has dried. If clamps are used, protect the veneer from them with a piece of scrap wood or thick cardboard inserted between the veneer and clamp. Immediately wipe off any excess glue that oozes from the joint.

Blistered Veneer. Blisters in veneer come from the same causes as loose veneer. They are more difficult to correct, however, because there is no easy way to get glue under the veneer. The best thing to do is to make a slit in the veneer with a razor blade at about the middle of the blister. Make the cut in the direction of the wood grain. Glue can then be worked under the veneer by applying the glue with a small spatula, working the blade through the split in the veneer.

Patching Veneer. When a section of veneer is badly damaged it can often be patched if a piece of the same type is available. The best shape for the patch is in the form of a diamond. The best way to insure getting the patch the right size is to place the new piece over the damaged area of old veneer and cut through both at the same time with a razor blade. Remove the patch and pry out the damaged section of the old veneer. Apply a thin coat of glue to the underside of the patch and on the base, and set the patch in place.

Drawers, Sticking. The usual reason for a desk or bureau drawer sticking is that the wood has absorbed moisture and expanded so it is tight against the framework. In all but the most expensive furniture, wood for the drawers, with the exception of the front piece and outside surface of the side pieces, is left unfinished. When the weather grows warm and damp, the unfinished wood easily absorbs moisture and expands. It's a wise precaution to coat all parts of a drawer with shellac so the wood cannot pick up moisture. This may also be done with the unfinished parts of any furniture to prevent moisture absorption.

Assuming the drawer is already stuck, the first thing is to get it open. Sometimes this can be done just by hard pulling but often such forcing will loosen joints. If time isn't a factor, wait until the outside air dries or the house heating system goes on, for then the wood will shrink as it dries and the drawer can be easily opened. A quicker way to get the drawer out is to place the piece near a source of artificial heat, such as a heat lamp or electric heater, and leave it there until the wood has shrunk enough to free the drawer. (Do not put the piece so close to a heat source that it may be damaged.) Once the drawer can be opened, and the wood has shrunk back to more or less its original state, coat the unfinished portions with shellac; and when this has dried, apply wax or paraffin to the top edges of the side pieces. This is where sticking usually occurs, and the wax or paraffin will act as a lubricant. Sometimes the top edges of the side pieces must be sanded down a bit before the lubricant is applied, to insure easy operation.

Drawers often stick because the bottom has sagged so that the front edge strikes the dividing rail. To remove them, take out the drawer underneath so that the loose bottom can be pushed up to clear the rail. Once the drawer is out, the bottom should be reglued to make it secure.

Tightening Loose Joints. A good deal of home-furniture repair work consists of tightening loose joints. Many joints in a piece of furniture are put together with glue only. Such a joint will fail because the piece is subjected to more strain than it is designed to take. Tilting back on chairs, for example, throws all the strain on two legs and subjects other joints to strains in directions they were never intended to handle. Glued joints will also fail because artificial heat and lack of humidity have dried out the wood and shrunk it so much that it breaks the glue seal.

Furniture is made up of many pieces of relatively light wood and the furniture's strength depends on secure joining of all the pieces. As soon as one joint loosens, the chair (or whatever it may be) should be taken out of service and kept out until it has been repaired. If it is left in use, the chances are that other joints will fail because they are subjected to more strain than if all the joints were tight and doing their job. Also, if there is any movement in the various parts because of loose joints, rungs and rails will tend to enlarge the holes into which they fit and make a good repair job more difficult.

Regluing a loose joint requires a certain amount of time; therefore, it's advisable to use only top-quality wood glues. All-purpose glues and adhesives, while excellent for many jobs about the house, are not as good on wood as glues specifically designed for it. White glue is exceptionally good for furniture. It is easy to apply and will not stain adjoining surfaces if wiped off before it hardens.

The ideal way to repair a loose joint is to take it apart, removing the old glue from both wood surfaces by sanding with fine sandpaper, then regluing the joint by applying a thin coat of glue to both surfaces. The surfaces are then joined together and clamped until the glue is hard. For most furniture repairs, however, it is impractical to take one joint apart, for this means that several or even all the joints must be disassembled. To save time and effort other means must be employed to tighten joints without complete disassembly.

Tightening Rails and Rungs. If the rail or rung on a piece of furniture is loose but still fits snugly into the hole in the adjoining member, pull it out as far as it will come without force, and coat the portion that fits into the hole with wood glue. Work the piece back and forth so that the sides of the hole become coated with glue. If the piece will not come far enough out of the hole to permit this, apply glue around the base and turn the piece up in such a way that the glue will flow down into the hole. This will only work when the rail or rung fits rather tightly into the hole. If the end of the rail or rung has shrunk or if the hole has become enlarged so the fit is very loose, glue alone will not hold. Then the joint must be made mechanically tight before it can be reglued. This can be done by one of several methods.

Assuming that the rail or rung cannot be pulled out of the hole, break off a few pieces of wooden toothpick or cut very small wedges out of hardwood. Coat these slivers with glue and drive them in between the rail or rung and the sides of the hole. Be careful not to make these wedges too thick or to drive them in with too much force, for this may crack the wood. When the wedges are all in place, cut off any pieces that project above the hole and let the glue dry.

If it is possible to remove the rail or rung, do so; then make a cut at the end with a fine saw. This cut should be about 1″ deep and made at the exact center of the end of the rail or rung. Remove the old glue from the end of the rung and from inside of the hole. Cut a thin wedge from hardwood and fit it into the cut so that it extends beyond the end for about ⅛″. Coat the end of the rung and the inside of the hole with glue and force the end of the rung into the hole. When the wedge at the end of the rung strikes the bottom of the hole, it will be forced into the cut, expanding the sides of the rung and insuring a tight fit.

Another trick for rungs and rails is to coat the ends with glue and then wrap silk thread around them. The thread will increase the diameter of the end enough to make a tight fit.

It is also possible to buy small barbed metal sleeves at hardware stores. These can be fitted on the end of the round rungs to hold them to the sides of the hole.

Dismantling Joints.   Sometimes so many joints on a piece of furniture fail that the only way to do a proper job of regluing is to take all or most of the joints apart and do a complete reassembly job. This requires time and patience, but it is often worth the effort.

Most joints in furniture are put together with glue, although some other device such as a wood dowel can be used to help reinforce the joint. In any event, if the glue is softened, the joint can be taken apart. A glued joint can usually be disassembled by softening the glue with water or steam. Sometimes it's possible to inject warm water into the joint with an eye dropper. Turn the piece to such a position that the water can flow down into the joint. When the water cannot be applied with an eye dropper, a small "dam" can be made of putty and built around the joint to hold the water in place until it can seep down into the joint. Steam will soften glue; a length of rubber or plastic hose attached to the spout of a teakettle will deliver a stream of steam that can be played into a joint. Steam and water are harmful to most wood finishes, so keep them off the finish as much as possible.

Sometimes glued joints are reinforced with metal pins; these must be punched out with a nail or punch before the joint can be taken apart. Wood screws are often used to reinforce joints; these screws are generally set well below the wood surface. The heads are covered with a plug made from a wood dowel or plastic wood. Before the screw can be removed, the dowel or plastic wood must be drilled out; this must be done with care so that the drill isn't damaged by striking the metal screw head. The screws may be very difficult to get out with an ordinary screwdriver because they are in so tightly. Try using a screw driver bit on a wood brace. If this fails to move the screw, hold a hot soldering iron to the screw head. This will heat the metal so that it expands; then, when it contracts on cooling, it will usually be easy to remove.

As each piece is taken apart, it should be marked in some fashion so it can be put back into its proper place. A small label tied to each piece is good, for it will not rub off in handling as will a pencil or crayon mark.

Assembling. The old glue should be removed from both surfaces as the joints are taken apart. Use fine sandpaper for this, and do not sand any more than is necessary to get off the old glue and smooth the wood. If the surfaces are sanded too much, the joint may not be tight when put together. In assembling the pieces, cover each surface with a light, even application of wood glue and then put them together. Each joint should be clamped in some way so as to hold pressure on it until the glue is hard. Various clamps are available for this. It is important that a piece of scrap wood or heavy cardboard be inserted between the clamp and wood finish so that the finish will not be marred by the clamp. A good clamp to use on many joints, especially on chairs, is made by tying the joint with stout cord and then inserting a stick under the cord. Twist the stick around to tighten the cord in the same fashion as a tourniquet. Be sure to protect the woodwork from damage from the string or stick.

Reinforcing Joints. To prevent certain joints from coming loose again, it is often advisable to reinforce them. Excellent reinforcements are square or triangular blocks of hardwood glued and screwed to the two pieces making up the joint. These blocks can be used on the undersides of chairs to reinforce legs and the seat, or on the undersides of tables to reinforce legs, tops, and aprons. They can be placed on the inside of drawers to give more strength to the sides and bottom. Only hardwood blocks should be used. The two surfaces to be glued should be sanded until they are very smooth. Holes should be drilled into the blocks before they are installed. When a block is to be glued to a portion of the furniture that has a finish on it, the finish should be removed by sanding so that the block can be glued directly to the wood.

Naturally, reinforcing blocks should be used only where they will not be visible.

Another, though less professional, method of reinforcing a joint is with a metal mending plate. These come in many sizes and shapes and are sold at most hardware stores. The commonest are the strap, a perfectly straight piece of metal, and the angle plate. Mending plates come with holes drilled in them so they can be fastened in place with screws. They are adequate for many jobs though not so effective as the wood blocks that are both screwed and glued in place.

Certain joints can be reinforced with screws. Most furniture is made of hardwood, so it is essential that a pilot hole be drilled first into the wood for the screw; otherwise it will be difficult to install and may split the wood. The pilot hole should be made with a wood twist drill and should be slightly smaller in diameter than the threaded portion of the screw. If the screw must be placed where it will be visible, the head must be countersunk and filled over with a wood plug or plastic wood. Directions for the proper installation of wood screws is given in the chapter dealing with tools and materials (page 34).

As a general rule, nails should never be used to reinforce or make repairs on furniture. They do not have the holding power of screws; and once they are in place, they are difficult if not impossible to get out should the occasion arise. If nails must be used, a pilot hole should be made.

Finishing and Refinishing Furniture

Few projects about the house can be quite as rewarding as finishing and refinishing furniture. Whether it's a new piece of unfinished furniture that you got from a furniture store or lumber yard, an old piece that you have salvaged from the attic or a second-hand furniture store, or an honest-to-goodness antique that you have picked up at an auction, you'll get a real thrill when the job has been completed and the wood has been given an attractive finish.

Finishing and refinishing furniture can be much more than just a worthwhile chore—it can be an engrossing hobby both for men and for women. It requires a minimum amount of equipment and it does not require an extensive work area.

Much money can be saved by doing the job yourself, so try to use the very best of materials. If brushes are needed, buy the best and save them for just this sort of work. Use the best grades of sandpaper, steel wool, and finishes. And, equally important, don't try to hurry the job. Never set a time limit on when the job must be completed, for this will usually mean hurrying, and this produces inferior work. Just as it takes time and patience to produce anything of value, so does it require the same ingredients to produce a fine finish.

Painting Furniture. Paint is the easiest kind of finish to apply; with certain pieces it can be one of the most attractive. The best kind of paint to use is a furniture enamel. On new work the wood should be lightly sanded and then coated with an enamel undercoater. If the wood has an open grain, it will save time and effort if you apply a wood filler before the undercoater. This will help ensure a smooth finish, with a minimum number of coats of enamel. After the filler is dry, sand lightly and then apply the undercoater. When this is dry, sand lightly again, dust and apply the enamel. Two or three coats with light sanding between coats will produce a good, durable finish. When the final coat is dry, wax will help to protect it. On old work it is seldom necessary to remove the old finish unless it is in very poor shape. Wipe it down with turpentine to remove old wax, polish, and dirt; then sand lightly. If there are areas where the old finish has been chipped off, patch these with several thin coats of enamel. Holes, cracks, and so on, should be filled with plastic wood or water putty, sanded smooth when the patch is dry, and then coated with enamel undercoater. An old finish in very poor condition should, of course, be removed with a paint remover; the wood should then be treated as if it had never been painted.

Paint is used as a finish when the wood itself has not much character. When attractive woods are involved, the finish you want is one that is transparent so that the natural color and grain of the wood will not be concealed. The most common kinds of finishes of the transparent variety are shellac, sealer, oil, and varnish.

Refinishing Old Furniture.   The first step is to remove the old finish. Whether it is paint, varnish, or shellac, the best way to do the job is with a paint-and-varnish remover. Directions for use of these materials have been given in the chapter on painting. Use the remover; then strip off the old finish one layer at a time. Don't be surprised if you find that there are many coats that must come off. Keep working with the remover until every last trace of the old finish has been eliminated.

Once you are down to the bare wood, you can determine whether or not bleaching is required. Avoid bleaching if possible, for needless to say, it not only requires time but also makes the wood rough so that sanding must follow. Try to avoid heavy sanding also, not only because it takes time but because it changes the color of the wood; this is especially true of old woods. Bleaching will be necessary, however, if there are dark spots in the wood that were not removed by the remover. Bleaching is also necessary if the wood was stained with a dark stain and if you wish to get a lighter color or if you wish to make a normally dark wood somewhat lighter. Bleaching wood has been covered in the chapter on painting.

Before you apply the new finish, go over the work and make any repairs on the piece that are required. Holes should be filled with wood filler or wood plugs. Loose joints should be reglued and reinforced if this seems necessary.

Staining.   Stains are used to change the color of the wood and to emphasize the grain. As a rule we don't need stain on a refinishing job because the wood usually has ample natural color and tone. If you have doubts as to whether or not to use a stain, try some on an inconspicuous area to see if it does improve the appearance of the wood. Certain kinds of finishes, such as sealer-stains, will add color, and will provide a protective finish. These are handy when a small amount of added color is needed. New wood, especially softwood, is often improved by staining; but you can't make a piece of pine into walnut simply by applying a walnut stain. Ordinary stains do not provide a protective finish, and any piece of wood must have this protective coating or else it will soon discolor from dirt.

Sealers.   These come clear or with stain added. They make a very durable finish and one that is easy to apply. Sealers are ideal for furniture that will have heavy use, for they are not easily damaged by heat or liquids. If they should be damaged, it's a simple matter to sand the area and then apply a thin coat or two of fresh sealer. Two coats of sealer are all that should be required. Buff with steel wool between coats. Allow fifteen minutes for the sealer to soak into the wood after application by brush; then wipe off the excess with a lintless cloth. Allow the sealer to dry overnight and then rub with 000 steel wool. Apply paste wax over the final coat.

Shellac. This has been used as a finish on fine furniture for many centuries. One of the best finishes to use on fine woods, it's an easy one to apply. Another advantage to shellac is that it dries in a matter of minutes. Use two or three thin coats—a 2- or 3-pound cut is fine. After a coat is dry, rub with 000 steel wool. Apply paste wax over the finish coat. Because shellac will not take as hard use as some of the other finishes, it is not the ideal one to use on children's furniture or on pieces that will get heavy use or will be marred by liquids or hot dishes. Use white shellac on light-colored woods and orange shellac on dark woods.

Varnish. A good quality furniture varnish makes a durable and attractive finish. The usual method of application is first to apply a sealer coat of shellac; this is then rubbed down with steel wool before the varnish goes on. The shellac sealer coat is important if the wood has been stained, for some stains bleed through varnish. One or two coats of varnish are adequate over the shellac. Buff with 000 steel wool between coats.

Oil. There are several prepared oil finishes available and they are among the easiest to apply. It's a matter of brushing on the oil, allowing it to soak in, and then wiping off the excess. Several coats are applied until the wood no longer absorbs any of the oil. Oil finishes can take a lot of hard use, and when they begin to show signs of wear they can be easily touched up by applying oil to the area. You can make your own oil finish with linseed oil thinned with turpentine, but the prepared ones are probably superior to what you can mix yourself.

CHAPTER 9

Exterior Repairs

Caulking—Filling Cracks and Joints. Cracks and open joints on the outside of the house are likely to occur where two different materials, such as wood and masonry, meet, or where exterior siding joins window and door frames.

The size of these openings may vary according to temperature and humidity. It is important they be filled with some substance to prevent moisture and air leaking into the building. The best filler is caulking compound.

This is similar in consistency to putty but, unlike putty, it never hardens. It will not crack or fall out should the opening shrink or expand. A tough skin, however, forms over the surface after application, tough enough so that it can be painted.

Caulking may be applied in several ways. The least expensive is with a caulking gun and a large container filled with bulk compound. The gun works much the same as a grease gun used in automotive work. The gun chamber is filled with compound; and then, as the trigger is pulled, a spring drives down the plunger, forcing the compound out through the nozzle. Nozzles of different shapes and sizes are available to fit various sizes of openings.

Guns of this type are efficient, but they are messy to use. Many homeowners prefer a more expensive but neater gun that takes a cartridge. With this, the compound-filled cartridge is slipped into the gun and tossed away when empty. The gun works on the same principle as the bulk-filled tool.

Another method of application is a compound in a tube similar to a toothpaste tube. A key is provided so that the tube end can be rolled up to force the compound through the nozzle. These are excellent for small jobs where only one or two tubes are needed. For very small cracks, a putty knife will do an excellent job.

Before a crack or joint is filled with caulking, it should be thoroughly cleaned to remove any dirt and loose matter. If the opening is wide and deep, both labor and compound can be saved if the opening is first filled with oakum. Oakum comes in rope form; it is made of jute fibers treated with tar. Oakum can be packed into the joint with a stick or caulking iron, and the compound applied over the oakum to provide a protective seal.

The best time for outside caulking is when the temperature is rather warm. When cold, caulking compound thickens and is hard to apply. If caulking must be done in cold weather, let the compound remain in a heated place overnight to keep it warm and easily workable.

Caulking compound comes in both light and dark shades. The light is preferred for most work around the home. The compound can be removed from hands and tools with a solvent such as turpentine or mineral spirits.

Caulking compound may also be used to fill cracks in outside masonry walls if appearance is not important. It is useful for filling in where plumbing fixtures such as bathtub or kitchen sink join walls.

Properly applied, caulking compound will last many years; but eventually it deteriorates and must be scraped out and replaced.

Asbestos Cement Shingles and Siding Panels. These are made of asbestos fibers and cement. They will not rot, burn, or be damaged by insects. But they are brittle, and occasionally a shingle or panel will crack and must be replaced. The old shingle can be removed by gently breaking it into several pieces and removing it piece by piece.

Pull out the exposed nails and use a hacksaw blade to cut off the nails concealed by the shingle above. Slip a new shingle of correct size and color into place. The new shingle will crack if a nail is driven into it without first drilling a hole through it. The hole should be about the same diameter as the nail used. Be careful when the nail is driven not to hit the shingle with the hammer, for this too will crack it. When the nail head is about ¼ " above the shingle, use a nail set to finish driving it in flush with the shingle surface.

A cracked asbestos board panel must also be removed and replaced, just as with a shingle.

Asbestos siding shingles and panels can be painted to change their color or to cover dirt stains. (See "Painting the House, Asbestos Shingles," page 88.) Rust and dirt stains can often be removed by scrubbing with a wall cleaner and warm water or with a special asbestos siding cleaner.

Brick and Brick Veneer Walls. Few homes built in recent years have solid brick walls. Most have only brick veneer outside walls. In this construction, the house is framed with wood and the sidewalls covered with wood or composition sheathing. A single course of brick is then laid up about 1″ from the sheathing but tied in to the framework by metal clips. This brick veneer serves as a coating against wind and rain, and it also provides a decorative finish. Bricks themselves do not usually require paint or other protective finish, because they seldom cause trouble; but the mortar joints can be trou-

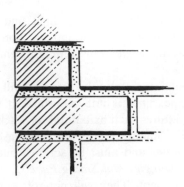

BRICK MORTAR JOINTS

blesome if poorly made or if the mortar was inferior and is porous or has cracked. These small openings allow wind-driven rain to penetrate the brickwork and flow into the small space between brick veneer and house sheathing. Eventually the moisture can seep through to damage the interior wall.

Walls of brick veneer usually have small holes drilled through them along the base to allow any water entering the wall cavity to run out. These are called "weep" holes; and if there are none, it's wise to make them.

Use a star or masonry drill about ½″ in diameter to cut through the mortar joints between bricks. Drill the holes so that they slant upward; and make them as close as possible to the base of the brickwork, but above the level of the wood sill. Set them every 16 inches.

Leaking Walls. If moisture seeps through a brick wall to the inside wall, it is undoubtedly the fault of the mortar joints. Inspect the wall for any joints where mortar has cracked or is crumbling.

The damaged mortar should be removed with a small cold chisel, and the opening dusted clean and dampened. Fresh mortar may then be packed into the hole. The mortar joint should be finished off to match the other joints. The best type of joint is where the mortar is formed so that it slopes slightly inward at the top, with the bottom flush with the brick face. This allows water falling on the joint to flow off quickly. If the mortar in the entire wall is porous, it is hardly worth the effort to cut it all out and replace with fresh mortar. In that case the best thing to do is either to paint the entire wall (which is expensive and hides the natural color of the bricks) or to coat the mortar joints with a clear masonry waterproofing compound. This will seal the open pores in the mortar and should eliminate the leaks.

If there is no caulking around doors and windows and the brick wall, water will eventually reach the inside walls.

White Discoloration on Brick Walls. See "Masonry, Efflorescence."

Stucco. Stucco is a mixture of portland cement and sand. It is applied to outside walls as an exterior finish. In some construction the stucco is applied directly to masonry blocks, while in other construction the house is framed with wood; and this is covered with a special stucco lath over which the stucco is applied.

Stucco is usually applied in three coats. Often small shrinkage cracks will appear in the top coat. These are nothing to worry about and can be filled by simply painting the wall. Large cracks should be patched, for these often go through all three coats of stucco and permit moisture to pass through the wall. The cracks should first be cut out with a cold chisel, so that the inside is slightly wider than the outside. Dust the opening clean, then dampen it and pack in patching stucco. Prepared patching stucco may be purchased in dry form at most paint and hardware stores. This only needs the addition of water to make it ready for use. Many come in colors to match the more popular stucco finishes. Patching compound can also be made at home by mixing one part portland cement with three parts clean sand, and adding enough water to produce a workable plastic. Pack the material into the crack and keep it damp for a few days until it has had time to dry and cure.

Particular attention should be paid to joints where stucco joins window and door frames. Moisture getting into these openings will be absorbed by the stucco, which, like a sponge, will keep the adjoining woodwork constantly damp. These seams should be filled with caulking compound.

Wood Siding. A common problem with wood siding is rust stains caused by nails. Unless the nails used are of noncorrosive material, such as aluminum, the nail heads must be set below the wood surface and the holes over the heads filled with putty and painted. If ordinary steel nails are used and not countersunk, remove the rust from the heads with steel wool, then drive the head ⅛″ into the wood with a nail set. Fill the hole over the head with putty; and, after giving this a day or so to dry, touch it up with paint.

Beveled Siding. Beveled or clapboard siding may warp slightly unless properly nailed. The remedy for a warped board is to drive in a few more nails. Use 8 *d* aluminum nails for this. If a piece of siding splits or is otherwise badly damaged, replace it. Note that each piece of siding is held in place by nails driven through both lower and upper portions of both boards, since each piece is secured to the one above. To replace, take small wedges and drive them between the damaged board that is to be removed, and the board above, then use a keyhole saw to make the two cuts. Pull out the nails from the lower portion and damaged section, then slip a hacksaw blade up to cut off the nails holding the top. The damaged section may now be taken out and used as a pattern for cutting a new piece to the correct length. Coat the ends of this piece with white lead, slip it into place, and secure it with aluminum nails.

Wood Shingles. Siding shingles occasionally warp; these can be split with a chisel and nailed back into place so that they will lie flat.

Aluminum Siding. In recent years, this material has become very popular for house siding because it is very durable and requires little upkeep. The most common repair consists of filling dents and holes, and these are easy to fix with plastic aluminum. Clean the metal and then apply the plastic aluminum. When dry, coat with paint. Aluminum siding does not require paint, but it should be painted for appearance's sake. (See "Painting the House, Aluminum," page 87.)

Grading of Soil. Many basements are damp only because the soil around the building is saturated with water. This is due to poor drainage. Whether the house has a damp basement or not, or even if it has none, it is wise to have the soil around the house well drained.

The soil should always slope down and away from the house. In good-quality construction, this is usually done when the house is built; but the ground around many houses today has little if any slope, and this allows large quantities of water to collect close to the house. The remedy is to bring in enough topsoil so that the earth can be properly graded. The land should slope away from the house for about 10 feet. When this slope is covered with grass, it will form excellent protection against excessive absorption of water.

If it is impossible to grade the earth properly, a concrete apron laid adjoining the foundation walls will help. This apron can also serve as a walk. It should be at least three feet wide and four inches thick, and pitched so that the rain falling on it will drain away from the house. The joint where the apron joins the house foundation should be filled with tar or caulking compound to insure that it is watertight.

Insect Screens. In all but a few areas, insect screens are a vital necessity during summer months. Screens for standard double-hung windows are usually installed outside, while screens for casement and awning windows that swing out are installed indoors.

Screening can be made of aluminum, copper, plastic, or steel. Frames are of wood, bronze, or aluminum. Iron screening, common a few years ago, requires much attention because it will rust unless it is kept painted. Copper screening, while it does not rust, will stain painted siding unless it is coated with paint or outside varnish. Aluminum and plastic screening need no protective or preservative coating.

If screens are taken down in the fall and stored for the winter, they should be washed before being reinstalled in the spring so that the dirt on them won't be rain-washed over the siding. It's not essential to take down screens made of noncorrosive materials. They won't be damaged by cold; and more harm may be done taking them down and putting them up again than if they are left in the windows.

From time to time, small holes may be punched in screens. These are easy to repair, either with special screening repair kits or with a piece of screening somewhat larger than the hole. Remove some of the crosspieces from each of the four sides of the patch so that the frayed ends extend ¼" or so beyond the solid portion. Bend these frayed ends to a 90° angle, and then place the patch over the hole so that the frayed ends go through the screen. Bend the ends over on the other side, and the patch will last indefinitely. Always use the same material as the screening to make your patch.

To be effective, every window that is opened in summer should be equipped with tightly fitted screens. Use caulking compound or weatherstripping to insure tight fits.

Attic louvers and basement windows should always be screened. Screen doors should have closing units so they shut tightly. Damage to the lower part of the screen by children or household pets can be efficiently prevented by covering the outside section with hardware wire mesh cloth.

Ladders. A good ladder is an essential piece of equipment for · the homeowner. When buying a ladder, get the best you can afford. Aluminum and magnesium ladders are excellent; they are light and will not decay or corrode. In fact, they are made to last indefinitely.

Wood ladders are good, if given proper care; but they should never be painted, for paint can encourage decay around the joints and hide flaws in the wood. A wood preservative should be used; this will protect the wood, yet leave it exposed so that if a crack develops, it can be easily detected.

When setting a ladder, make sure both legs are on firm ground. If the earth is soft or uneven, use wide, 2″ thick planks for a solid base. The ladder should be set so that its base is one-fourth its height away from the wall against which it rests. It's wise to tie a rope to the bottom rung and fasten it securely to a portion of the wall against which the ladder rests. This will prevent the bottom of the ladder from slipping. Never place a ladder in front of a closed door, for someone suddenly coming out may knock it down.

It's often necessary to set a ladder just where the top rests against a window. The trick here is to tie a piece of 1″ x 3″ lumber across the ladder top so that when in position, the board will rest on either side of the window frame, thus carrying the weight and keeping the ladder top a safe distance from the window glass.

Rainfall Disposal. Every house should be provided with some means of carrying off and disposing of the large volume of rain that falls on the roof during the year. Unless there is such a system in good working order, water will seep into the earth around the building and cause wet basements, wood decay, peeling paint, eroded lawns, and even termites.

The basic rainfall-disposal system consists of the runoff from the roof, the downspout and leaders that carry water from the gutters to the ground, and a storm sewer or dry well that safely disposes of the downspout discharge.

Roof Gutters. Gutters are made of aluminum, copper, galvanized iron, or wood. Aluminum and copper gutters won't rust or corrode and do not require protective coating. It's wise, however, to paint the

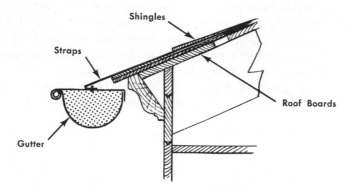

outside of copper gutters with trim paint or spar varnish to prevent staining of adjoining surfaces. The outside of galvanized gutters should be painted, for when the thin zinc coating wears off, the steel under it will rust. The best way to preserve the inside of galvanized gutters is to coat them with a thin application of roofing cement. Use a fiber brush to remove dirt and rust before applying the roofing cement.

Wood gutters should be painted on the outside with trim paint and lined inside with roofing cement. Small holes in gutters may be patched with roofing cement and a piece of tar or building paper.

Gutters should have a slight downward pitch toward the end connected to the downspout or leader. If there isn't enough pitch, or if a gutter section has sagged, water cannot flow easily into the downspout. This can cause the gutter to overflow and hasten rot and rust.

The best way to check a gutter's pitch is to pour a pail of water into it at the opposite end from the downspout or leader. Watch the flow of water if it collects at any point in the gutter, mark this and then adjust the hangers or install additional hangers so the sag or low spot is eliminated. Gutter hangers are usually set under the roofing; but when adding hangers, nail them over the roofing and then give the heads a coat of roofing cement. Hangers may be purchased at most lumber yards and hardware stores.

Keeping Gutters Clean. It's important to keep gutters clean at all times, but especially so in the fall if there are trees near the house that shed their leaves. Wet leaves can be very corrosive to metal gutters; and, as they absorb moisture, layers of thick, wet leaves can add enough weight to pull the gutter loose. You can save yourself the work of having to clean gutters by equipping them with guards. These wire coverings clip up under the roof and prevent leaves and debris from getting into the gutters. The downspout or leader opening should also be equipped with a special strainer made for the purpose.

Ice and Snow in Gutters. Ice and snow may slip off a roof, accumulate in gutters, and pull them loose. This is often caused by improperly hung gutters. The outside edge of the gutter should be

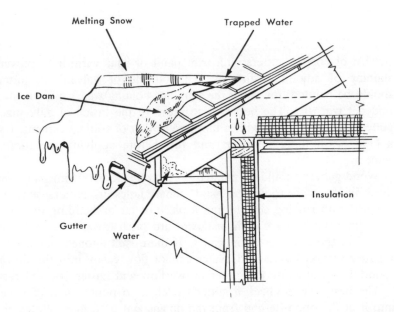

lower than the edge of the roof eave. Sometimes it's possible to adjust a gutter to get the outside edge below the eave. If this doesn't prevent accumulation of ice and snow, the best thing is to have an electric heating cable installed along the roof eave. (See "Ice Dams on Roofs," pages 137-38.)

Downspouts. Downspouts or leaders don't often become clogged, especially if fitted at the top with a strainer. It's a good idea, however, to flush out downspouts with a garden hose each year to remove any accumulation of debris. In many installations there is an elbow or turn at the bottom of the downspout, and water dripping from the gutter will often hit this elbow and make an annoying sound similar to a dripping faucet—only louder. This can be eliminated by cementing a piece of felt to the inside of the elbow so that water falling in the downspout will strike the felt instead of the metal under it.

Often a house rainfall-disposal system will stop with the end of the downspout, and all water flowing off the roof will discharge into the soil near the house. This can keep the earth constantly damp, which makes it attractive to termites and encourages woodwork decay. The downspout discharge should be carried a safe distance away from the building. To be safe, the water should be carried eight or ten feet.

This can be done by digging a shallow trench and laying a line of clay drain tile or bituminous pipe. This line should be tightly connected to the downspout. If the soil is absorbent, this is all that's required; but if not, it's best to run this line into a dry well. The discharge from the gutters should never be connected into a septic tank or cesspool that also handles house sewage. Some communities allow rain discharge to be run into city sewer lines; but others forbid this practice, since, during heavy rains, the flood of water will overflow raw sewage at the plant.

Building a Dry Well. The purpose of a dry well is to handle rain discharge from the roof. The simplest kind to make is to dig a hole large enough to accommodate a wooden barrel. Knock the bottom and top out of the barrel and sink it into the hole. Fill the barrel with rocks or chunks of masonry to within five inches of the top. Bring in the line from the downspout so that it discharges into the barrel, then cover the barrel top with insect screening. Replace the soil; and the dry well is ready.

Larger dry wells can be made in the same fashion as cesspools. These are holes lined with rocks or masonry blocks laid without mortar. The tops of these wells should be covered with a reinforced concrete cover set below the finish grade.

Rodents. The best way to keep rodents, such as rats, mice, chipmunks, and squirrels, out of a house is to make it impossible for them to get in. As a rule, rats and mice gain entrance along the lower sections of the house; squirrels and chipmunks look for openings in the upper sections.

The house exterior should be examined closely; and all openings, no matter how small, should be closed with either concrete or metal. Basement windows should be tight, and, as an added precaution, covered outside with wire mesh. Unused drains opening into the basement should be covered or filled. Attic louvers and windows should be covered with heavy wire and the upper house inspected for openings. Squirrels and chipmunks often use tree limbs to reach the roof, so it's wise to keep branches cut back far enough so they don't provide an easy bridge to the building.

The house and immediate grounds should be kept free of rubbish, and garbage should be stored in metal or plastic containers with tight lids.

A vigorous cat can usually deal with the mouse problem, but grown rats are too large and vicious for many cats to tackle. A terrier is a good rat catcher, but it doesn't have the cat's single purpose and patience; rats, which are highly intelligent, soon learn how to avoid the dog.

Traps, properly placed and set, are effective for rats and mice. Poisons such as red squill, harmless to other animals, will kill rats.

To deal with squirrels and chipmunks, close any openings they may be using. Do this during the day when they are likely to be out foraging. To make sure they are out, burn a sulphur candle in the nesting area. The fumes will drive out even the most obstinate rodent. Then close the openings.

Roof Repairs and Maintenance

While the homeowner shouldn't have much difficulty making repairs on a roof covered with asphalt or wood shingles, roll or built-up roofing, it's best to leave slate, tile, and asbestos shingle repairs to experts. The latter materials are brittle; and without expert knowledge, a great deal of damage may be done to a roof by simply walking over it.

There's always a certain risk involved while on a roof, so it's important to take all safety precautions. Never work on a wet roof, for it may be slippery. Wear shoes with rubber soles. When inspecting a roof with a steep pitch, use a rope for support. The rope can be tossed over the ridge and fastened to a window frame or other solid object on the opposite side of the house. If a lot of work is necessary, it's worthwhile to employ one of several safety devices used by professional roofers. One of these is the so-called "chicken ladder," which consists of a 1" x 12" board with wood cleats nailed across it a foot apart. One end of the board is fitted with wood or metal brackets, which are slipped over the roof ridge so that the ladder extends down toward the eaves.

Another device is a special bracket nailed to the roof to support a 2″ x 4″ that can be used as a foot rest.

Roof Leaks. It's usually easier to find the location of a small roof leak from the underside of the roof in the attic or crawl space, than from above. Go under the roof during a rain; and when the spot where the water comes through is noted, shove a piece of stiff wire through the opening so that the leak's location can be seen from above after the weather clears. It may be necessary to drill a small hole through the wood sheathing to accommodate the wire.

Temporary repairs of small leaks can be made from the underside of the roof. To do this, coat the underside of the roof sheathing around the leaky area with roofing cement. Take a piece of 2″ x 6″ stock cut so that it fits snugly between the roof rafters. Coat the face of the board with roofing cement and push it up so that it comes over the area on the roof boards which you also coat with the cement. Secure the 2″ x 6″ in place by toenailing it to the roof rafters. Use 16 *d* nails for this. Toenailing will drive the board up snug against the roof sheathing.

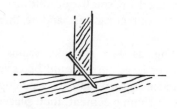

TOENAILING

Asphalt Shingles. When lightweight shingles are used on a roof with a very low pitch, the shingle ends will often be blown up by high winds, allowing rain to get through. Even if there's no leak, the wind can eventually tear the shingles or otherwise damage them. This can be corrected by lifting the tab (the lower unfastened end) of each shingle and putting a dab of roofing cement on the exposed lower portion of the shingle. Press the tab down and the shingle will be firmly secured. Start this job at the shingles along the eaves and work up to the roof peak.

Small holes in asphalt shingles can be closed by filling with roofing cement. For torn shingles, nail the two halves down, then coat the torn area with roofing cement. Put a dab on each nail head to keep water from seeping in around the nails.

Asphalt shingles soften when warm, and then they can be damaged by being walked over. It's best to make repairs on cool days or in the morning before the sun is hot. On the other hand, don't work with asphalt shingles when they are very cold, because then they are brittle.

When an asphalt shingle roof is in very poor condition, the best thing to do is to add a new roof. It's not necessary to remove the old shingles. In fact, assuming the roof framing is strong enough to carry the extra load, there are several advantages in leaving the old shingles in place. They provided added thickness, which makes the roof tighter and the house warmer in winter. Also, the time required to remove the old shingles and dispose of them can add considerably to the cost of the new roof.

The life of an old asphalt shingle roof can be extended by having it coated with one of the several special compounds made for this purpose. These coatings can also be used to change the color of the roof if this is desired.

Roll Roofing.   This consists of heavy paper, 36″ wide, applied in strips, each strip overlapping the adjoining one by several inches. Roll roofing is often used on small outbuildings and is inexpensive and easy to install. It isn't attractive, and is therefore seldom used on houses.

Holes in roll roofing, as well as leaky seams, can be filled with roofing cement. Tears or large gaps should be covered with a piece of roll roofing several inches larger than the opening. The underside of the patch is coated with roofing cement, then placed over the damaged area, and nailed around the edges with large-head roofing nails. Coat the top and edges of the patch with roofing cement.

Wood Shingles.   Old or poor-quality wood shingles will sometimes warp and leak. To fix warped shingles, split them lengthwise with a chisel and slip a piece of roofing or building paper under the two halves. Nail them back into place with shingle nails and dab cement on each nail head.

Leaks in the roof may be fixed by slipping a sheet of building paper or metal, such as copper or aluminum, under the shingles around the leak.

Wood shingles should never be painted, but they can be stained to give color. While this is easier before the shingles are on, it may be done after they are in place.

New wood shingles can be applied over old ones even if the latter are in bad condition or rotting. As soon as they are covered, they will dry out and decay will cease. The usual method is to trim back the old shingles about four inches along the eaves and roof edges, then fasten a piece of 1″ x 3″ board along these lines to serve as a nailing base for the new shingles and to provide a clean joint.

Asphalt shingles can also be applied over old wood shingles to reduce costs of reroofing.

Roof Leaks, Flashing.   The weakest point on any roof is where two roof angles come together to form a valley, or where the roof joins some vertical surface such as a chimney or adjoining wall. (This occurs where a one-story porch roof meets an outside wall.) These joints are usually made tight with flashing, which is usually made of copper, aluminum, or galvanized iron. If a leak occurs around valley flashing, and there are no visible holes, it can be assumed that water is running up under the shingles that partially cover the flashing and is then getting under it. If the roof is of asphalt shingles, the shingle ends can be lifted and roofing cement worked in under them to bond the ends to the flashing. With wood and other rigid shingles, this can't be done; but roofing cement may be carefully applied along the shingle ends to make a tight seal with the flashing.

The flashing around a chimney runs under the roof shingles and then comes up the chimney sides. The flashing ends are bent over so they can be slipped into the joints of the chimney and held in place by mortar. If the flashing ends pull out, clean out the old mortar from between the masonry, force the flashing back into the joint, and pack the joint with fresh mortar. Chimney flashing is made of many pieces of metal, and there can be leaks between them unless the work has been done properly. The best remedy, short of hiring a roofer, is to coat all the flashing liberally with roofing cement.

To prevent rust, galvanized iron flashing should be painted. This is not required for aluminum and copper flashing.

Ice Dams along Roof Eaves.   It is not uncommon in cold climates for ice and snow to accumulate along the eaves of the roof. These ice and snow dams are a common cause for leaks in the roof. Dams are produced by heat loss through the roof melting the snow on it so that the snow slides down toward the eaves. When this accumulation strikes the overhanging portion of the roof, which is usually not over a heated portion of the house and therefore much colder than the main area of the roof, the snow and water freeze, producing a dam.

Insulating the underside of the roof cuts heat loss to a minimum and can help stop these dams from forming. Leaks along the eaves can often be prevented by having a wide strip of flashing installed under the shingles.

One of the best ways to prevent dams from forming is to install a heating cable along the eaves or in the gutters. These cables will operate on household electric current. They can easily be attached along the edge of the roof by means of metal clips, or simply placed in the gutters. When there is a chance that snow and ice dams will form, the current is turned on to prevent the snow and water from freezing when it reaches the eaves or gutters. These cables are sold through hardware and electric stores, and are not excessively expensive.

Termites

Termites are insects that infest and destroy wood. They live in large underground colonies and are found in most parts of the United States, with highest concentrations in the warmer and more tropical areas.

Once entrenched in a building, termites can cause great damage, attacking wooden beams, posts, flooring, and other woodwork. They feed on the cellulose in wood. Because they work beneath the surface, they are often not discovered until the structure they have undermined is accidentally broken into or is so eaten away that even slight pressure will break through the thin crust remaining.

While somewhat antlike in appearance, termites are of a different order from true ants. Like ants, they live in a highly organized society, but, unlike the ant, the male, or king, termite not only helps to start the nest but remains with the queen throughout life. There are three caste groups: kings and queens, soldiers to guard the colony, and workers. The workers do the actual damage to wood.

The termite colony, which nests in warm, moist soil, maintains contact with its food supply through these workers, which are pale, soft-bodied, and wingless. They gain access to the house through wood that is in contact with the ground, through small cracks in the foundation walls, or by means of small earthen tunnels that they construct over various obstacles to reach their food supply.

At certain times of the year, the young kings and queens, called "reproductives," swarm out of their nests to form new colonies. The reproductives are black, with narrow bodies and long, membranous wings. They are sometimes mistaken for flying ants, but are straight-sided, lacking the tightly constricted "waist" of the ant. They are usually about half an inch long. They are the only members of the colony to come out into the open. They are no immediate menace to wood, for when out they remain only long enough to shed their wings and to pair. They then go back into the ground to start a new colony.

One sign that termites are about the property is the finding of these wings which have been shed by the reproductives. Bodies of those that have died may also be found at this time. Both wings and bodies are sometimes found in the house itself, on window sills, or around doors. These findings do not necessarily indicate that termites have already begun their destructive gnawing, but can be a clear warning that they are in the vicinity and preparing to go to work.

In order to make sure that the woodwork close to the ground has not been infested, it is a good idea to prod all suspect wood with a sharp-pointed tool such as an awl. An icepick also makes an accept-able probe. For deeper probing into heavy beams and sills, a long drill is useful. If the points of any of these instruments pierce the wood easily or break through into a cavity on slight pressure, it may be an indication of decay or dry rot, or it may be termite-infested wood.

Ridding the House of Termites. If a swarm of flying termites is observed around the house, and there is time, you may be able to knock many of them out with an insect spray. You probably won't get all of them, however, and the ones who get away will soon begin to form new colonies. It is the better part of wisdom to concentrate on getting rid of the colonies already established, and wood already infested. It takes termites some time to get established, so there is no point in becoming highly alarmed. In other words, don't panic; the house will remain standing. But get rid of the insects without delay.

Since termites breed and thrive in moist ground, they must keep their connection lines to the ground open at all times, in order to obtain the moisture without which they cannot live. The best way to destroy both the colony and those already in the house is to break this connection and stop the traffic going back and forth from house to nest.

One effective way to do this is to saturate the soil around and under the building with poison. The termites will not penetrate the poisoned soil as long as the chemicals remain active. The success of the operation depends on proper impregnation of all earth under and around the house. It is often necessary to drill holes through concrete foundations, drives, walks, and basement floors, so that the poison can be forced under these surfaces. Unless the poison barrier extends completely around the house, the treatment will not be effective.

Because of the need for such relatively drastic measures, it is obvious that this work is best done by a professional termite exterminator, preferably one in the general locality. A competent exterminating company will provide a guarantee for several years and will return at regular intervals to inspect the premises and add more poison, as needed. While this may be somewhat costly, it will ensure the job being done properly and will probably save money in the long run.

It is possible, however, for the homeowner to attempt the job himself if he so desires. There are several termite poisons on the market designed for home use. These are sold with full instructions, which should be followed to the letter for a successful result.

Chemicals most commonly used for this saturation process are chlordane and pentrachlorophenol. Kerosene can be fairly effective when used for this purpose, although for briefer periods. It has the disadvantage, also, of being being both inflammable and harmful to plants and lawns.

It is important to check foundation walls and other masonry for cracks or openings that might provide entry for the termites. These should be filled as soon as possible. Also, destroy any earthen tunnels found. Make sure, wherever possible, that no unprotected wood or woodwork remains in contact with the ground. Wooden posts and piers should be replaced with concrete or masonry, or set in a tight concrete or sheetmetal lining after being treated with a wood preservative.

In addition, keep the area around the house free of waste lumber, dead tree stumps, etc. Try to keep foundation plantings, especially those with woody roots, at least 18 inches from the house, for the roots can be used as a pathway inside. Make sure that earth close to the foundation is properly graded and that gutters are properly installed to prevent collection of rainwater and ensure proper drainage.

Preventing Termites from Entering the House. The most effective way to prevent termite destruction is to take precautions as the house is being constructed. The installation of a termite shield is

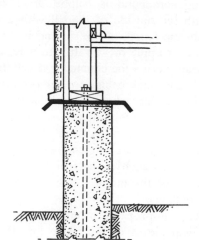

TERMITE SHIELD

excellent protection. The shield is made of sheet copper, which is placed between the top of a masonry or concrete foundation wall and the wood sill above. The copper sheet should be several inches wider than the wall on which it rests, so that there is an overhang of at least two inches on both sides of the foundation. This copper shield is then bent down at a 45-degree angle. It must extend entirely around the house foundation. Many new houses have this shield, and for them there is little chance of termite infestation.

Windows

Windows, Leaky. Damp spots and peeling paint or wallpaper on interior walls around a window usually indicate that water is seeping in around the window frame or windowsill.

Inspect the outside of the frame to make sure that the joint where the frame joins the siding is filled with caulking compound.

The position of the damp spots on the interior wall may not always indicate the exact location of the leak, for water may be entering at one point and flowing some distance before showing on the side wall.

Leaks often occur along the underside of a window sill; filling this joint with caulking compound is helpful. Even better is to cut a channel underneath the outside of the sill with a wood gouge. This channel should run the length of the sill and be ½″ across and ¼″ in depth. Add paint or apply preservative to bare wood. Wind-driven rain will not be able to cross the channel and will drop to the ground.

Many window frames leak because water is trapped on the surface of the sill. This often occurs where a combination storm window and screen with a permanent metal frame is set into the window frame. In summer, rain may pass through the screening and be trapped on the sill. If it remains on the sill long enough, it will find a small crack and run off into the wall cavity. The remedy is to drill small "weep" holes along the base of the metal frame so that any water trapped on the sill can easily flow off.

A poorly built or improperly installed wood window may have cracks where vertical pieces of the frame join the sill. These joints should be cleaned and packed with white lead thinned to a paste by the addition of turpentine.

Metal windows sometimes leak because sash or frame has become bent and a tight fit can't be made. It's virtually impossible to realign the frame or sash; the best thing to do is weatherstrip the window so that a tight joint is achieved.

Windows, Replacing Glass.   Most window sashes installed recently are easily removed. Taking down the sash and putting it on a worktable will make the job of replacing a pane of glass much easier than trying to do the job with the sash in the window frame.

First, the broken glass must be removed. This should be done with care. Wear gloves. Sometimes it's possible to pry the glass loose from the putty, but you may find it necessary to remove the putty first. Putty can usually be taken out with a wood chisel. If it is so hard that it will not respond to this treatment, warm it with a hot soldering iron.

After the old glass is out, clean off the old putty and get out the small triangular glazier's points that hold the glass in the frame; they can be pulled out with a pair of pliers. Clean the recess into which the pane fits, and then coat the exposed wood with linseed oil or a thin coat of paint. This is necessary to prevent the bare wood from absorbing the oil from the putty, thus causing the putty to dry and crack.

The window glass should be cut about ¹⁄₁₆″ to ⅛″ smaller on each side than the actual opening. This allows for irregularities in the glass edge left by cutting. It is also best to measure all four sides of the opening, for many sashes, particularly in older houses, won't be absolutely square.

The wood frame around the opening into which the pane fits is made with a shoulder, and the glass should fit snugly against this. The shoulder should be given about $\frac{1}{16}''$ application of putty. The pane is pushed into place and should make contact with this thin bed of putty along all four sides. This thin putty bed will insure a tight seal between sash and pane.

The glass is held in place by glazier's points. These can be forced into the wood with a screwdriver or chisel. They should be placed about every four to six inches, points down. Force the points deep enough into the wood to make them secure, still leaving enough metal above to hold the pane tightly in position. The final step is application of the strips of putty that form a watertight joint between glass and wood sash. Getting this putty strip smooth and even will take a little practice. An ordinary putty knife will do, but there are special tools designed for just this sort of work. After the putty is in place, let it dry for a day; then apply a coat of paint. Some carpenters claim that the paint should be applied while the putty is still wet.

Some of the latest types of wood windows are made so that a pane of glass cannot be replaced without taking the sash apart. If you are not going to do the work yourself, you may find it less expensive in

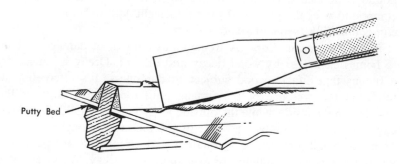

Putty Bed

SHOWING HOW PROPER BEVEL IS OBTAINED

the long run to buy a new sash rather than hire a carpenter or glazier to take the sash apart to replace the broken pane of glass. The four sides of the sash are held together with metal pins, and these can be punched out with a nail set. Once the pins are out, the four sides of the sash can be pulled apart. The glass fits into grooves cut into the four pieces of the sash frame; and once the frame is apart the old glass can be removed. Clean out the putty or glazing compound from the grooves and replace with fresh compound. Set the new pane into the groove of one side of the frame and then fit the other three sides into place. Press the pieces together so that the pins at the four corners can be replaced.

Metal Windows. In some metal windows, the glass is held in place by means of small metal clips attached to the metal frame. In other types, the glass is held by metal strips screwed to the sash. Some metal windows are glazed on the outside, some on the inside.

To take out the glass, either remove the glazing compound to expose the clips, or remove the metal beading by taking out the screws. Then scrape away the glazing compound.

Metal windows should be glazed with double-strength glass instead of the ordinary single-strength glass used on wood windows. Also, metal windows are glazed with glazing compound instead of putty. Glazing compound remains more flexible than putty.

A thin bed of glazing compound is first applied to the sash opening, and the glass is then set in place. Check to be sure the compound makes contact with all areas of the glass and there is no place where the glass comes in direct contact with the metal sash frame. If clips are used, these are now replaced; and a coating of glazing compound is applied over them. If dealing with metal strips, apply the compound over the glass and then attach the strips. Wipe off excess compound with turpentine and a cloth.

Wood Decay and Rot. A tremendous amount of damage is done to homes each year by wood decay and dry rot. Decay is caused by a fungus that attacks wood subject to dampness. It's often difficult to detect the presence of the fungus until too late; it destroys the wood from the inside, while the outside looks perfectly solid. Wood decay is most likely to attack a house in a damp area among trees. Parts of house woodwork where ventilation and circulation are poor and where there is little sunlight are also subject to decay. Wood decay is common on those parts near the ground or in direct contact with soil, but woodwork against masonry may also become infected.

Wood damaged by decay can be found only by careful inspection, and usually it's necessary to prod with a sharp tool such as an awl.

If the point goes in easily, it usually means damage by decay or termites.

To prevent wood decay and dry rot, wood should be pressure-treated with a wood preservative at the lumber yard or during manufacturing. Wood can also be treated by the homeowner with a preservative applied by brush or by soaking in the preservative. This is best done before installation. Many modern wood preservatives serve as a base for paint, and this makes them more acceptable than older ones, such as creosote which, while effective, will bleed through paint applied over it.

In replacing wood damaged by decay, make sure the new lumber has been treated with a preservative.

The danger of wood decay and dry rot can be minimized by seeing to it that no woodwork comes within 18 inches of the ground. It's also essential to keep woodwork from prolonged dampness. Plantings should be trimmed to allow sun and air to reach the lower areas of the house. There should be sufficient openings under wood porches, steps and crawl spaces to insure good ventilation.

During warm, humid weather, a musty odor will indicate areas where ventilation is poor and dry rot and decay likely to occur.

Wood preservatives can be injected into cracks around window and door frames and where woodwork joins masonry. These will help reduce the hazard of wood decay.

Certain woods are more resistant to decay than others. Red cypress is excellent. But ordinary woods may be made impervious to rot by treatment with a wood preservative.

CHAPTER 10

Heating and Cooling

Heating

Any domestic heating system can be divided into two parts, each dependent on the other, one active, one passive. The active part is the actual mechanical system: boiler, furnace, and the equipment required to produce heat. The passive part is in the house itself: the insulation, storm windows, and other devices that reduce heat loss and prevent cold drafts. A house can never be really comfortable in winter unless both heating system and house have been designed and prepared to maintain cold-weather comfort.

Forced Hot-Water System. The main component of this system is the boiler, in which water is heated to around 180°. The water is then piped to radiators, convectors, baseboard units, or coils in the house floor, walls, or ceilings. These heat exchangers transfer heat from the water to the air through radiation and convection. A small pump called a *circulator* is connected at the boiler site; it brings cooled water from the units about the house to the boiler for reheating and then forces the heated water from the boiler to the units.

Early hot-water systems depended on gravity to keep the water moving, but today's circulator is much more efficient. Near the boiler is a horizontal tank called an *expansion tank* which contains a certain amount of air and in which the heated water may expand.

Heat for the boiler is provided by an oil or gas burner. With automatic heat, oil or gas, the system's operation is controlled by the house thermostat. When the air temperature around the thermostat drops below its setting, the burner goes into operation, heating the boiler water. At the same time the circulator starts pumping water through the system.

The heated water from the boiler circulates through the room heat exchangers until the air temperature reaches the thermostat's setting. At this point the thermostat shuts off both burner and circulator. The

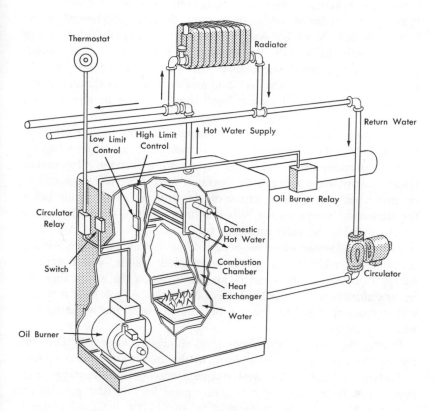

FORCED HOT-WATER SYSTEM

boiler water temperature is also controlled by a high-limit control switch that prevents the water from overheating. When the water reaches the required temperature setting, the high-limit switch shuts off the burner but allows the circulator to operate until cut off by the room thermostat.

Frequently, in such a system, water for cooking or bathing is heated by a special coil set inside or outside the boiler. In this type of installation there will be a low-limit control switch to allow the boiler to maintain hot water without circulating it through the heating system.

This enables the boiler to produce domestic hot water during the summer months without allowing heat to enter the radiators.

In a hot-water system, the boiler, as well as all pipes, radiators, convectors, baseboard units, or heating coils, must be filled with water. If any part contains air rather than water, this area will be only warm instead of hot. Most hot-water boilers are equipped with a gauge showing both the water's altitude and its temperature. The altitude gauge has two arrows: one is black and stationary and set when the system is installed; the other is white and movable and shows the true altitude of the water. The white hand should always be directly over the black for properly efficient operation.

Most modern forced hot-water systems are fitted with a pressure-reducing valve that automatically feeds water into the boiler when the system's pressure drops below the valve setting (around 12 pounds). Older systems have a manually operated feed valve which should be opened when the movable arrow on the altitude gauge drops below the stationary hand's setting. When adding water to the boiler, add it slowly, opening the valve only part way.

Do not add water when the boiler is hot!   Water entering a boiler contains air, which, in a properly designed system, will eventually escape from one of the system's air vents. When the air escapes, the water's altitude will be lowered. Because of this, if you have a system with a hand-operated feed valve, be sure to check the water level at weekly intervals.

During the summer, the water level should be kept full. This will reduce the rust that tends to form in the iron parts of the system.

Failure to Heat.   The most common reason for a radiator, convector, baseboard unit, or coil giving poor heat is that part of the system contains air. In more modern and better designed systems, there will be sufficient automatic vents to get rid of the air before it causes trouble. In older systems, hand-operated rather than automatic air valves are used. These are usually found on hot-water radiators, set near the top. The valve can be opened with a small key provided for the purpose; at the same time water should be fed into the system at the boiler, unless the boiler is equipped with an automatic reducing valve.

When venting a radiator, hold a small pan or saucer under the air valve, for as soon as all the air is out, water will squirt through the opening. This means that the radiator is now filled with water, and the air valve may then be closed.

Another reason for a unit failing to heat is that it is so far removed from the boiler that before hot water reaches it, the house thermostat has cut off the burner and circulator. One way to improve this is to insulate the pipes to these distant units.

Although the hot-water system gives an even heat, it cannot produce it as rapidly as some other types. This means that if the house is cool and the thermostat is set up to demand heat, it may be several minutes before the radiators or heat exchangers grow warm and more minutes before the rooms begin to warm. This delay is even greater when hot-water coils are set in a concrete floor, because although once the mass of concrete is warm it will remain so for some time, when it cools there is a lag until it warms again.

This lag can be eliminated by turning up the thermostat a few degrees in late afternoon just before the sun sets. This will start the boiler and circulator bringing up heat, and by the time the outside temperature falls, the house system and air inside will be warm. Or an outside thermostat, working in conjunction with the inside thermostat, can be installed. When the temperature drops, the outdoor thermostat will anticipate the situation and demand heat from the boiler even though the air temperature around the inside thermostat is still above the setting.

Inadequate Heat. When a system fails to heat the entire house properly, make sure heat loss has been reduced to a minimum by means of insulation, weatherstripping, storm windows, and caulking. If these are adequate, it means there is insufficient radiation in certain rooms or possibly throughout the entire house. It's often possible to correct this by replacing radiators and convectors with larger units, or by the addition of extra ones. As a rule, boilers are oversized and thus more equipment can be added without worrying about installing a larger boiler.

Stale Air. With some types of forced hot-water systems, particularly those with radiant coils in the floors, the air in some rooms may become uncomfortably stale. This is due to lack of circulation. The easiest thing to do is open a window just a crack at the top. Fresh, cold air will enter and create enough disturbance to put the air in motion without chilling the room. A small portable fan may also be used.

Forced Warm Air. This system consists of a furnace fired by oil or gas. The air is heated by flowing around (but never inside) the combustion chamber in which the fuel is burned. When the room

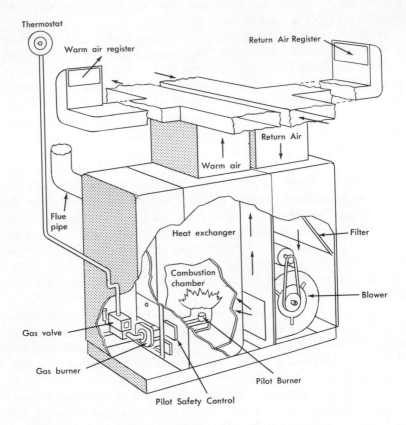

FORCED WARM AIR SYSTEM

thermostat demands heat, the burner starts; and when the air temperature around the combustion chamber is sufficiently high, a blower goes on and the warm air flows through metal ducts to registers located in floors, walls, and sometimes ceilings. The warm air flowing from the registers forces the colder air in the room down toward the floor. Special registers called *cold-air return registers* are connected to ducts to carry the cold air back to the furnace. Cold air passes through a filter in the furnace, where dust and dirt are removed, then through the blower and into the area around the combustion chamber for reheating.

Maintenance. Besides the necessary attention to the burner, the furnace will require periodic servicing. It is most important that the filter be cleaned or replaced when badly soiled. A dirty filter will reduce the system's efficiency considerably. Some filters can be cleaned by tapping them on a newspaper to catch the dirt. Others must be replaced. (The legend on the filter will tell you whether it can be cleaned or must be replaced.) If you must have new filters, buy a few extra from your dealer so that they will be on hand when needed. Clean or replace a filter at least twice during the heating season. Even more frequent changes may be required. The filter's location is marked on the furnace.

Blowers, blower motors, and belts should be checked twice each season. Turn off the electricity to the furnace so that it can't start while you're at work. Inspect the motor to see whether it has cups that need oil. If the manufacturer doesn't specify a particular grade, use a #10 motor oil. Check the belt between motor and blower; if it is worn or frayed, replace it. Check the blower for bent blades and dirt, for these can make the system noisy.

Cold Floors. Warm air from the registers flows upward; cold air is pushed down, where it often remains, making the floor chilly. While this can sometimes be corrected by installing additional cold-air returns, it can also be eliminated by adjusting the furnace to continuous air circulation.

Continuous Air Circulation. Until a few years ago, it was usual for a blower to operate at infrequent intervals but for long periods, and then only when the air temperature in the furnace was high. It has been discovered that the best way to run a forced warm-air system is to have the blower run at frequent intervals, and, during very cold weather, to run continuously. The furnace controls can be set so that the blower goes on when the furnace air is between 90 and 100 degrees, a much lower setting than if the blower is to operate at infrequent intervals.

When this adjustment has been made—and it should be made only by a competent serviceman or heating contractor—there will be a constant but slight movement of air through the room registers at all times. This gives more even heat in the house; and because of the constant air circulation, it will prevent cold floors. Also, it does away with the annoying cold or hot air blast that comes through a register when the blower goes into operation after being off for any extended period.

Many homeowners resist adjusting the system to continuous operation because they feel the constant operation of the blower motor will increase power bills and reduce the unit's life. But it costs very little to operate these small motors all day, and in some ways it's easier for the motor to run continuously than to start and stop under the old system adjustment.

Drafts.   Uncomfortable drafts may be due to several factors other than air leaks in the structure. A cold draft may come through a register when the furnace blower goes on. This happens because cold air in the room drops into the registers and ducts and is forced up by the blower. The cold-air flow from the registers lasts only a few seconds, but it can be annoying. This can be eliminated by having the furnace adjusted for continuous air circulation.

Cold drafts across rooms and down stairs are caused by a lack of cold-air returns. A well-designed system will have a sufficient number of returns placed on inside walls to allow cold air in the room to return easily to the furnace for filtering and heating. However, if there are too few, the cold air may have to travel some distance to find a return. The only effective remedy is to install additional cold-air returns.

Ducts and Registers.   Even with a filter, a certain amount of dirt will get into registers and ducts. Registers may be cleaned with a vacuum cleaner. Most of them are easy to remove, so the adjacent ductwork can also be cleaned. Most furnace service companies are equipped with large, heavy-duty vacuums to clean all ductwork. This may be required from time to time.

Most modern ducts are made of aluminum or glass fiber, because these require no insulation. Insulation may be required on galvanized steel ducts when they become dull and lose their natural insulating qualities.

Noises in the System.   Expansion and contraction of metal parts around a furnace often cause crackling noises which may be carried through the house by the metal ductwork. A slight vibration of the furnace when the burner or blower is operating can also be annoying, since the sound will be amplified by the ductwork. If the furnace cannot be silenced by leveling and being firmly secured to a concrete base, a fabric sleeve may be inserted in the ductwork. This will break the continuous metal link between the furnace and the room registers.

A furnace may also be noisy because of a worn blower belt or bent fan blade in the blower. Even an accumulation of dirt and grease on the blower blade can cause noise.

Odors in the System. The air heated in a furnace never comes in contact with the burners or with the fumes resulting from fuel combustion. The burner is set in the firepot, and its only opening is into the stove pipe connected to the chimney. If an unpleasant odor comes from a register, the system should be shut down and the firepot carefully checked for leaks. This check should always be made by a competent serviceman. Incidentally, have your furnace thoroughly gone over by a serviceman before each heating season to be sure it's in proper working condition.

Uneven Heat. As with other systems, there may be rooms in the house heated by forced warm air that never reach a comfortable temperature because the thermostat shuts off the furnace before these rooms get their full share of heat. These usually are the rooms farthest from the furnace. In a well-designed system, the ducts to distant rooms are larger than those to rooms nearest the heater. Large ducts carry more air, and carry it faster, than small ducts; and there is less heat loss. Uneven heat can also be overcome to some degree by proper balancing of the system.

Usually there are dampers in ducts at points close to the furnace. They can be adjusted so that a greater amount of heat flows through some ducts and a lesser amount through others. On installation, these dampers are usually set to provide the best possible balance, but the individual requirements of the family may make changes desirable. And, of course, not all systems are properly balanced when installed.

The easiest method is to call in a heating contractor and have him balance the system to your needs. He'll have special instruments to measure the temperature and velocity of the air from the registers. If you don't wish to go to this expense, you can do the job yourself through trial and error. It's a simple process to adjust the dampers with a pair of pliers. Close down on those to rooms near the furnace, and open the ones to rooms far away from it, or to the rooms where more heat is wanted, such as children's rooms or bathrooms.

Steam Heat. This system uses a boiler in which water is heated to the point where steam forms. The pressure created by the steam in the boiler forces the steam through pipes into radiators. Steam is very quick; it takes but a few minutes for it to flow up and heat the radiators. Then, when the steam cools, it condenses back into water and flows from the radiator back to the boiler for reheating.

Some systems have a single pipe from boiler to radiator that carries steam from the boiler as well as the return water. In other systems each radiator has two pipes: one for steam, the other for water. Most homes use the cheaper one-pipe system.

Unlike a hot-water system, only the boiler contains water, and even this is only partly filled. If there is no mark to indicate how much water should be let into the boiler, add water and keep it about at the halfway mark on the glass water gauge. *Never add water to a hot boiler!*

In a one-pipe system, it's advisable to have all pipes insulated so that distant radiators get their full share of heat before the thermostat turns off the burner. Each steam radiator must have a small air valve to let air escape so the steam can enter. These valves may be replaced with adjustable air valves which allow air to escape slowly or quickly. If the air escapes slowly, the radiator will heat slowly, whereas if the air flows out quickly, the radiator heats quickly. The air valves on radiators near the boiler should be adjusted to let air out slowly, and valves on distant radiators should be opened as wide as possible.

Adjustable air valves are sold at plumbing and hardware stores and heating concerns. They are easily installed by unscrewing the old valve from the radiator side and inserting the new one in the same opening. Be sure to do this when steam is not coming up, or else close the radiator shutoff valve.

Nonheating Radiators.   Often a radiator fails to deliver heat because the air valve is clogged. Placed at the side of the radiator, this little valve is so designed that when steam comes up it opens and lets any air in the radiator escape, making room for the steam. When the steam strikes the interior of the valve, the valve closes, preventing the steam from escaping. If the valve is clogged or worn, it won't open; and as the air can't come out, there will be no place for the steam and the radiator will stay cold.

Air valves can be cleaned by taking them off the radiator and soaking them in white gasoline. Don't use ordinary automotive gasoline, which contains lead. Soak the valve for 15 minutes, and then flush with fresh gasoline. Let it dry; then replace it. Old valves that are worn inside or coated with paint should be discarded. New ones are not expensive.

Steam radiators are provided with a shutoff valve. Sometimes this is turned off accidentally, preventing the radiator from heating.

Pounding Radiators.   Radiators and pipes in a one-pipe steam system will often make a loud noise when steam comes up. This can be caused by the shutoff valve being only half open. It should be either wide open or tightly shut.

Pounding in pipes and radiators can also be caused by water that has condensed in the radiator and is trapped either there or in the pipes. The trapped water interferes with the passage of the oncoming steam, and pounding and hammering result.

If the pounding is in the radiator, slip some ¼″ wood blocks under the legs at the other end from where the pipe enters the radiator. These will lift the radiator high enough so that the water trapped in it will flow back to the boiler. Sometimes thicker blocks will be needed to change the pitch sufficiently to provide good back-drainage.

Sags and low spots in horizontal pipe runs will trap water; these can be corrected by installing pipe straps and supports.

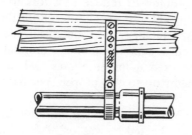

HANGER FOR PIPE

Electric Heat. While electric energy has been utilized for many years to provide heat in the form of electric space heaters, it has only been in very recent years that electricity has been utilized for central heating. Today many homes are designed and built to be heated by electricity and this method of heating will become more common in the years to come.

Electricity provides a very comfortable, clean, and convenient method for central heating. It is also a method that can provide individual controls for every room in the house. The most common type of installation utilizes the resistance principle—the same principle that provides electric heat in an electric toaster, iron, or portable electric heater. In some installations the resistance coils are placed in baseboard units somewhat similar in design to the baseboard units used in hot-water heating. These units are installed along the base of the walls. Another method of installation is to have the resistance coils imbedded in the ceiling. It is also possible to have the installation where both baseboard and ceiling coils are used. Electrical furnaces and boilers are also available and these function basically in the same manner as any furnace or boiler except that electricity provides the energy to heat the water or warm the air.

Electric central heating requires an absolute minimum of maintenance. With a resistance type of installation there would be, for all practical purposes, no maintenance other than an occasional vacuuming of dust that might settle on baseboard units. Where an electrical unit is used to provide the heat for a furnace or boiler, there will, of course, be the need of maintenance of the moving parts of the furnace and the care of the boiler circulator, etc. The primary considerations in regarding electricity as a choice of heat are that the local power rates are favorable and that the house is properly insulated and weatherproofed to reduce heat loss to a minimum. Local electric utility companies can provide you with the necessary specifications to insure satisfactory and economical installation.

While most electric heat installations are put into new houses, this system can be used in older houses and in remodelings if the house can be brought up to the proper specifications as far as heat loss is concerned.

Space Heaters.   Many small houses, vacation homes, and dwellings in warm climates are heated by gas or oil-burning space heaters. A space heater works much like a warm-air furnace, but it has no ductwork. Air circulates around the firepot, where it is warmed, and then flows from a register in the heater. Some space heaters are set in the floor; others are set in the walls or are free-standing.

If a house is compact, a space heater can do a good job. Sometimes, for better distribution of heat, a small portable fan can be set almost at ceiling height to force the heated air from one room into another or from ceiling to floor.

Any fuel-burning space heater should be vented to the outside by a stovepipe and chimney. This goes for oil, kerosene, gas, or coal burning equipment. Any fuel that burns produces certain gases which can be dangerous if inhaled. It's also important to be sure there is proper air supply to the room or rooms where the heater is located. Burning fuel uses oxygen; and unless there is a fresh air supply, the oxygen content of the room will become dangerously low. This is especially important if the house is tightly built and fitted with storm windows and weatherstripping, leaving little if any space for air leaks.

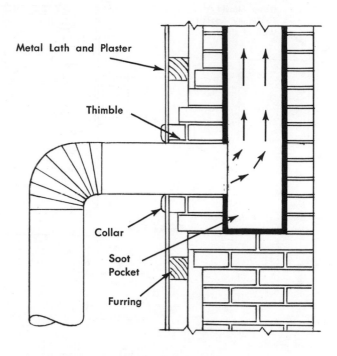

Metal Lath and Plaster

Thimble

Collar

Soot
Pocket

Furring

SOOT POCKET

Chimneys and Stovepipes. Any fuel-burning equipment requires a chimney to allow combustion gases to escape from the house. The furnace or boiler is connected to the chimney by a metal or asbestos-cement stovepipe. It's important that stovepipe and chimney, as well as joints between them, be tight, for leaks permit gases to enter the house.

Inspect the stovepipe and connections to the chimney at least once a year. Metal stovepipes in a damp basement may rust after a few years and should be replaced. Make sure the joint between pipe and chimney is tight. This may be done by filling in around the pipe with asbestos cement, cement mortar, or furnace cement. The stovepipe should not protrude into the chimney flue but just to the edge of it, so as not to block it.

Masonry chimneys should be lined with clay flue tile and should be tight and free from obstructions. If coal or oil is burned, the chimney

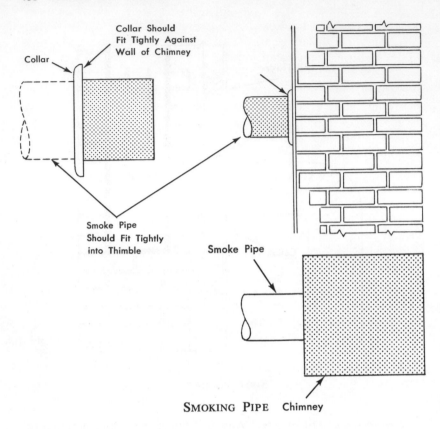

Collar

Collar Should
Fit Tightly Against
Wall of Chimney

Smoke Pipe
Should Fit Tightly
into Thimble

Smoke Pipe

SMOKING PIPE   Chimney

may require cleaning from time to time to remove soot. This can be done by putting some stones or bricks in a burlap bag to provide weight, and then filling the bag with old rags or excelsior. Tie a rope to the bag and lower it down the chimney a few times. This will loosen the soot and it will fall to the chimney base, where it can be removed through the clean-out door provided for the purpose. A thick accumulation of soot in a chimney can cause a serious fire.

Until recent years, most chimneys were built for use with coal-burning heaters. If your heating system has been converted from coal to gas, have the local gas company check the chimney. Often an old type of chimney that is not adequate for gas can be made so by inserting a liner in the old flue.

Oil Burners.   Oil burners should be carefully inspected just before the heating system goes into operation each fall. This job should be done by a qualified serviceman. Many fuel-oil delivery concerns have men trained for this, or you can use your local oil-burner serviceman. In any event, it is far better to have this job done by an expert than to attempt it yourself.

In many homes the oil burner is set in a small closet or utility room. When the burner is being checked, be sure it's checked with the closet door closed. A burner requires a large amount of air for proper operation, and often the vents or louvers in the utility or closet door aren't adequate to supply the burner with enough air. If the door to the heater room is left open when the burner is checked, a true picture of normal operation is not given.

In a one-story house where the heater is set in a room on the main level, there is often a draft across the floor of the adjoining rooms when the burner is in operation. This can be eliminated by running a vent into the attic or attic crawl space from the heater room so that the air for the burner is drawn from the attic rather than from the living areas.

Failure to Operate. When a burner fails to operate, there are several points to check before calling a serviceman. First, make sure the thermostat is set high enough to demand heat. Move the thermostat control back and forth a few times, in case a speck of dirt has lodged inside to prevent proper electrical contact. Next, check the burner emergency switch located outside the heater room. This is an ordinary electric wall switch, but it has a red plate on it. Sometimes, by accident, a member of the household will throw this switch to the "off" position. Next, check the fuse to the oil-burner circuit to see if it has blown. If it has, replace it with a fuse of the same rating as the old one.

One common reason for a burner not to operate is that there is no oil in the storage tank. Some tanks have gauges, but they are not always accurate. The best way to check the tank is to remove the cover on the fill pipe and measure the contents with a long stick.

An oil burner's motor is protected from overheating and overloading by a small built-in switch that turns off the motor in case of trouble. When this occurs, a little red reset button on the motor will pop up. As soon as the motor has cooled or the overload no longer exists, the button can be pushed down and the motor will start. If it pops up again, more serious trouble is indicated and a serviceman should be called.

Another reason for failure of an oil burner is that the relay or "stack switch," which is mounted on the stovepipe from heater to chimney, may be out of adjustment. This is a safety device that will turn off the burner motor should the fuel fail to ignite within 90 seconds. Sometimes this relay switch gets out of order and stops the burner even though operation is normal. Flicking the little lever on the switch will usually start the motor again. Should the fuel fail to ignite, the switch will once more turn off the motor. Again, if this happens, a serviceman should be called.

Most hot-water boilers have a low-water control unit that prevents operation of the burner should the water level in the boiler be too low.

Failure of Electric Power. If there is a failure of electric power, turn off the burner emergency switch and keep it off until power has been fully restored. This is done because the voltage may be low while the lines are being repaired, and this low voltage can damage the burner motor. After power has been restored and the house lights are burning brightly without flickering or dimming for several minutes, it may be assumed conditions are normal and the burner can be re-started.

Noisy Oil Burners. A burner may hum a little if not sitting level. Loud hums may indicate serious trouble with the burner or motor. A serviceman should be called.

Smoking Oil Burners. After an oil burner has been in operation for several minutes, it should not smoke. If it does, it needs adjusting. Smoking will occur when a burner first goes on because the heater firepot is cold and fuel combustion isn't complete. After a minute or two the firepot will become so hot that combustion of fuel will be complete and there should be no more smoke.

Oil Storage Tanks. The small oil storage tanks (275 gallons) are usually located indoors; the larger tanks (550 gallons) are set underground outside. Each tank has a vent pipe so that air can enter to replace the oil as it is pumped or drawn to the burner. These vents should be fitted with a cap so that snow or rain can't get into the tank. Under no circumstances should the vent be clogged, because this will prevent oil from flowing to the burner. Be sure that children aren't allowed to push snow, mud, etc., into these vents. Inside oil tanks can be given a coat of paint to make them more attractive. They'll need a sealer coat of aluminum paint, and then they may be painted the color of your choice.

It's a good idea to have an oil-storage tank filled at the end of the heating season and kept filled during the summer months. This prevents condensation inside the tank. The water resulting from condensation will collect at the tank bottom and cause rust and trouble inside. There are special compounds that can be added to the oil in the tank to discourage condensation; these are sold by many fuel-oil delivery concerns.

Radiators, Convectors, Etc. Radiators produce heat by radiation as well as by convection. To insure maximum output, they should be placed where they have good air circulation and where nothing interferes with the radiant rays coming from them. Radiators, both steam and hot water, should never be coated with a metallic paint such as aluminum or bronze, for this cuts down heat output. They should be painted with a flat paint or radiator enamel. This can be applied directly over a previous coating of metallic paint and it will restore efficiency to the unit. The metallic paint does not have to be removed before the paint or enamel is applied.

Radiators should be kept clean. Any dust and dirt on them will act as insulation, and reduce their heat output. Dust and dirt on radiators will cause dark stains to appear on walls behind radiators. Use a special brush or attachment on the vacuum cleaner to get between the radiator sections.

Radiators shouldn't be recessed into walls. This reduces their heat output. A poorly designed enclosure can cut down heat output considerably. The enclosure should have several inches clearance between it and all sides of the radiator for proper air circulation. There should be a large opening at the bottom of the enclosure so that fresh air can enter, and an equally large one at the top to allow the heated air to flow out.

Convectors. These units should never have drapes or furniture placed against them because they will interfere with air circulation. Most convectors have removable front panels; these should be taken off at frequent intervals so the unit may be cleaned. A heavy coating of dust on the convector's metal fins can reduce heat output.

Baseboard Units. Baseboard units are of two kinds: the radiant type and the convector. The radiant panels are somewhat similar to a radiator in operation, and they produce heat by both radiation and convection. They are usually made of cast iron. Convector baseboard units produce heat by convection; therefore, they shouldn't be concealed behind draperies or large pieces of furniture, which will check the circulation of air.

Thermostats. Almost every member of the household is familiar with the thermostat. This little device controls the heating system's operation. From the standpoint of comfort, the thermostat is a vital part of the house. Unless properly located and adjusted, and in good working order, the house will never be quite comfortable.

The thermostat should be in a centrally located spot, such as the living room, dining room, or family room, where it will be subject to the true air temperature of the house. It should never be near an artificial source of heat, such as a radiator, register, or fireplace, or near a door or window. Even the small amount of heat from a TV set, a radio, or an electric light can prevent the thermostat from giving a true picture of the house's temperature. If it is near a heat source, the house will be cool; since the thermostat is warm, it isn't demanding heat from the system. If in a draft from a door or window, or even in the path of drafts flowing across a room toward an open fire in the fireplace, the thermostat will demand heat not really required and the house will be uncomfortably warm.

The best height for a thermostat is about five feet off the floor, on an inside wall, set between wall studding. Thermostats operate on a low-voltage system, and it is not difficult to shift them to a better location. Simply turn off the electric power to the heating system, remove the thermostat from the wall, and if necessary splice the wires so that the thermostat may be moved to its new location.

Many otherwise excellent heating systems fail to function properly because an inferior thermostat is used to govern their operation. With an old or low-cost thermostat, there will often be a lag from the time the air temperature drops well below the setting and the time the thermostat finally demands heat. Newer and better quality thermostats react to a small change in temperature. This means they demand and get heat before the room cools, and also turn off the heat before the room is overheated.

Thermostat Setting. The correct setting of a thermostat is up to the individual household. Young, active adults will find a lower setting more comfortable than that required by older people and the very young. The most satisfactory setting for the entire household seems to be between 72° and 74°. Certainly any heating system will function more effectively if the thermostat is left at one setting most of the time. Find the setting most comfortable to the entire household. If some members feel this too high, they can wear lighter clothing; and those who feel it low can wear something heavier.

A certain amount of fuel can be saved if the thermostat is turned down a few degrees before retiring, but it's best not to set it below the 65° mark because the house will grow so cold during the night that the fuel saved will be used in the morning to warm the house. Some thermostats can be set to turn themselves down a few degrees at night, and then up to normal daytime setting an hour or so before the family gets up, insuring a warm house in the morning.

When it's very cold, it's best to set the thermostat a degree or two above normal. In spite of wall insulation, storm windows, and double glazing, the cold exterior walls and windows of the house reduce our body heat. This will happen even when the air temperature around us in a room is adequate. This is why we feel cold on very cold days even though the air temperature in the room may be at 72°. As we have said, the problem can also be eliminated by installing an outdoor thermostat to work in conjunction with the indoor one. The outdoor thermostat measures the outdoor temperature and slightly elevates the control point of the indoor thermostat as the weather grows colder. As the weather moderates, it lowers the control point. This arrangement is especially suitable to homes with radiant-heated concrete floors where there may be a considerable lag between the time the thermostat demands heat and the slab becomes sufficiently warm to produce heat.

Fireplaces. In spite of modern heating systems, open fireplaces continue to be an essential feature of the most modern homes. Unlike a central heating system, a fireplace is inefficient as a heat producer; but it lends cheer and its own special warmth to a room.

Sometimes a fireplace may smoke. This can be caused by a down draft. The chimney top should be at least 2 feet higher than the roof's highest point. Even with an adequate chimney, some fireplaces need a hot fire to keep them from smoking. When first lighted, the flue is cold. Twist a newspaper, light it, and hold it up the flue for a few seconds. This warms the air, making it rise and insuring a good draft when the fire is lit. Never use a fireplace to dispose of trash and old papers. This is not only unsightly, but also it may cause smoking.

Fireplaces also smoke if there is not enough air in the room. Open a door or window when you start your fire. Many homeowners have a register in the floor in front of the fireplace to insure an adequate air supply and eliminate cold drafts flowing across the room to the fire.

Don't store fireplace wood in the house. It often contains insects that will leave it for the house woodwork, and if not used within a reasonable time it becomes so dry that a large log will be consumed in minutes.

Unoccupied House in Winter.   If you go away for several weeks during the winter, leave the heating system operating with the thermostat at 55°-60°. This requires little fuel to maintain. If you do this, the plumbing system won't have to be drained and other steps taken against freezing. Ask a neighbor or friend to check your home every day to make sure the heating system is functioning, for many families have gone away, only to return and find that because of power failure, a blown fuse, or a clogged oil line, the heater has gone off, subjecting the plumbing to serious damage.

If you plan to be away all winter, the plumbing should be drained and the heater turned off. Below-freezing temperatures won't harm the normal house or equipment if there are no liquids that can freeze. (See "Plumbing, Draining the System" page 188.)

Relative Humidity.   This refers to the water-vapor content in the air at a given temperature. House air must contain some moisture for health and comfort. Experts find that a humidity of approximately 35%, when the outside temperature is above zero, is about right for most people. Below zero, the relative humidity should be around 25%. The relative humidity in the house can be measured with a hygrometer, an inexpensive instrument as important to comfort as the thermometer. If the hygrometer shows that the relative humidity is too low, several steps can be taken. The humidifying device on the furnace, which adds moisture to the air as it's heated, may be turned too low. If there is no humidifier, one may be easily installed. There are electric humidifiers to use on systems that do not lend themselves to installation of a central humidifier on the heater itself.

Excessive Moisture in the Air.   Most homes today suffer from too much humidity. The result is that condensation (the appearance of water or ice on a surface) collects on windows and walls in cold weather, and sweating occurs on toilet bowls, flush tanks, and cold-water pipes. Excessive humidity also causes peeling and blistering of the paint on outside walls, and mildew on wallpaper or paint on interior walls.

This was not a problem in older houses, because they were not so tight. Today, houses are compact, with insulated walls and roofs, weatherstripped windows, and caulked joints. Desirable as this may be, it can add up to trouble if the problem of excessive moisture gets out of hand.

The amount of moisture that air can carry depends on temperature. The higher the temperature, the more water vapor. Water vapor seeks even distribution, and there is always a flow from moist to dry air. House air usually has more moisture in winter than the outside air, because the house is warmer. When warm moist air strikes a cold surface, such as a window or a cold pipe, the temperature is lowered and vapor is deposited on the cold surface as water. If it is very cold, frost or ice forms.

Eliminating Excessive Moisture. If the hygrometer shows the relative humidity to be over 40%, or if you have sweating windows and peeling paint, the house has a moisture problem. Remember that water vapor flows from moist to dry air; and this means that no matter where the moisture source may be, once you've eliminated it the air in the house will be properly humidified.

Check your furnace humidifier; if it's operating, turn it off, for obviously you don't need it and it has no automatic cut-off. Make sure automatic clothes washers and dryers are vented to the outdoors, either with a vent or with an exhaust fan. If you must hang wet wash indoors, be sure the room has good ventilation either from a fan or from an open window. Too many indoor plants also produce vapor. Wipe your floors with a damp mop instead of flooding them. If you have a gas furnace or boiler, have your local gas company check the chimney and flue to make sure they are adequate, because burning gas produces moisture and, unlessly properly vented, can add a great deal of moisture to the air.

Earth floors in basements or crawl space can give off large amounts of moisture even though the soil looks dry. It's best to cover the earth with a plastic vapor barrier and then with concrete, but strips of waterproof building paper, lapped at the seams by four inches, or polyethylene sheeting spread over the earth will help considerably. Crawl space should have vents, and there should be at least two square feet of vent for each 100 linear feet of foundation wall.

It's impossible to remove all sources of water vapor entering a house, but these suggestions will help reduce the amount. Exhaust as much moist air as possible with exhaust fans in the kitchen and bathroom. Of course, the fans will draw heat from the house, but they need to be operated only when water is boiling, or food is being cooked, or when baths are being run or showers being used. If there is no exhaust fan, an open window will help.

Most homes have an attic louver or vent to allow warm, moist air collecting there to escape. These should never be closed during cold weather. If your attic or crawl space is damp in winter, or if moisture shows on the underside of your roof sheathing or on the nails protruding through it, your ventilation is poor. Larger louvers or a fan should be installed. If there are no louvers, but there are windows, open one.

Condensation on Windows and Walls.   Condensation can be eliminated, assuming the house air isn't too damp, by preventing windows and walls growing too cold. Storm sash or insulating glass may be used on windows, although even with storm windows, sometimes condensation will show on the inside glass; this indicates that the storm sash isn't fitted tightly enough. Caulking or weatherstripping should give a tight seal. If moisture collects on the storm sash glass, it means that water vapor from inside the house is flowing through and around the inside window and coming in contact with the cold outside glass surface.

Sealing the joints between the inside sash and window frame with weatherstripping or masking tape may help, but usually the storm sash needs venting to let the moist air escape. Many storm sashes have small vents at top and bottom of the frame. If there are none, drill a half-inch hole at the top and at the bottom of the frame.

Moisture on interior walls usually indicates that the wall has not been insulated or that the air-moisture content is so high that even the drop of a few degrees when the air strikes the wall is enough to make it unload some of its moisture. Condensation on interior masonry walls can be eliminated by setting a false wall over the masonry. The false wall of plaster or wallboard is set a few inches from the masonry by wood furring strips. This air space will prevent the false wall surface from being chilled.

Reducing Heat Loss.   An effective way to cut fuel costs and make a house more comfortable during the winter months is to minimize heat loss. Happily, what we do to reduce heat loss will usually reduce heat gain and thus make the house cooler during hot weather.

Insulation.   This is the most important single item in preventing heat loss or gain. The largest amount of loss or gain occurs at the housetop, so this is where the greatest insulation is needed. Around 5″ to 7″ of insulation, or insulation having a minimum R (insulation) value of 19, should be fitted between the roof rafters or the attic floor joists. Any existing insulation should be checked to see if it is of adequate thickness or provides the required R value. Make sure the entire area is covered; during installation, some spaces may have been missed, and this can account for much heat loss. Insulation is sold at building-supply and mail-order houses or lumber yards, and the

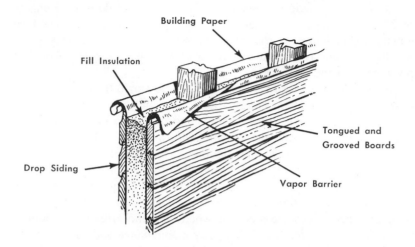

manufacturers usually furnish complete instructions. Installation is not difficult.

Sidewalls should have the equivalent of 3″ of insulation or insulation with an *R* value of 11. If the walls aren't insulated, you can hire a firm to blow insulation into wall cavities. The other method is to cover the interior wall surfaces with furring strips and apply decorative insulating board or wallboard over this.

Floors. Cold floors are often caused by improper heating, but some floors are cold because of excessive heat loss through the floor or because there is an unheated area under it. If they have no basement or crawl space beneath them, floors should be insulated by applying insulation between the joists. Where insulation is provided with a vapor barrier, this side should face up against the subfloor. Some concerns make special floor insulation for easy application between joists. Floor insulation should be 3″ to 3½″ thick, or the equivalent of 13 *R* value.

Cold Concrete Floors. A concrete slab floor in contact with the earth will lose most of its heat around the edges, whether it has heating coils or not. In good construction, the edges will be insulated; but sometimes this has not been done. Matters can be improved by digging a trench around the slab perimeter and inserting sections of 2″ rigid foam insulation to protect the slab edges. The rigid insulation should run as far down as the footings supporting the slab edge, but even 2′ of it will help.

Where it's impossible to insulate, or insulation alone isn't sufficient, the floor can be made warmer by installing a wood flooring. Lengths of 2″ x 4″ "sleepers," treated with wood preservatives, are laid face down and anchored to the concrete with mastic or masonry nails. Set the sleepers 16″ from center to center, and over this lay ¾″ plywood or wood subflooring.

Storm Windows and Insulating Glass.   A single thickness of window glass is an excellent conductor of heat, and an ordinary window can cause serious heat loss in winter and heat gain in summer. The best solution is to equip the window with a storm sash. On double-hung windows, the sash fits outside; on casements and awning windows that swing out, the storm sash is usually installed on the inside. The interval between the window and the storm sash gives an air space which acts as insulation.

Storm sash frames are made of wood or metal, usually aluminum. Aluminum frames require little if any maintenance and are easier to handle. Storm sashes should fit tightly; it's wise to seal them with caulking compound or weatherstripping.

Because it is difficult to install storm sashes on large picture windows, these are often made with insulating glass. This consists of two pieces of glass spaced a fraction of an inch apart and sealed along the edges so that there is no movement of air between the two surfaces. Insulating glass is much more expensive than ordinary plate glass, but it is a worthwhile investment for large glass areas in cold climates.

It is also possible to obtain standard-size window sashes with insulating glass. This is expensive but it eliminates the need for storm sashes.

Weatherstripping.   Weatherstripping windows and doors helps to prevent heat loss and annoying drafts. Inexpensive felt weatherstripping, which will last a year or two, can be easily installed with tacks or an adhesive. More expensive metal stripping will last almost indefinitely, but it should be installed by a professional. There is a special caulking tape that makes an excellent seal against air and heat loss; it requires no special fasteners because it will adhere to any clean surface.

Caulking.   Structural leaks can account for heat loss as well as drafts. These can be sealed from outside with caulking. (See "Exterior Repairs, Caulking," pages 124-25.) Pay particular attention to seams where siding joins window and door frames and the joint where the house sill and siding joins the foundation wall.

You don't need to consult an expert to tell whether or not your house is properly insulated and otherwise protected against excessive heat loss. Put your hand on an inside wall on a cold day. If the outer walls feel cooler than the inside partitions, it means that the outside wall is poorly insulated.

After a snowstorm, if the snow melts off your roof before it melts on the roofs of your neighbor's house, you may be sure your roof needs better insulation. Snow can also help you determine how well a concrete slab floor has been insulated. If the snow melts quickly around the house, it means that heat is flowing out along the edge of the slab.

Another way to judge heat loss conditions is by the setting of the thermostat. If you have to keep inching it up during cold weather, above 75°, to make the place comfortable, there is either too little insulation or you have too many cracks around the doors and windows.

Cooling the House

In many areas, cooling the house in summer is as important as, or more than, warming it in winter. There are few sections where cooling in one form or another is not desirable at certain periods of the year.

Many things may be done to make the home cooler. What is done depends on the degree of coolness desired and the amount of money available to accomplish this.

Insulation. This is a must, whether you plan central cooling or have a limited budget for summer cooling. Insulation will make the house cooler and reduce the operating cost of window and central air conditioners while making them more effective. (It also cuts down heat loss in winter.) Use 6 inches of insulation at the roof and 3 inches in the wall. The heaviest heat gain occurs at the roof, so this is the part to insulate first.

Shading Devices. A house may be kept several degrees cooler simply by shading it from the hot sun. Shade trees are fine, although it may take several years for them to grow to an effective size. Window and porch awnings help, and so do devices such as louvered fences set a short distance from the house.

Light-Colored Roofs. Dark roofs absorb heat from the sun and warm the house; light-colored roofs reflect the heat and cool it. When

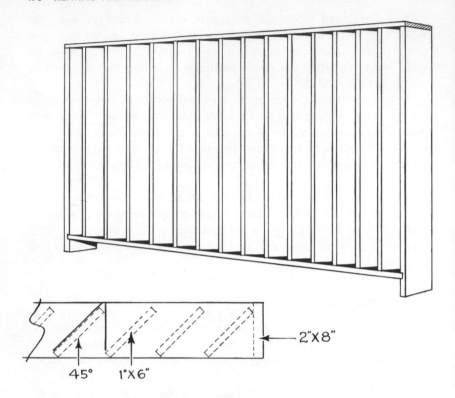

2"X8"

45°   1"X6"

LOUVERED FENCE

and if you re-roof, use as light a color as you can if you wish to keep the house cool.

Fans.   Properly used, fans make the house interior more comfortable in several ways. They drive out hot air from inside the house, allow the cooler outside air to enter. But even when there's little if any difference between inside and outside, the fact that air is moving makes us more comfortable.

Attic exhaust fans can reduce the amount of heat entering the house by as much as 25%. These are usually mounted in the floor of the attic, but they can be installed in almost any central location as long as they can exhaust to the outside. Attic fans may be used on any style of roof. They should be permanently installed and controlled by a wall switch or a switch and thermostat. The fan's size will depend on the house and its location. In the South, the fan should be able to change the house air every minute; in cooler sections, it can take 1½ minutes to do the job. If it is impossible to install an attic fan, a large exhaust fan can be installed in a window.

Operating Attic Fans.   An attic fan should not be turned on early in the morning, for then the house is cool and the outside air is probably warmer than the inside air. Instead, close the windows, especially those on the east and south sides of the house. During the morning, the fan should be operated for a minute or two at frequent intervals to remove the air that is beginning to heat under the roof or at the ceiling height of the rooms. When the house temperature is near that of outdoors, open the windows on the shady side and allow the fan to draw in the cool outside air. When the sun goes down, the air close to the earth cools fastest, so open the windows near the ground and let the fan suck in the air through these. At night, close off all the rooms but the bedrooms, and open the bedroom windows so that the fan can pull cool air through. A timer on the fan is helpful, for it can turn off the fan, allowing the house to fill up with cool air, which will be there in the morning when the family awakens.

Although they are effective, fans are not in a true sense air-conditioning units. Such a unit lowers the air's temperature by mechanical means, removes excess moisture, filters it, and circulates it.

Window Air Conditioners.   Many homeowners have found that one or two window air conditioners do the best job for them. Two of these units, in conjunction with a fan, can cool an entire house. The fan is used to pull the cold air produced by the units into other areas of the house.

When possible, window units should be set in windows on the shady side of the house or, if this is impossible, an awning should be used to protect the outside portion of the unit from the sun. Rooms in which units are installed should be insulated and windows made tight against air leakage.

Many air conditioners fail to function properly because of dirty filters or low voltage. Filters should be cleaned or replaced at the start of the cooling season and again at midpoint. Low voltage can cause a unit to burn out or to operate at reduced efficiency. Dimming of house lights when the unit goes on usually indicates low voltage, and it's wise to have an electrician check the system to see if an additional circuit may be required.

Through-the-Wall Units.   These are similar to window units except that an opening is made through the outside wall and the unit is permanently set in. This type may be financed through FHA improvement loans, since they are a permanent part of the house. They are used in both old and new houses where it isn't practical to install a central air-conditioning system to handle the entire house.

Central Air-Conditioning Systems.   Much progress has been made in the past few years in perfecting central air conditioning for average-cost houses. Unlike older units, the present ones do not require large amounts of water; they operate on the air in the same way that a window unit does. The least expensive central unit is one that can be installed in conjunction with a warm-air furnace so that the same ductwork and registers may be used for heating in winter and cooling in summer. Many concerns make warm-air furnaces especially designed to accommodate a cooling unit. The cooling unit can be put in during installation of the furnace or added later.

When a house is heated with forced hot water or steam, the most practical cooling method is to install window or wall units; but in new construction, there are special units that operate on hot water in winter and chilled water in summer. It is also possible to install an air conditioner with ductwork separate from the heating system.

The main problems that occur with a central air-conditioning system are caused by faulty installation and improper maintenance. These are areas that cannot be handled by the amateur; they require the services of a very competent serviceman.

Heat Pumps.   This is a combination heating and cooling system that operates on electricity. It works on the same basic principal as an air conditioner in that it removes heat from one area and discharges it into another. In summer, the pump takes heat from the house air and forces it outdoors, like an ordinary air conditioner. In winter, the process is reversed and the pump extracts heat from the outside air and puts it into the house. Even with very low temperatures, air contains a certain amount of heat; this makes the operation of the heat pump possible.

Naturally, the lower the outside temperature, the more the pump must work to provide heat to warm the house. For this reason, when heat pumps are used in very cold climates, they are usually hooked up with a resistant-type electric heater to provide additional heat when required.

At this time, heat pumps are most effective in warmer states where the outside temperature seldom drops to a very low reading; but every year these units become more efficient and are thus able to operate in colder climates. The beauty of the heat pump, besides the fact that it doesn't require fuel, is that it doesn't need an expensive flue or chimney, and it is both noiseless and clean.

CHAPTER 11

The Plumbing System

You will have better luck dealing with the plumbing system in your house if you have some idea of how it is supposed to function. So before flying off in all directions with a pipe wrench, take a minute to study the diagram in Figure 1 and read the next few paragraphs with as much interest and care as you can muster.

The illustration shows a typical domestic plumbing system. Plumbing systems today are fairly standard. They will differ in general layout, but all will have the same basic elements.

You will notice that the plumbing system is divided into two parts. There is the fresh-water system consisting of hot- and cold-water pipes that go from the supply to the various fixtures and faucets about the house, and there is the drainage, waste, or sewer system that carries waste from the fixtures out of the house to the street sewer, septic tank, or cesspool.

Points of interest in the fresh-water system are the shutoff valves that control the flow of water to various parts of the system. The main shutoff valve allows all the fresh water in the house to be turned off in one fell swoop. The branch shutoff valves control the flow of water to the various fixtures and branch lines. It is helpful to label each shutoff valve with a tag designating the part of the system that it controls. In this way, when and if trouble occurs, a lot of time won't have to be wasted locating the proper valve to turn off.

First, of course, you'll have to find the valves. Sometimes they are in the basement or basement crawl space. In homes with slab floors, the valves are often found in small closets off the bathroom or kitchen or in the utility room.

Water in the fresh-water system is always under pressure, so before making any repairs be sure to turn off the shutoff valve that controls the section where repairs are to be made. If you fail to do this, you may be in for quite a soaking.

The house drainage system is not under pressure; it depends on

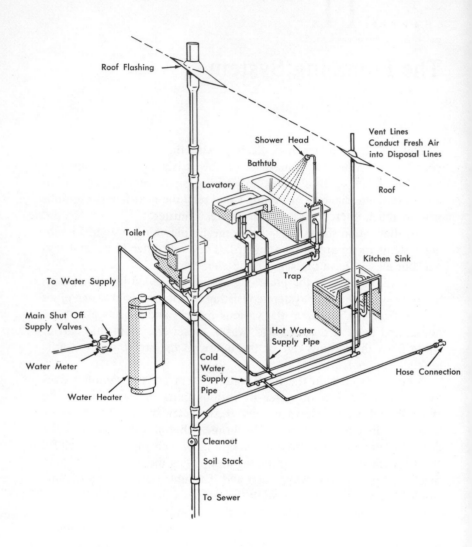

Roof Flashing

Shower Head

Vent Lines
Conduct Fresh Air
into Disposal Lines

Bathtub

Lavatory

Roof

Toilet

Kitchen Sink

To Water Supply

Trap

Main Shut Off
Supply Valves

Hot Water
Supply Pipe

Water Meter

Cold
Water
Supply
Pipe

Hose Connection

Water Heater

Cleanout

Soil Stack

To Sewer

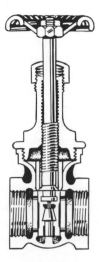

GATE VALVE

gravity to bring the waste water away from the fixtures. The entire system is given a slight downward pitch so that waste flowing out of a fixture will flow through the pipes and out of the house. Among the more important parts of the drainage system are the curved sections of pipe under each fixture. These are called *traps*. They prevent sewer gas from coming up through the fixture drains. They are also the points in the drainage system most likely to become clogged. In the case of sinks and lavatories, the trap is right under the fixture and easy to reach. Traps for showers and bathtubs can sometimes be reached from the floor below if they are over an unfinished basement or crawl space. Sometimes they can't be reached at all, which can be a nuisance. Some tubs and showers use a drum rather than a curved trap. A drum trap is shaped like a cylinder and is set into the floor with a metal lid flush with the floor. The lid can be unscrewed so that the trap can be cleaned. Toilets have built-in traps. We will go into these later when we come to the subject of clogged toilet bowls.

All fixture drains eventually connect into the main house sewer line that runs through the house and connects at the base to the underground sewer line. Near the base of the house sewer line is a clean-out plug that can be removed to clear obstructions in the house sewer line or the underground sewer line.

You will note that the drain pipes increase in size as they run from fixtures to the main sewer pipe. This is an important point to keep in mind, because when a branch line becomes clogged, it is often possible to push the obstruction along until it reaches a larger size pipe where it can flow through without further aid.

Tools and Equipment. You can do most ordinary household plumbing repair jobs with a screwdriver and an adjustable wrench large enough to take a 2″ nut. Pliers, especially water-pump pliers, can be used in place of a wrench; but pliers are likely to slip and damage the plating on certain fittings as well as damage the shoulders on the nuts. Even when using a wrench it's wise to protect plated fittings with a cloth or masking tape. One piece of equipment you will find most useful is a rubber suction plunger often called a "plumber's friend." This is handy for clearing stopped-up drains. You should

FORCE CUP OR "PLUMBER'S FRIEND"

also have a box of assorted faucet washers and some graphite im-pregnated wicking used for packing faucets and valves.

Leaky Faucets. The illustration shows a typical compression faucet in general use today. When water continues to drip out of the spout of a faucet after the handle has been turned as far as it will go, the trouble is usually a worn washer. This can be corrected in the following manner: Turn off the water supply to the faucet at the nearest shutoff valve. Use the wrench to loosen the big packing nut on top of the faucet body. Turn the nut counterclockwise to loosen it. When the nut is free from the threaded portion of the faucet, turn

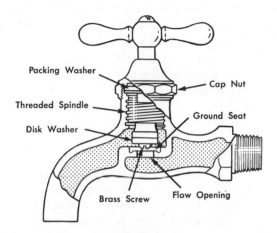

the faucet handle as if to open it. You'll find that the faucet spindle will unscrew out of the faucet. At the end of the spindle you'll find the washer, held in place by a small screw. Take off the old washer, and replace it with one of the same size and shape. Put the spindle back in place, and turn the handle to close it. When the spindle is once again inside the body of the faucet, replace the packing nut. The trick here is to tighten the packing nut enough so that water won't leak out around the stem to which the handle of the faucet is attached, but not to screw it so tight that the faucet handle can't be turned with relative ease.

Sometimes even a new washer won't prevent a faucet from leaking. This means that the metal washer seat inside the faucet is probably worn. One remedy is to replace the faucet, but this is expensive. You can smooth off the worn seat with a tool called a valve-seat dressing tool, but this job is best left to a plumber. However, there are several patented faucet inserts designed to correct this situation. These are available at most hardware stores, and they are inexpensive and do a good job. Usually the hardware clerk can explain how the particular brand he handles should be installed.

Faucet leaks often occur around the packing nut, either at the base or around the opening where the faucet stem passes through the nut. First, try tightening the nut. If this doesn't stop the leak or makes the faucet handle too difficult to turn, shut off the water to the faucet and unscrew the packing nut. Take off the faucet handle so that the packing nut can be slipped off the stem. Inside the nut you'll find the packing. Remove the old packing and apply the same amount of new, winding it around the stem in the same direction that the packing nut is turned to tighten—clockwise.

The actual working parts of kitchen sink, bathtub, and shower faucets are not always easy to reach. Sink faucets are often concealed in a box, and this must be removed before you can work on the faucet. Tub and shower faucets are often recessed in the wall, and before you can get at the packing nut or washer it may be necessary to first remove the handle, the plate that covers the opening in the wall, and other items of trim.

Noise in the Plumbing System.   A plumbing system should make no noise. When it does, it means that something is out of order; and this should be attended to at once, before serious damage occurs.

If a faucet chatters when open, or partially open, the cause is usually a loose or worn washer. Tighten the set screw that holds the washer in place or replace the washer.

Loud hammering in pipes when a hot-water faucet is opened indicates steam in the hot-water pipes; this means that the hot water is too hot. Reduce the temperature on the thermostat of the hot-water heater to around 140°, and the hammering should end.

If there is a hammering or banging in either the hot-water or cold-water lines when a faucet is turned off, you have what is called "water hammer." This occurs when the water under high pressure, and traveling at a fast rate through the pipes, is brought to a sudden stop by the closing of a faucet. Closing the faucet slowly will often eliminate this condition, but the best solution is to have a plumber install a special shock-absorbing fitting in the supply lines, or a vertical length of pipe with a cap on the end on branch lines. Water hammer is not only annoying, but it can become so violent as to open joints in the system and thus cause leaks.

Many plumbing systems are noisy because the pipes are not held securely in place, and they shake when water passes through them. This can be corrected by installing additional pipe supports.

Drain and waste lines become noisy if there is a partial stoppage at some point. A flooded cesspool or septic tank will also cause noise in the drainage system.

Stopped-up Drains.   Drains seldom stop up all at once. First they get the "slows," and get slower and slower until they finally stop. The best time to fix the drain is when you first note signs that it is slowing down.

The first place to look for a stoppage in a fixture drain is at the trap. Most traps have a small clean-out plug at the base, and if this is removed you can often work a piece of wire into the trap and pull out the obstruction. If the trap doesn't have a plug, take the entire trap off and clean it out. Some traps are removed by loosening two large nuts, one at each end. Some newer traps are held in place by friction washers, and if you give them a hard pull they'll come off. Traps always contain water; so before you remove the plug or the trap itself, have a pail handy to catch the drainage from the trap.

Should the stoppage not be in the trap but rather in the line running from the trap to the house sewer line, other methods must be used to remove the obstruction. One method is to employ the plumber's friend mentioned earlier. The trap and clean-out plug should be in place, and there should be enough water in the fixture so that when the rubber suction cup is placed over the drain opening, the rim of the cup will be under water. Hold one hand over the overflow opening of the fixture, if there is one, or plug it with a piece of wet cloth. Pump up and down on the handle of the plunger. The alternating suction and pressure created by the suction cup will often loosen the obstruction and push it along to a larger-size pipe. Once you feel the obstruction is loose, pour plenty of water down the drain to help flush it into the sewer line.

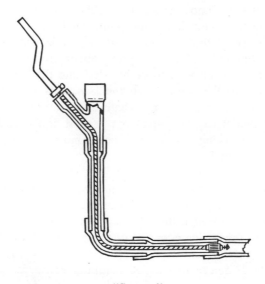

"Snake"

Another way to push an obstruction through the line is with a "snake." This is a long coil of flexible steel with a point on the end. You can often rent one of these from a hardware or plumbing store. Remove the trap and insert the point of the snake in the pipe, and keep pushing and pulling until you have either pushed the obstruction into the main sewer line or pulled it out through the trap opening.

Chemical drain cleaners are useful when certain obstructions can't be reached with a snake or other mechanical means. These are strong substances, so they must be handled with care and used according to the directions on the label. Pour the cleaner into the line as near the stoppage as possible, and then resign yourself to a little waiting. It may take a considerable amount of time for the chemical to eat through the obstruction. Chemical cleaners are good where the obstruction is caused by objects that can be readily dissolved, such as rags, grease, and food particles. They are useless if the stoppage is caused by metal, wood, etc.

Kitchen sink drains usually give the most trouble, because both grease and food particles wash down the drain into the trap. Keep as much grease as possible out of the drain by wiping the grease off your pans and dishes before washing them. And don't believe that old story that coffee grounds are good for drains—they are not. In fact, unless your sink is equipped with a garbage grinder, keep as much solid matter out of the drain as possible.

Toilet bowls give almost as much trouble as kitchen sinks. Toilets have a built-in trap, and this is the point where trouble occurs. Try the plumber's friend first, for in most cases this will do the trick. If it doesn't, get hold of a coil-spring auger from a hardware or plumbing store. This device can be inserted into the bowl so that the point goes up into the trap. When the handle is turned, the point rotates; and this either breaks up whatever is causing the trouble or catches it so that it can be pulled out. You'll find it easier if there are two people working the auger—one to hold it in place, and the other to turn the handle.

Clogged Underground Sewer Lines. A stopped-up underground sewer line will keep a fixture drain from working properly. Often a stoppage in the underground line can be cleared by inserting a large snake into the line through the clean-out plug located near the point where the main sewer line goes out of the house. This is rough work and is best done by a plumber.

Tree Roots in Sewer Lines. A common cause for stoppage in

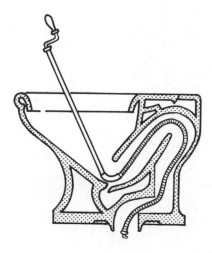

WATER-CLOSET BOWL SHOWING USE OF COIL SPRING-STEEL AUGER

an underground sewer line is tree roots. A small crack in the line allows the fine roots to enter, and once inside they quickly spread and grow until they form an almost solid obstruction. The roots can often be removed with a large snake, but it's heavy work. Two pounds of copper sulphate crystals (sold at hardware stores under various trade names) dissolved in water and poured down a drain near the sewer line can also be effective if conditions are not too serious. This treatment can be repeated every month or so, if required. In most communities, there are firms with special equipment designed to cut out the roots. The best remedy, but also the most expensive, is to dig up the old line and have a root-proof one installed.

A flooded septic tank or cesspool will put the house drainage system out of order. This condition is most likely to affect those fixtures close to the ground. If several fixture drains start acting up all at once, check the septic tank or cesspool.

Leaky Flush Tanks. Before you can make repairs on the inner workings of a standard flush tank, it is necessary to know how this strange collection of rods, valves, floats, etc., functions. Shown here

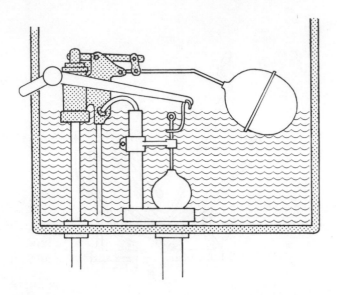

FLUSH TANK

is a typical flush tank. When the toilet is flushed by operating the handle, the flush ball valve is lifted off its base, allowing water to flow from the tank into the bowl. This flushes the bowl. As the water level in the tank drops, the float ball (made of copper, glass, or plastic) drops with the water, and this opens the inlet valve that is connected to the float by a metal rod. The water then enters the tank to fill it for the next flushing. At the same time that the inlet valve opens, the flush ball valve drops back into place at the bottom of the tank to shut off the flow of water into the bowl. Water continues to flow into the tank until the float ball reaches the shut-off level. Running up through the middle of the tank is the overflow pipe. This takes care of emergency situations when the tank may get too full of water. If this happens, the water will flow through the overflow pipe into the bowl and then down the drain line. Unless there is a stoppage in the trap of the bowl, the bowl can't overflow, no matter how much water runs into it. A little tube from the inlet valve to the top of the overflow pipe refills the bowl with water after it has been flushed.

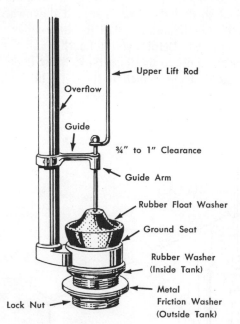

Upper Lift Rod

Overflow

Guide

¾" to 1" Clearance

Guide Arm

Rubber Float Washer

Ground Seat

Rubber Washer
(Inside Tank)

Metal
Friction Washer
(Outside Tank)

Lock Nut

The most common trouble with flush tanks is the continuing trickle of water into the bowl long after the bowl has been flushed. The way most of us try to solve this problem is to jiggle the handle; and while sometimes this works, sometimes it does not. Often the cause of the trouble is that the metal rods that connect the flush ball valve to the handle are bent or out of alignment so that the valve can't drop down easily into place. Bending the old rods straight or installing new ones usually corrects this situation. Hardware stores sell special fittings that help insure that the valve will fall back into place. Sometimes the trouble is due to a worn flush ball valve that no longer makes a tight seal at the bottom of the tank. Ball valves are sold at most hardware stores, and they are easy to install, since they screw right into the rod. Another cause for leakage is dirt or rust around the valve seat, over which the ball fits. Clean off the seat to insure a tight fit.

Sometimes you'll find that water continues to flow into the bowl by means of the overflow pipe. When this occurs, it means that for some reason the water supply to the tank is not being shut off at the proper time. You might first try bending the rod that connects the valve to the float so that the float is forced downward just a bit. If this doesn't help, the chances are that the inlet valve washer is worn and must be replaced. Before you take the valve assembly apart, shut off the water supply to the flush tank. Most tanks have a shutoff valve directly under them, which is handy. The inlet valve washer

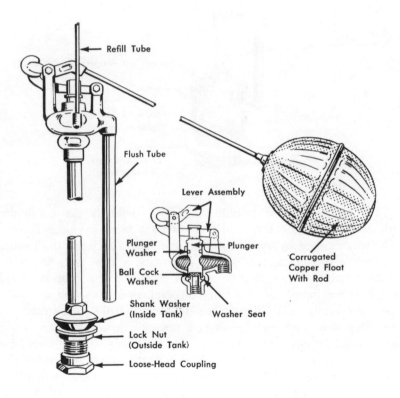

is attached to a valve plunger, and this can be removed from the valve assembly after you have loosened one or two thumbscrews. Replace the washer with one of the same size and shape. A worn inlet valve washer can also cause a whistling when the flush tank is being filled.

The parts of most flush tanks are standard and interchangeable, but there are some exceptions. If you need a new part, it's usually best to take the old one to the hardware store so that you'll be sure of getting the correct replacement.

Hard Water. In some areas, the water contains calcium and magnesium carbonates which make the water "hard." These salts react with the stearate and alkali in soaps to form precipitates. With this type of water, more soap is needed to get yourself and your clothing clean. You can use hard-water soap to wash yourself, and a detergent for your clothes; or you can invest in a water softener. This unit contains exchange resins plus sodium chloride, better known as common salt. In the softener, calcium and magnesium are exchanged for soluble sodium compounds before the water enters the house system.

A small softener costs about $130, but an automatic unit can run as high as $300. A tank of saturated salt solution is connected to the softener. Once or twice a week, the resin bed has to be backwashed to cleanse it of slime; in most softeners, this is automatic. After the backwash, your water may be cloudy for a few hours, but it will soon clear.

Red Water. Rust in the water in old houses often comes from rusting pipes and tanks. The only solution is to replace these with items of noncorrosive materials, such as copper.

Many ground waters contain small amounts of ferrous salts, usually in sulfate form, as well as the calcium and magnesium compounds mentioned. The softener will eliminate this iron, provided there isn't too much of it. If the softener can't do the job alone, then you'll have to install an aerator and filter or a special chemical unit ahead of the softener to remove excess iron.

Dirty Hot Water. When a hot-water faucet is opened and a stream of rusty or dirty hot water comes out, it usually means that the sediment in the hot-water heater should be drained. Don't use any hot water for several hours; give the sediment time to settle on the tank bottom. Then open the drain faucet at the base of the tank and let the water run until it is clear. That's all there is to it. If you do this little chore at fairly frequent intervals (every two weeks or so, depending on conditions), you shouldn't be troubled with dirty hot water. By the way, while some of the discoloration in the water may be due to rust from iron tanks and pipes, it is often nothing more than the foreign matter found in almost all water, turning a reddish color when it is heated.

Inadequate Hot Water. We run out of hot water for about the same reason that we run out of money—because we use more than we have. In both instances, the solution is simple: either get more or use less, and certainly don't waste what you have.

You can get more hot water by installing a larger hot water heater and tank or an auxiliary unit. This may be the only solution when a growing household is trying to get along on an undersized heater and tank. There are, however, other remedies. An obvious solution is to get the members of the household to practice a little economy in their use of hot water. It is not necessary to turn a hot-water faucet full blast when you wash your hands, and you can get quite as clean in a shower that lasts five minutes as you can in one that goes on for half an hour. If the family won't cooperate, you can have a plumber install "flow-control" fittings in the hot-water pipes; these insure that no matter how far open a faucet is turned, only a certain amount of hot water will flow out. These flow-control fittings, by the way, are very good to have if your hot water comes from a coil in the central-heating boiler, for these coils can only produce so many gallons of hot water per minute; and it's easy to use the water faster than it is heated, unless there is some sort of built-in control.

You can conserve what hot water you have by insulating the hot-water pipes. This can be especially helpful if they run for any distance or pass through unheated portions of the house. You can get pipe insulation from lumber yards, plumbing supply stores, and mail-order houses.

Septic Tanks and Cesspools. If you live where there are no city sewers, you will probably have either a septic tank or a cesspool. These are totally different in operation. The only thing they have in common is that both usually go out of order when you have a house-ful of guests and when no one can come around to do anything about it for a week or so.

If you have a septic tank, the main thing to keep in mind is that it must be cleaned out every few years. If it is not, the semisolid sludge that collects at the bottom of the tank will eventually get deep enough to put the tank out of operation. This means a flooded septic tank. There are firms that will periodically inspect septic tanks to determine whether they need cleaning, and if they do, the workmen will pump them out. As a general rule, the tank should be cleaned when the sludge is half way up from the bottom of the tank to the scum that floats on the surface of the liquid. If the tank is undersize,

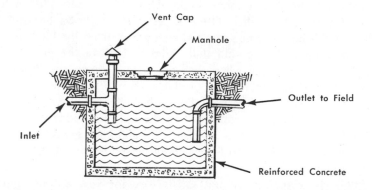

cleaning may be required at rather frequent intervals. It's wise to have the tank inspected at least once a year.

Besides cleaning, a septic tank needs a little consideration to keep it in good working order. You should not, for example, connect the discharge from gutters or a swimming pool into the tank, because too much water will flood it. Excessive use of high-foaming detergents in household equipment can harm the action of the tank for a period of time. Low and non-foaming detergents are perfectly safe to use with a septic tank. Chemical drain cleaners, used in moderation, won't harm the tank; but if used daily (and this should not be necessary unless there is something seriously wrong with the drainage system), they can slow down the operation inside the tank. Kitchen sink garbage grinders are safe to use with a septic tank, but the tank may require more frequent cleanings unless it was originally sized to handle this job.

If you don't know the exact location of your septic tank, it's an excellent idea to find out where it is and mark the spot so that when cleaning or repairs are necessary, the tank can easily be found.

Cesspools. Unlike the septic tank, which is a hygienic method of disposing of household waste, the cesspool is simply a large hole in the ground lined with masonry and fitted with a cover. Waste flows into the cesspool and is eventually absorbed by the surrounding soil. Cesspools are not watertight, and they are not meant to be. The main trouble with cesspools, aside from the fact that they can contaminate the surrounding soil and nearby water supply, is that they often overflow. Sometimes they overflow because too much water runs into them. Sometimes they overflow because the soil is so wet that it can't absorb any more liquid. This often occurs after a long spell of very wet weather. Often a cesspool overflows because the soil around it has become saturated with grease from the kitchen sink. Certain compounds are sold that claim to remove the grease from the sides of a cesspool when they are poured down the drain, but most experts claim that these products are not too effective. As a general rule, when a cesspool floods because of grease, the only thing to do is dig a new one next to the old and connect them up. The old cesspool will act as a grease trap and keep grease out of the new one. Even better is to forget about cesspools and install a well-designed septic tank.

Although cesspools are not satisfactory for year-around houses, they can be perfectly suitable for vacation houses—assuming that they are kept a safe distance from the fresh-water supply.

Draining the Plumbing System.   If you are going to leave a house unheated in an area where freezing conditions occur, the plumbing system must be drained and prepared to prevent damage to it and to the house.

First, you must drain all the water out of the fresh-water system. Turn off the hot-water heater, shut off the water supply to the house, open all faucets, and then open the drain tap (usually found at the lowest point in the system. If there is no such tap or plug, disconnect the pipes at the lowest point in the system to allow any water in the lines to drain off. Horizontal lengths of pipes usually have a slight downward pitch for draining; but if they don't or if they have sagged, disconnect them where possible for safety's sake. Many of the shut-off valves will have little knurled knobs on the side; these should be opened to allow water in the valves and in the adjoining pipes to run out. Drain the hot-water heater, the boiler, and the radiators. If the house is heated by warm air, drain the water from the furnace humidifier. If the house is heated with radiant coils in the floor, have a plumber come to blow these out with compressed air, or have them filled with a special antifreeze. Drain water-storage tanks and water pumps. Pumps usually have to be taken down for proper drainage.

As far as the drainage system goes, pour about a quart of kerosene slowly down each fixture drain. This won't freeze, and won't evaporate, as will alcohol, and will keep sewer gas out of the house. Empty the flush tank, and sponge out any water that remains at the bottom.

Use a pan and sponge to remove as much water as possible from the toilet bowl, and then pour in about three quarts of kerosene. You don't have to worry about the rest of the drainage system, the septic tank or cesspool.

Thawing Frozen Pipes. When a fresh-water line freezes, the first thing to do is to turn off the water supply to the affected line. This will eliminate possible water damage should the freezing have split the pipe.

The safest way to thaw a pipe is with plenty of towels and boiling hot water. Spread the wet hot towels over the pipe; and when they begin to cool, pour boiling water over them. A blow torch is, of course, much faster than towels; but there is a fire hazard involved in using a torch. You must also be very careful not to hold the torch in one spot too long. If you do, the intense heat will not only melt the ice but also turn the water into steam which can do damage. If you use a torch, play it back and forth along the pipe, working back from the open faucet. Electric heaters can also be used to thaw frozen pipes.

When an underground line freezes, the best approach is to call a plumber who has the equipment necessary to thaw the line with electricity. This does the job without the need for digging up the line.

Frozen drain lines can be opened by pouring hot water down them. There are also chemicals available for thawing drain lines, but these must never be used on fresh-water lines.

Sweating Flush Tanks, Bowls, and Pipes. At almost any time of year it is possible to find moisture collecting on the sides of flush tanks, toilet bowls, and cold-water pipes inside the house. This is caused by condensation of warm moist air as it comes in contact with the cold surfaces.

Condensation on flush tanks can be controlled in several ways. One method is to purchase a special metal pan that fits under the tank and catches the water dripping from the sides. There is a small tube that allows the water caught in the pan to drain into the toilet bowl. These pans are sold at hardware and department stores. Another solution is to line the inside of the tank with insulation made for this purpose and sold through hardware, plumbing, and mail order shops.

The best way to prevent sweating on both tank and bowl is to warm the water inside the tank so that it won't chill either container.

There are little electric heaters made for this job, or you can have a plumber connect a hot-water line and a mixing valve into the supply line to the tank so that the water temperature in the tank and bowl will be kept high enough to prevent sweating.

Sweating cold-water pipes are easy to correct. Just cover them with some form of insulation. There is a special wrap-around insulation made for this job, and another one that is applied much like paint. Insulation used to prevent heat loss in hot-water and heating lines will also work on cold-water pipes.

Inadequate Water Pressure. In many homes, the pressure of the water is so poor that when a faucet at a lower point in the system is opened, the flow through a faucet at a higher point almost comes to a stop. In a properly functioning system, there should be adequate water pressure to all faucets even if they are all open at the same time; otherwise, the water pressure is inadequate for modern needs.

Low water pressure is sometimes caused by rust or mineral deposits on the inside of the pipes. This occurs most often in houses with galvanized-iron pipes, because, unlike copper or brass, these pipes are subject to corrosion and their rough interior encourages the formation of mineral deposits. The only practical way to correct this condition is to replace the existing lines with new ones, for there is no effective way to clean them out. Copper tubing is best as a replacement, because, as it is flexible, it can be threaded up through walls without the need of much structural work. The old pipes are disconnected and left in place, because they would be difficult to remove without a great deal of labor.

Inadequate pressure can also be the result of undersize pipes. The branch lines to the various fixtures are often too small to meet requirements.

Houses at the very end of city water mains sometimes are troubled with low water pressure; and unless the city can and will rectify this, you'll have to deal with it yourself. Some families have solved the problem by installing their own pump and storage tank to boost the water pressure. The necessary equipment for this kind of installation costs around $100 plus the labor.

Leaky Water Pipes. The only real remedy for a leaky water pipe is to replace it, but there are some temporary measures that give good results. One of the best is to split a length of plastic pipe or garden hose and slip it over the damaged section. Secure it at both ends with automobile radiator hose clamps. Another remedy is to cut out the damaged section of the line with a hacksaw and insert a length of plastic pipe.

Pipes sometimes leak around fittings. These leaks can sometimes be stopped by tightening the fitting or taking it apart and coating the external threads with pipe dope or pipe compound. Leaks around copper fittings are something else again, for these are usually made tight with solder; the only solution is to melt the solder and start off fresh. This job is best left to a plumber.

Leaks in cast-iron pipe used on drainage systems can be repaired with iron cement or liquid steel. Leaks in lead pipe can sometimes be sealed by punching the metal to close the opening. Don't try to use solder on lead pipes, because it doesn't work.

Leaky Shut-Off Valves. The main spot for leaks in valves is around the packing nut. Turn off the water supply, loosen the packing nut, and replace the packing. Some valves use the same type of packing used in faucets; others use washers.

CHAPTER 12

Masonry

Concrete

Concrete is a mixture of portland cement, sand, and gravel. Portland cement is not the trade name of a particular cement; it refers to a type of cement in common use today. It is so-called from its first use on the Isle of Portland in England. When mixed with water, portland cement undergoes a chemical change that makes it a strong binding agent. Cement has little strength in itself but mixed with sand and gravel it forms a rock-like substance known as concrete. Concrete is used when maximum strength and watertightness are required, for foundation walls, floors, driveways, and swimming pools.

Mortar. Mortar is a mix of portland cement and sand. It doesn't have the strength of concrete, for it lacks the large gravel particles. However, it is a good adhesive, and is used to lay brick, concrete, cinder block, and stone.

Grout. Grout is a mix of portland cement and water. Sometimes very fine sand is added to give it more body. It's used to fill in small cracks in concrete and masonry walls and to insure a good bond between a fresh layer of concrete and old masonry. To apply a cement-mortar coating to a masonry wall in poor condition, first brush on grout. It should be thin enough so that it can be applied with a brush.

For most small projects and repairs involving concrete, the homeowner will find packaged cement most suitable. It's available at hardware stores and lumber yards. It comes packaged in a variety of sizes, and the cost is moderate. The ingredients have been mixed under ideal conditions, and only the addition of water is required.

It is more expensive than concrete mixed on the job, so it isn't commonly used for large jobs such as driveways, foundations, and floors. Here your best bet is to rent a concrete mixer or order the needed amount from a firm specializing in transit concrete. Usually these large trucks can deliver all the concrete needed in one trip. The cost isn't great and you're sure to get good quality materials. But be sure to have enough helping hands around to work the concrete as it comes off the truck.

If you prefer to mix by hand, or with a rented mixer, you'll have to be certain your proportions of cement, sand, and gravel are correct. For most house jobs, a good mix is one part portland cement, two parts sand, and three parts clean gravel. Each sack of cement contains one cubic foot, so in using this formula you'll need two cubic feet of sand and three cubic feet of gravel for each sack. This mixture won't produce six cubic feet of concrete despite the fact that the total amounts of the ingredients add up to six. The fine cement particles will fill in voids between the sand grains, and the sand and cement will then fill in around the particles of gravel. Thus, only about four cubic feet of concrete will actually be produced.

Tables I and II show the more common concrete mixes, the amount produced for each sack of cement, and the amount of water required per sack. The water needed will differ somewhat according to the moisture content of the sand used. If the sand is very damp or wet, less water will be required than if it is dry. The water needed will also vary depending on how the concrete is to be used. If the concrete is to be poured into forms it should be more fluid than if it is to be shaped without forms.

Sand and Gravel. It's essential for strong concrete that both sand and gravel be clean. Dirt particles will produce weak spots. Suitable sand and gravel can be purchased at lumber yards or masonry supply houses. They are usually sold by the cubic yard, but it's possible to buy less.

Mixing Concrete by Hand. Concrete for small repair and improvement jobs can be mixed by hand. This may be done in a metal wheelbarrow or on a concrete floor or a wood platform. First, pour out the required amount of sand and spread it in the form of a ring. Pour the required amount of dry cement into the center of the ring and mix cement and sand together with a hoe or shovel. When the mixture has a uniform color, it should again be spread into a ring and the required amount of gravel added. Mix the gravel into the sand and cement, again form a ring, and slowly pour in the water.

Avoid pouring the water too forcefully. If you do it will flush the cement off the sand and gravel. Use a hoe to mix the water into the dry ingredients. Concrete is properly mixed and of the correct con-

TABLE I.   HOW TO SELECT THE PROPER CONCRETE MIX

KINDS OF WORK	Add U. S. gal. of water to each sack batch if sand is			Suggested mixture for trial batch			Materials per cu. yd. of concrete		
					Aggregates			Aggregates	
	Very wet	Wet (average sand)	Damp	Ce-ment, sacks	Fine cu. ft.	Coarse cu. ft.	Ce-ment, sacks	Fine cu. ft.	Coarse cu. ft.
6-Gal. Paste for Concrete to be Watertight or Subjected to Moderate Wear and Weather									
Watertight floors, such as industrial plant, basement, dairy barn; watertight foundations; driveways, walks, tennis courts, swimming and wading pools, septic tanks, storage tanks, structural beams, columns, slabs, residence floors, etc.	4¼	5	5½	1	2½	3½	6	15	21
				Maximum size aggregate 1½ in.					
7-Gal. Paste for Concrete not Subjected to Wear, Weather or Water									
Foundation walls, footings, mass concrete, etc., for use where watertightness and abrasion resistance are not important.	4¾	5½	6¼	1	3	4	5	15	20
				Maximum size aggregate 1½ in.					

sistency when it can be squeezed into a ball in the hand and still plastic enough to hold its shape.

Placing Concrete.   It's best if fresh concrete is poured into the forms within 30 minutes after mixing. Beyond this, the concrete begins to set; and if it hasn't been placed, it will not obtain its maximum

TABLE II. HOW TO ESTIMATE MATERIALS REQUIRED FOR 100 SQ. FT.
OF CONCRETE OF VARIOUS THICKNESSES

Thick-ness of con-crete, in.	Amount of con-crete, cu. yd.	Proportions								
		1:2:2¼ mix			1:2½:3½ mix			1:3:4 mix		
		Ce-ment, sacks	Aggregate		Ce-ment, sacks	Aggregate		Ce-ment, sacks	Aggregate	
			Fine, cu. ft.	Coarse, cu. ft.		Fine, cu. ft.	Coarse, cu. ft.		Fine, cu. ft.	Coarse, cu. ft.
3	0.92	7.1	14.3	16.1	5.5	13.8	19.3	4.6	13.8	18.4
4	1.24	9.6	19.2	21.7	7.4	18.6	26.0	6.2	18.6	24.8
5	1.56	12.1	24.2	27.3	9.4	23.4	32.8	7.8	23.4	31.2
6	1.85	14.3	28.7	32.4	11.1	27.8	38.9	9.3	27.8	37.0
8	2.46	19.1	38.1	43.0	14.8	36.9	51.7	12.3	36.9	49.3
10	3.08	23.9	47.7	53.9	18.5	46.2	64.7	15.4	46.2	61.6
12	3.70	28.7	57.3	64.7	22.2	55.5	77.7	18.5	55.5	74.0

Quantities may vary 10 per cent either way, depending upon character of aggregate used. No allowance made in table for waste.

Courtesy Portland Cement Association

strength. It's never a good idea to try to make concrete that has started to set more workable by addition of water.

Concrete should be shoveled into the forms in layers not much deeper than six inches. Each layer should be spaded so the concrete will become compact. The strength and watertightness of a concrete mass will depend on how well it has been compacted. Fresh concrete should be covered with burlap, building paper, or straw, and kept damp for a week to ten days. The strength of concrete depends on a chemical action that requires water. The longer the concrete is kept damp, the longer this chemical process continues and the stronger the result.

Forms. On many jobs, forms will be required to hold concrete in place until it hardens. Concrete has considerable weight, so the forms must be sturdy. Ordinary ¾" tongue-and-groove boards are good for forms and so is ¾" exterior plywood. Forms should be supported about every two feet with pieces of 2" x 4" and must be built so they can be easily taken apart without damaging the concrete. One way to do this is to drive the holding nails only part way in, leaving the heads up so they may easily be pulled out with a hammer. Special concrete-form nails are available with two heads, one set a fraction of an inch below the other, and these are excellent.

Sometimes the forms are coated inside with oil or grease to make them easier to remove; but this is not good practice, for the oil or grease may discolor the concrete. Concrete doesn't stick easily to wood, and therefore there is seldom any trouble removing the forms if they can be taken apart. Be sure that all nails are on the outside of the form.

Where a curved form is required, tempered hardboard or sheets of galvanized iron can be used.

Forms shouldn't be removed until the concrete is thoroughly cured and hard; two weeks should be allowed.

When concrete is to be poured into a hole in the ground, it's often possible to dispense with forms. If the earth is firm and holds its shape, make the sides of the hole as vertical as possible and then line them with building paper. This is to prevent the moisture in the wet concrete from being absorbed by the earth.

Surface Finishing. When forms are used and an attractive surface is desired, it's important to have forms made of materials that will impart a smooth surface to the concrete. In these cases, plywood or hardboard forms are desirable.

For driveways, walks, terraces, and floors, the concrete surface must be smoothed with a trowel or wood float. Directly after pouring, the concrete should be made as smooth and level as possible by laying a piece of 2″ x 4″ stock across the work and, with someone at either end, working this over the surface.

Final troweling is done about two hours after pouring. By this time the concrete should be stiff enough to be worked over with a steel trowel, which will make it compact and produce a smooth, hard surface. On walks and driveways it is desirable to have a rough surface to provide traction and eliminate slipperiness in wet weather. This is done by working a wood float over the surface instead of the steel trowel.

Concrete in Freezing Weather. Concrete work should never be done when the temperature is below 40° or when there is a chance of freezing weather before it has had ample time to cure and harden. Contractors often pour concrete in below-freezing weather, but they avoid trouble by heating the sand, gravel, and water and also by using certain chemicals added to the mix that chemically generate heat and keep the fresh concrete from freezing. These devices aren't practical for the homeowner, so the best advice is not to work with concrete in cold weather.

Repairing Poured Concrete. Cracks in poured concrete can be repaired with cement mortar or prepared packaged concrete patching material sold at hardware stores. Mortar for patching concrete is made by mixing one part portland cement with three parts fine sand and adding sufficient water to produce a putty-like substance. As portland cement is usually sold in 94-pound sacks, it would hardly be worthwhile to buy a bag just to get enough for a small crack. Usually it is easier and cheaper to use the prepared packaged concrete patcher. All cracks in poured concrete may be repaired in more or less the same way. The crack should be cut out, wide and deep enough to allow the patching material to be packed in. Use a cold chisel and hammer to enlarge the crack and, if possible, cut the opening so that the inside will be slightly wider than the outside. This makes a key which helps hold the patch in place. The crack should be dusted out with a tire pump. Wet down the inside and then pack in mortar or patching compound. A small trowel is good for this, but it can be done using your hands and a putty knife.

Foundation Walls. Cracks sometimes appear in foundation walls, usually when the house is new. They are caused, as a rule, by the small amount of settling that occurs in any new house, but they are not serious. They do not indicate that the foundations are unsafe. But they can allow water to get into the basement or crawl space, and they also offer an avenue for termites and other insects to reach the house's wood porticos. For these reasons, cracks in foundation walls should be repaired. It's best not to make these repairs immediately in a new house, for the settling process may still be going on and patching will be a waste of time if the cracks continue to enlarge. Mark the top and bottom of the cracks, wait a few months to see if they grow larger. When the spread has stopped, the crack is ready to be patched.

It's best if a crack is filled from both sides, but this means digging a trench to reach the outside of the foundation and most people are content just to patch from inside. Often, caulking compound or tar is used in place of mortar; these repel insects and keep out moisture unless there is a good deal of pressure behind the water. Where there is a serious water problem, cement mortar should be used.

Drives and Walks. Cracks in drives and walks may be fixed in the same fashion as cracks in a concrete wall. The crack should first be cut out with a cold chisel, widened inside, dusted, and wet down. Only mortar is suitable for cracks in drives and walks. Tar or caulking compound will be picked up by tires or shoes and tracked over the concrete.

When some of the concrete has broken, it should be removed or broken into small pieces to serve as a base for new concrete. A sledge is a good tool for breaking up concrete, but a heavy cold chisel and hammer may be used. If the patch is to hold, it should be about 4 inches thick on a walk and about 6 inches thick on a driveway.

Cut the edges of the surrounding concrete so they are vertical. After wetting the base and edges, fill in the hole with concrete (see "Mixing Concrete") or a packaged gravel-mix concrete. The patch should extend about $\frac{1}{8}''$ above the body of the concrete, for it will shrink a little as it hardens; and if it is only flush when wet, it will form a depression when it hardens. Keep the patch damp and covered with a piece of burlap, cloth, or even hay for about a week to insure that it cures slowly and gains maximum strength.

When an entire section of a concrete walk or drive is badly damaged, it should be broken up and a fresh section installed. Use a cold chisel to trim off the concrete edges on each side of the hole, and then cover these edges with a sheet of roofing paper. This is allowed to remain when the concrete for the section is poured, for the paper will serve as an expansion joint. Wood forms must be set along each side of the walk or drive to hold the concrete in place until it has set. Usually two lengths of $2''$ x $4''$ or $2''$ x $6''$ lumber, set on edge and supported by stakes driven into the soil, will be adequate for these forms.

Retaining Walls. Cracks in concrete retaining walls may be caused by a general settling of the structure, but often they are due to the tremendous pressure of water held in place by the walls in the early spring. If this is the case, repairing the cracks is a waste of time until some method is devised to relieve the water pressure. The simplest way to do this is to drill a series of holes through the base of the wall so that water on the other side may flow out. Holes in concrete may be made with a star drill or one of the devices mentioned in "Drilling and Cutting Masonry." In addition to the holes a trench must be dug along the front of the wall to carry off the water that flows through the holes. This trench should run to a dry well or drainage ditch. Another way to remove water from behind the wall is to dig out the soil so that a line of drain tile may be laid in back of the wall. Four-inch-diameter perforated drainpipe is good for this, or lengths of clay tile may be installed with a space of about ¼" between the tiles. The tops of these spaces should be covered with tar paper to keep soil out of the system. Fill in around and over the pipe or tile tops with gravel and then topsoil. The line must be pitched so that water entering it will flow out at one end.

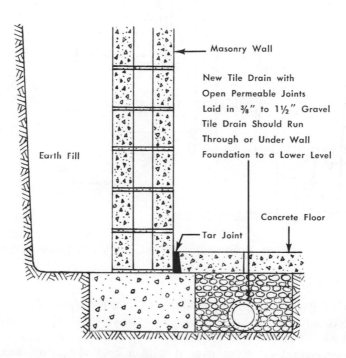

Masonry Wall

New Tile Drain with
Open Permeable Joints
Laid in ⅜" to 1½" Gravel
Tile Drain Should Run
Through or Under Wall
Foundation to a Lower Level

Earth Fill

Concrete Floor

Tar Joint

RETAINING WALL

Pools. Cracks in poured-concrete swimming pools should be cut out, always with the inside of the crack wider than the outside. Wet down the crack and then fill with cement mortar made with one part cement to two parts sand. As soon as the patch is in place, fill the pool so the patch is covered and keep it covered with water for about ten days. This will insure the patch curing slowly to make it waterproof.

Resurfacing Floors and Drives. When the concrete surface of a

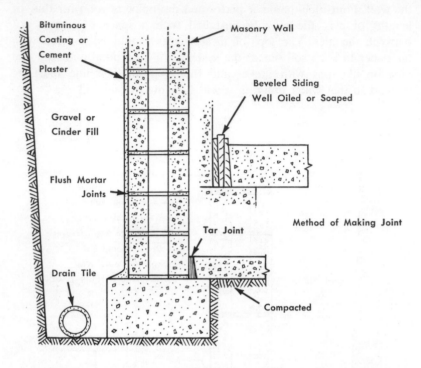

Bituminous Coating or Cement Plaster

Masonry Wall

Beveled Siding Well Oiled or Soaped

Gravel or Cinder Fill

Flush Mortar Joints

Method of Making Joint

Tar Joint

Drain Tile

Compacted

CROSS SECTION OF FOUNDATION WALL SHOWING DRAIN TILE AND PLASTER COAT

drive or walk is in poor condition, or has low spots where water collects, the best remedy is to resurface the concrete. Grease, oil, and paint should be removed (see "Removing Stains") and then the surface roughened by going over it with a cold chisel and hammer. Sweep the surface clean and then coat with a grout made by mixing one part portland cement with one part clean, fine sand and enough water to give the mixture the consistency of thick paint. The grout is most essential, for it insures a good bond between the old concrete and the fresh coating. The new concrete must be applied before the grout has become dry; therefore it is best to apply the grout to only a few square feet at a time. Trowel the 2-inch topcoat of concrete over the area that has been grouted, and then apply grout to the adjoining section. Continue in this fashion until the entire surface has been grouted and coated with fresh concrete.

Sanding and Dusting. If concrete is improperly cured or mixed, it will tend to dust or sand after it hardens. This is not a serious situation, but it makes it difficult to keep the concrete floor clean, because no matter how often it's swept, more dust or sand will appear. In most cases this can be corrected by coating the surface with a commercial concrete hardener sold at hardware and paint stores. These transparent hardeners flow into the concrete pores and act as a binder, preventing particles of sand and cement from coming loose. They also make the concrete less porous and easier to clean, since grime and dirt cannot get into the pores but remain on the surface. Paint will also prevent concrete from dusting. Any paint suitable for use on concrete will stop sanding and dusting if the condition isn't too serious. In severe cases when sanding and dusting are accompanied by flaking of the surface, the best remedy is to remove the loose surface concrete with a cold chisel and apply a top coat (see "Sealers").

Removing Stains from Concrete. Concrete is somewhat porous, so liquids or substances likely to cause stains are quickly absorbed and hard to remove. The longer the stain remains, the more difficult it is to eliminate. Where appearance is important, as in a basement gameroom floor or terrace, it's best to seal the concrete with a sealer, hardener, or decorative stain or paint.

Masonry Blocks

These blocks come in many sizes and shapes, the most common being the rectangular block 8″ high and 16″ long. When gravel is added to the cement and sand used to make these blocks, the result is a concrete block. When cinders are used in place of gravel, it is

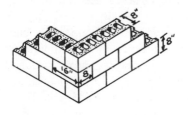

CONCRETE BLOCKS

a cinder block; and in some areas where pumice is used, it's a pumice block. Concrete blocks are heavier and harder to handle than cinder or pumice blocks. They are, however, stronger and usually less porous.

Masonry blocks are used for foundation and basement walls, for outside house walls, and for steps, retaining walls, and fences. Sometimes they are coated with cement plaster on one side for appearance's sake. The hollow spaces inside the blocks make them lighter and easier to work with. Like brick and stone, masonry blocks are put up with cement mortar.

On many jobs, masonry blocks are used in place of poured concrete, but they are not so strong or so watertight. A wall of masonry block contains hundreds of mortar joints, any one of which can cause trouble, for unless well-packed with mortar, there is a good chance of water seeping through. So a masonry-block basement wall is likelier to pose a more serious waterproofing problem than one of poured concrete. If there is strong water pressure behind the wall, one or more blocks may actually be pushed out of alignment.

Faulty Mortar Joints. The most obvious points for trouble in a masonry-block wall are the mortar joints. When a crack shows or the joint leaks, the old mortar should be cut out with a cold chisel and, after dampening the masonry, fresh mortar should be packed in.

Blocks, Working With

Concrete and cinder blocks are handled in much the same way as bricks except that they don't need to be dampened before laying and they should be laid with a straight portland-cement mortar—one part portland cement and three parts sand. Blocks are usually hollow in the middle; these holes do not need to be filled with mortar. Blocks are 8″ wide and so a single row laid one on top of the other will form an 8″-thick wall. Headers are not needed, but it is important that the vertical mortar joints do not fall directly over one another.

Rust Stains. These sometimes appear on cinder blocks. They are caused by small iron particles in the cinders used. Moisture in the blocks makes the iron rust, and this flows through the block and shows up as a reddish stain. To correct this, take a cold chisel and cut out the area until the cinder causing the trouble is located. The offending cinder will look like a rusty pebble and is easily detected. Remove it from the block and patch the hole with mortar.

Bulging Walls. Occasionally a basement, foundation, or retaining wall of block will bulge, and some blocks may crack due to pressure behind them. This can be serious. Rather than try to repair it yourself, call in a competent mason or contractor.

Pointing Up Mortar Joints. The wall should be carefully inspected, and any cracked or shrunken mortar joints should be marked. Use a small cold chisel to cut out the faulty mortar for a depth of about one inch. The more old mortar that can be replaced with fresh, the better will be the job. Dust out the seams, wet them down and then pack in fresh mortar. A more compact and water-resistant joint will result if the mortar is applied in thin layers which can be easily compressed. A small masonry trowel is best for this, but the mortar can be applied with the fingers or with a small stick. The mortar joint surface should be finished off to match the rest of the wall. It's easier to finish off mortar joints if the mortar is allowed to set until it is thicker and easier to work. Some mortar is sure to get on the bricks, but if they are damp it won't be absorbed and can easily be brushed or rinsed off. This should be done before the mortar dries.

Porous Mortar Joints. In some cases, the mortar used on bricks is of such poor quality or so badly applied that water will seep through even though there are no cracks. Then it's easier to coat the mortar joints with a waterproofing compound than to cut out and replace the mortar. Clear waterproofing compounds made for this are available at hardware and masonry supply stores. They can be applied to the mortar joints alone or to the entire wall.

Damaged Brick. Should a brick become cracked or discolored, the best thing to do is to replace it. The old brick is removed by cutting out the mortar. Select a new brick of the right size and color and soak it in water for about 10 minutes. Butter all sides except the outside face with mortar and force the brick into position, then trim off mortar that oozes out around the joints.

Decayed Bricks. In some older houses, bricks have been used for foundation walls and other areas where they are exposed to extreme dampness. Often the brick surface will flake. To remedy this, chip off the surface of the brick with a wide cold chisel until the solid core is reached. Then spray the bricks with water and coat them with a cement plaster made with one part cement and three parts sand. Add enough water to make a workable plastic. Apply this in a coat about 1/4″ thick, leaving a rough surface. When hard, wet down and apply a second coat of the same thickness.

Cleaning Brick. Mortar stains can be removed from bricks with a solution of one part muriatic acid to 10 parts water. Directions for mixing, handling, and applying muriatic acid are given on page 207.

Bricks around a fireplace often become stained with soot. This can usually be removed by scrubbing with a fiber brush and a gritty cleaning compound. Wet down the bricks and scrub with the brush and cleaner, then rinse with fresh water. If the soot has penetrated the bricks deeply, cleaning may have to be done with a rotary wire brush in an electric drill. Wear goggles for this work. Fireplace bricks are less likely to absorb soot, and will be easier to clean, if sealed with an application of a clear masonry sealer. Painting the bricks will make them easier to clean but will, of course, change their color.

Stone

Except that stone is a natural material, stone walls are much the same as masonry-block and brick walls, since all are put together with mortar. When a stone wall leaks, the fault is nearly always in the mortar. This should be removed and replaced in the same way as the mortar on block and brick. Sometimes a single stone will crack, allowing water to enter. Small cracks can usually be sealed by filling them with a clear waterproof compound.

Stone, Working With

Stone is much more difficult to work than either brick or block, for it's usually of irregular shape and design. The minimum thickness of a stone wall should be about 16 inches. It is laid up with the same mortar used for block.

Stucco

This is a cement plaster made of portland cement and sand. It is generally used for exterior siding. Usually it's applied over a special noncorrosive metal lath or over masonry block or tile. As a rule, stucco is put on in three coats to bring it to a thickness of about one inch.

Cracks in Stucco. Small hairline cracks may show on the surface or top coat of a stucco wall. These aren't serious, for they do not

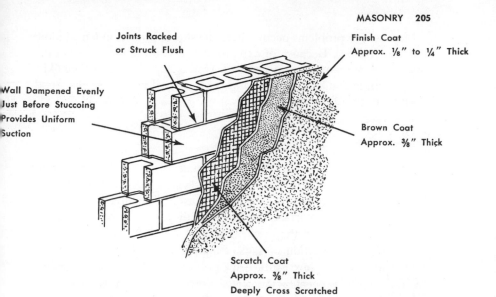

Joints Racked
or Struck Flush

Finish Coat
Approx. ⅛" to ¼" Thick

Wall Dampened Evenly
Just Before Stuccoing
Provides Uniform
Suction

Brown Coat
Approx. ⅜" Thick

Scratch Coat
Approx. ⅜" Thick
Deeply Cross Scratched

STUCCO WALL ON CONCRETE BLOCK

allow moisture to penetrate the wall. On the other hand, frost getting into them can enlarge them. Therefore it is a good idea to fill them with portland-cement paint, stucco paint, or a waterproofing compound. Cracks that go through the stucco are more serious, for these permit moisture to get into the wall. The cracks should be enlarged with a small cold chisel and the edges dampened. They can then be filled with cement mortar or with a special stucco patching compound which can be bought in colors to match painted walls.

Stucco applied over masonry block or tile seldom gives trouble, for there is seldom any movement of the base. When applied over lath there may be movement of the lath because of movement and shrinkage of the wood framework to which the lath is attached. This can cause stucco to crack or fall out. When a stucco section bulges or falls out, enough stucco should be cut back and a patch installed. Apply two coats. The first should be forced into the lath so that the stucco interlocks with the lath. Leave this first coat with a rough surface, and keep it damp and covered for 4 or 5 days, until it hardens. Dampen again and apply the finish coat, keeping this damp and covered for about a week.

Stucco that is leaky because it is porous can be sealed by coating with a stucco paint or clear waterproofing compound.

Most stucco problems occur where the stucco joins wooden windows and door frames. Because of expansion and contraction, cracks often appear where wood and stucco meet. Unless kept sealed with caulking compound, moisture will get in and rot the wood and cause the woodwork paint to blister and peel.

Efflorescence

This shows as a white crust or crystals on masonry. It is most noticeable and least desirable on brick because of the color contrast. The deposits are caused by salts in the masonry dissolved by moisture and carried to the surface. Most often they are found around the mortar joints between the brick, block, or stone, for the mortar contains a heavy proportion of salts. Efflorescence will, however, sometimes appear on the face of the brick or block itself. It is most common on new masonry because the water used in mixing the concrete or mortar brings the salts out. After a few months, the masonry will have dried out and you can relax.

When efflorescence shows on old work, it usually means that moisture is seeping in at some point. The commonest spot is at the top of the wall, either where an outside wall joins the roof, or at a chimney top or garden wall. A masonry wall such as this should be covered at the top with a cement cap about three to four inches thick and pitched so that water falling on it will flow off. If there is no cap or the cap has cracked, water is sure to get into the masonry wall and cause efflorescence. Faulty mortar joints or cracks in masonry allow moisture to enter the work and will cause trouble.

One problem in tracing the cause of efflorescence is that it doesn't necessarily show at or near the spot where the water is seeping in. Often water will penetrate the wall and flow through the interior by means of mortar joints until it finds a weak spot on the other side where it seeps through and deposits the salts. This may be many feet away from the point where the water entered, and it may take quite a bit of sleuthing to locate the exact spot where water is getting in.

When new masonry has had time to dry out and that efflorescence has stopped, or when an old wall has been repaired so that water can't get in, the white crystals on the surface can be removed. With luck, rain will wash them away; but if they are heavy, it may be necessary to scrub them off with water and a stiff fiber or wire brush.

If they prove very stubborn, they can be softened and removed with a solution of one part muriatic acid and ten parts water.

Muriatic Acid. This is sold at hardware stores and masonry supply houses. It is a powerful acid, so it must be handled with care and kept away from children and animals. When working with the acid, it's wise to wear old clothes for it can burn fabric. Rubber gloves and goggles should be worn. Scrub with a long-handled brush so that the chance of splashing acid on the skin is kept to a minimum.

Pour the needed amount of fresh water into a wooden, earthen, or enamel container and then add the acid. Never pour the acid in first for the mixture may splash. Dampen the masonry with a garden-hose spray, then apply the acid with a long-handled brush. Try to keep the acid off mortar joints, for it will soften them. Let the acid remain for about ten minutes, and then scrub. When the discoloration is gone, rinse by hosing and then neutralize the last traces of acid on the masonry by applying a solution of one pint household ammonia to two gallons of water.

Drilling and Cutting

The ease with which masonry may be drilled depends on its type and on where the hole is to be made. Some forms, such as brick and cinder block, are rather soft and easy to drill, as are some stones— for example, sandstone. Granite on the other hand, is not. Unless very inferior, poured concrete is also hard to drill. Mortar joints are easier than solid masonry sections, so when it's possible it is wise to locate the hole in the mortar rather than at other points.

Star Drill. The star drill is the most primitive way to drill through any masonry. This is a steel rod with a star-shaped point. They come in many sizes and are inexpensive. The drill is held in one hand with its point against the masonry. The drill end is then struck a sharp blow with a mallet, and after each blow the drill is rotated a quarter turn. This prevents the point from being damaged and makes drilling faster. From time to time the drill should be pulled out and dust blown from the hole. Wear goggles and a pair of heavy work gloves when using a star drill.

Masonry Drills. Carbide-tipped masonry drills are designed for use in electric hand drills. They are much faster than a star drill and require less effort. The common household ¼" electric drill will handle the ¼" carbide-tipped drill; but be careful not to let the drill get too hot, for this will burn it out. The household drill should be used only to make holes for masonry anchors, not to drill completely through solid masonry. For this, and where holes larger than ¼″ are needed, rent a heavy-duty ½″ electric drill designed for rugged work.

Jackhammer. When very large openings in solid masonry must be made, or when heavy concrete must be broken up, a jackhammer should be used. This, along with an experienced operator, may be rented on a day-to-day basis from a local masonry contractor.

Cutting Masonry. Masonry can be cut with a cold chisel and hammer or with a special blade designed for use on an electric saw.

Bricks

Bricks are made of baked clay. They are joined with mortar in the same fashion as masonry blocks. Since bricks are a good deal smaller, there will be more mortar joints in a brick wall and, therefore, more chance of trouble if the bricks are not properly laid.

Leaking Brick Walls. Bricks are not used today for foundation walls. They are used for exterior siding, usually as a brick veneer. When an exterior brick wall lets water leak through, the common cause is the mortar joint. Sometimes the mortar has cracked or fallen out; in other cases, it has shrunk enough to pull away from the brick and there is a small channel through which water can pass. While somewhat porous, the bricks themselves seldom make a leaky wall. Usually it is the fault of the mortar joints.

Bricks, Working With

Bricks are ideal for a number of projects around the house and garden. They are cheap, easy to handle, and can be purchased at almost any lumber yard or building supply house. One great advantage bricks and blocks have over poured concrete is that work may be stopped at any time without harmful effects. This makes them ideal materials for the weekend mason.

While there are many kinds of bricks, the three basic types are: common, face, and firebrick. Common brick is about 8″ long, 3¾″ wide, and 2¼″ thick. It can be used for almost every job except one where it will be subjected to intense heat, such as inside a fireplace. Face brick comes in many shapes and sizes for decorative facing.

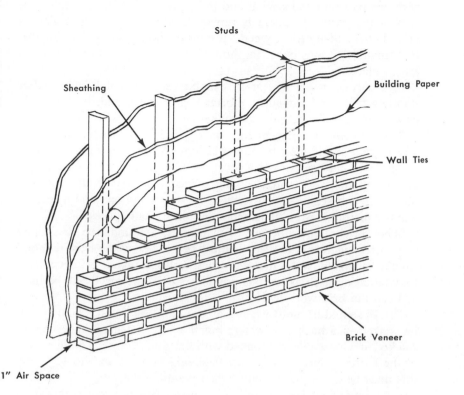

Studs

Sheathing

Building Paper

Wall Ties

Brick Veneer

1" Air Space

Firebrick can withstand great heat and is used to line fireplaces and outdoor cooking units. Unlike common and face bricks, firebrick is not applied with ordinary mortar but with a special fire clay made to withstand high temperatures. Firebrick is usually 9″ x 4″ x 2½″.

Bricks, Secondhand and Seconds. For many projects, home masons prefer secondhand bricks, or "seconds" (new bricks with flaws). Secondhand (used) bricks may have a more attractive color than new bricks and you may be able to pick up old bricks from house wreckers or secondhand building supply houses. If you buy them with the mortar still on, they're cheaper; but it takes time to chip away the old mortar. Because of present popularity the seconds, oddly, are often more expensive than new bricks without flaws.

Mortar. The best mortar to use on brickwork exposed to weather or set below ground is made with one part cement to three parts clean sand. Otherwise a cement-and-lime mortar is best; this is made with one part portland cement and three parts sand, but about 10 per cent of the portland cement is replaced with hydrated lime. This is more buttery than ordinary cement mortar and so is easier to handle. For small brick jobs about the house, excellent ready-mixed mortars are available.

Mix only as much mortar as can be used in a half hour. After standing for over 30 minutes, mortar begins to set and, having made its initial set, will not produce maximum strength when applied.

Tools Required. Except for trowels, the tools needed for brick-laying are found in most home workshops. A hammer and cold chisel are used to cut bricks, and a level, rule, and cord are essential for laying out the work and checking to see that it is both level and plumb. It is best to use two trowels, a fairly large one and a smaller one for the finish work and for getting into small spaces.

When bricks are to be laid with mortar, a foundation or footing of poured concrete is needed. It must be set below the frost line and should be slightly wider than the brick wall and about 8″ deep. This foundation must be as level as possible, for if uneven, it will be hard to keep the brickwork level.

Bricks should be moist when they are laid. For small jobs they can be soaked in a bucket of water; but if many are used, they can be stacked in a loose pile and soaked with the garden hose. The thickness of the mortar joints between bricks should be from ⅜″ to ½″, and this must be taken into account when planning the job.

Each horizontal layer is called a *course.* Bricks laid lengthwise to the wall being built are called *stretchers,* and bricks laid at right angles are called *headers.* The minimum thickness of a brick wall is 8 inches. Two rows of stretchers, with mortar between, will produce an 8-inch-thick wall, and so will a header course where 8-inch bricks run at right angles to the walls. Headers are used at intervals to tie stretcher courses together. The number and location of header courses will determine the wall's pattern. Four stretcher courses, followed by a single header course, is called a *common bond* wall. The *English bond* or pattern consists of alternate courses of headers and stretchers. Sometimes a course consists of both headers and stretchers, as in *Flemish bond.* If, for the sake of appearance it is desirable not to have headers in a wall, then metal strips must be used to tie together the two rows of bricks making up the stretcher course. These are imbedded in the horizontal mortar courses and do not show.

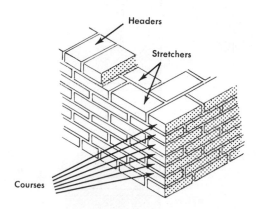

Mortar Joints.   Many kinds of mortar joints are used to produce different effects. The best is the flush joint, in which the mortar is cut off flush with the brick face. The weathered joint is more difficult, but it is excellent for outdoor work because it easily sheds water. Struck and raked joints should not be used if they will be exposed to weather, for they hold, rather than shed, moisture.

When the concrete foundation is hard, it is ready for the brick. Lay the first course dry to see whether the thickness of the mortar joints should be varied one way or the other in case any bricks must be cut to fit the foundation wall's length. If the wall is to have corners, these should be built part way up first and then connected by the intermediate bricks. To keep the wall from swinging in or out, attach a cord at each end in line with the outside wall face and slightly above the course being laid. A level should be used from time to time to check the wall corners to be sure they are perfectly upright and to check the top of the work to be sure it stays horizontal.

Only as much mortar as can be covered by three or four bricks should be applied at a time to the foundation and succeeding brick courses before they're set in place. They can then be tapped to produce tight-fitting end joints. The success of any brick wall depends on getting all the joints well packed with mortar.

Like most jobs, working with brick takes practice, and no one

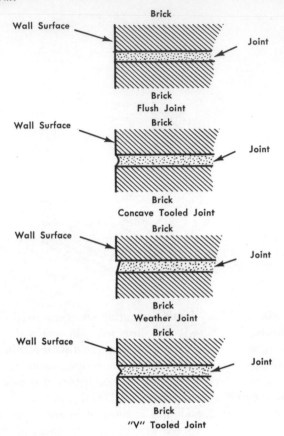

Wall Surface → Brick — Joint
Brick
Flush Joint

Wall Surface → Brick — Joint
Brick
Concave Tooled Joint

Wall Surface → Brick — Joint
Brick
Weather Joint

Wall Surface → Brick — Joint
Brick
"V" Tooled Joint

MORTAR JOINTS

should expect to turn out a perfect job the first time. Pick a minor project and acquire some skill before taking on large jobs.

Damp and Leaky Basements

Before spending time and money trying to cure a damp basement, the exact cause of the dampness must be diagnosed. Many home-owners have wasted a great deal of time treating basement walls with various waterproofing agents when actually the walls were watertight and the dampness came from an entirely different source.

In a new house, the basement is almost sure to be damp, because a large amount of water is used to mix the concrete for the floor and often for the walls, and it takes several months for this moisture to dissipate. Good ventilation and artificial heat will accelerate this drying-out process, but it will still take several months. However, if the basement is still damp after six months, it is time to look into the matter.

If a basement is damp and yet no leaks are found in the walls, the floor, or the joints between them, it's safe to assume that the condition is not due to water from outside flowing through the masonry but is caused by condensation. The floor and most basement walls are in direct contact with the soil, which is usually colder in both summer and winter than the house air. When warm, moist house air strikes these cold surfaces, condensation occurs and a moisture film is deposited. This is often called "sweating." It may show on basement cold-water pipes. The condition can be so severe that rivulets of water flow down the walls or across the floor.

Dampness due to condensation can't be eliminated by water-proofing the floor and walls; it must be corrected by removing moist air from the basement or by warming the surfaces so there won't be a great difference in temperature between them and the surrounding air.

It's often possible to remove a good deal of moist air by improving ventilation and circulation. Most basements have far too few windows, and these are often kept shut all the time or are surrounded outside by plants and shrubs which reduce the airflow through the windows and even add moisture to the air. If basement windows are left open on warm, dry days and plants or shrubbery near them are moved or at least cut back, it will help dry out the cellar. An exhaust fan or portable electric fan placed in one of the windows so that fresh air is pulled through will prove helpful. Such forced ventilation should be attempted only when the outside air is dry, not on warm, humid days.

Dehumidifiers.   Another way to reduce basement air moisture is by a dehumidifier. This device may operate either with chemicals or a machine similar to an electric refrigerator. The chemical type is less expensive; it consists of a container filled with calcium chloride, or some similar substance, which absorbs moisture from the air in the same way that salt picks up moisture on damp days. These are effective, but eventually the chemicals will have absorbed all the moisture they can hold and must be renewed. Calcium chloride, along with containers for it, can be bought at many hardware stores and lumber and building supply yards.

The electric dehumidifier is more expensive than the chemical, but it is automatic. Basically it consists of a coil, compressor, and fan. The compressor chills off the liquid in the coil just as a refrigerator compressor chills the coil in the freezer compartment. The fan pulls the basement air across the cold coil, which causes the moisture to condense on the coil. The liquid drops into a pan which is emptied periodically or may be connected to the house drainage system. A dehumidifier of this kind can remove many gallons of water from the basement air daily. Electric dehumidifiers are sold by appliance stores, discount houses, and department stores.

Insulating Walls and Floors. Another way to check condensation is to warm your basement walls and floors so that their surface temperature will be close to that of the outside air. If this is done, there will be little condensation even when it is humid.

The most practical way to warm an existing masonry wall or floor is to cover it with a false surface. The standard method of covering walls is to fasten 2" x 2" or 2" x 4" wood furring strips to the wall and cover them with wallboard such as gypsum or insulating boards. Plywood, hardboard, and asbestos board are also suitable.

Before installing the wall, it's wise to give the inside face of the basement wall a coat of asphalt paint, as good insurance in case slight cracks develop. The asphalt paint prevents leaks and protects the wood furring strips from any dampness in the masonry.

The wood furring strips should be installed 16 inches on center and are usually set vertically unless the wall is to be covered with narrow boards such as pine or insulating plank. In the latter case the furring strips are applied horizontally, 24 inches apart. Furring strips can be attached in one of several ways (see "Hardware, Fastening Devices"). It's usually not necessary to insert insulation between the furring strips, because the dead-air space created by the furring strips between the masonry wall and the new wall surface is an efficient insulation in itself and prevents the new wall surface from becoming cold. A strip of insulation should, however, be laid between the furring strips at both top and bottom of the wall. This insures that once the new wall is in place air will not be able to flow up through the cavity between the new wall and the masonry wall.

After the furring strips are in place, the wallboard covering can be laid. When you buy this, insist that the manufacturer's instruction sheet is supplied. This gives all needed information for actual laying of the wallboard.

Installing a Floor.   Condensation dampness isn't as common on basement floors as on walls, for the reason that the earth under the floor is generally so far down that it stays at approximately the same temperature the year round. Condensation on concrete floors is more likely to occur on shallow slabs in one-story homes or on porch and terrace floors. A false floor over the concrete one can eliminate the condition.

The first step is to lay 2" x 4" strips to serve as a nailing base for the new floor and to keep it several inches off the concrete. These strips, called "sleepers," should be spaced 24 inches from the center and fastened in the same fashion as the furring strips. Over these are set sheets of ¾" plywood, with the good side up. Use screw-type nails to fasten the plywood to the sleepers, and then cover the plywood with an asphalt or linoleum floor tile.

Leaky Basements.   When water flows through a crack or seam in the basement walls or floor or seeps through porous masonry, it means that water is collecting along the outside in sufficient amount, with enough pressure behind it, to create a serious waterproofing problem. Correcting this can be a difficult and often expensive business.

Before attempting to repair the basement floor and walls, make sure everything possible has been done to prevent large amounts of water from collecting near the house. Discharge from roof gutters should be carried a safe distance away from the soil adjoining the basement and there should be no low spots where water can collect near the building.

Leaks Through Cracks and Seams.   Frequently a basement will leak only at spots where there is a crack in the wall or floor or at seams, such as mortar joints between masonry block or where the floor joins the wall. If not too serious, these openings can be filled efficiently by yourself without calling in a professional. Repairs of this type should be made during dry weather, when no water is coming through the crack or seam. The crack or faulty mortar joint should be cut out to a depth of about ¾" and made about ¾" wide, with the inside slightly wider than the outside. Mix one part portland cement with two parts clean fine sand and add just enough water to let the mortar form and hold its shape. Dust out the orifices, wet them down, and then pack in the mortar, using a wood or metal rod so that the mortar will be tightly compressed.

In serious cases, a continuous flow of water will pour through a joint. Cut this out in the manner suggested above and start filling from the top down with the same cement mortar. Do not try to fill the entire seam or joint with the mortar; if you do, the pressure of the water will force the mortar out before it can harden. Leave an opening at the bottom for the water to continue to flow out. When the mortar patch is dry and hard, fill the opening at the bottom where the water is flowing through. For this a special fast-hardening hydraulic cement is used. This can be bought at hardware and building supply stores. Add water to the hydraulic cement and hold a wad large enough to fill the hole in your hand until you can feel it hardening. Now force it vigorously into the hole and hold it there for a minute or two. It hardens very quickly and after a minute will usually hold itself in place. When a leak occurs at the seam where wall and floor meet, cut out the seam with a cold chisel to a depth and width of about ¾", with the cut in the shape of an inverted V (see illustration).

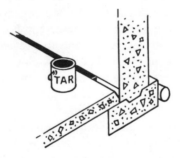

BASEMENT FLOOR JOINT

Hot tar is the best filler for this type of repair. If tar is used, the joint should be dried out first by running the flame of a blowtorch along it. The hot tar is then poured in and allowed to come a fraction of an inch above the floor surface. Tar is the best filler for this because of possible expansion and contraction of the floor and the walls, and a filler that is somewhat elastic is most desirable. The joints, however, may be filled with cement mortar of the type used for wall cracks and seams.

Waterproofing the Outside. When leaks or seepage occur over a sizable area of a basement wall, the most effective method of waterproofing is from the outside. Unfortunately, this is also the most expensive and time-consuming operation of all, for it involves digging a trench outside the basement wall down to the footings under the wall. The trench must be wide enough so that a man can work freely. When the entire wall has been exposed, it should be brushed clean and any cracks or faulty mortar joints repaired. It is then coated with two coats of cement plaster and, finally, two coats of hot bituminous compound. When this work is being done, lay drainage tile along the trench bottom. This should be pitched so that water entering the system will be carried off to a dry well or storm sewer.

Waterproofing from Inside. While not so effective as waterproofing from the outside, waterproofing from the inside is much easier and can, unless conditions are severe, do the job efficiently. When seepage is slight, two coats of portland-cement paint may be adequate. These paints make a strong bond with the masonry and are often dense enough to prevent seepage. Also, even if they are not adequate, they serve as a suitable base for other waterproofing. There are many waterproofing compounds available and, when properly applied, they will serve well. But they must be applied strictly according to the manufacturer's directions since their success depends as much on proper application as on the compound's formulation.

An excellent and also inexpensive way to waterproof a masonry wall from the inside is with two coats of cement plaster. This must be applied only to a wall free from paint and other waterproofing, with the exception of portland-cement paint. While it's possible to remove oil and rubber-latex paints from a wall with a strong solution of trisodium phosphate and water, and while whitewash and similar water-thinned coverings will respond to 20 per cent solution of muriatic acid and water, the best method of removing paint is by sandblasting. This will have to be done by a professional. Grease and oil stains can be removed with benzine.

The walls should also be brushed down with a stiff brush to remove dirt and loose matter. Spray the walls with a garden hose until they are thoroughly damp, then apply a grout made by mixing portland cement and water to the consistency of paint. Apply this with a brush. Over it goes the first coat of cement plaster, made with one part portland cement and two-and-a-half parts clean, fine sand; it should be about ½" thick. This coat must be applied before the grout is dry, so do not cover the whole wall with grout but work on an area of a few square feet at a time.

After the first coat of cement plaster is on, scratch it by going over it with a wire brush or a piece of metal lath. This provides a key for the second coat of plaster. Give the first coat 24 hours in which to set. Dampen it, if necessary, with a fine garden spray to prevent it drying out. The first coat should be damp when the second coast of plaster is applied, in the same thickness as the first. The second coat should be troweled to a smooth surface and kept damp for at least two days.

Leaky Floors. The best remedy for water seepage up through a floor is first to cover the floor with waterproofing membrane followed by a 2-inch-thick top coat of fresh concrete. This job is difficult, because the entire floor must be treated at the same time. Equipment resting on the floor, such as heating units and hot-water heaters, must be removed during the application. The old concrete floor should be covered with sheets of tar roofing paper, the first layer cemented to the floor with hot tar, and the second layer, running at right angles to the first, cemented with the same material. Run the paper up along the walls to the height of about a foot. A coating of hot tar is then mopped over the top layer of paper and the 2½" concrete topping is applied.

Sump Pumps. It may be that it is either impractical or too expensive to waterproof a basement effectively. In that case the best solution is to install a sump pump, which will automatically remove any water that enters the basement. The pump should be located at the lowest point of the floor where the water normally collects. A hole is made in the floor and a length of tile pipe set, with the top flush with the floor surface. Water in the basement will collect in the tile pipe. The pump is so installed that the float and intake pipe are inside the tile. The discharge from the pump should be connected into the house drainage system or run outdoors some distance from the building. When water in the tile reaches a predetermined level, the pump, which is electrically operated, will start and the water in the tile or pipe will be removed.

CHAPTER 13

Electricity

Household Wiring

Electricity generated at the local power station is carried into the home by either two or three heavy wires. Two wires give the house a 120-volt system; three make 240 volts available.

Volt is the term used to indicate electrical pressure. Volts are not current, but they force current through the line; thus, the greater the voltage, the greater the flow of current.

It's important that the homeowner know whether his house is wired for 120 or 240 volts; many heavy-duty appliances operate on 240 volts and cannot be used on a 120-volt system. To run a third wire into the house is an expensive operation.

Wires from the street are called *service entrance wires,* and are installed and maintained by the power company. Neither the homeowner nor an electrician may handle these wires unless authorized by the power company; and installation of a third wire, if needed, is done by the company.

The service entrance wires pass from the street directly into an electrical meter which measures the amount of power consumed. From the meter they tie into the main distribution box, which usually has a switch to cut off all power in the house if that is necessary. This is the main switch, and every member of the household should know its location in case of an emergency. The main distribution box also contains the main house fuses. There is seldom need for the homeowner to touch these, for they rarely need replacing.

From the main distribution box, the wires go to the *branch-circuit distribution box,* from which electricity is carried to the house outlets. It's at this box that the homeowner becomes involved. Each house or apartment contains a certain number of circuits made up of two wires. Usually the wires are in a rigid or flexible metal cable. One wire is covered with black insulation and is the "hot" wire; the other is white and is the ground, or neutral, wire. Each circuit has its own protective fuse and a number of outlets, and it can handle just so much current.

The unit measuring a current rate of flow is the *ampere* or *amp;* this is the current pushed through the lines by the volts. To obtain electricity, there must be a current flow in amps and the pressure to force the amps through the lines is expressed in volts. The current a branch circuit can handle depends on the wire diameter. A thicker wire can carry a heavier current than a thin one. If too much current is forced through a wire, it will overheat and burn through its insulation, which can start a fire. For this reason, each branch circuit is protected by a fuse or circuit breaker, located in the branch-circuit distribution box, sometimes called a fuse box or circuit breaker.

Branch Circuits. As we have said, the amount of current that can be carried by a branch circuit depends on the size of the wire; and since these wires run through walls and floors, they cannot be easily changed. A NO.-14 wire is suitable for lights, lamps, radios, TV sets, vacuum cleaners, and small appliances. This wire can carry up to 15 amps current flow at 120 volts without overheating; it is protected by a 15-ampere fuse or a circuit breaker that cuts off the current if it exceeds 15 amps. Toasters, waffle irons, and other appliances that require more current, usually located in the kitchen, may require a circuit with the larger NO.-12 wire. These circuits are fused with a 20-amp fuse or circuit breaker. Both circuits use 120 volts.

Individual Circuits

The third type of house circuit is the *individual circuit.* This serves a single piece of major equipment, such as on oil burner, water pump, electric water heater, air conditioner, range, etc. It may use a 120 or 240-volt circuit. Wire and fuse size depend on the appliance's demands. As these circuits contain no outlet other than the one into which the single appliance is connected, they seldom cause trouble. General-purpose and small-appliance branch circuits are the ones in which difficulties can occur.

Capacity of a Circuit. A circuit's capacity is determined by the wire size used when installed. As mentioned, with a NO.-14 wire a 15-amp fuse or circuit breaker gives protection; with a NO.-12 wire, the heavier 20-amp fuse can be installed.

The amount of electrical energy a circuit supplies is measured in *watts.* Volts multiplied by available amps gives the wattage. Thus, a 120-volt system, protected by a 15-amp fuse or circuit breaker, can supply 1800 watts. The term *watt* is familiar; it measures the capacity of light bulbs, and voltage and wattage are printed on each bulb. Equipment, too, usually carries a plate giving the required watts for the appliance. The heavier the wire and larger the fuse, the more watts. A NO.-12 wire with a 20-amp fuse can supply 2400 watts, and the heavier wires used for ranges and hot-water heaters can supply even more.

Circuit Breakers and Fuses. Each circuit has a fuse or circuit breaker; its primary purpose is to protect the wiring from overheating from an overload or a short circuit. An overload is caused when appliances demanding more wattage than the circuit can supply are plugged in at the same time. A short occurs when two exposed wires touch, either in the wiring or in an appliance. Without a safety device, an overload or short can make the wires so hot that they will start a fire. The fuse or circuit breaker protects against such fires by shutting off the current when there is overheating of the wires.

There are main fuses controlling all current into the house, but these are heavy-capacity and will not interrupt the current flow before the light wires are overheated and begin to burn. By having fuses for each circuit, only the current to the shorted one is cut off, and the rest of the house wiring continues to function. Fuses and circuit breakers, like the safety valve on a steam boiler, prevent serious trouble.

Circuit Breakers. Circuit breakers have only recently been installed in houses, but they are growing more popular. The branch distribution box holding the circuit breakers has a faceplate containing several switches that look like ordinary wall switches. Each controls one house circuit. When there is an overload or short, the heat generated in the wires releases the switch, which moves from ON to OFF. When the trouble has been removed, the switch can be put back to ON by first pushing it to OFF and then to ON, restoring the current. No replacements are needed in a circuit breaker.

Fuses. The branch-circuit distribution box holding the fuses usually has a cover which, when lifted, exposes the fuses. The most common type is the plug fuse, which screws into a metal socket in the box. Each circuit has one fuse. The plug fuse has a glass top; inside there is a small metal strip, visible through the transparent cover. The circuit current flows through this strip, and when there is a short or overload the heat generated melts the strip and cuts off the electricity. The metal strip is designed to melt at a lower temperature than that which would cause the wiring to overheat and burn through its insulation.

It is not difficult to tell if a plug fuse has blown, because the glass or mica top will be discolored. When a fuse blows, it is useless and must be replaced.

Nontamperable Fuses. One danger with the ordinary plug fuse is that it can easily be replaced with one of much heavier capacity, which is comparable to tying down a steam boiler's safety valve. If a 15-amp fuse, offering adequate protection on a circuit with NO.-14 wire, is replaced with a 20-, 25-, or 30-amp fuse, the overload can start a wiring fire before the fuse blows. Therefore, it is important to replace a blown fuse with one of the same or even less capacity. To prevent anyone from installing higher-capacity fuses, nontamperable fuses are available. These have a special adapter designed to take only a fuse of given capacity. Once an adapter is screwed into the box, it can't be easily removed and only the correct fuse can be used in it. Such fuses are often used in apartments or rental units where a tenant may try to get more juice out of the circuit.

Multiple Fuses. Changing fuses is bothersome; if one blows and there is no replacement handy, it means a hurried trip to the hardware store. To eliminate this, multiple fuses can be used. They screw in as do ordinary fuses, but they contain six or more elements. When one element blows, the fuse can be turned to another.

Multiple fuses are rated the same as ordinary ones and offer the same protection. They cost more than plug fuses, but actually they are half a dozen in one.

Time-Delay Fuses. When an appliance motor starts, it draws more current than it uses while it is running, in the same way that a car requires much more power to start than when it is rolling on the highway. The starting-load demand of an electric motor is so great that it will often blow a fuse. Special plug fuses, called time-delay fuses, may be used; these carry, for 30 seconds or so, 100 per cent more current than they are otherwise capable of handling. This lets the motor start without blowing the fuse; but, once started, it offers the same circuit protection as an ordinary plug fuse. They are excellent for window air conditioners, power tools, and similar appliances with large electric motors. (They are not needed on heating devices, because these don't draw much more current on starting than at other times.)

Cartridge Fuses.   These are used primarily for the main house switch or for heavy-duty equipment such as ranges. They are held in place by clips, and they can be removed simply by pulling them off the clips.

Changing Fuses.   When a fuse blows or a circuit breaker opens, the first thing to do is to locate the trouble and correct it; otherwise, the new fuse, when inserted, will blow or the circuit breaker will pop back to OFF. (See "Correcting Overloads and Short Circuits.")

In older houses the fuse box is rather primitive, simply a metal box with a hinged cover. On one side there is usually a switch which is the main house electric switch. *Always pull the main switch before replacing a fuse;* otherwise you may receive a severe shock. In more modern boxes, plastic panels are fitted in. Each panel has a handle by which it may be pulled out. On the reverse side of one panel are the main house fuses, and, once removed, power to the box is cut off. The plug fuses are located directly under the panel containing the main fuses, and it's a good idea to pull it out before changing a fuse.

If the main switch is pulled or the main fuse panel removed, current to the house is automatically cut off. Therefore, you will need a flashlight to replace the fuses if the box is in a dark area or if you are working at night. If located in a basement with a damp floor, a wood grating should be available to stand on, otherwise you may drop dead as a cinder, and looking rather like one. Plug fuses are usually easy to unscrew by hand. Insert a fuse of the same capacity, and then throw the main switch or replace the panels.

Locating Circuits.   Every house has a certain number of circuits, and each goes through a fuse or circuit breaker. To keep the system in good order, the homeowner must know which fuse controls which circuit and what outlets are connected to it.

The way to determine which fuse controls a circuit is to turn on the house lights and then loosen one fuse at a time or throw a circuit-breaker switch to OFF. Each time, a certain number of lights will go off. Write down the location of the outlets affected by each on a piece of paper and paste this near the fuse box or circuit breaker. This will save you or an electrician valuable time when major work has to be done. It is also a good idea to jot down the capacity of each fuse so that the circuit's load may be calculated.

Determining Loads.   Every circuit has a certain rated capacity determined by the wiring and fuse sizes. Each NO.-14 wire branch circuit with a 15-amp fuse will handle up to 1800 watts; a NO.-12 wire circuit with a 20-amp fuse will handle up to 2400 watts. Once the number and locations of outlets in a circuit are known and its capacity determined, it is a simple matter to find out how much demand is being placed on the circuit. The number of watts needed to operate an appliance is usually given on a plate fastened to it. Light bulbs are rated by wattage; a 100-watt light bulb requires 100 watts of current from the circuit. Items such as lights, radios, TV sets, and small motors need relatively small amounts. Heating appliances demand a tremendous wattage, and some, such as electric broilers, require over 1800 watts, higher than can be supplied by an entire NO.-14 wire circuit. Below is a table showing the average requirements for a number of common appliances.

TABLE OF WATTS

Appliance	Watts	Appliance	Watts
Air conditioner	750–1250	Iron	1000
Blanket	200	Mixer	100
Broiler	1400–1650	Radio	30
Coffee maker	1000	Refrigerator	150
Dishwasher	1300	Sewing machine	75
Dryer	4500–9000	Skillet	1100
Fan	50–345	Television	250
Freezer	350–450	Toaster	1150
Heater	1000–1650	Vacuum cleaner	340–700
Heating pad	60	Waffle iron	1000
Hot plate	1650	Washer	400

Some appliances, such as power tools, are rated in amperes rather than watts. You can find the wattage by multiplying the number of amps by 120 volts. For example, if the plate on a power saw states the saw requires 1.5 amps, multiply this by 120. The answer is 180 watts.

The total wattage needed for all household appliances is often far greater than the circuits' capacity, but it is not likely that all these devices will be used at the same time.

Overloaded Circuits. When several appliances on the same circuit are turned on at the same time and they demand more watts than the circuit can supply, the circuit is overloaded. Today, most household electrical troubles are caused by overloading. A familiar sign of overloading is dimming of the lights when an appliance is turned on. What happens is that there is not enough voltage in the line to provide current for all the appliances, and instead of the full 120-volt pressure, it drops to 90, 80, or even less voltage. The circuit wires heat up, and a fuse blows or a circuit breaker opens. Often the overload isn't quite enough to open the circuit but does decrease efficiency. Poor reception on a TV set may be due to low voltage. Failure of coffee makers or toasters to come up to the desired temperature can be caused by low voltage; and electric motors may burn out, which is costly. To insure proper functioning, the wattage needed by all equipment, and the circuit capacity and outlets, should be known.

Correcting Short Circuits and Overloads. When a fuse blows or a circuit breaker opens, the trouble must be found and corrected. House wiring seldom is the cause, for, being inside walls and floors, it is not subject to wear and tear, and usually it has been carefully inspected prior to installation.

Usually at fault are the cords, plugs, or the appliances themselves. If you are in trouble, unplug all cords from outlets. The fuse can then be replaced or the circuit breaker closed. Unless the fault is in the house wiring, the circuit will stay closed and you can take your time in finding out the cause of the trouble.

First inspect all your extension and appliance cords for loose plugs or frayed insulation. If the two wires in the cords plugged in are touching each other, you have a short circuit, which often occurs when cords are poorly made or roughly used. If all your cords and appliances seem to be in good shape, figure out their wattage to see if the circuit may have been overloaded. If you find this is so, move some of the appliances to another circuit or be careful not to use all of them on the same circuit at the same time. If the circuit is not overloaded and you cannot find a short, plug in each appliance one at a time. When the one causing the trouble is on, the fuse will again blow, thus exposing the culprit. If, on close inspection, no short can be found, have the appliance checked at an electrical store, or buy a new one.

Inadequate Wiring. Most houses, even those built in the last few years, do not have either enough circuits or the capacity to handle the electricity required. Adding new circuits is expensive. First, the service entrance capacity may have to be increased. Many old homes have a 30-ampere service capacity, which means that with a 120-volt system the total available current is only 3600 watts, not high by today's standards. To raise this to present minimum house capacity of 100 amps, at 240 volts, calls for a third-service entrance wire with a new distribution box and additional circuits. Homes with a 60-ampere, 240-volt entrance are a little better off, as they have a 14,500 watt capacity. To get more juice from this system will require a new service-entrance distribution box, a new or additional branch-circuit distribution box, and the required number of circuits. Houses built today usually have a 100-ampere, 240-volt service entrance with a capacity of 24,000 watts, which, for the moment, seems adequate. Increasing house service entrance capacity and adding circuits is no job for the average householder; it should be done by a qualified electrical contractor.

Even when the electrical system's over-all capacity is adequate, the number of outlets may be insufficient and inconveniently located. Many people try to meet this situation by stringing extension cords from existing outlets. This is not only unsightly but can be dangerous to limb and property.

The best way to extend existing wiring is with metal raceway or plug-in strips. A raceway is a small, square length of metal enclosing the wires. It can be fastened to walls or woodwork. The metal covering may be painted to match walls or woodwork. At the end of the raceway is a metal box containing a duplex convenience outlet. The wires at the other end of the raceway are connected to the house wiring, usually at an outlet. Metal or plastic plug-in strips are similar to raceways, and they are designed to provide numerous outlets along the strip; but they do not increase the circuit's capacity. Remember that just because the plug-in strip contains a number of outlets that does not mean you should use them all at once. The strip can handle only as much demand as the circuit can supply. Strips should be wired directly into the house wiring at a nearby outlet. While the homeowner can install the raceway or plug-in strip, it's best that the actual connections into the house wiring be made by a competent electrician.

Appliance Cords and Plugs

Repair or replacement of cords and plugs on electrical devices is a familiar household job. Since they must be light and flexible and are subjected to considerable handling and wear, cords eventually become worn or pull loose from their plugs. The plugs also break or wear and have to be replaced. Most short circuits are due to faulty cords and plugs. Inspect them at frequent intervals; and if the insulation is frayed or cracked, hook up new cord, and reconnect loose plugs.

Three basic types of cords are designed for home appliances. For lamps, radios, TV sets, and items requiring little current, and where the cord is not subject to heavy wear, rubber or plastic-covered *rip cord* is suitable. This is designed so that the two wires can be separated by ripping them apart, making connections easy. This type of cord should never be used on any appliance that produces heat, such as a toaster or an iron, or as an extension cord for such appliances.

For heavy wear or where it runs the danger of getting damp, a rubber-covered S-cord should be used. This is excellent for vacuum cleaners, waxers, portable power tools, and portable lamp cords in the garage, basement, or workshop.

For heating appliances, only the standard heating appliance cord, with a protective covering of asbestos fibers and an outer fabric covering, should be used. Each wire has its own insulation inside the asbestos lining. This is the only cord for appliances that develop heat, such as toasters, hair curlers, hot plates, roasters, broilers, waffle irons, etc. If any other type of cord is hooked to these units, the heat developed inside the cord will burn off the insulation and cause a short circuit.

Care of Cords. Improper use of appliance cords can lead to short circuits, electrical shocks, or serious fires. Cords must never be stapled to the woodwork or run under carpets, for an insulation break may go undetected and start a fire. If there are small children in the house, all cords must be inspected frequently, kept free from loose connections or breaks in the insulation, and should be out of the children's reach until they are old enough to learn not to touch them. Cords should not be placed where they may come in contact with a radiator, plumbing fixture, or water pipe. Also, do not splice wires. This admonition may be in vain, for many people will do it anyway, but the fact remains that a spliced wire can seldom be as mechanically and electrically sound as an unbroken piece of wire.

To disconnect a cord from an outlet, never pull the cord; this may rip the cord away from the plug. Instead, grasp the plug firmly, and pull. Similarly, when disconnecting a heating appliance, always turn it off first and then pull the plug from the wall rather than the plug from the appliance. To say it in its simplest form: Always remove the wall plug first. As to removing appliance plugs, because of the construction of the plug on the appliance, more sparking occurs when this is removed than when the plug in the wall is pulled. The arcing eventually pits the prongs of the appliance so that a poor electrical contact results.

Wall or attachment plugs come in many shapes and sizes. They may be made of plastic or rubber. The plastic plug is smaller than the rubber one and is less conspicuous but not so durable. Plastic plugs are suitable on lamps and on any device where the plug will not have rough treatment. The commonest type of plug is one made of plastic or rubber with two terminal screws inside. The wires are fastened around the screws to provide a secure electrical and mechanical connection. Many appliances today come with prongs; in others, the wires are soldered directly to the prongs. There is no way to fasten loose wires on these plugs, so the easiest thing to do is to replace the plug with one that has terminal screws.

Another popular plug has no terminal screws, but has a clamp that secures the wire to the plug. There are small prongs in the plug that penetrate the insulation around the wires and make the electrical contact when the wire is forced in place and held there by the clamp.

Another useful type is the rubber plug with a metal clamp securing the wire to the plug. These are good for vacuum cleaners, for if too much strain is put on the wire, the plug will pull from the wall rather than the wires pulling from the plug. When a piece of furniture must be set close against a wall containing an outlet, special flat plugs with the wires coming from the base of the plug are available. These require less space than ordinary plugs.

The standard plug has two prongs, but there are plugs with three prongs for special equipment and with special convenience outlets (see "Grounding").

Appliances often fail to operate because the plug prongs are bent, dirty or rusty, and as a result do not make a contact inside the outlet. Dirt and rust may be removed by rubbing the prongs with fine sandpaper; prongs can often be bent back into proper shape. On cheap plugs, the prongs will not hold position long and they should be replaced.

Attaching Plugs.   To fasten lightweight rip cord to a plug with terminal screws, first cut the cord end off clean and slip it through the hole in the plug base. Separate the two wires to a length of about three inches and then tie them in a knot as shown. This is called an "underwriters' knot," and its purpose is to prevent the wires from pulling loose from the screws should they be given a too strong tug. The knot will fit into the space provided in the plug base and hold the wires secure. Certain smaller plugs do not have any space for the knot, and in this case, do not tie one. Assuming there is space and a knot has been tied, pull on the plug so that the knot fits down securely into the base. Now remove about ½" of insulation from

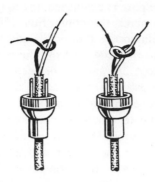

UNDERWRITERS' KNOT

the ends of the two wires. Be careful not to cut through the wire when doing this, for appliance cords are made of wires containing many fine strands. When the insulation is off, twist each wire to insure that there are no loose strands, and bring each wire around a prong and then around the terminal screw. Make certain to wrap the wire in the same direction the screw is turned to tighten it, otherwise it will work loose when the screw is tightened. Use a screwdriver. When the screw is tight, trim off any loose strands of wire with a sharp knife or razor blade.

Braided cord and heavy-duty S-cord with rubber outside insulation are attached in the same way as rip cord, except that the outside insulation must be carefully removed for about three inches after the wire has been fitted through the plug opening. When removing the outside insulation, be careful not to cut into the inside insulation around the individual wires. The cotton fiber under the rubber insulation of an S-wire should be removed.

Appliance Plugs. These plugs are used to connect the appliance cord to the appliance; they are found on most heating units, such as irons, toasters, etc. The most common type is the rectangular plug. This comes in three standard sizes. Some equipment requires a special plug. Should one of these go dead, take it to the hardware or electrical store so as to be sure of getting the correct replacement.

The standard heating-appliance plug must be disassembled before it can be removed. This is done by taking out the screws holding the two halves together or taking off the metal clips. The halves will then fall apart. Inside are two small metal sleeves, to which the cord wires are fastened. When the plug is connected, the appliance prongs engage with these sleeves to make the connection. The appliance plug is molded inside to accommodate these clips and wires.

To fasten the cord to the plug, first run the cord through the spring protector. Remove about 2½″ of the braided outer insulation, being careful not to cut the asbestos covering of the individual wires. Set the wires into the grooves provided in the plug to determine exactly how long they must be to reach the terminal screws on the metal clips; it will probably be about ½″. Cut the wires to the correct length and remove about ½″ of the rubber and asbestos insulation from the ends. Fasten the wires to the terminal screws and trim off any loose strands. Fit the clips into the space provided and set the wires into their individual grooves. The asbestos protective covering should come to the point where the wire is connected to the terminal screws. Fit the end of the spring protector into its recess and reassemble the halves of the plug.

Wall plugs for appliance cords are installed in the same fashion as plugs for braided and rip cords.

Rewiring Lamps

The standard lamp socket operates either by a pull chain, a key, or a push bar; but regardless of the type of switch, the manner of attaching the cords to the socket is the same. The usual reason a socket needs to be replaced is because the switch has broken, and the light cannot be turned on or off. The lamp may also need a longer cord, or the cord may be worn out.

The outside of the standard socket is made up of two parts. One is the brass shell, threaded at the end in order to be screwed into the lamp. The brass shell can be separated from the cap by pushing in on the sides where the word "push" is engraved. Sometimes this can be done with your fingers but often a screwdriver blade is needed. When the sides of the shell are pushed in, it can be separated from the cap. The body of the socket will then be exposed. This consists of the switch mechanism and a threaded metal tube into which the bulb screws. Inside the brass shell is a fiber jacket which serves as insulation and prevents the socket from coming into contact with the metal shell. Another piece of insulation inside the cap serves the same purpose. These two pieces of insulation should always be in place when the socket is put back together.

The cord wires are connected to the socket body by terminal screws. To remove the wires from an old socket, disconnect them from these screws. If there is an underwriters' knot, untie it. The cap screws onto a threaded sleeve projecting from the lamp, and often this is held by a set screw which must be loosened before the cap can be turned.

If your only problem is to replace a worn or broken socket, slip the wires through the new socket's cap and secure them to the threaded sleeve. Tie the underwriters' knot and fasten each wire to a terminal screw. Fit the shell over the socket body and then put the shell back into the cap.

Many socket caps and shells are interchangeable, so you may find that it is not necessary to remove the old cap when replacing the socket body.

To replace a lamp cord, take the socket apart so that the wires can be disconnected from the terminal screws. If the lamp is a simple one, the new cord can then be run to the socket and the wires hooked to the screws. But with many lamps, the lamp body must be taken apart, in order that old wires may be removed and new ones run to the socket. Most lamps are put together in more or less similar fashion. A narrow pipe runs through the center and the cord through this pipe, which is threaded at each end. Around the pipe end at the base of the lamp is a nut and a washer. When these are removed, the pipe can usually be pulled out of the lamp top. In a single-socket lamp, the socket cap will be screwed to a small length of brass pipe which in turn is connected to the longer pipe length through the lamp. With more than one socket, there will be a round metal box directly below where the wires from the sockets are hooked to the main lamp cord. This assembly box should come apart easily when the lamp is broken down. The wires inside can then be separated and the old cord taken out. The new cord can be fed through the lamp base and pipe and brought to the socket or box where the connections are made.

Safety

Some people are so afraid of electricity that they would rather spend hours in a dark house than change a fuse or flick a circuit-breaker switch. Others, even more misguided, ignore the danger involved. A little knowledge will prove a useful and protective servant.

A paramount safety rule is never to handle plugged-in electric appliances when your hands are wet. Dry skin is a poor conductor of current, and if your hands are dry, you can touch an appliance with an open circuit and feel only a small, tingling shock. On the other hand, if your hands are wet, the resulting shock may be fatal. For the same reason, electrical devices should never be handled when any part of your body is in contact with dampness, water, or a plumbing fixture. Many serious accidents occur every year because houseowners take their radios or portable TV sets into the bathroom and handle them while in the tub or in contact with a metal fixture. The same holds true of the kitchen when a radio is placed near the sink. No electrical device, no matter how little current it draws, should ever be put where it can cause this problem.

Bathroom and kitchen lights should be controlled by switches rather than pull cords. If this is impractical, the pull cords should be fabric rather than metal, for a metal chain makes a strong conductor between the hand and a possible open circuit inside the lamp socket. Fixtures in bathrooms, kitchens, and damp basements should, where possible, be made of porcelain rather than of metal.

In repairing cords or appliances, always disconnect them first from the convenience outlet. If the house fixed wiring must be worked on, pull the main house switch to OFF or remove the fuse controlling that particular circuit. Current to some devices may be shut off by a wall switch, but someone may come along and accidentally turn on the switch while the wires are being handled.

Grounding

House wiring system circuits are made up of two wires. One is covered with black insulation and the other with white insulation. The white is the ground wire and is grounded near the main distribution box by a wire running to a water pipe or metal rod driven into the ground. The white wire is never fused and never broken by a wall switch.

The black wire is the "hot" wire, and it is broken by the fuse or circuit breaker and by wall switches. Wall receptacles, switches, lamp sockets, and such devices are equipped with terminal screws to which the circuit wires are attached. The black wire should always be attached to the brass or gold screw; the white wire should be attached to the nickel-plated or silver screw. If not hooked to the proper screws, there is a chance that someone touching the metal lamp socket or switch plate will get a shock. The reason for grounding is to provide protection against this. Metal outlet boxes, pipes, or flexible metal conduits bringing wires to the boxes must also be grounded, as are fuse boxes and distribution boxes.

Certain motor-driven appliances, however, must be provided with additional grounding to prevent any chance of a shock. This may occur if a wire inside becomes loose, or if insulation is worn off the wire sufficiently to allow current to flow into the appliance's metal. If this occurs, even though the appliance is turned off, you can receive a serious shock. If the appliance is properly grounded, a short circuit would blow the fuse, and this would indicate that something was wrong.

Electric ranges are grounded when installed. Water heaters do not require a separate ground because they are connected directly to the metal pipes of the plumbing system. On the other hand, washing machines need a ground wire, and this is not always hooked on because these machines can be installed without an electrician. Grounding should be done with a NO.-12 wire fastened to a pipe in the plumbing by means of a metal pipe clamp. Clean the pipe with steel wool so that the clamp makes a good contact, and use a clamp of the same material as the pipe. If the pipe is galvanized iron, use a galvanized clamp; if the pipe is copper or brass, use a copper clamp. The other end of the wire should be attached to the grounding terminal screw, usually located on the back of the machine. If there is no such screw, loosen any screw on the machine frame and scrape off some of the enamel so that when the wire is under the screw head it will be in contact with bare metal and not the enamel coating. The ground wire should not be removed once it is in place.

Power tools, such as drills and portable saws, are equipped with a three-prong plug, the purpose of which is to insure proper grounding; but this is suitable only where a special three-hole convenience outlet is available. These tools may be used on a standard two-hole outlet with a special adapter, a special plug that will accommodate the three-prong plug at one end. The adapter's other end has the standard two prongs to fit into the outlet. On the adapter's side is a short wire that is connected to the setscrew holding the outlet plate in place. This is the grounding wire; and once hooked to the outlet's metal plate, which is grounded, the tool will also be grounded. Some portable appliances come with a standard two-prong plug that has a short wire running from its side. This wire should be connected to the setscrews on the outlet plate when the tool is being used. If such portable appliances aren't grounded, you may receive a serious shock when you use them.

Convenience Outlets, Replacing

When a device is plugged into an outlet and fails to work, check the plug first. The prongs may have been bent out of shape or be coated with rust or dirt. If the plug is in good condition, try another appliance in the same outlet. If this too fails to operate and the wall switch controlling the outlet is ON, check to see if the fuse has blown. If the fuse is good, it can be assumed that the trouble is in the outlet, in which case a new one must be installed. Standard duplex receptacles for outlets are sold at hardware and electrical stores. Even if the outlet is a single, it can be replaced with a duplex receptacle.

First, remove the fuse or open the circuit breaker so that no current can possibly flow through the outlet. Remove the plate covering the outlet by taking off the setscrews, exposing the receptacle. It will be connected either to two or four wires. If it is the last outlet in the circuit there will be two wires; but if there is another outlet beyond, there will be four: two to bring current to the receptacle and two to carry current to the next outlet. Each receptacle is provided with four terminal screws so that it can be used in any position in the circuit.

The old receptacle is removed by taking out the two screws holding it to the box. It can now be pulled out a short way for the wires to be disconnected by loosening the terminal screws. Clean the wire ends with sandpaper until they are bright. The black wire or wires in the outlet box should be hooked to the brass terminal screws and the white wire or wires to the nickel-plated terminal screws. The wires should go through the screws in the same direction that the screws are turned to tighten, and the screws should be tight enough so the wires cannot be moved. Put the receptacle back in the box, secure it with the two screws, and replace the plate over the outlet.

Ceiling and Wall Fixtures, Replacing

Shut off current to the fixture, then drop it. This is done in one of several ways. Some lightweight fixtures contain two or more setscrews which fit into a metal strap connected to the outlet box. When these are removed the fixture can be pulled away so that the wires are exposed. With heavier ceiling fixtures, there is a metal pipe connected to the outlet box. The fixture fits over this pipe and is secured by a nut. Once the nut is removed the fixture will slip off the pipe. Wall and ceiling fixtures come with two short wires, one black and the other white. These are spliced to the black and white wires from the outlet box. The splices are made by wrapping the wires around each other and then covering them with friction tape or special plastic solderless connectors. Splices to be covered with friction tape should be soldered, but they seldom are. Solderless connectors are threaded on the inside; and if the wires are properly spliced, the connector will screw over the splice to provide reinforcement as well as insulation.

Separate the wires. The fixture can then be removed. When the new fixture is installed, it may be necessary to get special fittings so that it can be fastened to the existing outlet box. When splicing the wires of the new fixture, the black wire must be spliced to the black wire in the outlet box and the white wire to the white. Clean off the ends of the wires with sandpaper before splicing, and make sure the splice is tight and there are no exposed wires.

Wall Switches, Replacing

Wall switches fail to operate when their inside parts become worn. Since there is no way to repair a worn switch, it must be replaced.

Shut off the current, either by removing the related fuse or by pulling the main switch. Remove the plate over the switch by taking out the setscrews, then loosen the screws holding the switch in the outlet box. There are two basic types of home switches. The more common is the *single pole switch,* used to control a light or outlet from one point; the other is the *three-way switch,* which is used to turn a light off and on from two different spots. Three-way switches are often used for hall lights, stairway lights, garage lights, etc.

A single-pole switch has only two terminal screws; a three-way has three, because three wires are necessary to make the connections. An ordinary single-pole switch cannot be used in place of a three-way switch; and unless the circuit has been wired for it, a three-way switch cannot be substituted for a single-pole switch. When buying a new switch, be sure to get the right type.

Single-pole switches are connected to two wires from the outlet box. One wire will be black, the other white. According to the electrical code, only a black insulated wire can be run to a wall switch;

but cables for house wiring are usually made with one black and one white wire. To eliminate the need for a special two-black-wire cable, the code states that for a wall switch a white wire may be used. Connections of the wires to the switch terminal screws are made in the same way as on an outlet.

In a three-way switch, there will be three wires instead of two, a black, a white, and a red wire. To avoid trouble in transferring the wires from the old switch to the new, pull the old switch far enough out of the box so that the terminal screws are exposed. Hold the new switch in the same position as the old. Remove one wire at a time and connect it to the corresponding terminal screw on the new switch. Check the connections to be sure they are tight, put the switch back into the box, and replace the screws and the switch plate.

Static and Electrical Disturbances

Some motor-driven appliances can cause static or poor reception on radios and TV sets. These will occur only when the motor is running, but they can be annoying. The problem often can be solved if the radio or TV is plugged into another circuit than the motor appliance. If this is not possible, or does not produce the desired results, a special condenser made to suppress electrical disturbances can be bought at a radio or TV repair shop. This should be inserted into the line between the motor and the house wiring. If used on the line between the wiring and the set, it will prove useless. These devices are often designed with prongs so that they can be plugged into the wall socket, and the cord from the motor-driven appliance is plugged into the condenser.

Electric Motors

Motors on refrigerators, air conditioners, and water pumps will last indefinitely if given a small amount of care, if not overloaded, and if they have an adequate amount of voltage.

Some motors require oiling; and if they do, there are small oil sleeves at each end of the motor, each sleeve fitted with a spring-loaded cap to keep out dust and dirt. Oil is applied simply by lifting this cap. Instructions on the type of oil needed and frequency of oiling are usually given in the manufacturer's instruction sheet; but if this is missing, get a NO.-12 or NO.-20 motor oil. Use an oil can, and fill the sleeves to the top. Wait a few hours, then fill them again. This insures that the wick inside the sleeves is thoroughly saturated with oil. Be careful that the oil does not get onto other parts of the motor or onto the wiring.

The outside house of a motor should be kept as clean as possible. If it is coated with dirt and grease, wipe it with carbon tetrachloride—but never with gasoline or benzene. (Avoid inhaling carbon tetrachloride fumes.) The vents at the end of the motor housing allow air to enter the motor to cool it while it is running. If these vents are clogged, the motor may overheat and burn out. The average motor is made to operate at about 72° above the air temperature around it. When running, it should be warm to the touch but not hot. If hot it may be overloaded, or the air vents may be dirty.

Most overloads on motors are caused by too much tension in the belt connecting the motor to the other part of the appliance. The belt should be loose enough to give a few inches when pushed down by hand at the center; but it should not slip when the motor starts, for this means that it is too loose. Tension on the V-belt can be increased or decreased by loosening the hold-down bolts on the motor, or the device to which it is connected, and moving one or both closer together or farther apart.

V-belts should be checked periodically to make sure they are not worn or badly frayed. If they are in poor condition replace the belts at once.

When there is a failure of the house current, due to a storm or other interruption, turn off or disconnect all electric motors and keep them off until the power has been fully restored. This will prevent motors from burning out because of the low voltage that often comes through while power lines are being restored.

Motors should never be allowed to get wet. Should this happen, however, possibly because of a flooded basement or because you have dropped it in the sink while cleaning it, do not operate it until it has been thoroughly dried—and this job should be done by a competent electrician.

Electric Appliances, Care and Repair

Most modern electric appliances are so complicated that their repair is beyond the average homeowner's ability. In fact, it is sometimes hard to find a local serviceman who is qualified to make repairs;

and often the appliance must be returned to the factory for servicing. Good quality equipment, if properly treated, should run for many years without servicing; and often when an appliance fails to operate it is not the machine's fault but a fault in the domestic electrical system.

As we have said earlier no appliance will operate unless it is getting sufficient voltage. If an appliance begins to operate poorly or fails altogether, check to see whether it is getting adequate voltage. Often it is a simple matter, such as a blown fuse caused by an overload or an improperly fitted plug, or even a dead wall outlet. Loose connections on the cord at the plugs can also be the cause of the trouble.

Instruction manuals usually come with appliances, and these provide information on care and maintenance. They should be carefully read. Many breakdowns are caused by failing to read and follow the manufacturer's manual.

Heating Appliances. All heating appliances must be equipped with a special heavy-duty heating cord. As we have said earlier, lightweight rubber or plastic cords should never be used, and these cords shouldn't be joined to standard appliance cords to lengthen them. The insulated cord should never be wrapped around an iron, toaster, or any other appliance while the appliance is hot. The heating element in any appliance is delicate, and it can be damaged if the appliance is roughly handled or dropped. Unless so specified, heating appliances should never be submerged in water. In some few appliances, such as some electric frying pans, and coffee makers, the heating element is sealed; and these may be immersed in water without trouble if directions so state. Toasters, broilers, or waffle irons should be wiped off with a *damp* cloth, and then only after being disconnected. Never use a *wet* cloth, for water may flow into the heating element. Never set an appliance in a place in your kitchen where it may fall into the sink while in operation, or where someone having one hand in water, or touching a metal sink, can handle it. Most heating appliances draw considerable current and should be plugged into a circuit with a 20-ampere fuse or circuit breaker and NO.-12 wire. If a slight shock is received when the appliance metal is touched, it indicates an open circuit inside; and the item should be immediately disconnected and repaired.

Servicing Appliances. While it is impossible for the ordinary homeowner to repair or service modern electric appliances, the cost of having the work done may be cut down. One way is to buy appliances with a manufacturer's guaranty or warranty covering a certain period. If anything goes wrong in this time, repairs will be made by the manufacturer or his local agent for little or no cost. Another way to save money on repairs is to take the unit to the shop, when possible, rather than to have a serviceman come to the house. Just as a doctor charges more for a house call than for an office call, so most servicemen charge more for a house call than they do if you bring the appliance to the shop.

Some items are too heavy to be carried, but there is also a way to save on these. Make sure that when you call the serviceman you furnish all pertinent information. Each appliance has a metal tag giving the manufacturer's name, model, serial numbers, and other data; and if this is given over the phone the serviceman may be able to bring along the right parts for the equipment, saving himself time— and saving you money.

Window Air Conditioners. While the larger air conditioners operate on 240 volts, the smaller types will run on 120 volts. Each unit, however, should have a circuit of its own. If the unit is plugged into a wall outlet in a circuit used for other devices, trouble can be expected. An independent circuit should be installed for the conditioner; but even so, if the outlet is a considerable distance from the fuse box, there may be a tendency for a fuse to blow when the air conditioner starts. This can be avoided if the fan is first switched on and then, after a minute or two, the cooling compressor. By doing so, there will not be a heavy demand for current as occurs when both fan and compressor are switched on simultaneously. A time-delay fuse installed in the fuse box will prevent fuses from blowing when the unit starts.

Many older units without thermostats will frost up if the outside temperature drops below a certain point. A thermostat may be installed to shut off the unit when the outside temperature is low, or a timer device may be put on to turn off the unit after the household is asleep.

Refrigerator and Freezer Units. The motors on these should be checked and serviced in accordance with the manufacturer's directions. Lacking this information, act as suggested in "Electric Motors." Cooling units of this type are equipped with a condenser resembling an automobile radiator. This should be cleaned from time to time with a vacuum or soft brush to remove dust and dirt from the fins. Many refrigerators today have automatic defrosting devices, and there are special units that can be installed to automatically defrost a conventional refrigerator. Lacking these, the refrigerator should be defrosted when the rime builds up to a thickness of over ¼ inch. Frost on the freezer compartment acts as insulation and prevents the full effect of cooling distribution. This means that with a heavy rime coating the refrigerator must work doubly hard to keep the box cold.

When a refrigerator seems to run almost constantly, it is often due to frost overloading. Opening and closing the refrigerator door too frequently can also cause overfrequent operation, and so can a worn door gasket that allows warmth to leak in. To check on this, close the door on a piece of ordinary bond paper. If the paper can be pulled out easily, it means that the gasket is worn and should be replaced.

CHAPTER **14**

Buying A House

The Cost

How much can you afford to spend for a house?

That's the first question you should ask yourself before you even start looking at the houses offered for sale.

The answer no longer depends solely on how much cash you have available. Modern mortgage financing has made it possible for the majority of American families to buy a home principally on credit, and most of them do so. Of course, you'll need some cash for a down payment and other expenses—but most of the money will come from a mortgage lender. This does not imply that cash is of no importance whatsoever; cash still remains a consideration. However, the old rules have fallen by the wayside over the years. At one time, it was customary to receive a mortgage for only half (often less) of the selling price, putting up cash for the entire balance. Then it became the general rule to receive a mortgage equal to two-thirds of the value of the house.

The question still remaining is the size of the mortgage that may be arranged, and also, its terms. The size of the mortgage available to you will probably give you the closest answer to the top amount you can afford. That's because experienced lenders won't let you borrow more than you can afford to pay. The lender is interested in getting his money back, plus interest and fees. He doesn't want to take over a foreclosed home; he's in the lending business, not the selling of houses; and he doesn't wish to foreclose, and he will do so only under the pressure of circumstances.

Let's consider the method by which a lender decides whether you can pay for the home you want him to finance. It can save you the heartache of finding the home you have long dreamed about and then discovering that you can't get the loan you need to buy it.

Rules of Thumb. There's an old, often-repeated theory that you can't afford to pay more than 2½ times your annual income for a home. There's another generalization that your carrying charges—regular installment payments on the mortgage (principal and interest), real-estate taxes, and fire-insurance premiums—should not total more than 25% of your annual income. Roughly these two formulas work out about the same. For the family making an average down payment, a house that costs more than 2½ times annual income will bring the carrying charges to more than the 25% maximum level.

Using these rules of thumb, and assuming you are depending entirely on your income to buy a house, here's about what you can afford to spend for a home.

Annual income	Top price of home
$ 5,000	$12,500
6,000	15,000
7,000	17,500
8,000	20,000
9,000	22,500
10,000	25,000
12,000	30,000
15,000	37,500
20,000	50,000
25,000	62,500–75,000

Although the same formula works up the income scale, generally when you get into the higher income brackets, you won't pay as much as 25% of your income for a home. Government statistics prove that the lower your income, the greater percentage of it you must spend on housing or other basic necessities. If your income is high enough, the amount you pay will depend more on choice than on actual necessity.

But whatever your income, you should never pay more than you can afford for a home. By the same token, you should never be afraid to pay what you *can* afford. But of course, personal matters may alter generalizations. Obviously, a couple with no children do not have the same problem as a husband and wife with six youngsters, all needing food, clothing, and, ultimately, college education. A childless couple, as a rule, will have more money available to buy and maintain a house than people who have the fixed and continuing expenses of a growing family. And as previously mentioned, if the lender will give you the mortgage you need, you can be reasonably certain, all things considered, that you are not going overboard financially. Your lender's judgment is based on long years of experience—his own experience and that of many others in the field.

How much reliance can you place on such easy rules of thumb? Can you actually rely on the mortgage lender's judgment? Like all formulas of this kind, they have a large measure of truth—but they're not the whole story. Furthermore, no two homeowning families are precisely alike.

It's pretty obvious, on analysis, why such rules of thumb can't tell the whole story. If someone has left you a bequest of, say, $10,000, you can buy a more expensive house (and pay a larger amount of cash) than another family with the same income but without the inheritance or a similar sum that it has managed to save.

For illustrative purposes, let's take the story of Ed Merideth. He was a rising young executive in one of the country's largest industrial firms. The Merideths had just found the house they'd been looking for, and they were sure they would have no trouble getting a satisfactory mortgage. Based on his income and prospects, he should have been able to get a substantial mortgage. But one lender after another refused him. A credit check had disclosed that Ed was over his head in debt. He was living at a scale beyond his means, had not only bought a new car for himself but another for his wife, both on the installment plan. With his country club expenses, and sending his son to college, there just wasn't enough left over to pay the expenses of a new home. To the experienced judgment of the mortgage lenders, the Merideths were not a good credit risk.

A Word of Advice. The lender will *automatically* draw a credit check on you when you apply for a loan. So it's often advisable to defer the purchase of a new automobile on time, or other large installment purchases, until after you've bought your home.

Estimating Your Ability to Pay. Let us assume that a suitable house has been found and a mortgage lender is approached with a view to obtaining a loan. He'll judge you personally, as an individual, not completely by any of the previously discussed rules of thumb. Here are the three factors he'll evaluate:

1. *Your effective income*—it must be dependable, continuing income. If your income varies substantially from year to year, it must be averaged out.

2. *Monthly housing expenses*—what it will cost you every month to occupy the house, including easily overlooked items such as maintenance, repairs, gardening, etc.

3. *Your debts and living costs*—the amount you owe, and the everyday financial obligations which everyone has.

Let's consider these items one by one. If the first (effective income) adds up to more than the other two, it is reasonable to assume that you'll get the mortgage you need.

Effective Income. The key word is *effective.* That means take-home pay after tax deductions and withholding taxes. It also rules out income that you won't get regularly, such as overtime or bonus pay, children's earnings, money from renting a room, or income from occasional or part-time employment.

Does your wife's income count? It will, but only if her work has become an accepted part of your family life. If you have married recently, or if she's been working only a short time, her income probably won't be considered as "effective income." However, if she's a professional person, such as a school teacher, you generally can count on her income as regular and continuing. In some cases, the lender may give you credit for half her income, even for recent employment, especially when she's begun to work regularly because your children are now old enough to take care of themselves. With young married couples, the wife's income is usually discounted, on the theory that she will probably have children and her income will stop.

Monthly Housing Expenses. First, compute the payments on the mortgage—principal and interest. These, as a rule, will be the same amount each month during the life of the mortgage. On other mortgages, the payments will be slightly lower each year. Then you add the following: (1) fire insurance and public liability insurance (2) taxes (3) an estimate for maintenance and repairs (4) an estimate for utilities (light, heat, water, and air conditioning) and (5) miscellaneous, such as garbage collection, gardening, etc. This gives you your monthly housing expense.

Your Debts and Living Costs. These must be divided into two groups—living expenses and fixed obligations.

Living expenses include food, clothing, insurance premiums, children's education, medical and dental care, automobile maintenance, transportation (commutation, etc.), recreation and entertainment, emergencies, and miscellaneous (dues, contributions, etc.).

Fixed obligations are regular, fixed installment payments for an automobile, appliances or furniture (if purchased on time), personal loans, plus miscellaneous items that vary from person to person (support of parent, income taxes not withheld, savings and retirement fund).

Of all the above items, the one that requires the most discussion and consideration is monthly housing expenses, and the most important item in that group is the first mortgage.

Payments on the Mortgage. The one unfailing item, and a large one, concerns the monthly payments on the mortgage. Assume, for example, that you need a $10,000 mortgage. How much will that cost you a month? (For a $20,000 mortgage, the figures that follow may be doubled, or they can be computed proportionately for larger or smaller amounts.)

The answer depends on two factors, in addition to the principal amount of the mortgage ($10,000), which has been selected for purposes of illustration. The two factors are the interest rate and the length of time agreed on to pay off the mortgage in full. Obviously, the higher the interest rate, the higher the monthly payments. On the other hand, spreading the time of payment over a longer period of time brings down the amount due each month; but, of course, this requires you to pay interest for a greater number of months to make up the difference.

Suppose we work out the cost in dollars and cents, based on a $10,000 mortgage. Let's start first with a 6% interest rate. Here's how the monthly payments (including reduction of principal plus interest) vary, depending on the time you take:

15 years $84.39
20 years 71.65
25 years 64.44
30 years 60.94

A similar table at a 5¾% rate illustrates the lower payments required with a drop of only ¼ of 1% interest. (Bear in mind that it adds up to a great deal of money over the years during which you're paying off the mortgage.)

15 years $83.05
20 years 70.21
25 years 62.92
30 years 58.40

No one should disregard the savings available through obtaining the lowest possible interest rate. To put the matter into concrete form, observe the figures for a 20-year mortgage. At 6% the payment is $71.65 a month, at 5¾% it is $70.21, or a difference of $1.44 a month. In one year the difference is $17.28; and over a 20-year term, it swells into $344.60. Bear in mind, this substantial saving involves only a difference of ¼ of 1%; if the mortgage bears interest at 5% or thereabouts, the savings are truly impressive.

You can see at a glance that stretching out the payments can cut down your monthly payments considerably, but your ultimate cost will be greatly increased. You'll pay almost $25 less a month by taking 30 years to pay instead of 15. (We're assuming the lender will give you 30 years; that's a problem for later discussion.)

What does all of this mean as a practical matter, and how does it affect you? First, extending the length of the mortgage may qualify you for a loan you couldn't otherwise get because it brings your monthly housing expense down to match your income. Looking at it another way, it qualifies you to buy a more expensive home, should you wish to do so.

Sometimes you have no choice, and the only available mortgage is over a longer period than you wish. But suppose your income is large enough to give you a choice—which type should you select?

You must remember that the longer you take to pay, the more the house will cost you. You have to pay interest for a longer time, and, of course, you have to pay for the use of that borrowed money. A $10,000 loan at 6% for 15 years will cost you $5,190.20 in interest. For 30 years, interest will come to $11,938.40—more than double, and even more than the principal! The difference between the two comes to more than $6,700, and is something you shouldn't forget—if you have a choice.

But don't let these rather surprising figures on the high cost of interest deter you from buying a home, even if you need a long time to pay it off. If you rent instead of buy, you'll be paying the landlord every month. You can be sure he makes due allowance for the fact that he has money invested in the property, and you'll be paying him for the use of his money just as surely you pay the mortgage lender for the use of his money when you buy a home. After twenty or thirty years of paying rent, you'll be no better off than when you started, for every dollar paid to your landlord will be gone. With a self-liquidating mortgage on your own home, you'll own it free and clear.

However, when you pay off a mortgage, part of your payments are for principal and the balance covers interest. That portion which goes toward reduction of the mortgage represents a savings every month. When your home is paid off, it will, as a rule, be worth as much or more than the amount you paid for it.

Furthermore, after having made payments for a number of years, you'll have created a substantial equity in the house, because part of your monthly payments are used to reduce the principal of the mortgage. If you need money, for example, to send a child to college, you might possibly refinance the mortgage and get the cash you need.

A Word of Warning. Very little of the principal of the mortgage is paid off during the first few years, because the payments, at first, are mostly for interest, inasmuch as the principal sum due is still large. In the later years, most of the payments will be for principal, because the amount due has been gradually reduced, and you are still paying the same regular installment although the total amount owed has been reduced.

Tax Advantages. You'll be able to recoup part of the expenses of paying for your home by deductions from your federal income tax. All your payments for interest on the mortgage during the year are deductible. So, too, are your payments for real-estate taxes. The savings here are considerable, especially if you're in a high tax bracket. In any event, they are definitely savings; and over the course of say, a 20-year mortgage, they amount to a considerable sum.

For example, if your real-estate taxes are $500 a year, and you're in the 40% tax bracket, you'll be able to save $200 a year in income taxes. In 20 years, the total saving will be $4,000.

If you add to this the amount you save from the interest deduction, the results are dramatic. For example, on a $15,000 mortgage loan, interest at 6% for 20 years totals more than $10,000. For the man in the 40% bracket that's another $4,000 reduction in income taxes—$8,000 in all.

Even if you're in the lower brackets, your deductions would surely come to at least $4,000 over the 20-year period. That's a benefit the renter doesn't get, although he's really paying off the same amount—but to the landlord, because the rental includes what the landlord must pay for real-estate taxes and interest on his mortgage.

Interest Rates. As a rule, there isn't too much opportunity to bargain about the interest rate on a mortgage. Lenders compete with each other for the available mortgage business, and somehow the interest rates are fairly stable in any particular area.

However, interest rates do vary from time to time within a given area. When savings by depositors are high, and lenders have a surplus of funds, interest rates naturally tend to go down. In reverse, when savings deposits are withdrawn and the lenders have little available mortgage money, rates go up. Obviously you'll obtain a lower interest rate if you buy a house at a time when money is "easy"—that is, plentiful.

Note. Interest rates vary from one part of the country to another. Generally, they're lowest in the East, highest in the West.

There is, however, one way that you may be able to cut down on the interest rate. Often this may be accomplished by making a larger-than-usual down payment on your prospective house. The more you pay in cash, the lower the mortgage, because the risk for the lender is smaller. As a practical matter, banks are often willing to accept a smaller interest rate if they feel the mortgage is gilt-edge—that is, one in which the amount of the mortgage is quite low in relation to the value of the house.

Sources of Mortgage Loans. Here are the main sources of home mortgage loans available in most parts of the country:

Savings and loan associations. These are generally referred to as S & L's. They are of two types: federal and state. These may be found in the telephone book in large cities or by looking around in the main part of the business district in small communities.

Mutual savings banks. Unlike other sources, these are limited to about 18 states, mostly in the East.

Commercial banks. Although these banks specialize in business loans, they will often lend on home mortgages, depending on the availability of their funds and conditions in the mortgage market.

Mortgage brokers. These individuals or firms act as agents for various lenders who wish to place funds in mortgages. They are one of the best sources of Federal Housing Administration (FHA) loans and Veterans Administration (VA or GI) loans, which will be discussed more fully under the important subject of down payments.

The Down Payment. You'll always need some cash when you buy a home, even if it is one of the lowest price. Of course, with expensive homes, the amount of cash required may be very substantial. True, the mortgage lender will finance the largest part of the cost, but he will never finance all of it. As a matter of fact, mortgage lenders aren't permitted to do so (except on a Veterans Administration loan). Lending institutions are regulated by the state and federal governments, and the amount of money they can lend is limited by law. (The law also sets a top limit on the number of years you can be allowed to pay off the loan.)

Furthermore, the regulations limit the lender as to the top amount he *can* lend you. He doesn't, and often won't, give you as much as the law permits; and, of course, the smaller the amount you are able to borrow, the greater is the amount needed for a down payment.

When money is easy, you have a good chance to get a top (large) loan, but when money is tight, you'll probably have to settle for less. It's a matter of bargaining and trading, somewhat like the give-and-take of selling a used car. Don't be reluctant to do a little bargaining yourself, if you have to; and if one lender won't give you as much as you need, check with other lenders in the area.

Three Types of Loans. The size of the down payment required will depend in large part on the *type* of loan you get. There are three types:

1) *Conventional loans.* This is any regular mortgage loan not insured or guaranteed by the government (FHA and VA). Down payments required on this type of loan are generally higher than on a government-backed loan. Not too many years ago, it was almost impossible to buy a home without making a down payment of at least one-third of the purchase price. But both state and federal laws have been liberalized, and the trend is to smaller down payments as well as to a longer payoff period.

At the present time, federal S & L's are permitted to make 90% loans. That means your down payment can be as small as 10%. But in actual practice, only a small percentage of federal S & L loans are as high as 90%, although the number is increasing. In most cases, you'll probably receive about an 80% loan—which means a 20% down payment. Of course, it should be remembered that mortgage conditions change from year to year.

A Word of Warning. The percentages here, and in all other cases discussed, refer to a percentage of *appraised* value, and not to a percentage of the price you pay for the home. Since lenders, especially on conventional loans, tend toward conservatism, their appraised value will generally be somewhat less than the amount you pay for the house. This should not disconcert you, nor should you necessarily feel that you are overpaying, merely because the appraised value is less than the price paid. Thus, if you get a 90% loan, your down payment will actually be more than 10% of the price you pay; if you get an 80% loan, your down payment will be more than 20% of what you pay.

If you get a loan from a state S & L, or from a mutual savings bank, the amount of the loan permitted varies from state to state. But in most states, you can get an 80% loan, and in some, a 90% loan.

Commercial banks, traditionally, have not made many home mortgage loans. Recently, however, they have expanded the scope of their home mortgage lending, and in many areas they are actively seeking and placing conventional home loans. However, they generally demand a down payment of about 25% of appraised value. Also, their maximum maturity (payoff time) is usually 25 years, contrasted with the 30 years often obtainable from the other lenders. As previously pointed out, you can save a great deal of money by making a larger down payment; and if you can afford to do so, because you have the available cash, don't overlook the commercial banks as a source of mortgage money. Also, don't disregard them when you're shopping around for the best possible mortgage terms.

2) *FHA loans.* These are loans insured by the Federal Housing Administration (FHA), a federal agency set up by the government to insure home loans for private lenders.

Some people are under the mistaken impression that FHA lends money to home buyers. FHA loans are made only by private lenders (banks, etc.) for whom FHA *insures* ultimate payment of the loan. Therefore, it is clear that the loan must be obtained from a lender, not from the FHA.

Because the loan is insured by the government, lenders feel more secure and tend to make larger loans than they ordinarily would on uninsured loans. Therefore, a home buyer who needs a substantial loan, because he can afford only a small down payment, must find a lender who will make an FHA loan. (Technically, lenders must be approved by the FHA in order to make these loans, but you'll find that almost all of the lenders will be approved.)

Just how small a down payment can you make on an FHA loan? Before considering the present FHA requirements, you must remember the following facts:

a) As in a conventional mortgage, the down payments are the *minimums* required, by the FHA. The lender, if he chooses, *can* require a larger down payment.

b) The amount you can borrow, and consequently the down payment required, depends on FHA appraised value, which may be lower than the price you have agreed to pay for the house. (But generally, FHA appraisals are more liberal than those on conventional mortgages.)

c) The FHA can, and does, change its regulations from time to time including the amount of the down payment required. But in recent years the trend has been toward lowered down payment requirements (and toward longer terms of maturity). In any case, FHA down payments will always be substantially lower than those on conventional mortgages.

d) The largest loan FHA can make (at present) on a 1-family house is $25,000. So if you're buying a high-priced house, you'll probably find that a conventional mortgage is best, all things considered.

FHA DOWN PAYMENT TABLE

FHA Value	Maximum Mortgage	Down Payment
$ 8,000	$ 7,750	$ 250
9,000	8,700	300
10,000	9,700	300
11,000	10,650	350
12,000	11,600	400
13,000	12,600	400
14,000	13,550	450
15,000	14,550	450
16,000	15,400	600
17,000	16,300	700
18,000	17,200	800
19,000	18,100	900
20,000	19,000	1,000
21,000	19,800	1,200
22,000	20,500	1,500
23,000	21,300	1,700
24,000	22,000	2,000
25,000	22,800	2,200
26,000	23,500	2,500
27,000	24,300	2,700
28,000	25,000	3,000

A quick look at these tables will show you how much less of a down payment is required with an FHA loan when compared with a conventional mortgage which carries from 10% to 20% of value. For example, on a $15,000 house, the FHA down payment is only $450 against a payment ranging from $1,500 to $3,000 with a conventional mortgage. On a $20,000 house, the FHA down payment is $1,000, contrasted with a payment ranging from $2,000 to $4,000.

On lower-priced homes, available in smaller communities where land costs are lower, the FHA down payments are extremely moderate. For an FHA mortgage on a $10,000 home, a payment of only $300 is required as against $1,000 to $2,000 with a conventional mortgage. However, in the $25,000 (and over) range there may be little difference between the two kinds of loans—that is, if your lender is willing to accept a 10% down payment on a conventional mortgage.

3) *VA loans.* These are the so-called GI loans, available only to veterans of World War II and to Korean veterans. They are of two types, *guaranteed loans* and *direct loans.*

Guaranteed loans are made by regular mortgage lenders, almost exactly like conventional and FHA loans. Direct loans, as the term implies, are made directly by the government through the Veterans Administration, but only in regions where mortgage money is not generally available. At present, these areas are generally in outlying and rural areas. In other regions, veterans must rely on the guaranteed loan program.

Both guaranteed and direct VA loans require no down payment, but the veteran must pay closing costs (discussed below). However, on a guaranteed loan, the lender *may* require some down payment (the no-down-payment provision merely gives him permission to make such a loan if he wants to).

Note. Under the present law, some World War II veterans will find their rights to a GI loan running out soon. Eligibility is based on a formula of 10 years from time of discharge plus one year for each three months of service. For some World War II veterans, time will run out starting July 25, 1962. It will run out for all World War II veterans on July 25, 1967.

Korean veterans follow the same formula, but their earliest expiration date is January 31, 1965, and the latest January 31, 1975.

Initial Costs. Many home-buyers receive a most unpleasant and unanticipated shock when the time arrives to close a deal for the purchase of a house. They have mentally figured on the down payment, but frequently they are not warned of additional, so-called "closing costs," which they are required to pay before taking title. These "closing costs" can often amount to a substantial sum. Here are the costs a home buyer is usually required to pay:

1) *Title Insurance.* This is actually an insurance policy that provides protection against claims of ownership to the property by third parties after you take title. Most mortgage lenders require that you obtain a title insurance policy to protect them against such claims.

The fee is fixed by the title insurance company, so there is nothing you can do to bring down its cost.

Unlike other forms of insurance, the title insurance premium is paid only once—at its issuance, usually at the closing.

Title insurance is necessary because there are sometimes defects in a title to property that even a thorough search of the title will not disclose. For instance, a missing heir may turn up or a deed may be forged, or any one of a hundred other complications may arise.

Warning. There are two kinds of title insurance—mortgage insurance and owner's title insurance. The lender, as a rule, will only require that you obtain mortgage title insurance—which protects him against losses, but does not necessarily protect you. As you pay off the mortgage, the lender's interest gradually becomes smaller. When he's finally paid off, the title insurance expires. If someone then makes a claim against the property, *you* have no protection.

It is important to obtain an owner's title insurance policy to protect you against claims to the property. Even false or doubtful claims can cost money for attorney's fees, to say nothing of the time lost defending your interests. With an owner's title insurance policy, the insurance company takes over the defense at its own cost, and you're protected against both valid and invalid claims.

It is important to take out your owner's policy at the same time as the mortgage title policy. That's because the title company, before it issues insurance, must make a title search of the property. Inasmuch as it is already doing the research for the lender, there's no extra work required on your behalf. Therefore, the cost to you is approximately one-half of what you would have to pay if you took out an owner's policy at a subsequent time. The first cost is the only cost to you; it covers you and your heirs as long as you own the property.

2) *Title Search.* There are some areas where title insurance is not required. If so, the lender will have his own attorney make a title search, and you are required to pay this expense. But there will be no extra charge for such a search if you are paying for the title insurance, discussed previously.

3) *Appraisal Fees.* The lender will have to make an appraisal of the property in order to determine how large a loan he can make. You'll have to pay him for this service. On an FHA or VA loan, the government sets the fee; it can be changed from time to time, but

generally runs about $20 or $25. On a conventional mortgage, the lender sets the fee, and it may run as high as $100.

4) *Credit Check.* The lender will want to check your personal credit record. Occasionally he will do his own checking; sometimes he will use an outside credit-investigating agency. In any event, you pay the charges; but they amount to only a few dollars.

5) *Origination Fee.* The lender will usually charge you about 1% of the amount of the loan to cover his basic costs in making the loan. Both FHA and VA limit this charge to 1%. Thus, on a $15,000 mortgage, this charge would be $150.

6) *Survey Charges.* The lender may, in some cases, require a survey of the property; if he does, you will be required to pay for it. In many cases, the property has been surveyed many times before, and you may be required to pay only a nominal amount for an inspection to see that there have been no changes since the last survey. As previously mentioned, a survey may not be necessary.

Prepayment of Insurance and Taxes. You'll have to pay these charges sooner or later, but you may not be prepared to pay them at the time of closing. Don't forget to find out what they amount to before you go to the closing. If due, be prepared to pay them at the closing.

Note. There's nothing you can do about taxes *after* you buy the property. But you should find out how high they are before you agree to buy.

Warning. There's little you can do about *honest* closing costs, which are a routine part of buying a house and obtaining a new mortgage. But there have been many incidents of *excessive* closing costs. You should protect yourself by getting competent legal advice *before* you sign any agreement to purchase, and before you make a deposit. Your attorney can protect you not only against excessive closing costs, but also in many other ways. A lawyer can usually tell you something about the reputation of the parties you are dealing with, and if necessary put a clause in your contract that will permit you to get your deposit back and call off the deal if the closing costs come to an amount over a specified (and fair) amount.

Remember, you must protect yourself, for you may lose your deposit if you can't go through with the deal. What's more, the seller may be able to collect damages.

However, don't get the impression that you will always, or even usually, be asked to pay excessive charges. Most people in business are basically honest, and they want the future business that comes with a good reputation. But even honest closing costs (and prepayments) can easily come to $500 or more, and you shouldn't commit yourself to buy unless you know that you can meet these payments. If you know what they are, and you are willing to pay them, then make your decision. Your attorney will know the approximate closing costs in the area where you are buying, so see him *first*. It may be too late after you've signed a contract, for he will be bound by the terms of the contract, and they are inevitably drawn in favor of the lender.

Searching for a House

Let us assume that you have decided that you wish to buy a house, you know how much you can pay, and you are now looking for one. What factors should you consider? A home is a long-term investment, and it involves a substantial amount of money. You'll probably be living there a long time. The postwar shortage of homes is now over, but still not every house represents a good investment; you may suffer a substantial loss if you make a poor choice.

The Community.   Modern transportation facilities and highways have given the vast majority of Americans a wide choice of communities in which to live. It's important to check various areas that might be suitable. Outwardly the same, there may be great differences between them that are of the greatest importance to you and to your family.

Taxes.   You'll naturally prefer an area where taxes are low. But remember that taxes are not determined by tax rate alone. They're also determined by the valuation practices of the local assessors. In some areas, homes may be valued at only 25% of true value; in others, it may run as high as 50% or even 70%. So you must take both the tax rate *and* the local valuation practice into consideration, and determine the amount of tax dollars you'll have to pay. Don't be misled by an apparently low tax rate.

Warning.   Rates and valuations can change. If the community is a growing one (many young couples with young children), it will soon need more schools, sewers, and other services in the near future. Then you may soon find yourself paying a great deal more in taxes than you anticipated. In some communities, taxes have risen substantially, or even fantastically, in recent years. The safest neighborhood for comparatively stable taxes is one that has already been fully developed, with good schools, adequate fire and police protection, a completed sewage system, and, most important of all, homeowners with a sense of civic responsibility and a community with a reputation for good government.

Also be on the lookout for those communities that raise taxes excessively when a home is bought by a new owner. The tax bill of the seller is not always a clear indication of what you—a new owner —will ultimately pay. Check the local assessment practices of the community. This can only be done by speaking to new residents of the community, who presumably have experienced exactly what will happen to you if you buy in that community. Ask them if their assessment and total tax bill increased when they first moved in.

Zoning. A good community has zoning laws that protect its homeowners. The zoning laws should clearly set forth the residential areas, so that homeowners won't find a garage or an open-air theater being erected next to their property. (Here, again, is a situation where your attorney can help you ascertain the facts.)

Avoid communities that permit easy variances in zoning laws— that is, permit political favorites or those who have good connections to make exceptions to the zoning law, and thus destroy the value of your property as a home.

Good zoning may also make a difference in your tax bill. Some residential communities do not make adequate provision for business and industrial areas. If they are permitted near your home, they will almost surely damage its value. But if the neighborhood is properly zoned, and business and industry restricted to known and specific areas, they can help cut down the tax burden on homeowners by bringing in additional taxes to the community. They can also provide services and shopping areas for yourself and your family.

Zoning laws may also prevent you from using the property in the way you had planned. For instance, you may want to convert the second floor of the house you are buying into a separate apartment, possibly for another member of your family or even for rental purposes. If the property is in a one-family residential zone, you won't be able to do so.

The same prohibition may apply if you want to use part of your house for an office, or partly for a business. Even though no alterations are required and you intend to operate your business in one of the rooms of the house, such use may be prohibited.

Zoning is even more important to the buyers of land who are planning to erect a custom-built home (or a prefabricated home). Some communities, in their anxiety to keep out families who will demand new streets and sewers, and whose children will require more space in schools than is presently available, have created zoning rules that may make it impossible for you to build the home you plan. For instance, one community may require a specified amount of acreage for a one-family zone, and restrictions of that type have been upheld in the courts. If you buy a smaller lot than the zoning ordinance requires, you can't build a house (or anything else, for that matter) on the lot you own.

Since zoning ordinances usually don't affect existing homes, present homeowners can still continue living in their "substandard" homes. You, too, as the buyer of one of these existing houses, will normally be able to continue its prior use, even though it doesn't meet the requirements of a new house you want to put up. This can lead to endless problems, hearings with the zoning commission, and inevitable disappointment.

The conclusion is obvious. Don't sign a contract until after you have checked the zoning ordinances. It will protect you against both undesirable uses by your neighbors, and the inability for you to use your property in the way you want.

The Neighborhood. Any experienced real-estate man will tell you that the single most important point to consider in buying a house is location. The word *location* refers in general to the neighborhood and to the people who live there.

What factors add up to a good location? That depends mostly on your personal preferences. You may prefer a neighborhood where most of the people are of a particular social level, or who are in about the same economic group as your family. Or you may prefer a "mixed" neighborhood, with more variation in groups, personalities, and economic levels.

Whatever your preference, be on the lookout for changing neighborhoods, where one specific group is moving out and another moving in. If that is the situation, be sure the incoming group is the type you want as neighbors. This is *not* a matter of snobbery or of undesirable class consciousness—it's a matter of making an easy and satisfactory adjustment to the community. Changes are not always for the worse; they can often be for the better; therefore, bear in mind that change alone means little. The important thing is that your neighbors should be of the type you expect and not come as an unpleasant surprise.

Location also means accessibility. Perhaps most important of all, if you have children, is accessibility to schools. Their school will probably be determined by the physical situation of your property. Inasmuch as almost all suburban schools are good, this should present no serious problems. However, schools do vary in methods; and if this is important to you be sure the house is in a school district acceptable to you.

Consider, too, the location of shopping areas in relation to the property you are considering. (If there's a second car available, you'll have a wider choice.) Wives often find that desirable stores are badly located in relation to the house, and this makes shopping a very wearing and time-consuming process. Deliveries of heavier goods from the shopping area are often delayed or refused, if the house is not conveniently located. Yet, being too close to a shopping area means early-morning noise and excessive traffic. Finding the proper location involves being not too close, nor yet too far away from a shopping area.

New House or Old.   A new house or an old one? That's one of the most basic questions presented to homeseekers before they start their search. The most important factor—but not the only one—is price. Generally speaking, older houses are substantially cheaper than new ones, all things considered. For some people, this makes the older house a necessity, not a matter of choice. If you have a large family and need a four-bedroom home, for example, it is likely that there will be a substantial difference in cost between a new house and an old one.

However, price may not be the only reason for preferring an older home. Often, the community you choose may be a neighborhood of older homes, with little or no land available for the construction of new houses. What land is available may consist of isolated lots; and a new house would, of necessity, have to be custom-built, which would cost considerably more than an older home, or even a new home in a development.

In considering the space you need, remember to distinguish between actual space and usable space. Many older homes have a great deal of wasted space. Newer homes generally are built in more compact fashion. Because of current high construction costs, most builders make use of every square foot of space. Therefore, if you are considering an older house, be sure that it has the *usable* space you require. Don't be deceived into thinking it has more space than the new house merely because it covers a larger area.

An older home also generally needs repairs and rehabilitation. A modern tiled bathroom and a streamlined efficient kitchen will cost several thousand dollars. Be sure to add the cost of these repairs to the purchase price to determine the true cost of the house.

Warning. Few people know enough about construction to estimate the cost of repairs and usually underestimate them. Before you buy an older house, you should get the advice of an expert, a professional builder or architect, who can tell you what you'll have to spend. In addition to the obvious items, such as a new kitchen or bathroom, he can inspect the plumbing and wiring and advise you as to their condition, and thus protect you from an unanticipated major expense.

When you have computed the purchase price of the older house plus the required repairs and alterations, you can then determine whether the house is a good buy compared to the new houses you have seen. The total cost of the older house should be substantially less than a new house with about the same space—at least 20% lower —before you should even consider its purchase.

One compensating cost factor is that the landscaping of an older house has usually been completed. The cost of landscaping is considerable, and most new homes provide, at best, only partial landscaping.

In discussing cost, we have not mentioned the land. Obviously, land costs vary, and the same house in one location may cost a good deal more or less in another location. Whether buying an older house or a new house, you can best determine the value of the land the way professional builders and architects do: by comparing the prices of other parcels of land in the area. When you get a price on a parcel of vacant land, be sure to consider the cost of clearing the property. This is a cost you won't have to meet when you buy an older house, or a new house in a development, or one already constructed.

On the face of it, this discussion of houses points out the seeming advantages of new ones. They contain all the modern conveniences most housewives want, such as modern kitchens and bathrooms. Space is efficiently utilized, and there is generally a choice of models to suit everyone's taste. You can choose a full dining room, or have a living-dining combination which cuts down the cost. There is no problem of repairs in the immediate future, so the price you pay is your total price.

The biggest disadvantage is the higher price you pay for a new home. But there is the consideration that when and if you resell, a higher price may be obtained. Of course, none of this takes into account the general spaciousness and charm that older houses often have and, unfortunately, many newer houses lack.

Another financial advantage in buying a new house is that more favorable mortgage terms are generally available. Mortgage interest rates are generally somewhat lower on new houses than on older ones. As we have seen, this difference can come to a substantial amount over the life of the mortgage, which often goes by with surprising speed.

In addition to the lower interest cost, new-home buyers generally obtain a longer payoff period on their mortgage. This longer period results in lower monthly payments, perhaps as low as those on a less costly older house. Of course, you'll have to pay off for a greater number of years, and whether you want to do so is something that only you can decide.

In making your final decision as to whether to choose a new house or an older one, one factor will outweigh everything else. As emphasized previously, location may well be the most important of all considerations. Make certain that the house you choose is in the neighborhood you like best, one that will give you the kind of life you are looking forward to. When you choose a house, you are also choosing your neighbors, your potential friends, the schools your children will attend and the friends they will make, and all the intangibles that make living in a house a way of life rather than merely shelter. Make sure your house gives you the way of life you are looking for.

Signing a Contract

Once you've made up your mind to buy a particular house, and have agreed with the seller on a price, a contract of sale must be signed. Even if you wish to, a house cannot be bought like a fur coat or an automobile, paying the cash and immediately getting title and possession. That is because a house is real property, not personal property, and is subject to special laws.

Buying a house involves many details that take time and effort.

Most important of all, the title will have to be checked carefully. The seller may have an existing mortgage, and you (or your lawyer) will have to check on the unpaid balance. There may also be other claims against the house (lawyers call them *encumbrances*). There may possibly be a mechanic's lien for work done on the house and still unpaid. Even if it's paid off in fact, you'll want it cleared on the record before you take possession of the house. A tenant may conceivably be in possession. If he has a lease, you won't be able to get possession until the lease expires. Even if he doesn't have a lease, you may have to spend time and money to get possession. All of these points indicate the complexities involved in purchasing a house and seeing that the contract is properly drawn.

Of utmost importance is the fact that you'll probably need a mortgage to help pay for the house. That takes time. The lender will want to check the validity of the title, and the value of the house, to determine the amount he's willing to lend, and he'll want to check your personal credit too.

A contract of sale helps to resolve some of these difficulties. It assures you that you'll get the house you want at the price you've agreed on. It gives you time to check the title and to arrange for a mortgage. But it also does something else. *It binds you to go through with the deal,* if the seller can deliver what the contract calls for.

So, before you sign a contract of sale, you must know exactly what you're signing and what the consequences are. It is always advisable to hire an attorney *before* you sign a binder or a contract of sale. The problems are so varied and so complex that the home buyer is not equipped to handle them himself.

Although it is impossible to foresee every contingency, you should assist yourself by knowing what the legal problems are. At the very least it will point out why you need the professional guidance of an attorney *before* entering into a contract.

The Deposit. Generally, when you sign a contract to buy a house, you'll be required to make a substantial deposit, often as much as 10% of the total price. Assuming that you later find out that you can't get a satisfactory mortgage to purchase the house, what happens to your deposit? If the contract says nothing on this point, the seller will usually refuse to return it. He will claim, and successfully, that the deposit is forfeited as damages for your failure to go through with the contract. Even if you go to court and possibly win, you will lose both time and money.

A properly-drawn contract of sale can, of course, protect you in such a situation, and many other situations not easily foreseen by most purchasers. It can provide that your deposit is to be returned, and that you are to be released from your agreement to buy the house, if you can't get a satisfactory mortgage.

Why can't you frame such a mortgage clause yourself without the assistance of a lawyer? It is theoretically possible, but as a practical matter it is much more complicated than it appears. Here's an example:

You enter into a contract for the purchase of a house. The contract provides, at your insistence, that the deal may be cancelled and your deposit returned if you do not obtain a "satisfactory" mortgage. A lender offers you a mortgage at 6% interest, to be paid off in 20 years. According to your calculations, you need 30 years to bring the monthly payments down to a satisfactory figure. Can you refuse to go through with the deal? Is that a "satisfactory" mortgage that compels you to buy the house, or must you default and lose your deposit? Obviously, there's no definite answer to this question. The main point is that such a question should never arise. A good contract of sale will spell out specifically all the details that will protect you, such as the interest rate, the length of the mortgage, and all the other details that can lead to disagreement and a lawsuit.

Will the seller sign such a contract that protects you, the buyer? If he's acting in good faith, and most sellers do, there is no reason for him to refuse. The same contract that protects you also protects him, by closely defining the terms of sale. He can, for instance, insert a clause that allows *him* to find a mortgage that meets the terms you want, or, if he wishes, to take back a mortgage himself for the balance over the down payment.

Here's another typical, knotty problem that may arise. At the time you are to take title to the property, the seller offers you a deed. Generally speaking, a warranty deed is always far better than a quitclaim deed (a subject we'll discuss later). Suppose the seller's deed to you is a quitclaim deed, an almost completely unsatisfactory type of deed. Can you refuse to accept it and insist on a warranty deed? In many states, the buyer must take a quitclaim deed if the contract of sale does not specify a warranty deed. But the question will never arise if a contract of sale is drawn up by an attorney who is familiar with the problems involved in the purchase of a house and who will make certain that the contract contains a clause giving you a warranty deed, if that is what you want.

Printed Forms. The seller may ask you, at the time both parties agree on the price, to sign a printed form of the type that can be purchased in stationery stores. One objection to such forms is that they are written to cover a general situation and there may be a specific situation in your case that it does not consider. Also, such forms have a tendency in their wording to favor sellers, since sellers are generally the purchasers of these forms. As a matter of fact, many sellers who are active in real estate have special printed forms prepared by their own attorneys; such forms will naturally be more favorable to the seller than to the buyer. It is customary for sellers to tell potential buyers that the printed form "doesn't mean anything." As a matter of fact, the reverse is true; it means a great deal and is completely binding, so don't sign it regardless of how innocent you may think the wording is. Also, don't give the seller a check for any amount as a "token of good faith," even if the seller tells you he won't deposit it and will return it if you change your mind. To be definite: don't sign anything except the formal contract with all the terms of sale carefully spelled out.

Let us assume another situation that frequently occurs: the potential buyer doesn't sign anything, but he agrees orally with the seller to buy the house. The deal is sealed with a handshake. This oral agreement is of no effect whatsoever. The law wisely provides that an agreement for the sale of real estate must be in writing; otherwise the deal is not normally enforceable by *either* the seller or the buyer. Even a written agreement under certain circumstances may not be enforceable because it doesn't contain the minimum requirements that the law demands. It is important *not* to give the seller a check as a deposit, particularly if it mentions the deal, since the courts often find this to be a "written agreement."

Although oral agreements are not enforceable, that does not mean that the deal must remain vague and undecided until it is finally put in writing in a lawyer's office. You can help yourself and your lawyer if you agree in advance *orally* on the main essentials of the contract.

Your lawyer will be concerned with protecting your interests and seeing that the contract contains the proper clauses. But it's your job, not your lawyer's, to decide on the price you're willing to pay for the house you want to buy. There's no point in going to him for a written agreement until you have agreed with the seller on the price and the general terms. It's your lawyer's job to see that you get what you've agreed on. You may agree orally, as mentioned before, with the seller on the terms. However, do not put it in writing until you are sure you are fully protected. As discussed previously, but worthy of repetition, do not sign any memorandums or receipts or give any deposits in advance of the signing of the actual contract.

The courts have unanimously refused to enforce oral agreements for the sale of land (that includes the house on the land). Even written agreements have been held unenforceable when they lacked certain minimum requirements. Contract requirements vary from state to state, and it is too complicated to list all the technical details that might arise in the courts. On the other hand, there are a few points that can save litigation and are vital in most states.

Contract Requirements.   1) The seller and the buyer should *both* sign the contract. However, this is not required in every state. In some, if only one party has signed the contract, he can be sued. In these states, if the buyer signs it, the seller can enforce it even if he himself has not signed it; but the buyer can't enforce the contract against the seller. Obviously, this is not a situation the buyer desires, so he should insist that the contracts of sale be signed by both parties.

2) The contract must be definite enough to identify the property being sold. Although it need not be in language as formal as that contained in a deed, it should make *absolutely* clear just what property is being bought and sold. At the very least, it should include the street number, city, and state. Property usually carries a "block and lot" number (found on tax bills, as a rule) and these should also be included in the contract. It's best, however, to give a complete legal description, which is the general practice of most lawyers in preparing a contract of sale.

3) Be sure the wife (or husband) of the owner signs the contract of sale. (This does not apply to sales of houses in a corporate development, or when the builder is a corporation.) In many states, the spouse has rights in the property that cannot be destroyed by a sale of the property. If the wife (or husband) has not signed the contract of sale and subsequently refuses to sign the deed, you can refuse to go through with the deal, and generally, get your down payment back (after considerable delay and trouble). But that's an unsatisfactory solution after you've spent several months looking for a house and have to begin all over again. If you decide to take title to the house without the second signature (of the other spouse) you may not receive a marketable title. In some states you may sue in court and receive a reduction in the purchase price, but this procedure is unsatisfactory and undesirable.

Note. A very few states still won't let a married woman sign a contract to sell real estate unless her husband also signs. In these states, the contract is void without the husband's signature. That means it's not enforceable by either the seller or the buyer.

4) Be certain the contract is complete—that is, it contains all the essential details that will make it unnecessary to negotiate later. Make sure it includes the purchase price and how it is to be paid (cash, or cash and mortgage). Be sure that if it provides for the seller to take back a purchase-money mortgage, all the terms of the mortgage are spelled out in detail—interest rate, amortization, the date the installments become due, and the termination date of the mortgage.

5) Include the type of deed that is to be given such as warranty or bargain and sale deed.

Some General Thoughts. By now, you should be alerted to the need for legal assistance. A contract for the sale of real estate is not a simple paper to be signed casually. It binds you to the payment of many thousands of dollars. Often it is the largest single purchase of a lifetime, and the moderate fee of an expert in such matters is a small price to pay for the protection received.

This basic premise holds true even if the seller is willing to sign a contract that requires no down payment or one so small that you wouldn't mind losing it should you change your mind. Once you've signed the contract, you're legally responsible for the consequences; and it is not always possible to avoid this, even if you forfeit your deposit. The seller can (and often does) bring suit for breach of contract, and you may find that the loss of your small deposit has grown into an expensive litigation involving thousands of dollars simply because you didn't go through with your legal obligation to buy the property. Even a small deposit may cause you untold headaches and expenses. Once again—never give a deposit, never sign a memorandum or "binder," without being sure that you are legally protected.

CHAPTER 15

Title Closing

Title is *closed* when the deed transferring ownership of the property is delivered by the seller, and the purchase price is paid by the buyer. The purchase price may be paid in full in cash or by check, but more often than not there is only a part payment in cash and the buyer takes the property subject to a mortgage.

The Time and Place of Closing. Ordinarily, the contract of sale sets forth the time and the place of closing title. There are times when these details are omitted from the contract, unintentionally or on purpose. If this happens, either the buyer or the seller must notify the other and give him a reasonable time to prepare for the closing of title. Of course, the time and place of closing of title may be changed by agreement between the buyer and seller; and very often this occurs, because not all of the details can be cleared up in time for the planned closing date.

Your attorney will usually contact the mortgage-lending institution, the attorney for the seller, and the title company, to fix a convenient date for title to close. The time and place of closing is then orally agreed on, or letters may be exchanged between the various parties to confirm the date of closing.

Even though the time of the closing has been specified in the contract of sale, either the buyer or the seller may notify the other that he desires to delay the date of closing of title. If either request a *brief* adjournment (say, for a week), it is extremely difficult to refuse. However, sometimes a party may request a delay for an unreasonable period of time (two or three months, for example). Either party can, if he wishes, accede to a request for such a long delay in closing title. Occasionally, a party may say that he will refuse to close title if a long adjournment is not granted. The best way to compel another party to close the title is by notifying him in writing (preferably by registered mail) that you are ready to close title on the specified day and that no further adjournment will be permitted.

Should the other party fail to appear at the time and place set for the closing, after such notice, his default should be noted and a formal offer to complete the contract of sale should also be made by the party present. This means the buyer offers to make payment in the presence of witnesses, and the seller's failure to appear and his consequent inability to furnish a deed to the premises would be noted. On the other hand, if the buyer fails to appear, the seller should make a token offer of the deed in the presence of witnesses, and inasmuch as the buyer is not present, there would be no payment of the purchase price. At this point, the contract of sale has not been fulfilled by the party failing to appear and a legal action could therefore be commenced against him. However, if the party who did not appear for the title closing has a good reason for not doing so (illness, etc.), the court may nevertheless allow extra time for the closing, as previously mentioned. One of the touchiest and most difficult questions to decide, if either the seller or buyer requests an adjournment of the closing or fails to appear, is whether to take a default or accede to the request for an adjournment, even though it is unwarranted. This is a matter that will have to be decided by your attorney. It is seldom advisable to refuse a brief adjournment and attempt to take a default if either side requests a short adjournment of the closing.

Nevertheless, it is vitally important that the time of closing be fixed with some degree of certainty. For example, if you are buying a new house and also selling your old one, the time of closing title to your new home may become vital. (This is discussed in more detail elsewhere in this book.) The purchaser of your old house may insist on closing title on a certain specified day, and this means that you must move from your old house on or before that day. If the seller of your new house does not close title on the day specified in your contract, and move before that date, and you have made plans to move in, it may become necessary for your family to move in with relatives, take rooms in a hotel, or arrange other temporary accommodations, until the seller is ready to close title. Your furniture will have to be placed in storage during this period, constituting an added expense and inconvenience. To avoid this awkward situation, it is suggested that the date of the closing be specified in the contract of sale, and that it be followed by the words "time being of the essence." If the seller does not object to this wording, it means that he must close title on the day specified or be responsible for any losses that you sustain. However, as a rule, the seller's attorney will object to the use of such strong affirmative wording, on the grounds that it is unfair to the seller. As a compromise, it is occasionally possible that the seller's attorney will agree to a "day certain" for title to close, and that if it does not close on that day, the seller must pay a sum of money to the buyer, usually at a daily rate, to compensate the buyer for any expenses that he may incur. This, in effect, provides a penalty to the seller for delaying the closing of title, and it is not likely that he will wish to incur this additional expense. There is then a strong incentive for the seller to make sure that he closes title on the precise day specified in the contract. The amount by which the seller becomes responsible to the buyer is usually fixed at approximately $20.00 per day on a typical small house, but may be more or less depending on the price and other circumstances. It might well be $100.00 a day on a very expensive house. If the seller refuses to agree to this provision, the buyer must take his chances that the seller will close title on the day specified in the contract.

The Actual Closing of Title. The closing of title is a meeting of the interested parties and their attorneys, at which time the legal documents are executed and transferred and the appropriate payments are made.

Persons Present at the Closing. The closing of title takes place at one of the following places: the office of the mortgage-lending institution, at the title company, or at the office of the attorney for the seller. The buyer and seller are present (often with their spouses) as well as the respective attorneys for the parties. If a mortgage is being made to the buyer by a mortgage-lending institution, an attorney for the mortgage lender will also be there. Also present at the closing will be a title closer from the title company. In some states the title is searched by the attorney for the buyer, in which case a title closer will not be required. If a broker brought about the transaction, he will usually make it a point to be present, in order to collect his commission from the seller. The broker will be required to give a paid bill to the seller as a receipt for the payment of his brokerage fees.

It is the purpose of this chapter to acquaint you with the people, the documents to be executed, and in addition, with the procedures that are customarily followed at the closing of title.

Identity of Persons at the Closing. It is always advisable to be sure that the persons who appear at the closing and say that they are the buyer (or seller) are, in fact, such parties. In most cases, there is little doubt of the person's identity; but there have been cases in which mortgages were executed and money paid and yet the documents were not actually signed by the proper party. Reasonable care must be taken to determine the identity of each person present. Large sums of money are changing hands at a title closing; and although mistakes are not frequently made, even one such mistake can be costly.

The easiest way to determine whether the buyer and the seller are the individuals named in the contract of sale is to require them to produce identification. The seller will probably have a prior deed, a receipt for taxes on property, a title policy, or an insurance policy to show that he is, in fact, the correct party in interest. As a rule, however, the attorneys present will identify the buyer and seller, and this should ordinarily be sufficient.

Documents Required at the Closing. The attorney representing the buyer must carefully check the written documents that the seller delivers to the buyer. In every case, this will include a deed transferring ownership to the buyer, and unless the property is purchased free and clear of a mortgage, a mortgage and a mortgage note (or bond) to be signed by the buyer.

Of course, particular emphasis must be placed on the deed. The deed should be a perfect copy, and it is advisable that it should not contain any erasures or even minor corrections. The buyer is entitled to a perfect deed to the property and one that conforms to the requirements of the contract of sale.

In many title closings, the buyer pays part of the purchase price by executing a purchase-money mortgage in favor of the seller, to secure payment of a portion of the purchase price. The purchase-money mortgage is usually prepared by the attorney for the seller. The buyer's attorney will carefully read this document to make sure that it conforms to the requirements set forth in the contract of sale and contains the appropriate provisions.

Other Papers Required. If the seller or the buyer is a corporation and not an individual, it is prudent to obtain a copy of a resolution of the board of directors of the selling corporation authorizing the transaction, and also a certificate of the Secretary of the corporation that the consent of at least 2/3rds of the stockholders has been obtained. After title has been closed, there can be no objection by a director or stockholder to the transaction, if such certificates have been obtained.

If personal property (refrigerator, garden furniture, etc.) is to be transferred by the seller to the buyer and it is not included in the contract of sale, the buyer may wish to obtain a bill of sale from the seller. This is a simple written document signed by the seller specifying that the seller owns the property listed and that he is transferring it to the buyer. Sometimes the purchase price for the personal property may be separate from the purchase price in the contract of sale.

If the buyer decides to take title and retain the existing mortgage which the seller has on the house, the *precise* amount (computed to the last penny) of the mortgage principal remaining unpaid may be credited to the buyer as part of the purchase price which he pays. The seller, or his attorney, usually contacts the mortgage lender several weeks before the closing and obtains a written statement on the lender's stationery of the exact amount of mortgage principal owed as of the date of closing. The mortgage lender will usually reply by letter setting forth the amount of the balance due on the mortgage. If this letter is signed by an officer of the mortgage-lending institution, it is usually acceptable at the closing for the purpose of determining the mortgage principal that remains unpaid. Sometimes the buyer will insist on a more formal document to fix the amount unpaid with certainty. In these cases, the officer of the mortgage-lending institution will sign an *estoppel certificate* which recites the amount of the mortgage and the amount that has been paid to date, leaving a balance due to the mortgage lender as of that date. This document is acknowledged before a notary public and is usually recorded in the land office of the county in which the real property is located. It thereafter prevents the mortgage-lending institution from claiming that any further sums (over and above the amount specified in the certificate) are due on the mortgage, because they are "estopped" from doing so.

All recent tax bills affecting the real property should be delivered by the seller to the buyer at the closing. These may include school taxes or city, county, village or town tax bills, depending on the locality and the nature of local taxes. There is sometimes a water or sewer tax bill as well; water or sewer bills that have been paid by the seller in advance are also turned over to the buyer at the closing. Any prepayment by the seller should be adjusted as of the closing date in the same manner as are taxes on the property. Wherever possible, these tax bills should show a receipt of payment from the seller on a certain day so that the buyer will not be required to pay these bills (or any penalty or interest that may have accrued due to the seller's failure to pay on time). The seller usually pays for the entire tax period in advance and the buyer will make an adjustment with the seller for any time within the tax period that he occupies the house. (This will be discussed subsequently.)

The seller should transfer to the buyer ownership of all insurance policies that affect the house at the closing. Usually this is limited to fire insurance and extended coverage including hail, windstorm, and other damage caused by an act of God. A public-liability policy protecting the seller from any lawsuit brought by a third person, claiming an injury was due to the seller's negligence, may *not* be transferred at the closing. It is considered personal to the seller, and insurance of this type should be obtained by the purchaser as a new policy. The transfer of ownership of the insurance policies may be made by calling the insurance broker, who in turn notifies the insurance company and confirms the transfer by letter some days later.

At the closing, the title company representative usually notifies the buyer that a title policy will be issued by the title company which will protect the mortgage lender (if the buyer has obtained his own mortgage loan) and also the buyer from any claim of ownership to the property by some third party. As a rule, the title policy is not ready for delivery to the buyer at the time of the closing; it is mailed to his attorney several weeks later. Until that time the title report, which shows that there is no objection to the title or that any objection has been waived by the title company, will be retained by the buyer or his attorney, pending the more formal certificate of the insurance. (Title insurance is discussed in more detail at the end of the chapter on insurance.)

Another set of papers may be required in order to furnish the buyer with a satisfactory legal title. These papers depend on the title search and what it reveals in relation to the property. Often the title search will reveal objections to a clear title or possible encumbrances.

Escrows. Escrows are frequently used when title to real estate is closed. By definition, escrow means that some third party (who is usually not personally or financially interested in the transaction), is asked to hold the article until the happening of a certain event. When that event happens, he will then transfer that article either to another party, or back to you, as provided in the agreement. Any article of personal property, but in particular money, deeds, and mortgages, may be placed in escrow.

On occasion there may be certain objections to the transfer of title that appear at the closing, such as a judgment against the seller or an unpaid tax or old mortgage that has not been satisfied before the closing. In such instances, it is usually possible to place an amount of money equal to the amount owed by the seller on the unsatisfied judgment, tax, or mortgage, in the hands of a third person until the objection to title has been cleared. When that occurs, these monies will be turned over to the seller by the escrow agent—the party holding the funds. However, in the event the seller does not succeed in clearing the outstanding objection, the buyer may find that he must pay this sum for the seller. In such case, rather than reach into his own pocket and pay off the amount owed, he may call on the escrow agent to release the money he is holding to pay such outstanding indebtedness of the seller and, in this manner, the buyer may avoid any responsibility for the seller's indebtedness.

The use of the escrow agent resolves many disputes which would otherwise prevent the closing of title. The buyer is well protected, inasmuch as some of the purchase price that would ordinarily go directly to the seller is held by a third party until the seller complies with the provisions of the escrow agreement, after which the funds are turned over to him. If the seller refuses or is unable to carry out the provisions of the escrow agreement, a portion of the purchase price has been held by the escrow agent for just this purpose and has never passed into the hands of the seller. The result is that the indebtedness is paid off without an additional burden to the purchaser.

The escrow agreement will usually contain the names of the buyer and the seller and the name of the escrow agent. In addition to cash deposits with the escrow agent, deeds, insurance policies, service contracts, mortgages and mortgage notes may all be held in escrow by an escrow agent until the happening of a certain condition. The conditions of the escrow agreement are then stated in detail, with directions as to what is to be done with the items held in escrow when a certain condition occurs (or does not occur) within a certain specified time.

Occasionally the escrow agent will charge for his services, but usually a third party can be found who is trusted by both the buyer and the seller who will hold the money or documents without charge. This is especially true in the case of an attorney for either the buyer or the seller who may accommodate his client by holding money or documents in escrow. Frequently, a title company will act as the escrow agent, usually for a moderate fee. When a deed is held in escrow, the transfer of title is not completed until the terms of the escrow agreement are fulfilled and the deed itself is delivered to the buyer. In many western states, particularly California, real estate deals are frequently made by "going escrow." Various institutions are authorized by the state to act as escrow agents, and the contract is made and title passes hands in this fashion.

Encumbrances that Affect Closing of Title.   An *encumbrance* may be a mortgage on the property, a judgment affecting the premises, a mechanic's lien, an unpaid tax or assessment, or even a restrictive convenant that affects the property. If the buyer accepts the deed while there are encumbrances on the property, he may be required to expend large sums of money which the seller, rather than the buyer, really owes. As soon as an encumbrance is uncovered, the seller should be notified in writing and given a reasonable time to remove the encumbrance or objection to the title. This may usually be accomplished (if the encumbrance is only a money obligation) by paying the mortgage, judgment, lien, or taxes that affect the property. However, it is not likely that a restrictive convenant, not mentioned in the contract of sale, may be readily removed, and therefore the buyer may decide not to take title to the premises. It is possible that the seller will agree to a reduction of the purchase price if he is unable to remove the encumbrance.

The encumbrance most frequently encountered is unpaid taxes; taxes of all sorts should be paid before the closing. Where there is an existing mortgage affecting the premises, and a new mortgage is to be placed on the property, the seller may not have sufficient funds to pay it off before the closing of title. Usually the holder of the mortgage will appear at the title closing or, in the alternative, authorize the title company to accept payment for the balance due on the mortgage at the closing from the seller, and also request the title company to file a satisfaction of the mortgage on behalf of the mortgage lender. In this way the encumbrance will surely be removed within a reasonable time after the closing of title. Another method of disposing of a money encumbrance (when it is difficult to obtain a satisfaction or discharge at the time of closing) is for the seller to make a deposit in *escrow* with the attorney for the buyer, or with the title company representative, of a sum of money sufficient to pay off and discharge the encumbrance. The buyer should insist that the full amount (or even somewhat more) be deposited, under an agreement that any balance not used to obtain the discharge of the encumbrance will be refunded to the seller. In the case of unpaid taxes, there is always the possibility that additional interest will be required to satisfy the obligation.

The contract of sale usually provides that encumbrances discovered by a title search may be disregarded at the closing, providing the seller deposits a suitable sum of money with the buyer or the title company representative, and that such encumbrances shall not be an objection to title if this is done. Such deposits with the buyer or the title company representative are generally effective to pay off mortgages or mechanic's liens that affect the property. Of course, as stated previously, this applies only to unpaid money matters—not to legal objections to titles.

If the title search reveals an *objection to title,* the seller's attorney should be notified in writing immediately, as far as possible in advance of the date of title closing. The seller (through his attorney) will then make an effort to remove this objection prior to the closing of title. Often, objections are merely simple matters, involving mistaken identity, and merely involve an affidavit by the seller that he is not the same person (as the title search indicates) who has a judgment of record against him, and who, by coincidence, has the same name as the seller. On the other hand, it might be a very difficult problem for the seller to remove an important legal objection to title. For example, the title report may show that a person in the chain of title had died during ownership of property, or that there had been a defective foreclosure proceeding. In such case, a will might have to be probated, or a foreclosure proceeding may have to be re-opened in order to name a defendant who was omitted in an earlier proceeding. These are merely examples of time-consuming and expensive proceedings that might have to be taken to correct the objection to title. Therefore, the buyer may refuse to take the "cloudy" title, or the buyer may take the title if the seller agrees to a reduction of the purchase price and the buyer is willing to assume the risk of taking title under the circumstances.

If there are no objections to title, no encumbrances affecting the property (or if all objections and encumbrances have been removed or will be removed to the satisfaction of the buyer at the closing), the title closing is ready to proceed.

Adjustments in the Amount to Be Paid by the Buyer. The contract of sale specifies the purchase price that the buyer will pay to the seller. Usually a portion of the purchase price is paid on the signing of the contract as a down payment, and receipt of this down payment is acknowledged by its seller in the contract of sale. The balance of the purchase price must be paid to the seller at the closing of title. Of course, the buyer may take the property subject to an existing mortgage, or by delivering to the seller a purchase-money mortgage for a part of the balance of the purchase, as previously mentioned. Nevertheless, there will inevitably be a certain sum of money due to the seller (represented by the difference between the selling price and the deposit plus the amount of the mortgage). In addition, there are always adjustments of the purchase price at the closing of title and the buyer may have to pay additional sums other than those specified in the contract sale. There are also allowances the seller must make to the buyer which will change the stated purchase price in the contract of sale. All of these adjustments are computed by the attorneys for the respective parties at the closing.

Closing Statements. At the closing of title the attorneys for the buyer and seller each prepare closing statements—that is, a financial accounting. The purchaser is charged with the various amounts he is required to pay, and in turn is credited with the amounts that have been paid (or with payments the seller is required to make). The difference between these two amounts is the sum that the buyer pays in cash. It may seem difficult, at first, to understand all of the various adjustments made at a title closing. It is always advisable for the attorneys for the buyer and seller to consult with each other and with their clients before the closing of title so that many of the debits and credits are agreed on before the closing of title. This will save time and help to make the closing of title run smoothly. Frequently, however, the attorneys are too busy to do this, and the actual computations are delayed until the day of closing.

The forms to be used for a closing statement sometimes appear on the back of the contract of sale. These forms list all the credits to the buyer and to the seller.

A typical closing statement for the purchase of a residential home is as follows:

Closing Statement
Premises 9905 Central Avenue
New Rochelle, New York

Title to 9905 Central Avenue, New Rochelle, New York, Section 3147, Lot 30, Westchester County, was conveyed on September 22, 1964, pursuant to a written contract dated August 4, 1964, between Henry Blake and Edith Blake, his wife, as Sellers, and Harold Davis and Jean Davis, his wife, as Purchasers. The closing took place at the offices of McGrath & Ballentine, attorneys, 1271 Park Avenue, New York, New York, at 2 P.M.

PRESENT AT THE CLOSING

HAROLD and JEAN DAVIS, Purchasers
HENRY and EDITH BLAKE, Sellers
STANLEY COLE, Attorney for Purchasers
GEORGE MCGRATH, Attorney for Sellers
WALTER WELCH, Title Closer for Title Guarantee and Trust Company

The following papers and documents, etc. were delivered:

BY THE SELLER

1. Bargain and Sale Deed with Covenant against Grantor's Acts.
2. Affidavit of Henry Blake, sworn to September 22, 1964, to the effect that to his knowledge there were no outstanding judgments against Edith Blake or Henry Blake.
3. Letter from Henry Blake to the First Industrial Savings Bank assigning escrow deposit of $264.94 held by First Industrial Savings Bank to Harold and Jean Davis.
4. Keys to premises.
5. Bill of Sale to personal property signed by Henry Blake and Edith Blake.

BY THE PURCHASERS

1. Certified check of Harold Davis to the order of Henry and Edith Blake in the amount of $23,884.42. See end of Statement.
2. Uncertified check of Harold Davis, drawn to the order of Henry and Edith Blake in the amount of $3,500 for personal property.

REVENUE STAMPS

Revenue stamps in the amount of $31.85 are to be attached to the deed by the Title Closer for the Title Company, and a check in that amount was given by Mr. McGrath to Mr. Welch.

INSURANCE

The premises were covered by a policy of Insurance in the face amount of $48,100, covering fire and all physical loss. The policy was for a period of five years, expiring September 2, 1966. The full premium for the five-year period is $527.62. The apportionment from September 22, 1964 to September 2, 1966 (one year, 11 months, 10 days) resulted in a credit to the Seller of $205.17. A certificate of this policy was delivered to the Purchasers by the Seller, and the Purchasers' attorney is arranging to have the policies assigned to the Purchasers.

CITY TAX

The city taxes for the calendar year 1964 were $961.60. Payment for the second half of 1964 in the amount of $480.80 was made on July 11, 1964. This prepayment was apportioned and resulted in a credit for the Seller for the period from September 22, 1964 to December 31, 1964 (3 months, 8 days) of $261.76.

SCHOOL TAX

The school tax for the fiscal year 1964–1965 is $534.00. The first payment was due on October 1, 1964. The school tax was apportioned and resulted in a credit to the Purchaser for the period from July 1, 1964 to September 22, 1964 (2 months, 22 days) or $121.63.

DEED

The deed was a Bargain and Sale Deed with Covenant Against Grantor's Acts, executed September 22, 1964 by Henry Blake and Edith Blake, his wife. Mr. Welch, the Title Closer for Title Company, took the deed for the purpose of recording it. It will be returned to the Purchasers' attorney.

MORTGAGE

There is a first mortgage, executed September 20, 1963 by Henry Blake and Edith Blake, his wife, as mortgagors, to the Industrial Savings Bank, 100 Chambers Street, New York, as mortgagee, originally in the principal amount of $20,000, due on October 1, 1983, with interest at the rate of $4\frac{1}{2}\%$ per annum. At the time of the closing, the principal balance of the mortgage was $19,422.41, which was verified by a letter from the mortgagee dated September 8, 1964. The Purchasers took title subject to the first mortgage.

ESCROW ACCOUNT

The escrow account held by the Industrial Savings Bank in the amount of $264.94 was assigned by the Purchasers to the Seller. This resulted in a credit to the Purchaser in the amount of $264.94.

MORTGAGE INTEREST

The principal balance outstanding on the mortgage held by Industrial Savings Bank on September 1, 1964 was $19,422.41. The mortgage interest at the rate of $4\frac{1}{2}\%$ was apportioned for the period from September 1, 1964, to September 22, 1964, and resulted in a credit to the Purchasers of $53.41.

PERSONAL PROPERTY

Personal property listed in a rider to the Contract of Sale was purchased from the Seller by the Purchaser for the amount of $3,500, and payment was made in that amount.

STATEMENT

DEBITS

Purchase Price	$47,500.00
Real Property Company, fire and physical loss policy, face amount $48,100—5 years, expiring September 2, 1966, total premium $527.62; apportionment from September 22, 1964, to September 2, 1966, 1 year 11 months, 10 days	205.17
Escrow held by Industrial Savings Bank	264.94

City tax for calendar year ending December 31, 1964, $961.60; second half prepaid July 11, 1964, $480.80; apportionment from September 22, 1964, to December 31, 1964   261.76

| | Total Debits | | $48,231.87 |

CREDITS

Paid on signing of contract $ 4,750.00

Mortgage, Industrial Savings Bank, principal due and payable October 1, 1983, at 4½% per annum; principal balance, September 22, 1964   19,422.41

Mortgage interest; apportionment from September 1, 1964 to September 22, 1964   53.41

School tax for fiscal year 1964–1965, $534; apportionment from July 1, 1964 to September 22, 1964   121.63

Total Credits $24,347.45

Certified check of Harold Davis required to close title $23,884.42

$48,231.87

Explanation of Closing Statement. The first charge against the purchasers is the entire purchase price, appearing under the heading of Debits.

In turn, the purchasers are entitled to a credit for the amount which they have paid on the signing of the contract as a down payment, and this appears as the first item under Credits.

Returning to Debits, the second item is an adjustment of the insurance policy, previously paid for (in advance) by the sellers, and they are entitled to a refund of the unused portion of the premium. The sellers are also entitled to a credit for the moneys they have on deposit with the bank in the escrow account in the amount of $264.94. When the present purchasers sell the house, they, in turn, will receive credit for the value of the escrow account from their purchasers. The last item appearing under Debits is an adjustment of city taxes; since these are partially paid in advance, the sellers are entitled to a refund.

Under Credits, we have already discussed the first item. The second entry covers the current amount remaining due under the mortgage, because the purchasers are assuming payment of this sum, and therefore are entitled to be credited with this figure. The mortgage interest is computed separately in the next entry, and the purchasers are entitled to receive a credit for a portion of the month, since the interest is not paid until the end of the month, and the sellers have lived in the house a part of the month, without having paid for their share of the interest. The next item is the school tax, which also results in a credit for the purchasers because the sellers have lived in the house a portion of the tax year without paying the tax.

Finally, the difference between the Credits and the Debits represents the amount required to be paid by the purchasers in order to close title.

Other Matters That Arise at a Closing

Computing Interest and Other Adjusted Amounts. The custom is that adjustments of interest and taxes are made as of the day immediately preceding the day on which title is closed. In computing interest or any other adjustable item, the 360-day method is used; thus, each month represents 1/12th of the annual charge and each day 1/30th of the monthly charge. However, this rule is not always observed; on occasion the buyer or the seller may request a computation based on a 365-day year and the number of days in the particular month. If there is no provision in the contract which provides that customary rules shall be followed, the buyer or the seller may insist on such a procedure. As a rule, the difference between the two methods of computing adjustments is not substantial.

Mortgage payments are usually made on the first day of the month. This payment usually includes interest due for the preceding month. For example, the interest paid on September 1 is the interest due for the preceding month of August. It follows that a closing during the month of September (for example, on September 15), means that the seller has not paid the interest on the mortgage for the first 15 days of the month of September while the seller occupied the home. The next monthly payment of interest on the mortgage is due on October 1. When the buyer pays this sum he will be paying not only for the 15 days of September in which he occupied the home, but also for the 15 days of the month when the seller occupied the home. There is, then, a credit due to the purchaser for 15 days of interest on the mortgage which the seller must allow at the closing of title since the purchaser must pay this sum to the holder of the mortgage on the property.

Purchase Money Mortgage. If the purchaser gives the seller a purchase-money bond and mortgage, the full sum of the bond and mortgage will be entered as a credit to the purchaser.

Taxes. The taxes on the house are also apportioned between the buyer and seller in the same manner that the interest on the mortgage is apportioned. Real-estate taxes are local taxes that vary from community to community. For example, there is almost certainly a school tax, and there may also be county, town, city, or village taxes. Local taxes that affect your house are not levied in a uniform fashion. For example, the school tax may be on a fiscal-year basis; that is, the amount paid may cover a period from July 1 in the current year to June 30 of the next year. Another local tax, such as the city tax affecting real property, may run on a calendar-year basis, covering the period from January 1 to December 31. Further, such local taxes are usually divided into two payments, each covering a period of six months. As a result, you might have to pay one-half of the city tax on January 1 and the second half on July 1; and you might be required to pay the first half of the school tax on April 1 and the second half on October 1.

It is customary for the seller to pay such taxes (if due) for the entire half-year, although he knows that the house has been sold and that the closing of title will take place before the end of that 6-month period. This means that he is entitled to an adjustment in his favor for any prepaid taxes from the time title is closed to the end of that particular half year. Usually taxes are apportioned on the half-year basis. If, as in our example, the buyers take title to the home on September 22, there would be an apportionment of the city tax for the period from July 1 to September 22, since the sellers had paid in full for a six-month period from July 1 to December 31. The buyers must therefore give the sellers credit for 8 days of the month of September and the entire months of October, November, and December, during which the buyers own the home and will pay no school tax because the sellers, in effect, had prepaid it for them. It is important to obtain satisfactory proof that the taxes have been paid by the seller. The best evidence of this is the paid or receipted tax bill. If this cannot be obtained, the title company will search the records to determine whether the most recent tax bill has been paid by the seller.

Water Rates. Although the water charges or sewer taxes on real property will usually not be substantial in amount (except in certain Western states where water is expensive), these charges are adjusted at the closing. If the seller has prepaid a portion of the water rates or the sewer taxes, he is entitled to a credit for the amount prepaid at the date of closing of title.

Insurance. It is the established custom for the buyer to take over any insurance policies that have been placed on the property by the seller during his occupancy, but this may depend on the terms of the contract of sale. If the buyer is not required to accept the transfer of existing insurance policies, the seller may cancel them at the short-rate cancellation basis and obtain a refund for any prepaid insurance premium; but short-rate cancellations cost the seller a pro-rata loss in the value of the policy. If the buyer takes over the policies, it is important to ascertain whether the insurance policy is still in effect at the time of the closing, and that the premiums have indeed been prepaid. This can be done by contacting the insurance broker, whose name usually appears on the cover of the insurance policy.

However, insurance that is transferrable at the closing of title (and for which premiums are adjusted) does not necessarily include insurance of the seller's personal property or a public-liability insurance policy. As a rule, only fire-insurance policies and other hazard or risk policies that affect the house are transferable. Public-liability policies, which insure owners against lawsuits initiated by persons receiving injuries while on the premises, are rarely transferable.

Fuel. In most cases there is some fuel in the house at the time of closing. The fuel may consist of coal, oil, or gas and may be used not only for heat but also for hot water or cooking. In the case of coal or oil, an estimate should be made of the supply of fuel left in the house by the seller, and this amount should be credited to the seller at the usual market price. In the case of city gas or electric heating, there is no reserve supply of fuel furnished by the seller and therefore no adjustment would be made.

Closing Statement. The various items of credits and debits should be set forth in the financial statement, as in the sample set forth above. The difference between the credits and debits indicates the amount that the purchaser must pay in cash at the time of closing. As a rule, the buyer's attorney will, in advance, make a rough estimate of the amount of money actually required to close title. Inasmuch as the *precise* amount can rarely be determined until the actual day of the closing (computing such items as the value of the fuel in the house, for example), it is advisable to obtain a *certified* check for the estimated amount and bring it to the closing. When all of the computations have been completed, the buyer can then write a check for the comparatively small amount to make up any difference. If the certified check is too large, the seller can write a check for this difference. A certified check is always required at a closing because otherwise the seller will refuse to pass title.

Other Amounts to Be Paid by the Buyer. Through custom, the buyer usually must pay certain additional sums of money other than that specified in the contract of sale. If, for example, a purchase-money bond and mortgage has been prepared by the attorney for the seller, the buyer will usually be charged at the closing for the preparation of this bond and mortgage. Although rates differ in various communities, the average payment due to the attorney for the seller for such services is about $20. In many communities, there is a mortgage tax charged by the county land office where the mortgage is recorded. (In New York State, for example, this tax amounts to ½ of 1% of the face amount of the mortgage. The mortgage tax, therefore, on a mortgage for $15,000 would be $75.) This sum is payable at the local county land office. It is usually given to the title closer at the time of the closing, and it is his duty to file the mortgage and pay the mortgage tax.

The buyer must also pay for the recording of the deed. This will probably be a small sum; it is usually computed at about 50¢ per page.

Another tax for which the buyer must pay are the revenue stamps to be attached to the deed. This is a requirement of the federal government. Before any deed may be recorded, revenue stamps in the amount of 55¢ for each $500 of the sale price of the real property must be attached to the deed and marked "cancelled."

As previously mentioned, the buyer must also pay the expenses for the examination of title whether this has been done by an attorney or a title company.

Affidavit of Title. In most states, the buyer or the title company will usually obtain from the seller a sworn statement that the seller is the owner of the home and that he has been in possession of it for a certain period of time. The seller should also state that his possession has been undisturbed by any other person, that his title has never been questioned, that there are no judgments against him, and other similar statements that might bear on his good title.

Signing and Delivering the Documents. After the attorneys for the purchaser and seller have inspected the documents presented by the seller and have approved them, and after the necessary adjustments have been made to the purchase price, there remains only the signing and delivery of the deed, the execution of the mortgage and bond, and of the various other documents. Finally, there is the payment of the balance of the purchase price by the purchaser to the seller.

Usually, payment is made to the seller by a certified check, and most attorneys request that this check be made payable directly to the seller.

Risk of Loss.   Should the house burn down or be damaged by fire or other hazards between the date on which the contract of sale was signed and the date on which title is actually delivered, it would seem that the seller who is still the owner and in possession of the home should sustain the loss. However, in the absence of a statute changing the rule, the risk of loss originally fell on the buyer. If there was no fire insurance on the house and it burned down before the date of closing of title, the buyer would nevertheless have to pay the seller the full purchase price. However, in most states today, statutes have changed this rule and in many states the risk of loss during this period is that of the seller and not the buyer. It is difficult to draw a satisfactory generalization on this point, because the law varies from state to state and title insurance is the best possible protection.

CHAPTER 16

The Land

Property. Property consists of all of the great variety of things that may be owned and used. Legally, it is divided into only two classifications: real and personal property. Land and the buildings on it are real property; everything else is personal property. Personal property includes the overwhelming majority of things that are used in daily life, such as cash, clothing, an automobile, a wristwatch, household furniture, to mention merely a few items. The land, and anything that is part of the land (such as trees and shrubbery), are regarded as real property. This distinction is extremely important to the homeowner.

There are times when personal property may become real property. A chandelier in a store, when it is sold to a customer, is clearly his personal property. But once it is installed in his home, in a permanent manner, as by fastening it to the ceiling, it becomes a part of the real property. Similarly, if a person rents a house and installs (for example) an oil burner, at the termination of the lease the oil burner may not be removed, for it has become a part of the real property and belongs to the landlord. The change from personal to real property may occur with dramatic suddenness. A workman, constructing a house, holds a brick in his hands; at that moment, the brick is personal property. A few moments later, when he has applied mortar to it and placed it on other bricks that go to make up a house under construction, it instantly becomes real property.

On the other hand, there are instances when real property becomes personal property. A tree, standing on the land, is usually regarded as real property. The moment the tree is chopped down and disconnected from the land, it becomes personal property, inasmuch as it is no longer a part of the land.

Whether the property you own is real or personal property, its ownership may be transferred to another person. The sale of personal property—a wristwatch, for example—may be accomplished by merely delivering it to another person in return for an agreed price. The sale of more important articles of personal property—an automobile, for instance—is usually accompanied by a document known as a bill of sale, or an agreement in writing signed by the seller. However, the sale of land is a much more formal affair which, by law, requires the signing of necessary papers by the seller. These papers are recorded in the land or registry office of the county in which the land is located. To understand the important problems that may arise when you sell your real property, you must first understand the nature of land.

The Nature of Land. Land is the surface of the earth, but it does not include the sea or other waters. To a lawyer or a real-estate man the word *land* has acquired a much broader meaning than the actual earth or ground. Land, or real property as it is sometimes called, is not only the ground within certain boundaries which you may own and occupy, but also the buildings, structures, trees, and shrubbery on your land, the minerals underneath your land, and the air space above it. If you own land, your ownership may be described as three dimensional, consisting not only of the surface of the earth, but theoretically extending down to the center of the earth and upward to the heavens.

Improvements on the Land. Any building or structure erected on your land is known as an *improvement* and immediately upon construction becomes a part of your real property. Building materials that are delivered onto your land remain personal property until actually used in the building itself.

Trees and Shrubbery. Trees, plants, bushes, and shrubbery are a part of the land on which they are rooted and from which they draw their support. Grasses and perennials growing on your land are also considered to be real property. However, a different and special problem arises when crops such as potatoes, corn, and wheat are raised on your land. Such crops require annual cultivation, as opposed to perennial trees and shrubbery. Growing crops are generally considered to be personal property (an exception to the usual rule) and may be sold by means of a bill of sale rather than by a formal deed. This rule permits a farmer to sell or mortgage his crops as personal property even before the crops have matured, while retaining ownership of the land on which the crops are planted.

Waters. There are two kinds of water that may be on your land. *Surface waters* take the form of lakes or ponds completely within the boundary lines of your land; they may result from rain or melted snow. You may do what you please with the surface water on your land, for it is considered to be a part of your land. But *natural waters,* such as rivers and streams, that flow across your land or form the boundary of your land are not owned by you alone, but by all of the landowners, upstream and downstream, who own land that adjoins the waterway, even though this may involve many miles and hundreds of owners. Since all of the adjoining landowners have their respective rights to use the river or stream, no single one of them may obstruct the waters in their natural movement and in their normal channel, by daming the river or filling in the bed of the stream, or otherwise interfering with its normal flow. Although a natural waterway may be used to irrigate lands (or for other uses such as turning the water wheel of a mill), substantially all of the water used must be returned to the channel in which the river or stream flows, and no one of the owners may remove substantial amounts of water from the natural waterway or cause an interruption in the flow of the water to the downstream owners.

Air Rights. Many years ago, common law ruled that the owner of real property owned all of the air space over his land up to the heavens. With the advent of airplanes and satellites, however, this rule no longer holds. The modern view appears to be that the owner of real property owns the air space over his land only to the extent that he requires it for the full use of his property. In effect, this permits you to erect as tall a building as you wish, providing it conforms with local zoning laws. It also permits the erection of sixty- and seventy-story buildings in New York City, since the owner of the land theoretically owns all of the air rights above his property. This means that no one may use the air space immediately above your land without your consent; for example, you may compel a neighbor to remove tree branches, wires, the overhang of his garage, or telephone lines that intrude into the air space over your land. However, you do not have ownership to such things that overhang your property even if they are there for long periods of time.

In recent years, especially in urban areas, there has been a great deal of publicity about valuable air rights being sold to building developers. Sometimes these air rights are directly over highways, railroad tracks, or subway yards. The utilization of the land for its original purpose is not hindered, since ample air space is left to the landowner for his requirements. The developer may then construct an apartment or office building in the air space over such facilities, making use of the valuable air rights the landowner had in the air space over his land. Recently the Supreme Court of the United States held that low-flying planes taking off from a municipal airport, and crossing a farmer's land at a height of less than fifty feet, frightening and disturbing his livestock and poultry, actually trespassed on the farmer's land, and he was awarded damages for the wrongful "taking" of his property by the municipality. At this writing, a whole series of other lawsuits by landowners adjacent to large airports are pending in state and federal courts, claiming damages for similar intrusions into the air space of the landowner, which is considered to be a part of the land itself.

Mineral Deposits. Mineral deposits that lie under the surface of the land are also a part of the real property even though no mention of their existence was made in the deed to the property. Obviously, mineral rights are a variable question. In Connecticut, for example, the chance of finding oil under one's property is quite remote, to say the least. In Texas or Oklahoma, on the other hand, mineral rights are an everyday question and are far from being merely theoretical or conjectural. In some states the ownership of minerals under land may be sold apart from the land itself, by special agreement. The sale of oil deposits under the ground creates an interesting and complex problem. Petroleum usually moves from place to place under the ground, and the separate sale of oil rights will transfer nothing to a new owner until the deposit is actually located and the oil removed from the earth. The more usual practice is to allow exploration under the surface of the land by a written agreement called an *oil lease.* This permits an oil company to place drilling rigs on certain described land, but only for a certain period of time. If oil is located and brought to the surface, it belongs to the oil company; but the fortunate owner of such land receives payments, called *royalties,* on every barrel taken from the land.

Boundaries. The boundaries of your land must be fixed with certainty so that you, and others, may know the precise location and exact extent of your land. Boundaries are usually described in the deed to the property. When an error appears in the description of the land, boundary lines become the subject of disagreement and protracted litigation will often result. In such cases, the court will hear the testimony of the buyer and seller and others to determine the exact boundaries of the land. But the court will not rewrite the deed.

Perhaps the easiest way of avoiding errors in the description is to have the new deed closely compared with previous descriptions of the land appearing in prior deeds or title insurance policies.

The boundaries of your land are most often described by what is usually called *metes and bounds*. An example of a description by metes and bounds is as follows:

> Beginning at the corner formed by the intersection of the southerly side of Central Avenue with the easterly side of Linden Street; running thence southerly, along the easterly side of Linden Street, 141.43 feet; thence easterly at right angles to Linden Street, 122.02 feet; thence northerly again parallel with Linden Street, 144.44 feet to the southerly side of Central Avenue; thence westerly along the southerly side of Central Avenue, 122.04 feet to the corner aforesaid, the point or place of beginning.

Another method of describing boundaries of your land (frequently used in rural areas) is to refer to natural or artificial objects on your land known as *monuments*. An example of this type of description might be the following:

> Beginning at the old stone mill at the corner of the southerly side of Central Avenue and running thence southerly along the easterly side of Linden Street to a granite stone marked with the initials G.H.; thence easterly to a stake in front of the old elm tree, thence northerly again to the old water mill; thence westerly along the southerly side of Central Avenue to the point or place of beginning.

The boundaries of your land may also be expressed by referring to "block" and "lot" numbers that have been assigned to the land by the county land office, although this practice may vary from state to state.

A description by metes and bounds is generally regarded to be more reliable, although any method or combination of methods that describes the boundaries of your land with certainty is regarded as sufficient. But remember that boundaries are sometimes determined by means other than description in the deed, such as by adverse possession, discussed subsequently.

When the boundaries of your land are described by using a monument such as a fence, a stake, or a stone wall, the boundary line runs to the exact *center* of the object selected as the monument. However, if a structure or building is used as a monument in a description of the land, it usually is deemed to stand completely within your land and the exact boundary line of the land is the outer wall of the structure selected.

Boundaries on Highways and Streets.   If your land adjoins a highway or street, you may also own the strip of land from the curb line of your property to the center of the street or highway. Of course, ownership of land in the highway is of little practical use to you, unless the public ceases to use it and the municipality decides to return full use of the street or highway to the adjoining owners. Until such time the public has the right to use the street or highway without interference from any adjoining landowner. But, for the purpose of drawing an exact boundary line to your property, the bed of the highway or street to the centerline often is included, and will frequently appear in legal descriptions. Of course, there may be instances where the seller does not transfer his ownership of this strip of land to you. An example of this may be seen in the following description.

> Beginning *at the corner* formed by the intersection of the southerly side of Central Avenue with the easterly side of Linden Street running thence southerly *along the easterly side of Linden Street* . . .

This description provides that the boundary shall run along the *side* of the street and not along the street itself. Such a description allows the seller to retain ownership of the strip of land between the street line and the centerline of the highway, even though he may have no reason for doing so. It should be pointed out, however, that in many cases his own deed did not give him any such rights, and therefore, he has nothing to convey to you. Many times this occurs because the seller and buyer failed to pay proper attention to the language used. Most deeds now contain a provision that the seller gives to the buyer whatever right, title, or interest he may have in the bed of the highway or street to the center line. This usually expresses the intention of the buyer and the seller in most cases. Of course, if the municipality owns the land in the bed of the street or highway, the seller cannot transfer ownership of such land to the buyer.

Water Boundaries.   If your land adjoins a non-tidal body of water, such as a river or stream, the legal boundary line of your land extends *under the water* to the midpoint of the river or stream. Reference in the description to a monument, such as a stake or pier on or near a body of water located on the shoreline, does not prevent ownership of the river bed from passing to the buyer, since it is almost impossible to locate a monument at the center line of a body of water. However, as in the case of adjoining highways and streets, the seller may retain ownership of the land from the shoreline to the midpoint of the body of water, if he expresses the intention of doing so in the deed, or if he does not use proper language to describe the land transferred to the buyer. None of the above applies to tidal waters—that is, those affected by the action of the tides. This covers property facing the ocean, for example.

Avulsion. The sudden loss of your land (*avulsion*) that results from the elements or acts of God will not affect the boundary line of your land. Wherever possible, you may construct a breakwater and attempt to recoup the lost soil or sand and to restore the physical boundary line as it existed before the loss. However, if your land is *gradually* eaten away by the erosion of currents or tides, the boundaries of the land are changed accordingly.

Accretion. The gradual increase in the amount of land which you own resulting from sediment and earth deposited on your land by currents or tides is known as *accretion.* Land added to your property by accretion is considered within the boundary lines of your land, and may, under certain circumstances, add to the size of your property.

The Use of Land

As a landowner you may use your land in any lawful manner and exclude anyone from entering on it. You may be surprised to learn that the ultimate ownership of your land is held by the state itself, at least in theory. However, all states permit individuals to own their own land, and states are not permitted by law to interfere with such ownership unless there is a public purpose for doing so, such as, for example, construction of a new highway. If the state or municipality should require some of your land for a public purpose, you must receive full payment for the land taken from you or adversely affected by such construction.

Needless to say, the most valuable incident of landownership is your right to occupy the land. If you rent your home to another person, you are separating your right to possession from your title to the land for the period of the lease.

It is a maxim of the law that a person in possession and occupation of the land has a better right to possession and ownership than anyone else *except* the true owner. Therefore, at any time, the owner may expel a person who is wrongfully occupying his land. However, the law requires that the owner keep a vigil on his land and not allow wrongful occupation to continue for long periods of time. If a wrongful occupation does continue for more than the period of time provided by statute, the person who has been occupying and using the land for the statutory period may acquire ownership of the land, and the former owner will not be allowed to assert his claim to ownership again. This is known as acquiring title by *adverse possession;* it is discussed later in this chapter.

Transfer of Title. The ownership of land may be transferred in a number of ways. The most usual method, of course, is by a deed in writing. A deed is a written, legal document that describes the land in detail and expresses the intention of the owner to transfer ownership to another. To be effective a deed must be signed by the owner and delivered to the new owner. Usually a deed is acknowledged before a notary public, and is then promptly recorded in the land or register's office of the county where the land is located.

Ownership of real property may also be transferred by a will. A transfer by will is known legally as a *devise.* It is usually accomplished by the executor of the estate delivering a deed to the beneficiary named in the will, after the will has been approved by the court. If the owner of land dies without a will, title passes by law to the heirs of the owner as provided by statute. Usually this means that the ownership of land will pass to the owner's surviving spouse and children in certain proportions, as specified by law. In New York, to use an example, the statute provides that the surviving spouse receives approximately one-third of the estate and the children two-thirds, but statutes of this type differ from state to state.

There are other means of transferring the ownership of land, but they are not so common as the deed or devise. When the owner of a tract of land that is under development sets aside streets or highways for public use, and then surrenders the areas set aside to the local government, the transfer is known as a *dedication.* A *public grant* is the special act of a legislative body transferring ownership of lands owned by the state or federal government to private interests.

Should the owner of land die without a will and without relatives, title to his land passes to the state in which he lives, under the ancient doctrine of *escheat,* although this is uncommon. The state or federal government may also acquire ownership of land by *eminent domain.* This is the right of the state or federal government to take all or part of your land for public use (such as a highway), providing that you are adequately paid for the land that is taken from you.

Adverse Possession. When title to land has been obtained by means of adverse possession there is rarely any deed of record showing that the wrongful occupant has become the true owner. This is because the transfer of title usually occurs by what lawyers call *operation of law* and without legal proceedings of any kind. The statutes either prevent the owner from expelling the wrongful occupant of the land after the statutory period has expired, or prevent the true owner from proving his ownership, after the specified number of years have passed. Most states require that the land be occupied for twenty years before the title of the owner will be extinguished by law. However, some states, such as California, Idaho, and Nevada, prescribe a period of adverse possession of as little as five years. The New York statute originally provided a statutory period of twenty years; but as more and more land within the state was developed, the legislature decided that a period of fifteen years was sufficient time. The longest period of time required by statute in any state is thirty years.

Adverse possession was much more prevalent before the turn of the century than it is today. When the frontiers of the country were virtually uninhabited, and large tracts of land were unoccupied, it was possible for a squatter to occupy someone else's land and claim it as his own, without the knowledge of the owner, for long periods of time. Today, except in mountainous areas and woodlands, it is likely that an owner will soon learn that someone is living on his land without his consent. Usually, the local real-estate broker, a neighbor, or a handyman will keep a vigil for the owner of even large vacant tracts of land and notify him of any unusual occurrences affecting his land. As soon as an owner learns of the wrongful occupation of his land, he should take immediate steps to expel the squatter so that the statutory period will not run against him.

Of course, the occasional squatter or trespasser is not entitled to claim ownership of the land by adverse possession. Only a *continuous* occupation of the land, in a manner that would be obvious to anyone who observed the property, may entitle the wrongful occupant to claim ownership of the property. Cultivating the land and erecting buildings and fences would show the casual observer that the land was occupied. It is this type of occupation that the owner is required, by law, to take notice of; and to protect his ownership of the land, he must expel the wrongful occupant within the statutory period. Temporary interruptions in the continuous occupation of the land for reasonable periods do not necessarily prevent the statutory period of years from running against the owner; and if another person takes possession of the land from the original squatter or wrongful occupant, the time of the occupation of each may be added together (in some states) to determine whether the statutory period has expired. A difficult problem is presented when the wrongful occupant occupies land for most of the year, but moves away during, say, the cold winter months. Often it has been ruled that the time continues to run as against the true owner, and that the wrongful occupant is occupying the property "continuously," as required by law.

The most frequent use of adverse possession today is in deciding disputed boundary lines between neighbors. A boundary line between the land of neighbors and accepted by both for the statutory period becomes the *actual* boundary line, even though it may in fact be wrong or differ from the written legal deed. Another typical instance of adverse possession occurs when a building on your neighbor's land overlaps onto your land and you do nothing about it. After the statutory period has expired, the part of your land on which your neighbor's building rests becomes your neighbor's property by adverse possession, and the encroachment on your land becomes a legal fact.

Easements.   An *easement* is the right of one person to use another's land for a particular purpose. For example, if your neighbor permits you to walk across his land to reach a street or highway, the use of this land becomes an easement. An easement permits you to enter upon his land for some definite purpose, but it does not permit you to take anything from the land.

If your neighbor permits you to enter upon his land and regularly take something, such as water, fish or game, stone from a quarry, or produce of any kind, this use of the land is known as a *profit à pendre* and not an easement.

When you have an easement to use your adjacent neighbor's land, the use is considered to be a right, or a part of your land, and it can be transferred with the land to a new owner when you sell or dispose of it. However, where the use permitted to you is based on land that is not adjacent to your land, the use is considered personal property and it cannot be transferred to a new owner.

Easements are created in various ways. Under certain circumstances, a continuous and obvious use of another's land for a long period of time creates an easement by *prescription* after the statutory period of time has expired (the period of time varies from state to state). It is similar to the transfer of ownership by adverse possession. However, it should be remembered that neither an easement nor a *profit à pendre* gives you any ownership in the land belonging to another. You are merely permitted to *use* the land of another for the established purpose—and no other.

Easements may be created by a written agreement known as a *grant;* a grant usually calls for the payment of a sum of money each year. However, an easement may result more or less haphazardly when a seller transfers a part of his land to a buyer. Then the use of pipes, drains, or sewer lines passing under the land of the seller to the land of the buyer is an easement obtained by the buyer, providing they were in existence at the time of the sale. The easement for the buyer's use is legally implied. A similar situation occurs when the part of the land sold to the buyer is landlocked by the seller's land or by the land of strangers and the buyer has no access to a street or highway adjoining the seller's land. In such case, the buyer has an implied easement to use the land of the seller to gain access to the street or highway, and, of course, to reach his land.

If you have an easement on the land of your neighbor to use a path across his land to reach a street or highway, you must use the most direct route across his land. Your neighbor is not required to maintain the path or make repairs along the way. Should the path be covered with snow in wintertime, the owner of the land is not required to clear it, that being the duty of the holder of the easement, should he wish to do so. The manner in which you have used your neighbor's land over the years will usually determine how you may use it in the future. You may not change the path or widen it; and your neighbor may not compel you to make a detour, nor may he narrow the path. It should be remembered that you and not your neighbor own this *use* of his land (although you have no ownership), and that you may transfer this use, but only to a new owner of your land, even without your neighbor's consent.

Fixtures

One of the most confusing points in a real-estate transaction is the meaning of the word *fixture*. A fixture is an article of personal property which, when affixed to real property, becomes a part of the realty. Fixtures are therefore included in the sale of real property, as a rule, even though not specifically mentioned or included in the contract. Obviously, such permanently-fastened items as a boiler or plumbing installation are included in the sale of a house, even when not mentioned. On the other hand, some items of personal property, readily removed from the house without damage, such as wall-to-wall carpeting, are clearly *not* included in the sale of a house unless specifically mentioned. However, besides these obvious and clean-cut differences, there exists a middle area that has many contestable items. The law with regard to fixtures is complex and variable, and a cautious buyer should always see that there is a complete list of every item intended to be transferred in the contract, if he expects to receive such object without argument. Typical of property subject to doubt are Venetian blinds, shades, awnings, storm windows, screens, and similar items; some of these have been held to be fixtures in some states, personal property in others. The problem is further complicated in the case of storm windows, for example, which are usually regarded as affixed to the realty. Often, storm windows are removed during the warmer months (thus changing them back to personal property), but they are customarily regarded as fixtures nonetheless, for they are regularly and normally a part of the realty and have a functional relationship with the property.

Generally, carpeting, draperies, mirrors hung on the wall, electrical appliances, and the like remain the personal property of the seller and do not become a part of the land or the home. The seller may take these items with him as his own personal property, in the same way that he would remove his furniture and clothing from the home before title is closed.

On the other hand, mirrors and shelves set into the wall, the removal of which would leave walls unfinished, plumbing materials which cannot be removed easily and would require costly replacements, a furnace in the cellar, storm windows, linoleum flooring, fireplaces, and other articles that complete the interior finish of the home, are considered to be fixtures that may not be removed by the seller.

The most important consideration in determining whether an article is a fixture, and a part of the property being sold to the buyer, is whether the seller can remove the article without causing more than trivial harm to the home. Pictures on the wall may be easily lifted away, and carpeting on the floor may usually be removed, leaving only very minor damage, but a furnace in the cellar of the home, if removed by the seller, might leave holes in the wall that the buyer would have to repair at a substantial expense.

There are times when it is difficult for either the buyer or the seller to determine whether a specific article is the personal property of the seller or a fixture which is a part of the home. *The best way to avoid problems that may later arise is to agree in writing that certain articles are included in the sale to the buyer.* This is usually done by a paragraph in the contract of sale, which may read as follows: "All fixtures and articles of personal property attached to or used in connection with said premises are included in this sale; without limiting the generality of the foregoing, such fixtures and articles of personal property include plumbing, heating, lighting, and cooking fixtures, air-conditioning fixtures and units, ranges, refrigerators, radio and television aerials, bathroom and kitchen cabinets, mantels, door mirrors, Venetian blinds, shades, screens, storm windows, storm doors, window boxes, mailboxes, weather vanes, flagpoles, pumps, shrubbery, and outdoor statuary."

The seller and the buyer may strike out any of the items which they agree that the seller should keep and remove from the premises. They may also specify additional articles of personal property that the buyer will receive with the home, such as appliances that are on the premises and the carpeting throughout the home. If this is done carefully, no dispute should arise between the buyer and the seller over fixtures or other personal property that the buyer observed in the home before the contract of sale was signed.

The Ownership of Land

If you are about to buy a house, an important consideration is the method by which you take title to the land. Title may be taken in your individual name, in that of your wife and yourself, in the name of several people, or by a partnership or corporation.

If a husband and wife buy a new house, either may be named in the deed as the sole owner of the land. If the husband owns his own business and the wife is not a partner, it may be advisable to name the wife as the sole owner of the property. Then if the husband's business sustains a financial loss and a judgment is obtained against him, his creditors may not automatically be able to compel the sale of the house to satisfy their claims. A similar result occurs if the husband and wife take title as tenants by entirety. This will be discussed later.

Co-ownership. If two or more persons own land together, they are considered to be co-owners. Co-ownership may take the form of a *tenancy by the entirety, joint tenancy, tenancy in common,* or *community property.* Each form of co-ownership has distinct characteristics. Usually co-owners are not considered to be partners. This means that one co-owner is without the authority to sell or mortgage the land without the other's consent. The co-owners share any rental they may receive for the property, and each is entitled to occupy an equal part of the land. Before deciding on the form of co-ownership, it is wise to determine whether the particular form of co-ownership gives you and your co-owner the right of survivorship. This means that on the death of one of the co-owners, his interest in the land passes to the other co-owner automatically, by operation of law and without the necessity of legal proceedings. If there is no right of survivorship, the interest of a deceased co-owner may be transferred by will or it passes to his heirs, rather than the co-owner, on his death. Another important consideration in selecting the appropriate form of co-ownership is that a co-owner usually does not actually own any particular part of the land itself. His ownership is regarded as an undivided portion of the entire tract of land. This means that two co-owners each own an undivided one-half interest in the land. A disadvantage of this type of ownership is that a prospective buyer may desire to have his portion of the land partitioned (divided) rather than share it equally with a stranger (who inherits the interest), and this in turn may affect the purchase price of the land.

Tenancy by the Entireties. A husband and wife may take title to their home as *tenants by the entireties.* Although the name is somewhat confusing, this form of ownership has nothing to do with landlord and tenants. It refers instead to a common-law principle that a husband and wife are, so to speak, one person, and they own all of the land acquired during their marriage as an entity. This form of ownership is still recognized in all states except the community property states where a modern substitute is used.

The most important incident of a couple owning their home as "tenants by the entireties" is that, on the death of either the husband or wife, ownership of the land is immediately and automatically transferred to the surviving spouse by operation of law without the necessity of legal proceedings. This is known as the right of survivorship.

Another important advantage of this type of co-ownership is that creditors of either the husband or the wife may not compel the sale of the house to satisfy their claims. The unity of ownership achieved by such co-ownership generally protects the home from creditors' claims, since neither the husband nor the wife may sell or mortgage their undivided share of the land without the consent of the other. (The rule in most states is that a creditor *cannot* acquire any rights to real property so owned. In a few states, however, notably Arkansas, Kentucky, Massachusetts, New Jersey, and Tennessee, one spouse's interest may be sold at a sheriff's sale, but the purchaser must take his ownership subject to the other spouse's interest.)

Although a tenancy by the entireties provides the fullest advantage to a husband and wife that co-ownership can provide, other considerations may play a part in deciding on the most desirable form of ownership. For example, a wealthy couple may desire to consult their lawyer and accountant before taking title as tenants by entirety since it may have important tax consequences. For estate-tax purposes only, a deceased spouse is considered to be the owner of all of the land, not just one-half, unless the surviving spouse can prove that he or she actually contributed to the purchase price of the home.

Another consideration is whether the husband and wife are happily married and likely to remain so. If not, ownership as tenants by the entireties may prove to be an awkward arrangement that may have important legal consequences if the marriage does not last. While a divorce or annulment will end this form of ownership, a separation will not. In such a case, although the husband and wife may be living apart, each would have the right to occupy the home, but neither would be able to sell or mortgage their share without the other's consent. This can lead to irritating or unpleasant situations, in which either spouse can put pressure on the other as to the occupancy, maintenance, or sale of the house.

To establish a tenancy by entirety it is only necessary that the deed or will granting ownership to a husband and wife read "Tom Wilson and Edith Wilson, his wife," or "Tom Wilson and Edith Wilson, husband and wife, as Tenants by the Entireties." If the deed reads merely "Tom Wilson and Edith Wilson," a *tenancy in common* and not a tenancy by the entireties is created. It is best, however, to include the words "husband and wife, as Tenants by the Entireties," after the names.

Joint Tenancy. A husband and wife may take title to land as *joint tenants.* An important consideration in creating a joint tenancy is the presence of the so-called *four unities.* The co-ownership must be (1) created by the same deed, (2) at the same time, (3) for the same duration, and (4) each joint tenant must have the same right to occupy the land. A joint tenancy has one similar characteristic to a tenancy by entirety—that is, the right of survivorship. On the death of a joint tenant his interest in the land passes to the other joint tenant by operation of law, without the necessity of legal proceedings. But a joint tenancy differs from a tenancy by entirety in several respects. The co-owners do not have to be husband and wife; this is most important, as in a case in which a brother and sister, for example, both own the house. Another difference is that any joint tenant may sell or mortgage his share of the land without the consent of the other joint tenant; but when he does so, the co-ownership becomes a tenancy in common (discussed below). A joint tenancy is established in a deed or will by such words as, "Fred Adams and Ruth Adams, as joint tenants." If the words used do not clearly express their intention to take title as joint tenants, the co-ownership is considered to be a tenancy in common.

Tenancy in Common. Co-owners of land most often take title to property as *tenants in common.* The most important difference between tenancy in common and other forms of co-ownership is that there is no right of survivorship. When one tenant in common dies, his interest is not transferred to the other tenant in common, but to his nearest of kin or according to his will. A tenant in common may sell or mortgage his undivided interest in the land to another without the consent of his co-tenant.

The sale of land to two or more persons creates a tenancy in common unless they make it clear that another form of co-ownership is intended. A tenancy in common may be ended by agreement between the co-owners, or by a court order known as a *partition,* which divides the land between the co-owners.

Community Property. Community property is an innovation in the law; it is of Spanish origin, and is recognized in California, Louisiana, Washington, Arizona, New Mexico, Nevada, Idaho, and Texas. In these states, a husband and wife share equally in all property, both real and personal, acquired by them *during their marriage* through their joint efforts. All of the community-property states recognize that a husband or wife may own separate property acquired by either before marriage, or by sale, gift, or inheritance after marriage, but the tendency in community-property states is to assume that all property acquired by husband and wife during marriage is community property. It is therefore important in community-property states that the husband and wife consent in writing to the sale of any land owned by either or both. It is also important to realize that in a community-property state a husband and wife may not own land as tenants by entirety or joint tenancy. Since there is no right of survivorship in a community-property state, at the death of the husband or wife, his or her interest in the land is transferred to a beneficiary named by will or to the surviving spouse and children. This creates an unsatisfactory situation because minors may end up owning an interest in real property (after the death of a parent) that may prove to be unduly burdensome and costly.

Dower. Many years ago, at common law, a widow was considered to be the owner of one-third of the land that her husband owned during their marriage. This right, known as *dower,* gave a married woman an interest in her husband's land which, however, did not become effective until his death. In this way, a husband could not disinherit his wife without her consent. In every case where the husband sold land, which he owned during his lifetime, the purchaser would require the wife to consent to the transfer; if she did not do so, when the husband died, the wife might claim one-third of the land purchased. In most states (but not all) the right of dower has been terminated by statute. Its modern-day substitutes differ from state to state. None of these substitutes, however, provide the full advantage to the surviving spouse of a tenancy by entirety.

Community-property states have substituted the joint ownership of husband and wife in place of dower. This gives the wife the right to immediate ownership of one-half of the land and personal property of the husband acquired during marriage through their joint efforts. In New York the substitute for dower is the wife's right (of election) to claim one-third of her husband's estate if he disinherits her in his will. However, there is no requirement that the husband retain any property in his estate until he dies.

Curtesy. At common law the corresponding right of the husband to dower was based on the use and occupation of land owned by his wife during their marriage. This was known as *curtesy.* Today, curtesy rights of the husband in real property owned by his wife no longer exist in any state and have been terminated by statute.

Corporations. A corporation may own land in its corporate name; and it is possible to form a corporation for the sole purpose of owning your land, although this might involve an expense of several hundred dollars. It is sometimes an advantage for a corporation, rather than an individual, to own land. The corporation is a fictitious legal entity and is in many respects treated as a separate individual. If a creditor has a claim against you, and you are a stockholder, director, or officer of the corporation, he cannot compel the sale of land held by the corporation to satisfy his claim. The corporation is considered to be a separate person, apart from its stockholders, directors, and officers. However, the creditor can take over ownership of your interest in the corporation, which in turn owns the land. On the other hand, a claim by a creditor against the corporation cannot be made against you individually. It therefore appears that there may be some advantage in having a corporation take title to your land. However, the costs of forming such a corporation and continuing its existence, together with the separate taxation in most states, are disadvantages that usually outweigh the desirability of forming a corporation for such a purpose. All in all, a corporation is not recommended for the ownership of a private home in the absence of special considerations, which should be discussed with an attorney in full detail. For protection of the family interest, it is usually far better to take title "by the entireties," that is, as husband and wife.

Partnerships. Although a partnership is not a legal entity, it may in most states own land in its partnership name. If you purchase land from a partnership, you should insist that *all* partners sign the contract of sale and the deed; otherwise it is possible that a partner who did not sign may claim that he did not approve of the transaction.

Minors. In most states, a person who is under the age of 21 years may own land, but he may not sell his land or devise it by will. There is always a danger in buying land from, or selling land to, a minor. Because of his youth, he is allowed to disaffirm the transaction at any time until he reaches the age of 21, and for a few months thereafter. If the land decreases in value, he is still entitled to receive the purchase price he paid, providing that he returns the land that was transferred to him. If you sell land to a minor, you should consider transferring title to an adult, such as the father, mother, or guardian of the minor, who will take title to the land as a guardian or trustee until the minor reaches maturity.

Condemnation

When land is needed for public use, it may be acquired by the United States government, the state, or a municipality within whose boundaries the land lies. It may also be acquired by semipublic-utility corporations, such as railroads, and public-utility corporations (under certain special powers). The right to take land for such public use is known as "eminent domain," and the process by which it is taken is known as *condemnation*. There are two basic requirements: First, the use to which the property is to be devoted must be a public one; and second, just compensation must be paid to the private landowner.

The power of eminent domain involves a condemnation proceeding. This may consist of a court proceeding initiated by the municipality or other public body that desires to acquire title to all or part of an individual's land. The just compensation, to which the landowner is entitled, is the *fair market value* of the land at the time it is taken by the public body. Often, where a dispute arises, the matter may have to be determined by a court or a jury. However, the condemnor (the party seeking the property), need not wait for possession until the trial has been held. Thus the United States government may file a "declaration of taking" in a condemnation suit; this immediately gives the government title to the land, and only the price to be paid remains open for determination. By condemnation, the public body seeking to obtain the land actually acquires title and ownership (unless the courts decide that title is not required and that merely an easement or right of use is sufficient, in which case the condemnor will acquire only the lesser interest). For example, when a railroad seeks to condemn land in order to build a right-of-way, or a city condemns land to build a street, or a telephone company condemns in order to be able to build telephone lines, as a rule only an easement will be granted across the property of the individual. The property owner will ultimately be paid in the course of the condemnation proceedings, but only a lesser amount, inasmuch as the original owner will still retain title to the land.

CHAPTER 17

Mortgages

Financing Homeownership

Most families would find it impossible to purchase a home unless they were able to borrow a large sum of money from a mortgage lender, thus reducing the amount of cash required. Only a very small percentage of houses are purchased on an all-cash basis. Without the mortgage lender, there would be few sales of old homes and fewer new homes built. The mortgage loan has played an increasingly important role in the purchase of homes since the depression of the 1930's. It was in this period that Congress established the Federal Housing Administration to rescue the depressed building industry. During the past thirty years, due to increased federal participation in mortgage loans, the earlier variations and complexities of mortgage-lending practice have become more standardized. Today, with standardized practices crossing state lines, mortgage lending has become a vast industry in which banks, savings and loan associations, insurance companies, and the federal government often cooperate to provide the loan that enables you to purchase your home with a minimum down payment, and with repayment of the mortgage spread over a long period.

Your Home as Security for a Mortgage Loan. When you purchase an automobile on credit, you sign a sales contract with the automobile dealer that usually provides that the dealer or the finance company or bank will retain legal *title* to the car until you have completely paid the purchase price and carrying charges. You, of course, receive *possession* of the automobile while you pay the monthly charges. When payment is completed, legal title to the automobile is finally transferred to you. This type of purchase has been made on credit. The automobile has been used as security for your payment of the amount of the sales price. If you fail to meet your payments, the seller will undoubtedly repossess your car and sell it to someone else. Although the purchase of a home differs from the purchase of an automobile in many respects, you may also use your home as security for a loan from a lending institution. This type of loan is known as a mortgage. The lender is known as the *mortgagee,* and you, the borrower, is known as the *mortgagor.*

Reasons for Mortgaging Your Home. Today, most homes in the United States are mortgaged. The total mortgage indebtedness is almost as great as the national debt, more than $240,000,000,000. There are many reasons why a mortgage may be sought (or required) by the buyer of a house. Of course, the single most important reason is that the purchaser does not have enough cash to complete the purchase without a mortgage. But there are other reasons as well.

Although you may have enough money to purchase your home without a mortgage, you should nevertheless give careful considera-tion to obtaining a maximum mortgage on your new home. Rarely will you be able to obtain a loan of any kind at lower rates of interest or at less cost. You will probably pay less for your mortgage loan than any other loan that you can obtain. For example, the interest on personal loans, improvement loans on real estate, automobile purchases, or other articles you buy on credit, can well average out to more than twice the interest payments on a home mortgage. This high rate of interest results from carrying charges or from a banking practice that allows banks to deduct the interest to be paid on the loan in advance. This has the effect of substantially increasing the actual rate paid.

If you borrow $2,000 for a home-improvement loan, and your rate of interest is 5% per year for a period of three years, your monthly payments will be $65.76 for a period of thirty-six months, and you will have to repay a total of $2,367.36. The cost to you of this home-improvement loan is $367.36. What is the cost of a mort-gage in this amount for the same period and at the same rate of interest? A mortgage loan of $2,000 will cost only $2,150 if repaid in three years time. Thus you will save $217.36.

The reason for this saving is that the interest on a mortgage loan is computed on the unpaid balance due. However, when you borrow $2,000 from a bank for a home-improvement loan, the bank will immediately discount the interest for the three years in advance. (To receive $2,000 you must borrow $2,252.92.) Then, in addition, the bank charges interest not on the $2,000 you actually receive, but on $2,252.92—the sum which you borrowed.

Therefore, on the assumption that at some time in the future you will probably require capital for home improvements or some other purpose, you will be wiser to secure a maximum mortgage when purchasing your home, rather than to borrow in the future on your promissory note from a bank, without your home as security.

There are other important reasons for considering a high mortgage on your new home. Since 1936 there has been a gradual, almost year by year, decline in the purchasing power of the dollar. This is inflation, as we all know. Inflation may prove to be favorable to the homeowner with a large mortgage. Since the mortgage indebtedness is a fixed amount, he should find the principal of the mortgage easier to pay as the value of the dollar decreases. Another benefit is that the value of your house will also increase as the purchasing power of the dollar decreases. You may know people who purchased their home years ago for $15,000 to $20,000. If they wish to sell their home today, after many years of residence, the sales price will almost always be substantially higher than the sum they originally paid. The buyer obtaining a mortgage on such a house might obtain a mortgage for more than its original value. If inflation continues, a $15,000 mortgage on your home today might be equivalent to only $10,000, comparatively speaking, ten years from now in relation to your ability to pay it off. Of course, the gamble on a continued inflation is a two-edged weapon. During the early 1930's the country experienced a deflation which had exactly the opposite effect on homeowners. Many homes were lost by foreclosure to lending institutions, when their owners were unable to repay the mortgage loans. Whether there will be an inflation or deflation in the coming years is a risk the homeowner must assume as a matter of course, together with all of the other members of the community. However, the trend for the past thirty years seems to be toward inflation, and in particular to favor the homeowner with a substantial mortgage loan.

The ideal time to obtain a maximum mortgage loan is when you purchase your home. If you need a mortgage after you have lived in the house for a period of years, many "closing" costs which have been absorbed at the closing of title will have to be duplicated. For example, the mortgage lender inevitably requires a title policy to protect him from a claim by some third party to the ownership of your home. You will probably also order a title policy to protect your ownership after title closes. If both policies are ordered simultaneously, there is a substantial saving to the buyer. Another saving to the buyer is that the mortgage loan may be obtained at a minimum charge. The buyer is usually assisted by the real-estate broker, who is anxious to get the best mortgage terms possible so that the sale will be made. The same real-estate broker, if asked to act subsequently as a mortgage broker, may charge for his services a mortgage commission of as much as 2% of the face amount of the mortgage loan.

Remember also that if you want to sell your house, the new buyer will inspect your mortgage just as carefully as you did when you bought the house. One of the best inducements to any buyer is a substantial mortgage at low rates of interest with many years to run. This reduces the buyer's monthly carrying charges on the house. The best time to obtain such a mortgage is when you purchase the house. Often one deciding factor in the sale of the house is the favorable state of the existing mortgage. For example, there are still mortgages in existence that were guaranteed by the Veterans Administration in 1947 at 4% interest per year. A mortgage of this type, needless to say, is far more desirable than a mortgage obtained from a bank, which requires 6% interest per year and has the same period to run.

The Mortgage Itself. During the early 1930's many homeowners lost their homes because they were unable to meet the mortgage payments. Many of these mortgages were *straight-term mortgages,* characterized by the level payment of interest for three or five years, with the payment of the balance of the entire mortgage loan on a certain future date. These mortgages were accompanied by personal bonds or "mortgage notes," with similar provisions, known as "balloon" notes. On their due dates, the entire unpaid balance had to be paid. The unhappy experience of the depression brought about a great change in the field of mortgage financing. Today, most mortgages are of the amortizing, or self-liquidating, type. This means that level monthly payments over the years are used to pay both the *principal* of the mortgage loan and the *interest,* and after the final monthly payment there is no balance to be repaid. In brief, the lump-sum or "balloon" payment has been completely eliminated. The borrower is advised to avoid the straight-term mortgage or any mortgage loan that contains a provision that the entire balance becomes due on a certain number of days' notice from the lender to the buyer. On this type of loan, the borrower may be placed in the position of requesting an extension of payments and finding that the lender refuses to accommodate him. The result may mean the loss of the house.

The usual form of mortgage loan today is the so-called "regular mortgage." As a rule, the provisions require that the borrower pay the real-estate and water taxes when due, maintain adequate fire insurance, and correct any violations of local ordinances. There may be many other requirements which a conscientious homeowner would do as a matter of routine without reading the fine print of the mortgage. However, should the borrower default in meeting any of the requirements of the mortgage, the lender usually will give him written notice of the default and request that he correct it within a certain period of time. If the borrower does not do so, the lender may take steps to take possession of the house, or he may remedy the default and charge the borrower with the cost of doing so. Should the borrower fail to meet his monthly payments of interest and principal, there is usually a provision to the effect that after a "grace" period of 15 to 30 days has expired, the lender may take possession of the home through court action by means of a proceeding known as a *foreclosure*. There is also an "acceleration" clause, which provides that on failure to meet the monthly payments of principal and interest, the entire balance of the mortgage loan becomes payable. This allows the lender to take court action to recover the entire balance of the mortgage loan without waiting months or years for all of the mortgage payments to become due. It is obvious, therefore, that defaults should be avoided at all costs.

The house and land, which are the security for the mortgage loan, are described in the mortgage in the same manner as in a deed. In fact, the mortgage in some states is the deed, and actually transfers ownership of the land to the lender until the loan is repaid. In these states (Alabama, Arkansas, Connecticut, Illinois, Maine, Maryland, Massachusetts, Missouri, New Hampshire, New Jersey, North Carolina, Ohio, Pennsylvania, Rhode Island, Tennessee, Vermont, and West Virginia) the *lender* is legally regarded as the owner of the land. In most other states (including California and New York) the lender is considered as having only a *lien* against the land until the mortgage loan has been repaid, and the lender does not receive ownership of the land.

In all states, the mortgage contains a *defeasance clause,* which states that on repayment of the mortgage loan, the mortgage is of no further effect. The importance of the defeasance clause has been lessened by modern statutes which provide that even after the borrower has defaulted in his monthly payments, the lender may not take possession and ownership of the house for a period that ranges from two months to two years. These statutes give the borrower an opportunity to pay the overdue monthly payments.

The mortgage always specifies the amount that has been lent to the borrower and the precise terms of its repayment. The interest rate is set forth, and the monthly payments are also specified. The rate of interest the lender may charge the borrower is often regulated by statute. Many states (such as New York) prohibit the lender from charging interest at a greater rate than 6% per year on the unpaid balance of the loan. If the lender charges more interest than that permitted by statute, he may be prevented from recovering both the loan and the interest due, and he may also be guilty of a crime. The maximum rates of interest that may be charged vary from state to state; and the penalty for charging more than the rate allowed by statute, which is a crime known as usury, differs also. However, in all states, a *corporate* borrower may pay any rate of interest no matter how high. The usury statutes apply only to the *individual* borrowers.

There is often a provision in the mortgage for the *prepayment* of principal and interest. An FHA mortgage must provide that the borrower may repay up to 15% of the principal in any one year without penalty and a greater amount in any one year on paying the mortgage insurance of ½% of the outstanding balance. Conventional mortgages, however, may not allow a prepayment of principal. A lending institution has a right to have its money working for it and earning the interest that was agreed on between lender and borrower. Whether the borrower is to have a right to prepay the mortgage principal must be negotiated with the lender; and it is an important consideration that may save a great deal if or when the borrower decides to take out a new mortgage on his home and prepay the balance of the old mortgage. If he can do so without a penalty, or at a penalty of as little as 1%, then he has a satisfactory mortgage provision that may possibly result in a considerable saving.

Both the borrower and his spouse must sign the mortgage whether or not both are named in the deed as owners of the house. This is done to avoid claims of dower rights, homestead rights, or other claims that one of the spouses might make, unless their consent to the mortgage loan appears in writing.

Most states require that the mortgage be executed before at least two witnesses and acknowledged before a notary public or other official. Some states still require a formal seal to be affixed to the mortgage. The mortgage is usually recorded in the land office of the county where the land is situated. There are some states in which a deed of trust, or a *trust indenture,* is used in place of the regular mortgage. In these states (for example: California, Illinois, Colorado, Missouri, Mississippi, Tennessee, Virginia, and West Virginia), the mortgage takes the form of a deed of trust and is delivered to a third party, not the lender, who holds the ownership of the property in trust until the borrower has repaid the mortgage loan to the lender. He then returns the deed of trust to the borrower.

A few states also permit an installment land contract, which has many similarities to a mortgage. The borrower, in possession of the land, does not receive ownership from the seller until the entire purchase price has been paid, usually at the rate of 1% (for both principal and interest) of the purchase price per month. Since a large part of the monthly payment consists of interest, the installment contract may take about 11 years to be completed. The few states that allow such a purchase of land all require that the seller, and not a lending institution, be named as the lender, thus making it somewhat similar in nature to a purchase-money mortgage.

Mortgage Amortization. Inasmuch as most mortgages are self-liquidating (amortizing) loans, you will pay ordinarily a level amount each month toward the interest and reduction of the principal. However, remember that the interest is first computed on the balance due and therefore the first payment is practically all interest and the last payment is practically all principal. About midway during the term of the mortgage the interest and principal payments are about equal. This means that if you sell your home several years after purchase, there is a hidden cost to you because most of your monthly payments have paid the interest on the mortgage loan and very little has been used to repay the mortgage principal.

Shopping for a Home Mortgage Loan. Local banks, and savings and loan associations, have been writing home mortgages for many years along established procedures. These institutions will lend from 60% to 80% (sometimes even more) of the appraised value of your home if you can meet their financial requirements. Mortgages of this type are known as *conventional mortgages.* The number of years the mortgage runs may be from fifteen (sometimes only ten) to twenty (or even thirty) years depending on the quality and condition of your new home, and conditions in the mortgage market.

If you are seeking a large mortgage and the smallest possible down payment, then it is not advisable to seek a conventional mortgage from a bank or savings and loan association. For the past three decades the Federal Housing Administration, and more recently the Veterans Administration, have been responsible for mortgage loans of as much as 90-100% of the value of a new house, and the time of the mortgage may extend as long as thirty to forty years. However, neither federal agency actually lends money. They merely *guarantee* that the mortgage loan will be repaid to the lending institution (bank, insurance company, etc.) if you fail to meet the payments. With the risk of loss so greatly reduced, and with the government's assurance that the mortgage loan will be repaid, most lending institutions will lend far more on an FHA or VA mortgage than on a conventional mortgage. The difficulty (from the borrower's point of view) is that the rates of interest are set at a rather low figure by the government on these mortgage loans, and often mortgage money may be lent (by a bank) at a much higher rate if the conventional mortgage is used. When this occurs, it may be difficult to obtain an FHA or VA mortgage except at a discount, or by the payment of service charges by the bank. However, when this happens, the government usually increases the permitted rate of interest on such mortgages so that the mortgage money will again be available. Another government agency will then purchase such mortgages from lending institutions at a discount to allow those lenders that want to dispose of their mortgages to do so. From the point of view of a prospective mortgagor seeking a suitable loan, the problem is that there are times (usually lasting for several months) during which it is difficult to obtain satisfactory FHA or VA mortgages. The approximate rate of interest on an FHA mortgage today is about 5½% per year and there is an additional mortgage insurance premium of ½% (to protect the government in the event that a foreclosure becomes necessary and the government has to repay the loan to the lending institution). The mortgage interest of a VA mortgage loan is somewhat less. It is more than likely that a bank, savings and loan association, or insurance company will ultimately write your mortgage. More than 80% of all mortgages are held by such lending institutions; the remainder are written by private individuals.

Purchase-Money Mortgages. On occasion, the seller of a house may be willing to permit the buyer to borrow part of the purchase price of the new home from the seller providing that the buyer signs a mortgage to the seller. This is known as a *purchase-money mortgage,* and if it is in addition to the mortgage of a lending institution, it is known as a second mortgage. Obviously the seller would ordinarily prefer to receive cash rather than a mortgage for a part of the purchase price. The buyer should therefore question the inducements of the seller in allowing a purchase-money mortgage. It may be that the home is overvalued and the seller intends to discount the purchase-money mortgage (by selling it to a bank or a mortgage company at a price lower than the face value) and thus obtain the price that the seller really desired. Remember that a second mortgage is not as secure as a first mortgage since the proceeds of a sale of the property on foreclosure must be used first to pay the first mortgage loan and the costs of foreclosure, before the holder of the second mortgage is repaid. Also, the interest rates on a purchase-money mortgage are usually more than the buyer would pay for a first mortgage. The seller should not, however, require a title search or a title policy for the purchase-money mortgage since he has transferred his home to the buyer. He should know that there are no other claims to ownership of the property.

A purchase-money mortgage, however, may be ideal for the buyer under certain circumstances. Assuming that he does not feel the house is overpriced, if the seller will accept a purchase-money mortgage it reduces the amount of cash required. If the purchase-money mortgage is placed on a house sold free and clear of an existing mortgage, it assures the buyer of a definite amount of mortgage, and saves a great deal of mortgage expenses.

A relatively recent development in home mortgages is that of combining life-insurance policies with a mortgage loan. In the event that the homeowner dies, the life insurance repays the balance of the mortgage loan. The mortgage interest rates on this type are usually lower because the borrower is actually maintaining life insurance with the lender. However, the insurance aspects of the mortgage loan may be difficult to separate from the mortgage loan itself, and this may result in problems in the resale of the home, unless the borrower is permitted to prepay the mortgage without penalty or assign it to a new owner.

Applying for a Mortgage. The mortgage lender will usually follow the rule of thumb that the mortgage loan should not exceed two to two-and-a-half times the borrower's gross annual income. For example, as discussed in the chapter called "Buying a House," if your gross annual income is about $8,000 per year, your mortgage should not exceed $20,000. The lender is concerned with your dependable income and your financial situation, but he is also interested in the appraised value of your home. Since the mortgage loan will vary from 66⅔% (perhaps as low as 60%) to as much as 90% (or possibly even 100%) of the appraised value, this value is an important limitation to consider. Many conventional mortgage lenders are extremely conservative in their appraisals of house evaluations, estimating them below market value.

When you are looking for a mortgage, you will probably apply to a bank, a savings and loan association, an insurance company, a mortgage concern, or a private individual. Lending institutions all require that you fill out an application form; the application asks you to describe your new house in detail and requires full particulars as to your financial condition. You must also submit a copy of the contract of sale to the prospective lender, so that he can verify the terms and price. If the initial review of your application is favorable, the lending institution will then order a credit report on you and obtain an appraisal of the prospective house. When the lending institution actually approves the mortgage loan, you will be notified by letter stating that the loan will be made. The commitment letter specifies the maximum amount of the loan and the terms of payment. You need not, if you wish, accept this commitment from the lender. But if you do, you must notify the lender *in writing* within a specified period of time, usually thirty days. Although you will learn quickly of the lender's willingness to mortgage your home if you seek a conventional mortgage, it takes a longer time for an FHA or VA mortgage approval. Sometimes the official approval of such mortgage loans will take as long as eight weeks. As soon as the borrower notifies the lender that he will accept the loan, the lender will order a title search on the property. The search will reveal whether there are any defects, or objections, in the title. If there are such defects, the mortgage loan may not be allowed, and the borrower may refuse title. As a rule, the borrower has a simultaneous title search made for his own protection; the title company may issue a separate title policy to the lender and to the borrower to protect their respective interests, but the premiums for the title policies are paid by the borrower. The lender will also order a survey to determine whether there are any encroachments on the land, that is, in order to ascertain if the buyer is actually receiving the land for which he has contracted. The borrower must also pay for the survey, which may cost as much as $50. The lender will also check the judgment dockets of the local courts to make sure that the borrower may not become involved with unpaid judgments entered by creditors who may ultimately collect the amount due by compelling the sale of the home. This search will also reveal whether there are any mechanic's liens against the house which might affect the full ownership of the borrower. Mechanic's liens are claims made by workmen or contractors who have not been paid for work performed on the house and have filed claims against the property. These liens must be disposed of before the buyer receives a satisfactory title, and before the lender will advance any mortgage money.

When all of the above searches and inquiries have been completed, the lender is ready to close the mortgage. Usually the mortgage closing and title closing occur simultaneously at the offices of the lending institution. When the title company, or the attorneys for the lender, are satisfied that all the requirements of the closing have been completed, a cashier's check or a certified check will be given to the borrower in the full amount of the mortgage loan, made payable to the borrower. The borrower will usually be asked to endorse the check to the seller. Sometimes the borrower and the seller may agree to divide the check for the full amount of the mortgage into several checks of different amounts so that the seller, the broker, and the lender may be paid exact amounts due to them. In these cases the borrower will always sign "payment approved" on the back of each check, which is endorsed to other individuals at the closing.

Conditioning a Purchase on Obtaining a Satisfactory Mortgage. Frequently a buyer's ability to purchase a house is dependent on his ability to obtain a first mortgage loan in the required sum. This is particularly true if the buyer has limited funds and would not have sufficient funds to close the deal if the mortgage loan was insufficient. The buyer who signs a contract of sale should make the purchase *conditional* on his obtaining a satisfactory mortgage loan. However, the seller is not usually willing to take his home off the market for a long period of time, only to see the sale fall through if the buyer is unable to obtain a satisfactory mortgage. The buyer and seller may agree to a provision in the contract of sale along the following lines:

> This contract of sale is conditioned on the ability of the buyer to obtain a first mortgage loan, in an amount of not less than $15,000, bearing interest at not more than 6%, payable in equal monthly

installments for a term of not less than 20 years. The buyer agrees to make diligent efforts to obtain such a mortgage, but if he is unable to do so after applying to two or more lending institutions, then and in that event he shall notify the seller by registered or certified mail within sixty days from the date of this agreement and the agreement shall be considered at an end and the deposit paid by the purchaser shall be refunded to him without any further obligation on his part.

The seller will not, as a rule, agree to an unreasonable length of time for the buyer to obtain a commitment, or to an unreasonably high mortgage loan, or to rates of interest that are not current, since the seller would then be giving the buyer a way out of the contract of sale. In effect, this agreement would institute an option to purchase the house if he desired, regardless of whether the mortgage sought might be obtained. However, there should be no objection by the seller if the buyer is seeking a reasonable mortgage and requesting a moderate period of time in which to do so. The seller's problem is that the sale or "no sale" of the home may not be final until the full period of sixty days has elapsed.

Assuming the Mortgage or Taking Subject to the Mortgage. Most buyers who accept the seller's existing mortgage on the home, and who do not desire a new mortgage, take title to the property "subject to the mortgage." This means that if the buyer fails to repay the amount of loan that was originally made to the seller, the lender may still foreclose on the home and sell it to a third party in order to obtain repayment. However, if there is any amount still unpaid (even after the foreclosure), the seller remains personally responsible for this deficiency on the mortgage note or bond which he signed, and the buyer has no personal responsibility. However, should the buyer "assume" the mortgage, the buyer also becomes personally responsible to the lender for any such deficiency. It is unusual for a buyer to assume a mortgage and this should always be avoided.

The Mortgage Note or Bond. The execution of a mortgage requires that the borrower sign two separate documents. The first is the mortgage note (or bond) which contains the personal promise of the borrower to repay the lender. The terms of repayment and interest are set forth in the note (or bond) in the same manner that it is set forth in the mortgage. If the borrower fails to repay the lender, the lender may sue the borrower on his personal promise for the entire balance or, more likely, the lender will proceed to take possession and ownership of the house under the terms of the mortgage. It is only when a sale of the home pursuant to foreclosure fails to produce enough money to repay the entire balance of the loan, that a lender then sues the borrower on his personal promise to repay the loan. At the present time, comparatively few lenders find it necessary to sue mortgagors for balances due on defaulted mortgages, for the foreclosed property almost always brings a price sufficient to take care of the mortgage. However, no one knows for certain what the future brings. During the depression of the 1930's, tens of thousands of homes were foreclosed and lawsuits brought to recover deficiencies between the amount of the unpaid mortgage and the amount realized on the foreclosure sale.

Default and Foreclosure

If you fail to maintain your monthly payments of interest and principal on the mortgage, the lender will be compelled to take some action against you. Usually, after your payments have been in default for more than ninety days, the lender will turn the matter over to his attorney with instructions to take ownership and possession of your home by means of *foreclosure*. But before such drastic action is taken, the lender will usually attempt to work out some arrangement with you. The lender may even be willing to reduce the monthly payments for a brief period of time, if this will, in fact, assist you during a period of financial distress. The lender, as a rule, is not anxious to foreclose on your home. There are several reasons for this. Foreclosure proceedings are expensive and time-consuming. The law of every state provides that the borrower has a period of time, after foreclosure proceedings have been commenced, to make the back payments due on the mortgage and "redeem" his home. This period of time averages about a year, and in some states it is as much as two years. This provision is known as the borrower's *equity of redemption*. The average cost of a foreclosure proceeding (where court action is required) is about $500, although in Illinois, the most difficult state in which to obtain a foreclosure, the cost is more than $1,200, and more than 17 months is required to complete it. The foreclosure sale of a house by the lender may not completely pay the balance of the mortgage loan, and although the lender may then sue the borrower on the mortgage note or bond (the borrower's personal promise to repay the loan) such lawsuits may be unrewarding if the borrower is in financial difficulty. However, when all other efforts to assist the borrower in continuing the mortgage payments have failed, the lender will have no recourse but to foreclose.

The number of home foreclosures in the United States has increased during recent years. There are a number of reasons for this. Of course, unforeseen catastrophies are always contributing factors; long illnesses, deaths, unemployment, and lengthy strikes have always had an effect on the rate of foreclosures. But strangely enough, the unexpected and most important factor that results in foreclosure is marital difficulty. If neither the husband nor the wife has any desire to remain in the home, the mortgage payments will not be made. Often, in order to put pressure on his wife in a divorce or separation proceeding, a husband will refuse to make the payments due on the mortgage. In this way, he may hope to make his wife accept a less satisfactory financial settlement because of fear of losing her home. The same may be true, although to a lesser degree, of a family who are dissatisfied with the house itself. They may have found that it is of poor quality and substandard construction and is in need of constant repair. Such a family is not likely to care what happens to the house and may, in fact, let it go by default and subsequent foreclosure.

Whatever the reason may be for the failure to make monthly mortgage payments, the lender will naturally attempt to recover the balance due on the loan, in the manner the law allows. The methods of foreclosing a mortgage differ from state to state. In all states, however, the lender is concerned with cutting off the borrower's equity of redemption so that full ownership can be transferred to the lender.

In many states, the only manner in which the lender may foreclose on the property is by a court action. After all of the court papers have been filed, the proper parties served, and the legal formalities complied with, a court decree will ultimately determine that there has been a default under the mortgage and that the lender has the right to foreclose. The court decree will describe the land and recite the full amount due to the lender. This decree also designates the person who is authorized to sell the land (the sheriff, as a rule), and may specify that notice of public sale shall be published in a certain manner.

The sale is usually made at a public auction. In the majority of these public auctions, the lender is the high bidder and obtains ownership of the house. The manner in which such public auctions are conducted, and whether the borrower's right to have the home sold at a maximum price has been protected have frequently been questioned, but it is still legal. In many states a statutory *right of redemption* then arises after the foreclosure sale. During this period the borrower may still reside in the house, and may redeem it at any time by paying the overdue installments plus the not inexpensive costs of foreclosure.

In a number of states there is no statutory period of redemption. These include Delaware, Florida, Indiana, Maryland, Mississippi, Nebraska, New York, North Carolina, Ohio, Oklahoma, South Caroline, Texas, and Wisconsin. This means that immediately after the foreclosure sale the deed is given to the purchaser.

In Connecticut and Vermont the same court procedures are followed, except that there is no public sale at auction. The lender obtains ownership of the home two to six months after the final decree.

In some states court procedures are not required in foreclosures. In such states (Colorado, Minnesota, Georgia, and a few others), the borrower receives a formal notice that the house will be sold on a certain day at public auction. Usually, in these states, the lender is *not* permitted to purchase the property at the public sale, and the house is sold to the highest bidder.

In Maine, Massachusetts, New Hampshire, and Rhode Island, the mortgage may be foreclosed by the lender by taking peaceful possession of the land and holding it for a period of time. The entry on the land is made in the presence of witnesses, and the borrower is permitted to redeem the land by making the overdue payments within a period of one year (three years in Massachusetts). If the borrower refuses to allow peaceful possession, the lender may obtain a court order giving the lender possession of the premises.

How effective are these mortgage foreclosure procedures, defaults, and rights of redemption? Less than 1% of the homes foreclosed on are ever redeemed by the borrower during the period set aside by the courts for this purpose. Furthermore, less than 7% of the dollar value of deficiency judgments is ever collected from the borrower. This means that the personal promise to repay the lender is of comparatively little value. Finally, the public sale is costly and time-consuming both to the lender and the borrower. In New York State, for example, during the year 1960, there were 40,853 foreclosure sales, and the mortgage lender was the highest bidder on 40,570 of these.

The homeowners who appear to be most vulnerable to foreclosures are the young families who have purchased their houses with a minimum down payment and a high FHA or VA mortgage, and when the house was priced beyond the means of the family. If a borrower has a large equity in the home, there is usually little likelihood that a foreclosure will ever take place.

Mortgages for Non-Home Purposes

Until recently, mortgages were only made for the usual, standard purposes—that is, to assist in the purchase of a home or to help pay for repairs or improvements to the property. However, in recent years, many aggressive and competitive banks have begun to encourage loans for non-home purposes, thus opening up an entirely new field of mortgage lending. Sometimes the mortgage loans are new loans, but more often they represent an increase in the amount of the existing mortgage.

Some of the non-home purposes include college education, purchase of a pleasure boat, medical bills of an extraordinary nature, and even European vacations. When the banks have an excessive amount of cash on hand, they tend to encourage these non-home purpose loans; at other times, when deposits are comparatively low, they are not nearly so anxious to make them.

What usually occurs is along the following lines. When a house is first purchased, the mortgage may well represent the top amount an institution will lend on the property. However, as years go by, the mortgage is reduced and the owner acquires a substantial equity in his property; often, this is accompanied by an inflation in the price of real property which further increases his potential equity. Thus, the amount that can be borrowed increases. Temptation usually exists, in one form or another, for a family to borrow money by means of an increase in the reduced mortgage. The banks usually say that they will lend for "any worthwhile purpose," but in fact they are not primarily concerned with the use to which the money will be put, because they rely primarily on the property itself to assure themselves of repayment of the mortgage loan. Their concern is chiefly with the size of the mortgage in relation to the value of the property; they are also interested in the potential borrower's credit record, his income, and his prospects for the future.

Merely because a homeowner has the opportunity to borrow money, he should not necessarily do so. However, if the family has decided to make a loan, they are far better off making a mortgage loan than in borrowing directly on a note or from a "family-finance" company. The reasons are simple. Interest rates are usually lower than on unsecured personal loans. Furthermore, mortgage repayment periods are almost always longer. In fact, it may often be advisable to consolidate a group of personal installment loans into an increased mortgage, and then pay off in full the personal loans which customarily bear a high interest rate and must be paid off in a comparatively short period of time.

18

Liens

A *lien* is a legal claim against real property, specially authorized by law in favor of certain creditors to secure payment of an indebtedness. It gives the lienor (the one entitled to the lien) a form of additional protection and security to assure that his debt will be paid, over and above an ordinary lawsuit. The lienor makes a written statement of his claim, signs it, has the signature acknowledged before a notary public, and then files it in the local land office. Only certain kinds of creditor are allowed to file a lien against real property and are permitted this kind of security for the payment of their debt. The principal liens allowed by the statutes of the various states are *mechanic's* liens, *judgment* liens, *attachment* liens, and *tax* liens.

Once he has filed his lien, the lienor must take proper steps to make it enforceable. The practices vary from state to state. There is usually a time limit within which a lien must be filed. If the creditor fails to record his lien within the statutory time period, his lien may be removed. He then must recover his claim against the property owner in the same manner as all other creditors (by lawsuit, etc.) who are not entitled to a lien.

The importance of a lien is illustrated by the following example: *A,* a contractor, performs work on *B's* home in the fair value of $5,000 (say, by building a new bathroom and kitchen). When *A* asks for payment, *B* informs him that he is heavily in debt and cannot afford to pay him. *A* files a mechanic's lien against *B's* house. Several weeks later, *B* files in bankruptcy alleging that his debts are greater than his assets and asking that the debts be discharged.

In the foregoing example, a general creditor of *B* (that is, one without a lien) would probably not recover anything on his claim. However, *A's* lien is still good and he may still compel the sale of *B's* home to recover the amount of his claim.

Very often statutes provide that legal action must be commenced by the lien creditor against the debtor within a certain period, usually one or two years, to compel the sale of the property and use the proceeds of the sale to pay the claim. If this is not done, the lien, even though properly filed and recorded, will fail (although certain states permit liens to be renewed from year to year).

Mechanic's Liens. In almost every state, workmen and suppliers who have not been paid for work or materials, which have benefited the real property of the debtor, may file a *mechanic's lien* against such real property. In many states the mechanic's lien roughly resembles, in its legal aspects, a mortgage, and it may be foreclosed just as if it were a mortgage.

The reason for affording a lien to workmen, contractors, and suppliers of materials for the construction or improvement of a house is to protect them in their contribution to the increase in value of the real property. The policy of the courts and the legislatures has been to encourage the building and development of real property within the states.

Mechanic's-lien laws differ from state to state, but the basic principles are much the same. Once a mechanic's lien has been properly filed and recorded, the owner cannot sell or mortgage his property in order to avoid payment. Any prospective buyer must take legal notice of the mechanic's lien affecting the property, and the property remains "burdened" with the lien. The form for a mechanic's lien is usually a simple one and may be readily filled out and filed. However, the foreclosure of a mechanic's lien is a complicated task that will require an attorney.

In some states, the claimant must show that he was hired directly by the landowner, or his agent, to do the particular job. In other states, it is only necessary to prove that the owner consented to the work being done. If the owner knows of the construction or improvement being undertaken, and fails to protest or give notice to the contractor or workman that he will not be responsible for the work, a mechanic's lien may be filed and recorded against his property even though someone else may have actually ordered the work. If his wife, or any member of his family, or even another relative orders certain improvements to be made on the house, his implied approval (by permitting the work to be done) subjects his house to a mechanic's lien. It is therefore important for the homeowner to make a timely objection to the work being done if he did not order it. He should immediately send a written protest to the contractor or workman stating that he did not order the work. It should be sent by certified or registered mail (return receipt requested) and a carbon copy of his letter retained.

Contractors and Subcontractors. Most of the states draw a distinction between contractors and subcontractors in the effect of filing mechanic's liens. A contractor is one who is hired directly by the owner to do a certain job. A subcontractor, in turn, is hired by the contractor to do only a part of the job.

On the other hand, some states give the subcontractor the right to file a mechanic's lien which in no way depends on whether the owner owes anything to the contractor. Even if the owner has paid the contractor in full for the complete job, the subcontractor who claims that he has not been paid by the contractor may nevertheless file and record a mechanic's lien against the owner's property and enforce payment. This, of course, poses a considerable danger to the homeowner who in good faith has paid the contractor in full.

In other states the rule is somewhat different. The subcontractor's mechanic's lien depends, ultimately, on the amount that remains unpaid between the owner and the contractor. In these states the subcontractor may give written notice to the owner as to the value of services to be rendered, and the owner may withhold this amount from payments made to the contractor. In such states, therefore, if the owner has in fact paid the contractor in full (before he is advised of the subcontractor's demand), the subcontractor will not have a lien against the owner's property. Furthermore, if the general contractor fails to complete the work, or does it improperly, the subcontractor will again have no lien. In any case, the subcontractor is not entitled to claim a greater sum than the total agreed on between the owner and the contractor.

Priority of Liens. The precise time when the claim for a mechanic's lien becomes in fact a legal lien against the real property differs from state to state. In some Midwestern states the mechanic's lien becomes effective as of the date when the work was actually begun by the contractor or the workman. In Massachusetts, Rhode Island, and Connecticut, and Illinois, the mechanic's lien becomes effective from the date that the contract for the work was agreed on. In other states, including New York, the mechanic's lien is not effective until a notice of the lien has been sent to the owner and filed in the land office of the county in which the real property is located; in these states a mortgage lender who has advanced money to the landowner before the actual recording of the notice of the mechanic's lien is fully protected. However, in most states, the mechanic's lien is effective at the time that the entire construction job was actually begun. Thus, a subcontractor who completed work on the roof of a building on July 1 would have a lien against the owner's property dating back to April 1, if that was the day on which the job began. In these states, no lien may attach to the real property until *visible* construction has begun, and thus a prospective buyer or mortgage lender who inspects the land before purchase, or before making a mortgage loan, will certainly know that construction is underway.

Several states, including Illinois, New Jersey, and North Dakota, have ruled that when a mechanic's lien is filed and recorded, it is considered *prior* to any mortgage of record, regardless of the respective filing dates. The same rule applies, but only to improvements that are removable by the owner, in Iowa, Arkansas, Missouri, Oregon, and Montana,

Notice and Filing of Mechanic's Liens.   Most mechanic's-lien laws require the contractor or workman to send a notice of his claim to the owner within a specified time, and the lien creditor must thereafter file and record his lien claim within a certain period of time, usually within four months following completion of the work. If the lien creditor fails to follow the procedure specified in the statute, the lien will fail and he will only be able to sue as a general creditor.

Construction Loans.   When a mortgage lender advances funds for the construction of a building, it is usually provided (in rather small print) that the mortgage shall be repaid from any compulsory sale and before any mechanic's lien, for work and materials furnished in connection with such construction, is paid. If this were not so, the mortgage lender might hesitate to lend money for construction, knowing that a lien might arise which would be prior in payment to the mortgage.

The Mortgage Lender's Problem.   We have previously described the relative position of the mortgage lender and the lien creditor. In many instances, the amount of a mechanic's lien is insignificant; but there are occasions when the claim may be substantial. A lien of substantial size will materially affect the relationship between the landowner and the mortgage lender. Almost every mortgage requires that the owner pay any mechanic's lien filed against the property within a specified period of time. If the landowner does not do so, the mortgage lender may pay the mechanic's lien in full, and add the amount paid to the next installment due on the mortgage. If the land-owner fails to pay this sum, the mortgage lender may then foreclose on the property, and under the acceleration clause (which is contained in almost every mortgage) claim that the entire balance of the principal is due. In some cases the mortgage merely states that on the failure of the landowner to pay the amount of a mechanic's lien affecting the real property within a specified time, the default of the landowner shall, *in itself,* be reason for the foreclosure of the mortgage. In either case, the owner of the land is placed at a great disadvantage; he must pay the lien or face the loss of his land.

This problem often arises when an unscrupulous contractor or subcontractor does the required work and then sends a bill for a sum greater than that agreed on. Sometimes the contractor or subcontractor may claim that the price of the work was changed because certain extra work was added to the original agreement. A dispute will arise between the homeowner and the contractor or subcontractor. The contractor or subcontractor may thereupon file and record a mechanic's lien against the owner's house and notify him of its existence by mail. When the mortgage lender learns of this, the owner will be notified that the mechanic's lien must be paid within a certain time or the foreclosure provisions of the mortgage will come into operation. If the lien placed on the property is larger than it should be and the homeowner feels that it is unjustified, a difficult problem arises. On the one hand, there is the mortgage lender, threatening that if the lien is not paid and removed from the records, the mortgage will be foreclosed. Against this is the fact that the mechanic's lien is unwarrantedly high, and the homeowner wishes to contest it by litigation, if necessary. When the homeowner is caught in this squeeze situation, his best move is to consult an attorney. The attorney will probably advise him that if the amount in dispute is material, an application may be made to a local court to remove the mechanic's lien and file in its place a bond in the form of an undertaking by an insurance company. The bond or undertaking provides, in effect, that the amount claimed will be paid by the homeowner if the contractor wins the case after a trial. The contractor or subcontractor will then be compelled to sue for the amount claimed, having the bond or undertaking (instead of the lien) as his security for payment of any judgment he may obtain. To the mortgage lender, the "bonding" of a mechanic's lien is almost the same as actual payment, since the house is no longer subject to a compulsory sale after foreclosure in order to pay the lien.

The mortgage lender has other means of protecting himself against a possible mechanic's lien. He may insist that the contractor's agreement contain a waiver of his right to file a mechanic's lien. However, the position of a subcontractor may not necessarily be affected by such an agreement to which he is not a party. This agreement may prevent the contractor from obtaining subcontractors to do a part of the job since they may be unwilling to lend their credit unless they have the security that a mechanic's lien affords them. However, this is not basically the homeowner's problem, and if his contractor agrees to waive the filing of a lien (in the event of nonpayment) it should be included in any agreement entered into.

One method of resolving the problem is to arrange in advance with the contractor to pay for the improvements by installments as the work progresses. Some mortgage lenders will insist on this, and owners are advised to follow this procedure wherever possible. The owner or mortgage lender, under this agreement, may withhold payment from the contractor of any amounts that may be due to a subcontractor until the time for giving notice of any subcontractor's mechanic's lien expires. However, many contractors will refuse to agree to this provision. A compromise can be made by the owner paying installments as the work progresses, but withholding 20% for a period of time after the work is completed.

In some states the owner or mortgage lender is protected from a mechanic's lien filed by a subcontractor, providing payments are made in accordance with sworn schedule of payments submitted by the prime contractor. It is assumed that such lists of payments made to the subcontractors are all-inclusive. However, it may be a wise move to issue checks made payable to the contractor and the subcontractors in their joint names, so their endorsements on the check will be considered payments in full.

The owner or mortgage lender may also require a bond or undertaking to be put up by the contractor, before beginning the work, to ensure that all subcontractors will be paid in full. When the final payment has been made, the contractor usually signs a statement to the effect that he has paid all the subcontractors in full for their services, or for materials they furnished, and also that there are no mechanic's liens pending.

Purchase-Money Mortgages.   If a buyer takes title to real property and at the same approximate time orders certain improvements made to the premises which subsequently result in a mechanic's lien being filed against the property, the question of priority of payment between the contractor and the purchase-money mortgage (the seller who takes back a mortgage for part of the purchase price) becomes even more complicated. When the seller has taken back a purchase-money mortgage on the house, most states will give the seller priority over mechanic's liens that were filed and recorded against the premises thereafter.

Lis Pendens. When litigation is commenced *directly* involving real property, there is usually a statute permitting the complaining party to file a notice, in the county in which the real property is located, notifying the public that such action has been commenced. This legal notification that a lawsuit is pending is filed by means of a document known as a *lis pendens,* literally "lawsuit pending." Today, in most states, a *lis pendens* may be filed in actions involving the possession, use, or enjoyment of real property or the foreclosure of a mortgage. A *lis pendens* may also be filed in actions to foreclose a mechanic's lien, to compel the removal of an encroachment, or to set aside a deed as a fraud on creditors. Almost any action directly affecting the real property of the defendant is subject to the filing of a *lis pendens,* but the types of action vary considerably from state to state depending on the local statutes. In every case, the action must affect either the title or ownership of real property as indicated by the statute involved. For example, if the action is brought merely to recover a sum of money from the owner of real property, the action has no relation to the debtor's real property and a *lis pendens* would be improper. It would also not be permitted in action for damages for trespass, or even for the dissolution of a partnership formed to deal in real property, or an action to foreclose a chattel mortgage covering personal property that may be located on real property, or an action by a real-estate broker for a commission on the sale of realty. In these cases, there is no action that directly affects the land and no *lis pendens* may be filed against the real property of the defendant.

The *lis pendens,* or notice of the pendency of a civil action, must state the names of the parties, the object of the legal action, and a brief description of the defendant's real property. Without a proper description of the property, the *lis pendens* is completely ineffective. If the legal action is settled, or discontinued, or a final judgment is rendered against the plaintiff who filed the notice, and the time to appeal has expired, or the plaintiff unreasonably neglects to proceed in the action, the court may direct that the *lis pendens* be cancelled by the county clerk. Sometimes the *lis pendens* may be cancelled by a deposit, bond, or undertaking which is placed on file in the court where the action is pending. The undertaking must provide sufficient security so that the plaintiff is assured of having the judgment paid. A *lis pendens* filed against the defendant's real property has the effect of limiting his ability to convey or transfer ownership of the property or to raise a mortgage. A purchaser would not, of course, take title to property on which a *lis pendens* is filed, without sufficient surety to guarantee him against loss.

The filing of a *lis pendens* is considered a notice to the public from the date of its filing, and particularly to a prospective purchaser or to a potential mortgage lender. Any person who obtains ownership of the property or lends money as a mortgage lender to the defendant thereafter is bound thereby and may ultimately have to pay any sum of money awarded by the court.

The purpose then of filing a *lis pendens* is to give legal notice of the existence of a claim to a prospective purchaser or a mortgage lender from the time that it is filed until the final judgment in the action. The *lis pendens* thereby preserves the creditor's rights from the time the litigation is commenced until its termination, and allows the successful party to collect on any judgment he obtains.

The primary object of the *lis pendens* is to give notice to persons who are not parties to the lawsuit of its pendency, and for that purpose, the *status quo* is preserved. A *lis pendens,* properly filed, may render title unmarketable. It would justify the rejection of title by a prospective purchaser, inasmuch as the purchaser is not required to investigate or obtain evidence as to the facts on which the action is based, or to determine whether it is maintainable. The mere fact of the existence of a *lis pendens* in the title report, as stated above, justifies a prospective purchaser in rejecting title. It will then be necessary for the seller (or his attorney) to obtain a bond guaranteeing payment of any judgment by an insurance company. If so obtained, the lien is then regarded as "bonded," and the objection to title is removed; the purchaser must then take title.

Judgments.   A court order directing that one litigant recover a specified amount of money from another party is known as a judgment. It may also become a lien—that is, a legal claim against real property which will affect the debtor's property. A lawsuit may arise out of an infinite variety of circumstances. For example, if a home-owner is involved in an automobile accident that resulted in injuries, a lawsuit would probably be commenced by the injured party to recover a judgment against the homeowner. If a judgment is won and the judgment is not paid it will result in a lien against the home-owner's real property. In most states the judgment, in the form of a court order, directs that the plaintiff recover a specified sum from the defendant. The judgment will become a lien when it is recorded or docketed in the land office of the county in which the homeowner's real property is located. It will also affect any real property the defendant acquires thereafter in that county.

In certain states, including Tennessee, Illinois, and Indiana, the judgment is effective as a lien against the defendant's real property from the time that it is issued by the judge. However, in most states the judgment must be filed, recorded, and entered in judgment dockets or books, alphabetically arranged according to the name of the judgment debtor, and which are maintained in the court clerk's office in the county where the real property is located. A prospective buyer, or mortgage lender, will request that these judgment dockets or books be searched by the title company before buying real property or lending money to the owner of real property. No one will buy a house, or lend money with that property as security, if there is a lien against it. The lien must be satisfied (by payment, or the filing of a bond). The length of time that a judgment remains a lien on the real property of the defendant differs from state to state. In most states a judgment will remain a lien for ten years from the time that it is filed and recorded. In New York, the judgment remains a lien for twenty years.

If the defendant owns land outside the county in which the judg-ment has been rendered, the judgment may be made a lien against the real property in another county by filing a *transcript* (actually a certified copy) of the judgment in the appropriate office of the county in which such property is located.

A judgment rendered by a federal district court is usually treated in the same way as one made and entered in a state court. The federal court judgment is also a lien on the real property of the defendant located in the county where the federal district court rendered the judgment. In some states the transcript of the judgment or court order must be filed in the land office of the county where the real property is located.

The judgment ordered concludes with the court's direction that an *execution* be issued against the property of the defendant. The execution is a legal order directing the sheriff (or other public officer) to sell the property of the judgment debtor to pay the judgment in whole or in part, if it has not been paid in cash. Usually the attorney for the plaintiff will cause the execution to be issued and forward it to the proper public official. The sheriff customarily serves a copy of the execution on the judgment debtor and demands payment of the judgment. If payment is not made within a specified number of days he will endorse upon the execution the fact that demand has been made. He will also endorse upon the execution the exact description of the real property owned by the debtor and *levy* upon it, which usually includes serving a paper giving the landowner appropriate notice. This means that such property has been set apart, as required by law, by the official, for public sale. Next, the official is usually required to publish notice of the forthcoming sale of the judgment debtor's property. At the date fixed for sale, if the judgment is still unpaid, the property is auctioned off to the highest bidder, who is often the judgment creditor, since he can bid up to the amount of the judgment and still not be required to pay cash for the property. Of course, the judgment creditor is required to pay for the costs of the sheriff or other public official in selling the property, and these incidental costs may be surprisingly high.

As in the case of mortgage foreclosures, there is usually a period during which the homeowner, whose real property is being sold to pay the judgment against him, can recover his property by making payment to the judgment creditor. This redemption period differs from state to state. In most jurisdictions, the redemption period is about one year, but it may run as long as two years. If no redemption is made by the homeowner, a sheriff's deed (or similar procedure through another public official) obtains a title that is somewhat doubtful and tenuous. At best, it is never completely satisfactory. Numerous objections may be raised to such ownership, depending on the legal technicalities with which the judgment was enforced and the manner in which the execution and sale was carried out. A buyer of real property at such a sale *must,* as a matter of common sense, obtain a title insurance policy which will, at the very least, insure him as to the value of the real estate he acquires, should his title later be questioned and prove to be vulnerable.

If the judgment has been paid in full, the original homeowner should receive a written, notarized statement from the judgment creditor that such payment has been received and a document is given, known as a *satisfaction,* which is signed by the judgment creditor and filed in the county where the judgment or transcript of judgment has been recorded. This satisfies the judgment, and it is no longer a lien against the real property.

In those states where the judgment itself does not create a lien against the real property of the judgment debtor, the execution to the sheriff, when issued, will create a lien. In these states, the lien dates from the day on which the execution was delivered to the sheriff or other public official, and the judgment ceases to be a lien against real property if execution has not been made within one year (occasionally two years) following the entry of judgment.

It has been mentioned previously that a judgment against real property may be enforced by compelling the sale of real property and turning over the proceeds of such sale to the judgment creditor. It is of great importance to any potential buyer to be assured that there are no existing judgments against the seller which are a lien against the property (or in fact any judgments against the seller that have not been paid) before the closing of title. Another important consideration is the priority of creditors who are entitled to a lien against real property, since a sale may not realize enough to pay all of them. Generally, the rule is that the creditor with a lien against the property who first files and records his lien, in the manner prescribed by law, is the first to receive payment on the compulsory sale of the premises by court order.

Attachments. While ordinarily a judgment does not actually become a lien against real property until the claimant wins the lawsuit, there is a special situation in which a creditor may be entitled to a lien against real property *before* a final judgment. If the claimant can prove to the satisfaction of the court that there is a likelihood that the homeowner whom he is suing (or is about to sue) will try to sell the property before a judgment can be obtained against him, the court may allow the creditor to attach the real property of the debtor in advance of obtaining a final judgment. Such an attachment is effective as a lien against the real property of the debtor in the same manner as a mechanic's lien or a judgment, and any subsequent buyer or mortgage lender is regarded as having legal knowledge of its existence from the time that it is filed and recorded in the land office of the county in which the real property is located.

The conditions under which an attachment may be allowed against the debtor's real or personal property differ from state to state. The plaintiff in an ordinary lawsuit (such as an automobile-accident case, for example) is not usually entitled to an attachment. As a rule, the plaintiff must show the court that there is (1) some likelihood that the debtor will actually sell or transfer ownership of his house to avoid paying any judgment that may ultimately be obtained, or (2) that the debtor is likely to leave the state, or (3) that fraud has been involved in the claim he has against the debtor. The court will usually require the claimant to file a bond or undertaking in court to pay the debtor's expenses should a judgment not be awarded to the claimant at the conclusion of the trial. If the court finds that the claimant is entitled to an attachment, it will issue an order, signed by a judge, known as a *writ of attachment,* and the writ will be delivered to the sheriff (or other public official). The sheriff is usually required to visit the property and either serve a paper on the party involved or post a notice of attachment, usually by fastening it to the door. He then endorses on the writ that he has "levied" against the debtor's property, and describes the real property of the debtor in detail on the papers. The sheriff must then file and record a certificate in the county office within which the property is located, describing the real property attached by the court order. An attachment creates a lien which, however, may only be enforced *after* judgment is awarded to the claimant. It is a form of protection to the claimant against the debtor's transferring ownership of his real property in order to avoid paying the judgment that may be rendered against him. However, from the point of view of a prospective purchaser of real estate, the title must be rejected because the writ of attachment constitutes a valid lien against the property. Unless the lien is bonded by a licensed bonding company, the title must be regarded as unacceptable to a prospective purchaser.

Other Liens against Real Property.   There are other liens that may affect real property. For example, unpaid federal income taxes may result in the imposition of a lien against the taxpayer's property by the government. If there is an unpaid state income tax, a similar result may be expected. This lien will usually affect real property owned by the taxpayer from the time that the assessment list is received by the tax collector. Since a prospective buyer or mortgage lender is usually unaware of the nature of such lists, the lien will have no effect on anyone except the taxpayer, unless a notice of the tax lien has been filed with the land office of the county in which the taxpayer's real property is located.

If the landowner dies and his estate is of considerable value, the failure to pay an estate (inheritance) tax may result in the filing of a lien. The decedent is entitled to an exemption of at least $60,000 from any federal estate tax, and possibly twice that much if he is married, before any federal estate taxes may become due.

A tax lien (for unpaid estate taxes) will be valid for ten years against the real and personal property of the decedent; the lien against real property will date from the decedent's death and affect real property even where title has been transferred to a surviving spouse. The theory is that the ownership of the property was as joint tenants or as community property, and therefore the surviving spouse retains the liability. It is of considerable importance to understand that tax liens do *not* have to be filed or recorded to be effective against the *heirs* of the decedent. However, a potential buyer, who has no knowledge of the tax lien or a prospective mortgage lender, will not be affected by this type of lien.

The Commissioner of Internal Revenue may issue a certificate that will effectively discharge the estate tax lien when he has reason to believe that the entire amount will be paid or when he has received payment in full. This becomes particularly important when a person dies and the family desires to sell the property in question before the estate is closed. A purchaser will surely refuse to take title until such assurance has been received. The federal estate tax lien may even affect real property transferred by the decedent within three years prior to his death, under an estate tax rule that all property of the decedent disposed of within such period may be subject to estate tax if made in *contemplation of death*. What this means, in plain language, is that a person who is seriously ill may not give away a large part of his estate in "contemplation" of death. Such gifts, although otherwise valid, are taxable as part of the decedent's estate. The federal estate tax lien will not affect most homeowners, for it is of little consequence unless the decedent has a large estate. However, caution is suggested when the homeowner has (or may have) large amounts of life insurance which must be included within his estate in computing the total amount that may or may not be subject to estate tax.

Failure to pay a federal *gift tax* (on large gifts made during a person's lifetime) may also result in a lien against real property. Like the federal estate tax, the gift-tax lien remains in existence for ten years. There are various exemptions for all taxpayers; without detailing these exemptions and exclusions, it is sufficient to note that each taxpayer is allowed to dispose of $30,000 by gift during his lifetime without paying a gift tax, and an additional $3,000 in any year to any person in his family without being liable for a gift tax.

What has been said concerning federal tax liens also applies to those states that have estate and income taxes, but to a lesser degree, since the tax rate is markedly lower.

However, depending on local laws, a lien may exist for various other unpaid state taxes. There may be an unpaid corporation franchise tax; this will become a lien against any real property owned by a corporation, and large corporations are often the sellers of real-estate developments. Sales taxes are common in the various states, and a lien may sometimes be filed against the real property of the debtor to recover such local taxes. Old-age assistance liens may occasionally be made when the homeowner has been receiving such assistance. There is even the possibility of a bail-bond lien affecting real property. The lien of general taxes and special assessments is discussed elsewhere.

Finally, there are certain "equitable" liens that may affect real property. As a rule, "equitable" liens arise only in unusual or complicated situations, but they do occur often enough to warrant caution on the part of a prospective purchaser. An example might arise when a decedent has willed property equally to three children and only one has paid the taxes and carrying charges on the real property, and the two others have refused to contribute their share. In such a case the court, on application, may give the person who has paid such charges an equitable lien against the real property and allow him to compel a sale, or enter into a sale, of the property, and retain, out of the proceeds of the sale, the amount he has paid on property expenses.

Homestead Rights and Exemptions

"Homestead" rights have been created to provide families with a last refuge from the stresses of financial misfortune. Technically, an owner's entire real estate may be sold by a court order to pay off creditors' judgments against him. If there were no limitations on this power of forced sale, a creditor could compel the sale of a home, and in effect throw the family into the street, leaving them dependent on charity or local relief. In order to prevent this, most states provide that a debtor's house (up to a certain limited value) cannot be sold to pay off his debts. To this degree, it is the policy of the law that the preservation of the family home is more important than the payment of debts to creditors.

The amount and the extent of the homestead exemption depends strictly on the statutes of the various states. Some states have limitations as to value and others have limitations as to area. Often there is a difference between a rural homestead exemption and an urban homestead exemption. However, in most cases, the amount of the homestead exemption does not exceed a value of $5,000. Often a sheriff's sale will be held without complying with the formalities of setting aside the amount of the homestead exemption, since land in the value of that amount would be left to the debtor and the remainder of the land would pass to a purchaser at the forced sale.

Of course, there are certain debts against which the homestead exemption will not apply. When a mortgage is foreclosed against the property of the debtor, there is no homestead exemption. The same is true of a mechanic's lien or a lien for unpaid taxes or special assessments foreclosed against the property. The homestead exemption does apply, however, against most general creditors.

Because it is the policy of the law to protect the family, the family must be actually living in the house that is to be protected by a homestead exemption, and the head of the family usually must be the property owner. In some states, there is a requirement that a proper declaration of homestead be filed.

Once the householder has complied with the local homestead statute, should the other members of his family move away and he remains, the homestead exemption will continue. On the death of the husband, the widow usually has the right to continue to occupy the home; and she receives her husband's title to the homestead exemption. In a few states, including Delaware, Maryland, Pennsylvania, and Indiana, a homestead exemption is not allowed; but, even in these states, a small amount of real or personal property is exempt.

In addition to the homestead exemptions, which vary from state to state, almost every state has certain other exemptions applying to homeowners. In recent years, these exemptions have been extended to household furniture, wedding rings, jewelry up to a certain amount (usually under $50), books and Bibles, appliances such as washing machines, drying machines, and refrigerators, and certain other kinds of personal property in the house, specifically defined by the exemption statute. The effect of these statutes is to make certain personal property, as well as the value of a portion of the real property, exempt from collection by any creditors of the owner. Bear in mind, once again, that this does not apply against a mortgage or lien, only against a *general* creditor. A mortgagee and a lienor are regarded as *secured* creditors.

CHAPTER 19

Property Taxes, Assessments, and Income Taxes

The owner of real property is concerned with two distinct kinds of taxation. *General real-estate taxes* imposed by the various local communities are routine, an anticipated consideration for the real-property owner. In addition, there is the over-all gain or loss that you may sustain on the sale of your real property for federal and state income-tax purposes. This consideration arises only when you sell your principal place of residence. This type of tax is called a capital gains tax. When it is due, it is paid directly to the federal and state governments at the regular time for payment of the respective income taxes. This will be discussed later in this chapter.

Local Taxes on Real Property. Each state government has the original power to tax real property within its borders. However, the power of taxation is seldom enforced by the state legislature itself. Instead, the right to tax real property is usually delegated to the local governmental taxing bodies, and any tax on real property in your community is probably imposed by the village, town, city, or county in which you reside, and in some cases by a school district within your county.

There is usually more than one local tax that affects your real property, such as, for example, a city tax and a school tax. In each case the amount of the local tax is determined by means of an assessment based upon the value of your real property. Once the assessed valuation of the property has been ascertained by the local tax assessor for the taxing body, it is multiplied by a certain percentage (the *tax rate*) fixed by law in order to arrive at the tax for the year.

The tax "year" may vary with respect to each local tax levied on real property. For example, a village, county, or city tax may cover the calendar year and is usually payable in two or four installments, each of which must be paid before a specified day (usually within 90 days). If taxes are billed in two installments, the first may have to be paid within the period specified following January 1 of that year (say, April 1), and the second half should be paid within the period specified following July 1 of that year (probably October 1). On the other hand, a school tax may be computed on a fiscal-year basis instead of the calendar year. In such a case, a tax bill for the entire fiscal year may be rendered you on September 1, covering the period from September 1 of that year to August 31 of the following year. The school tax can usually also be paid on a semiannual basis. In such a case, the first half may then fall due on September 1, payable within a specified period following that date, and the second half falls due and is payable six months later (on March 1) of the following year or within a specified additional period thereafter.

Computing the Local Real-Estate Taxes. In arriving at the assessed valuation of real property, the local tax assessor is required to classify and describe each tax lot within his jurisdiction. The entries in the tax assessor's records must be sufficient to identify each tax lot by describing the approximate number of square feet (or acres) contained in each tax lot. A tax lot may not correspond to the boundary lines of the land owned by the homeowner and, in fact, the land may comprise several tax lots or make up only a part of one tax lot. (This would occur, for example, if you owned only one lot in a large development.) When the local tax bill is sent to you, a description of the tax lots that comprise your land should appear on the bill. The official description of your land for tax purposes is necessarily condensed on the tax records, but the description must be sufficient to identify the property that is being assessed. The tax assessor then prepares an *assessment roll,* the form of which is usually prescribed by local statute. From this, a tax map is customarily prepared and approved by the state tax commission. A number is then assigned to each tax lot shown on the map, which can then be further identified from the official records of the tax assessor. If the description in the official records of the tax assessor is insufficient to enable anyone to locate the land with a reasonable degree of accuracy, no subsequent taxation based on the assessed valuation of the land is lawful. However, most American communities are so built up and developed that this is an extremely unlikely contingency at the present time. Even in undeveloped regions of the western United States or in the new states of Hawaii and Alaska, tax records are generally in fairly good shape, and it is rare for a taxpayer to find any difficulty in identifying his property on tax assessment rolls or maps.

Although taxing procedures differ widely in detail from state to state and even from locality to locality, all real property subject to taxation is assessed by a local tax assessor either at its full value or at a certain percentage of its full value. The full value of your real property is the price the property would sell for under ordinary circumstances. It is the actual cash value in the real-estate market at the time of the assessment in the opinion of the assessor (which may or may not be correct). There is no reduction in this valuation because of any mortgages affecting the property. The buildings on the land and the probable cost of replacing them, and the market value of a similar piece of land, are the important considerations for the tax assessor.

In arriving at the assessed value of the land for tax purposes, the purchase price of the land paid by you (even though it was acquired shortly before the assessment) does not necessarily establish the true market value of the land. It is only one factor that the tax assessor will weigh in determining the true value. It is always possible that you have either overpaid or underpaid for the land. Another factor in determining the assessed valuation is the assessed valuation fixed for the preceding year. But land values change, and they are not permanently fixed by the tax assessor. However, obviously the assessed valuation should not vary by substantial amounts from one year to another. Each taxpayer should receive notice that he has the opportunity to question each new assessment as it is fixed.

Occasionally, the landowner will feel that his land has been overvalued by the tax assessor and that the taxes on his property are too high. In that event, the landowner may apply to the tax assessor or the local board to revalue his land; if his application is refused, a further application may be made to a court to review the assessment, alleging that the land has been overvalued. Real-estate taxes must be as equal and uniform as possible, bearing in mind that no two pieces of property are identical. This court proceeding to review an assessment is known as a *certiorari*. The court will carefully consider whether the assessment has been set at a reasonable figure. The landowner has the burden to prove that the assessment is higher than it should be. This may be done by showing that other comparable property in the vicinity has a lower assessment, that recent sales of similar property are lower, or other convincing arguments. If the court finds that the assessment is unreasonable, unlawful, erroneous, or unequal for any of the reasons claimed by the landowner, it may order that a correction of the assessment be made in whole or in part. The court order should conform the assessment of the landowner's property to the valuations and assessments of other similar property in the community on the same tax roll to secure an equality of assessment. The ideal goal—uniform assessed valuation—is difficult to attain, and usually the court will intervene only if the tax is obviously excessive or erroneous.

Assessments for Local Improvements. There is a definite distinction between general real-estate taxes and *assessments*. A general real-estate tax is imposed by the local tax district on all the real property within its jurisdiction. Assessments, on the other hand, have specific reference to public improvements that are especially beneficial to a particular group of individual landowners and are imposed in proportion to the particular benefit that their land will derive from the specific improvement. For example, the county, village, or city may order a repaving of the road in front of your house, or the construction of sidewalks, street lighting, or the laying of a sewer line underneath your street—an improvement that will service your house. In such cases, you and your neighbors must pay a proportionate share of the cost of these specialized improvements, and a share of the cost is apportioned to you. This is called an assessment. However, if the primary purpose of an improvement is to serve the general public, such as a school or a courthouse, it is not usually financed by special assessments.

Among the important considerations when you buy real property are to determine whether sewer lines have already been connected and whether the street in front of the house is likely to be paved or widened in the near future. In such a case, you may reasonably expect an assessment to be levied in addition to your local general taxes, which you will have to pay at the time the improvement is made or shortly thereafter. For example, if the pattern of public improvement in the area surrounding the property indicates that sewers will soon be installed to replace cesspools you may assume that a special assessment will soon be levied against your property. However, if you buy a house where these improvements have already been made, and a search of the county land records shows that the assessments have been paid by the seller, or the seller is required to pay outstanding assessments before the closing, you may then be reasonably sure that you will not be assessed for these improvements, which, of course, would add to the cost of your home.

As a rule, assessments for such public improvements are made after the work has been completed, sometimes even before it has begun. You may count on the fact that all of the homeowners who are to benefit by the improvement will be assessed in proportion to the amount of land they own and the benefit that their particular land is to derive from the public improvement. It would be unlawful to assess one property owner and not another when both are beneficially affected.

If your assessment for the public improvement is not paid, it becomes a lien against your real property. Unpaid assessments must be collected by a foreclosure proceeding rather than by an action against the individual owner. Usually this procedure is a last resort and is seldom enforced by local tax-collecting agencies. But more important is the fact that unpaid assessments constitute a lien against the property.

Since the ownership of land obligates the owner to pay for public improvements that benefit his land, the local government authority may repair crosswalks along the streets adjacent to the landowner's property, or construct and repair sidewalks, curbs, and gutters on such a street, and the landowner may be assessed for the value of the improvement to his property. An important consideration of the lien against real property (which arises when a landowner does not pay his assessment) is that the mortgage lender usually is not affected by the foreclosure of such a lien. It is only the property owner who may lose his land if he does not pay. The proceeds of sale will be used first to satisfy the mortgage lender and then to pay money due to the local authorities.

Tax Liens.   Until the local tax or assessment is determined with respect to the landowner's property, there can be no tax lien against his land. After due notification has been given to the landowner that payment must be made within the statutory period, followed by failure to pay, and after the filing of a tax lien, there is the possibility that a tax foreclosure may result. Thereafter, if still unpaid, the property will be sold at public auction and the taxes or assessments against the land will be paid from the proceeds obtained at the public sale. The foreclosure of a tax lien on the property is similar in many respects to that of the foreclosure of a mortgage. The landowner must be duly notified of the imposition of the tax or assessment. Usually the statutes provide that two or more years must pass from the time the local tax or assessment becomes a lien affecting the property before foreclosure may commence. When the statutory period has expired, the local authorities are permitted to foreclose on the land in a *summary* manner. This means that the foreclosure of the lien affecting the land takes place rather quickly, and the landowner may not then complain that he has not been given time to make the payments. There is always a waiting period (say, two years, as previously mentioned) but once that time has expired, the tax foreclosure will usually proceed rapidly in favor of the local governmental authority. This rather swift procedure is permitted because the landowner has presumably known of the tax lien for at least two years and has failed to make payment. As long as he has had a reasonable opportunity to complain of the assessment, or to pay it, and he has taken no steps in either direction during the statutory period, the local governmental authority is allowed to foreclose the lien in the summary manner provided by law. The duty rests on the landowner to keep himself informed of his local real-property taxes or assessments. If he fails to do so, it is his misfortune and he suffers the consequences. It is important, therefore, to read over *carefully* all notices, bills, and papers sent by the local government.

The landowner must, as previously mentioned, keep himself informed of tax liens or assessments that affect his property, and indirect notice by publication may be deemed sufficient for a tax foreclosure proceeding. This is true legally, even though he does not read the publication in which the notice appears. At any time before the tax foreclosure is completed under the law, the landowner may pay the tax or assessment affecting the property, together with interest and any penalties described, and prevent the compulsory sale of his land.

Tax Foreclosure Proceedings. The proceedings for tax foreclosures differ in the various states. There is, however, a typical and usual manner of foreclosing on the property of an owner who is delinquent in paying his taxes or assessments. The local governmental authority files a list of delinquent taxpayers in the land office of the county where the property is located. Such filing is the equivalent of notice to the landowner that he is delinquent. Following this, as already described, a publication in a local newspaper for a number of weeks should notify the landowner that he is delinquent and that tax foreclosure proceedings will be undertaken if payment is not made. As a rule, most people do not read these notices, for they rarely appear as other than small advertisements in closely set print, difficult to read. Any person having an interest in the real property may then serve a written answer to the foreclosure proceeding commenced by the governmental agency. The answer is usually filed in the court in which the action has been commenced and a copy served on the attorney for the tax district who has commenced the proceeding. If there is a mortgage lender who has a mortgage on the property, he, too, must be notified of the tax foreclosure. Usually, the mortgage lender will be protected and the mortgage paid off by the sale of the property before the tax or assessment is paid to the governmental authority.

Once in court, these foreclosures receive special treatment. Tax foreclosures are usually determined quickly. The proceeding is preferred over most other cases that are to be tried by the court. In some states, a court will order the sale of the property and will also determine the disposition of the proceeds of the sale. A court order will direct that the collecting officer of the tax district prepare and sign a deed to the party purchasing the property at the tax sale, and that such a tax deed shall be a lawful transfer of the property. The foreclosure of a tax lien usually does not terminate the restrictions in a deed, or any easements that affect the property. A new owner must recognize such burdens to his land in the same manner as the old owner.

Income Tax

A separate and distinct consideration is the profit or loss involved in the sale of your house. This is not a daily or yearly consideration; it will arise only when you sell your home. For many years, the federal and state governments have attempted to strengthen home ownership by granting special tax treatment to the homeowner.

When you sell your house, it is quite possible that you will receive more than you paid for it. This is especially true in areas where inflation has caused land values and construction costs to increase over the years. Whenever a profit is realized on the sale of your house, it must be considered as income for federal tax purposes, although the profit on the sale of a house is seldom treated as ordinary income. The gain realized on the sale of your house is the difference between the price you receive when selling and the price you originally paid for it. Such gain is regarded as capital gains, not as ordinary income. Under unusual provisions of the federal tax laws, the gain is taxable in a special manner. Should the sale of your home result in a loss, however, no such loss is allowable as a deduction from your taxable income for the year.

If you have owned your home for more than six months before selling it, the profit is considered a capital gain, as mentioned above; and the tax will be no more than 25% of the profit. If your ownership has been less than six months (which is not likely), the tax must be computed at your normal tax rate for ordinary income and you will not be allowed to claim a capital gain. However, there is some advantage in the way you may be able to report this short-term capital gain on the sale of a house held for less than six months. Such a short-term gain may be reduced by setting it off against any capital losses that you have sustained during the year (as in the stock market, for example).

If the sale of the taxpayer's house is followed within one year by the purchase of another house; or by occupation of a newly constructed house within 18 months, construction of which was begun within one year after the sale; or when a new residence had already been purchased within one year prior to the sale of the old house; then no tax need be paid on any gain made on the sale of the original house. This special tax treatment is particularly advantageous to homeowners in a period of inflation. The law, in effect, postpones the date of payment of taxes on any gain realized on the sale of a house until the taxpayer sells the last house in the series of houses and does not buy another. The cost of each new house purchased over the years is not, for tax purposes, the price the taxpayer paid for it, but it is considered to be the price he received for the sale of his old house. This special tax treatment may be a little difficult to understand. Here are some examples:

John Richmond purchased a home in 1950 for $15,000, and sold it last year for $20,000. He bought (and occupied) another house within one year following the sale of the old home, for $20,000. In this transaction, the gain of $5,000 is not regarded as a gain for income tax purposes. However, had the new house cost less than $20,000, there would be a taxable gain on the difference between the sales price of the old home and the cost of the new home. For example, had Mr. Richmond purchased a new home for only $17,000, there would be taxable gain of $3,000 to report as a capital gain. This taxable figure is reached because Mr. Richmond emerged from the transaction with a $3,000 profit. On the $3,000 profit, he would pay a *maximum* tax of 25%.

In order to avail himself of the benefits of this "reinvestment" privilege, the homeowner, as stated previously, must occupy the new house within one year from the date of the sale of the original home, or he must commence building a new home within one year after the sale, and actually occupy the new home within eighteen months following the sale of his prior home. If the homeowner does not invest, in a new home, any part of the proceeds he receives for the sale of his old home, the entire profit that he realized on the sale will be fully taxable.

This process of sale and purchase within the time period prescribed may be repeated indefinitely; and as long as the taxpayer observes the above-stated rules, the accumulated gains on each side may possibly *never* be taxed. For example, if the owner dies while still owning the last home he purchased, the tax on any of these capital gains will never have to be paid. The reason is that the new owner, who received title under the will of the deceased owner or by the laws of intestacy, takes the property by inheritance; and no capital gains tax need be paid. It is possible, however, than an *inheritance* tax may have to be paid. However, under federal tax laws, the first $60,000 of the taxpayer's estate is exempt; and if the taxpayer is married, the exemption is ordinarily doubled. This means that there may be no inheritance tax unless the estate valuation exceeds $120,000. Inasmuch as statistics reveal that a person who becomes a homeowner is likely to remain one for the rest of his life, there is always a good chance that the gains realized on the sale of a home will never be taxed at all.

The special tax treatment afforded to homeowners who replace their former residence by purchasing a new home, within the required time period, is permitted for only one residence at a time. The sale of a second residence (such as a summer home in the mountains), which is not the *principal* residence does not receive this special treatment; and any gains realized on the sale must be included in the regular taxable income for the year in which it occurs.

If there is a loss on the sale of a home, which sometimes occurs, no tax advantage accrues to the taxpayer, because the taxpayer is not allowed to deduct the loss from either his ordinary income or his capital gains.

The cost of repairs that the seller made to the home over the years of his ownership is not a deductible item for tax purposes. These expenses are considered to be normal upkeep—a part of the regular cost of home ownership. However, the cost of repairs and painting when specifically made in order to sell the property are considered as part of the cost of sale, and these may be deducted from any profit realized. Peculiarly enough, this may be done even though the homeowner should have made such repairs years before. To be deductible, these expenses must not be for permanent improvements or replacements, and they must be paid within 30 days after the residence is sold. In addition, all of the repairs must have been made during the 90 days preceding the day on which the contract of sale was signed.

To give an example, Robert Robinson decides to sell his residence. He had purchased it 5 years before at a cost of $17,500. To make it more attractive to prospective buyers, he has had it painted at a cost of $600 and immediately paid for the work done. He sold the house the next month for $25,000. The broker's expense and other selling expenses, including newspaper advertisements, and gardening during the preceding 90 days, amounted to $1,500. The sales price for tax purposes is $25,000, less the cost of painting the house, gardening, newspaper advertisements, and the brokerage commission; the adjusted cost is now $19,600. The gain would be $5,400, not $7,500, because $2,100 has been added to the original cost price. If he buys a replacement residence within the time prescribed, as previously pointed out, no part of the gain will be taxable. However, if he fails to purchase a new residence, a tax would have to be paid on $5,400.

The taxpayer is not required to occupy the old home until the actual date of its sale. The same tax exemption is available to him even though he has already moved to his new home (if purchased within one year preceding the sale).

The ownership of stock in a cooperative housing corporation is treated as equivalent to the ownership of a residence, providing that the owner of the stock uses the apartment or house as his principal place of residence.

Any gain the taxpayer realizes on the sale of his home should be reported in Schedule D of Form 1040. If the replacement is not anticipated, the tax is paid for the year in which the sale took place. If the taxpayer is undecided whether he will replace the residence with another within the time period allowed, he may *report* the sale for the year in which it took place but he need not pay any tax on it until a final decision is made (within a year of the sale). If he then does not purchase a new home, he should file an amended return for the year in which the sale took place and pay any additional tax required. In any event, all of the details with respect to the sale of a home are to be reported in Schedule D in detail.

CHAPTER 20

Insurance for Your Home

It may seem difficult to believe, in this era of high-pressure advertising, that many homeowners still do not fully understand the importance of adequate insurance protection. Although almost every homeowner needs and carries fire ("home") insurance, such a policy, in and of itself leaves the homeowner otherwise unprotected from many of the risks attendant to home ownership. For example, a visitor may fall and suffer severe personal injuries as the result of a defect in your sidewalk or because of a broken stair on your property leading to the entrance. A claim made against you will not be covered by a regular insurance policy. Also, if you hire someone to make repairs on your property and if in the process he is injured, he may make a claim against you; and this, too, will not be covered by ordinary insurance. If your house sustains damages as the result of high winds, you will not be covered by a regular home insurance policy unless it has been "extended" to cover wind damage. It should be apparent that a homeowner must have other insurance protection in addition to that offered by the usual fire (or "home") insurance policy.

Standard Form of Fire Insurance Policy. Most states have adopted, by statute, standard forms of fire insurance policies which every insurance company within the state must use. These fire insurance policies are more favorable to the homeowner than the policy formerly issued by insurance companies, which, as a rule, paid only for damage specifically caused by fire.

There are several approved forms. The most common type is the basic *dwelling-and-contents* form; this policy protects the homeowner against the perils of fire and lightning. You may also take out "extended" coverage against damage from wind, hail, explosion, riot, smoke, and various other hazards. If an endorsement to this effect is added to the policy, it is known as *extended coverage;* and of course your insurance premium will be slightly higher. Under the basic dwelling-and-contents policy of fire insurance, the insurance company pays only the *actual cash value* of the property destroyed. The actual cash value is not necessarily the market value, the original value, the sentimental value, or even the actual replacement value of the property destroyed. Rather, it is the cost of replacement with materials of like kind and quality—but with depreciation on the original property deducted.

Suppose, for example, that a fire destroys the roof of your home, and a contractor estimates that the replacement cost of the roof will be $1,000. How much can you collect from your insurance company? Assuming that you carry sufficient insurance to cover the full amount of the loss, the insurance company adjuster will allow you the actual cash value of replacing the roof, $1,000—but less a deduction for depreciation of the old roof. If the house was purchased new, and is now 10 years old, and the roof's estimated life span was 20 years, then the old roof has depreciated by ½ of its original cost and you will receive only $500 from the insurance company as its cost of replacement less depreciation.

Obviously, this is not the most satisfactory kind of insurance, since the amount you receive from the company does not fully reimburse you for your loss.

Broad Dwelling-and-Contents Form. This form of fire insurance policy offers a much more extensive form of protection. In addition to the coverage in the basic form, it includes such risks as vandalism, malicious mischief, damage caused by burglars, burning or bulging of steam or hot water systems, overflow of steam or water from interior plumbing, heating, or air-conditioning systems, and many other types of damage. Under this type of coverage, the insurance company will even pay the full cost of repairing the roof of your house if it collapsed due to the weight of ice or snow.

Very important in considering this kind of fire insurance with extended coverage, is that the *full replacement cost* is paid for any damage and no deduction is made for depreciation (assuming that you carry the amount of insurance required). Once again, you will not receive the cash value, the market value, or the original value of the property that has been destroyed. You will receive instead the full cost of replacement. Of course, it is obvious that insurance of this type (without deductions for depreciation) is more expensive than ordinary insurance.

Dwelling Buildings Special Form. A fire insurance policy of this type with extended coverage is extremely broad in its protection.

The insurance company will pay for any damage on a replacement-cost basis, as in the broad dwelling form. This policy will cover every risk, except those which are specifically excluded. The excluded risks are usually certain types of damage that occur over long periods of time, such as gradual deterioration, termite damage, or damage caused by water erosion. A policy-holder receives payment on claims even when the damage is caused accidentally, such as when a can of paint is carelessly spilled on the floor or walls. As might be expected, this kind of insurance is also more expensive.

Some General Thoughts about Insurance. Of course, none of these three basic policies covers household goods or personal property, nor do they afford protection to you for injuries sustained by a person who visits your home. These policies are simply fire insurance policies with extended coverage which allow you to recover for certain additional kinds of damage to your home (not to its *contents,* however, except under very special coverage).

The homeowner should also understand that, as a rule, fire insurance covers a loss by fire only. Under an ordinary fire insurance policy, damage caused by heat from steam is not covered, nor is damage caused by smoke from a fire that is confined to the place where it would ordinarily be. For example, if a house sustains smoke damage from a fire in the fireplace (the fire remaining confined to the fireplace), there is no recovery under an ordinary fire insurance policy; such a fire is called a "friendly" fire. Damage caused by smoke or soot issuing from defective furnaces is not covered either. It is only when a fire has escaped from the place in which it was intended to burn that the insurer becomes liable. Such a fire is then called a "hostile" fire. However, for an extra premium the company will add a rider to the policy extending the coverage to include damage caused by a "friendly" fire as described above.

Still another important consideration is to make sure that you can recover 100% of your loss. To be sure of this, you must usually carry an amount of insurance equal to at least 80% of your home's *replacement* value. If you do not do so, the insurance company will only pay you the larger of either of the following amounts: 1) The actual cash value of the insured loss with depreciation deducted, or 2) The proportion of replacement cost that the amount of your insurance bears to 80% of the full replacement cost.

For example, if wind destroys the roof of your house, and the replacement cost is $1,200, you must first ascertain what it would cost to replace the entire house. If the replacement value is $20,000, the estimated life span of the roof is 20 years, and the roof is 10 years old, how much would you collect? If you carry $16,000 of insurance (80% of replacement value of the home) you will receive the full $1,200 under the Broad Dwelling-and-Contents form of insurance or the Dwelling-Building Special form of insurance. But if you carried only $12,000 of insurance you would receive the better of these alternatives: 1) The actual cash value ($1,200) less 50% deduction for 10 years of wear ($600), or 2) The proportion of the replacement cost that $12,000 bears to $20,000 (60% of $1,200) or $720.

In this case you would be paid $720, the larger of the two amounts. If you had been fully insured, the company would have paid you $1,200. The 80% provision will not ordinarily apply to losses that are less than 5% of the dwelling insurance but not more than $1,000.

There may be other hidden benefits in a fire insurance policy, of which most policyholders are not aware. For example, you are usually allowed to apply up to 10% of the amount of the house insurance you carry to cover damage to buildings not connected to your home, such as a detached garage. If your house is insured for $20,000, you are protected against a loss as high as $2,000 on the detached garage. Remember, however, that if the detached garage is worth more than $2,000, you should carry additional insurance to protect it against additional loss.

There is another hidden advantage in the standard form of policy. If you rent a portion of your property and it is made untenantable because of an insured damage, loss of rent (or a fair rental value whether rented or not) is covered up to 10% of the amount of your dwelling coverage.

The usual fire insurance coverage also provides that the cost of hotel and restaurant bills expended during the period when you are of necessity out of your house while it is being repaired, will also be paid. This payment is limited to 10% of the amount of your dwelling coverage.

Another special provision in the standard form of fire insurance policy allows you to apply up to 5% of the amount of your home insurance to cover trees, shrubs, or plants destroyed by fire or other insurable dangers. However, there is usually a limit of $250 for any one tree, shrub, or plant; and damage from certain dangers, such as windstorm, are not covered.

A further advantage in the standard form of fire insurance policy with extended coverage is that 10% of the insurance may be applied to cover property that is temporarily out of the house destroyed by fire or any other insured risk.

In the standard fire insurance policy, the insurance company is also liable for an explosion caused by a fire, and any breakage, water damage, and damage by chemicals used in an effort to extinguish the fire.

Who May Insure Your Property against Loss. The homeowner or the mortgage lender are the usual parties who insure the house against loss by fire or other dangers. An outsider or stranger has absolutely no right to insure your property against loss. The insurance companies have considered the moral hazards of allowing an outsider to insure property he does not own or have any interest in, and have refused to issue any policies of this type. The companies will only issue policies in favor of those who have a *financial* interest in the property. The clear rule is that the party insuring the property must have an *insurable interest* (meaning monetary interest) in it.

It is important that the insurance company be advised precisely as to who owns the property. For example, if three people own a building jointly and each one were allowed to take out fire insurance with a different company (without disclosing his partial ownership), the building would be insured for three times its actual value. In such cases, the various insurance companies will each claim that the insurance policy is unlawful. It is therefore important that the names of the owner and the mortgage lender be accurately stated to the insurance company on the application form.

The insurance company will also refuse, or try to avoid making any payment if the hazards of a fire are unwarrantedly increased by the owner. For example, suppose you intend to take a long trip. There may be a clause in your insurance policy that provides that if your dwelling is vacant or unoccupied for, say, more than 60 days, the fire insurance provisions of the policy may not be applicable. (If furniture remains in the dwelling, it is not vacant; but if the owner has left the dwelling, it may be regarded as unoccupied.) Then you should have your insurance representative add a special provision to continue the insurance in effect in your prolonged absence.

The Rights of the Mortgagee. The homeowner, as *mortgagor,* and the mortgage lender, as *mortgagee,* each have an insurable interest in the house. Both interests may be and usually are covered in one insurance policy, but each may take out a separate policy. The unpaid principal of the mortgage is the limit of the insurable interest of the mortgage lender. Inasmuch as he is entitled to payment first, under the usual form of mortgage, any payments made by the insurance company for fire losses to the mortgage lender reduces the amount of the mortgage debt by that amount.

Formerly it was the custom for the mortgagor, or homeowner, to take out insurance in his own name but to assign the policy (with the insurance company's consent) to the mortgage lender. But this method did not adequately protect the mortgage lender, since the homeowner could wrongfully violate conditions of the insurance policy and the mortgage lender would be unable to collect insurance if a fire resulted. Today, the usual form of fire insurance with extended coverage provides that no wrongful act on the part of the homeowner can cause the insurance to be cancelled with respect to the mortgage lender. This means, in effect, that there are really two separate insurance agreements: one between the insurer and the homeowner, and the other between the insurer and the mortgage lender. Violations that would invalidate the first of these contracts will still leave the second contract intact.

In the event that the homeowner does not advise the insurance company of the persons who actually own the house, or he misrepresents or conceals other important facts from the insurance company, or he increases the hazards of fire in violation of the policy, the mortgage lender will not be affected. More important, if the insurance company and the homeowner should agree on an amount to be paid for a loss sustained by fire, the agreement does not necessarily prevent the mortgage lender from claiming an additional amount unless he has consented to the payment agreed on.

However, under the standard form of fire insurance policy, the mortgage lender must notify the insurance company of the commencement of any foreclosure of the mortgage; notify the company of any change in ownership or occupancy of the house; submit proofs of loss after a fire in the event that the homeowner fails to do so.

The insurance company may decide to rebuild the destroyed premises rather than make any payment to the homeowner or to the mortgage lender; and the mortgage lender as well as the homeowner, under the usual form of insurance policy, must accept this. (As a practical matter, this is rarely done.)

Liability Insurance. There have been an increasing number of lawsuits brought against homeowners by people who claim to have been injured while on the premises. The list includes invited guests, tradespeople (delivering merchandise), and solicitors (who want to sell something, and are, in point of fact, uninvited and even unwelcome). If any of them are injured while on the premises, they may sue. For protection, a *liability insurance* policy is necessary. It is an essential type of insurance for all homeowners. The basic limit of a policy in most states is usually set at $10,000. However, higher limits will be written for a relatively small extra cost. A $100,000 policy costs only 50% more than one for $10,000. Assuming that a homeowner had a $10,000 policy, a court award of $25,000 would mean that the homeowner (and his property) would be responsible for the $15,000 balance.

Liability insurance (sometimes called *public liability* insurance) protects you against lawsuits brought by persons who have been injured (or who claim to have been injured) on your property, or even by anyone who is injured or damaged by you (or a member of your family) while away from home. However, this does not include automobile accidents, which are specifically excepted from the policy. Basically, it covers ultimate legal liability (that is, a judgment rendered against the homeowner); and it also pays the costs of defending lawsuits, whether or not there is ultimate legal liability.

The liability insurance policy usually contains a *medical payments* clause, which provides payments for medical bills for anyone accidentally injured while on your property, or by you or members of your family, whether or not you are legally responsible. Furthermore, you are protected for accidental damage caused by you to the property of others. The basic policy will limit payments in the latter two cases to the rather small amount of $250, but it is possible to increase the limits of medical payments (at extra cost) if you desire.

Small-boat owners are usually covered in the operation of a family boat, unless it exceeds a specified length or horsepower. Here, too, property coverage can be increased by your insurance agent.

A *comprehensive personal liability* insurance policy of this kind will protect the homeowner from any claims for personal injuries received by workmen who are repairing the house or working on the property, but generally it will not protect against obligations required under your state workmen's-compensation laws. The effect of these laws depends on whether the injured workman is deemed to be *your* employee or is considered to be an independent contractor. (The legal distinction between an "employee" and an "independent contractor" is too complex for discussion at this time.) The definition of "employee" varies from state to state, so it is necessary to check this point with your insurance agent to determine whether you need workmen's-compensation insurance in addition to liability insurance.

If you hire a contractor and he employs several men, you should receive a certificate showing that he carries the necessary liability and workmen's-compensation insurance. If he is not so protected, check with your insurance agent to verify the contractor's status and your possible legal obligations. Any written agreement for the proposed work should state that your contractor carries public liability insurance and, if he is subject to the workmen's-compensation laws of your state, that he has adequate coverage.

Burglary and Theft Insurance. There is a *burglary-and-theft* policy available which is an accepted way to insure against loss by burglary, robbery, theft, mysterious disappearance, and similar risks. (Legally, burglary involves breaking and entering a house, whereas robbery is taking property from a person.) This form of insurance policy will protect not only property in your home but also property at certain additional specified places such as a bank, a safe deposit company, a public warehouse, or a friend's home where you have left property or loaned it for safekeeping. If your coverage is $1,000 or more, there is usually an *off-premises* clause that protects your property against such loss anywhere in the world. The off-premises coverage usually provides that if you borrow a friend's car and it is stolen, you are covered for the loss.

This form of insurance provides unusually broad protection, and is subject only to a few exclusions, such as aircraft, automobiles, trailers, and motorcycles, which must be insured by their own special policies.

Homeowner's Policies. The so-called *homeowner's policy* is rapidly growing in popularity. It is available in every state except Alaska, Hawaii, Mississippi, and Oregon. A homeowner's policy is an almost complete package that combines property insurance, burglary and theft coverage, comprehensive personal liability, and fire insurance.

Several advantages in this type of policy accrue to the homeowner. In the first place, there is only one policy to consider, combining all of the terms and provisions formerly covered by several policies. Next, the homeowner receives broader protection at lower cost. With some variations, costs can be reduced as much as 20% to 30% compared with the same coverages written under separate policies.

How Much Insurance? To determine the correct value of real and personal property, an appraisal should be made by an expert. At the very least, consult with your insurance agent. He is familiar with values in your area, and he undoubtedly will be able to estimate the amount of insurance you should carry on your house. It is better to be overinsured than underinsured. If the estimate of your property is more than its actual value, the additional cost in premiums will be small. Remember that unless your insurance equals 80% of the *replacement* value of your house, it may not be possible to collect full replacement costs on fire losses over $1,000. A good rule to follow is to insure your house for at least 80% of its *actual cash value.*

The limits of liability insurance should be at least equal to your net worth, but it is often advisable to insure for twice your net worth. In view of the large recoveries in recent years in court actions for injuries caused by negligence of homeowners, it would not be improper, in any event, to carry liability insurance of at least $100,000 on your home. The cost in excess premiums is not much greater than the cost of inadequate coverage, and the protection is essential.

Title Insurance

Another kind of insurance protection usually acquired by the buyer of a house is called *title insurance.* After signing the contract of sale, the buyer (or his attorney) applies to a title insurance company and agrees to pay a specified *single* premium for the company's title insurance policy. The title insurance company examines the prior record of ownership of the property and insures the buyer against any defects in the title or claims against the ownership of the property that were not disclosed by the investigation. The buyer (or his attorney) receives a report when the examination has been completed by the title company. The report describes the property in legal form, sets forth the name of the present owner, describes any existing mortgages, and lists all objections to full ownership. This report tells the buyer the exact state of title to the property, including any possible unpaid taxes, etc. If there are no objections to title, or the objections have been removed, title is closed and the title company issues a policy of title insurance to the buyer. The title insurance policy agrees to insure the buyer's title, describing exactly what is insured and the amount of insurance, and sets forth a schedule of exceptions to such insurance, if any, and the conditions of the insurance policy.

The title insurance policy undertakes to indemnify the buyer of the house against any loss or damage not exceeding the specified amount of the policy, usually the purchase price of the house, which the buyer may sustain by reason of any claim against his ownership due to liens or incumbrances existing as of the date of the policy.

The title insurance company usually agrees to defend the buyer at the company's cost and expense in any action brought against the buyer, based on a claim of title or incumbrance prior to the date of the title insurance policy.

There are some states in which title insurance policies are not customarily used, and in these states an attorney for the buyer will make his own study of the record of title to determine whether the buyer will obtain good title at the closing. The attorney will then give the buyer his opinion as to whether the title is clear.

In most states, however, the title insurance policy is utilized in order to give the buyer of a house greater protection. The premium for such a policy is paid only *once,* at the time of its issuance. In the event that a mortgage loan is obtained by the buyer, the mortgage lender will almost always require a title insurance policy for its own benefit. In such cases, the buyer will have to pay the title insurance premium for both mortgage lender and himself. However, when simultaneous title insurance policies are issued to the mortgage lender and the buyer, there is a saving of approximately 15% on the total cost of premiums on the two policies. The title insurance policy will protect the buyer for as long as he owns the property, whether for one year or a lifetime. The amount of title insurance on the buyer's property should be the equivalent of, or slightly in excess of, the purchase price. It should be remembered that, due to inflation, the value of real estate may increase over the years; and in such a case where the buyer has purchased a home for $20,000 (which is subsequently worth $30,000 due to an inflationary increase in value), a title insurance policy in the face amount of $20,000 will not be increased unless the buyer specifically requests that the coverage be increased to match the market value of the home. In many states, on payment of an additional premium, this type of title insurance coverage may be arranged.

Visitors

Every man may use his own land and the buildings on it for all reasonable purposes; and if he exercises ordinary care and skill in maintaining it, he will not be responsible to a person who enters on his land and is injured. The owner may be held responsible for a *negligent* act on his part, or that of his servants or employees, if a visitor should sustain injury or damage while on the land. The landowner must use reasonable care to keep the land and the buildings on the land in good repair so that a foreseeable injury will not result to a person who comes on the land. For example, if a chimney or wall should fall and injure someone while visiting on the property, and the landowner had any *notice* that the structure was in poor condition before the accident, he may be held responsible for the accident.

In recent years, however, more and more courts are finding landowners responsible for injuries sustained on their land by visitors, seemingly in disregard of the requirement of notice. For all practical purposes, the only way to protect yourself against this potential liability is by holding adequate insurance. The reason for this is simple: Even though you may ultimately defeat such a lawsuit, you will have to hire a lawyer and supervise the defense of the case. With proper insurance, all of this responsibility (including the payment of any judgment) falls on the insurance company.

Business Visitors. The owner of land must use care to keep his premises in a safe condition for the access of persons who come on his land by invitation for the transaction of business or for any other purpose beneficial to the landowner. If your premises are in a dangerous condition, you must give such visitors a special warning of the danger to enable them to avoid potential injury. Of course, an invitation to someone to come on your land for business purposes may be implied—for example, the person coming on the premises in connection with a matter of mutual interest, or in the usual course of his business (such as a mailman) comes on the land with an implied invitation.

In most states, the care a landowner must use for the benefit of his social guests who come on his premises is far less than what he must exercise toward gardeners, postmen, or other business visitors. In many states the host is under no duty to use care to discover and repair defects on his own premises before a guest is injured. He must only make sure that there is no increase of an already existing hazard or the creation of a new hazard. Otherwise, a guest accepts the premises of his host as he finds them and he need only be warned of any concealed defects on the premises known by the owner.

If an individual comes on your land without any invitation and without any business to transact, that is, comes on your land without being invited and without permission, he is considered to be a trespasser. To such persons, the only requirement of the landowner is to refrain from inflicting any intentional or wilful injury on him. This is true even if the premises are not enclosed with a fence or any other means of keeping persons without permission from coming on your property. The fact that there is no fence enclosing the property is not considered to be an invitation (implied or otherwise) to such persons. A special situation exists with respect to children, however. If they enter on your premises, even though uninvited and obviously for no business reason, the landowner is frequently held responsible. The only way to protect against this potentially dangerous situation is by carefully enclosing the property (although children may even defeat this by climbing over the fence) or by adequate insurance coverage.

The owner of an *unfinished* building does not, by leaving it open and unenclosed, give any permission or any invitation for the entry of a stranger. He is therefore under no obligation to make it safe for access or while such a stranger remains there. Even persons who have a right of way over the land occupied by the uncompleted building are considered to be trespassers if they enter the building.

Driveways. A driveway is regarded as proper and necessary to the use of residential premises. At the point where it crosses a public sidewalk, the driveway may be depressed, with curbing placed along its sides to define its limits and to keep vehicles within its bounds. The pedestrian who walks along the sidewalk adjacent to the street is not entitled to an absolutely level and unobstructed passageway, but it is always advisable to keep the sidewalk in good repair. Where the driveway crosses the public sidewalk, it, too, must be maintained by the owner in reasonable condition. There would, however, be no responsibility on the owner's part to a woman who caught her heel on the edge of a concrete driveway at the point where the end of the driveway was adjacent to a sidewalk and the level of the driveway was 1 or 2 inches below that of the sidewalk.

A property owner has the right to close the entrance to his property by means of a chain stretched between metal posts or brick pillars on either side of the drive without any special notice.

Steps and Stairways. It is not uncommon for a person to fall down a flight of stairs even when there is no defect in the stairway or its covering. A heel may catch on the edge of a step or its carpeting, and a fall may result. The responsibility for such a fall ordinarily lies with the person who placed his foot on the carpeting or the staircase. However, the width of the stair tread and the height of the riser may be regulated by an ordinance covering public buildings, and bannisters and handrails may be required. But in the absence of an ordinance, the construction of a stairway will only furnish grounds for suing if it is clearly dangerous to anyone who uses it.

If the defect is slight, such as a depression caused by wear on the surface of an outdoor step, this usually does not constitute a dangerous condition, and the owner is not required to prevent or remedy the situation. (But a torn carpet may be the basis of liability.) However, in view of many verdicts rendered in favor of persons injured on steps, public liability insurance may be the only practical solution.

Floors and Floor Coverings. Floors constructed of marble or hardwood are by their nature somewhat slippery, but the use of such materials is not of itself dangerous. The same is true of concrete floors. A floor deliberately made slippery for dancing by wax does not present a negligent condition, thus, a slippery floor intended to be used for dancing in a rumpus or playroom is not ordinarily regarded as an act of negligence on the part of the owner. Even a difference in level between two sections of flooring will not constitute negligence when it is obvious. But liability may follow when the difference in levels is accompanied by dim lighting or other obscuring conditions. The washing of floors is, of course, recognized as a necessity, and a floor being washed is usually wet and slippery. Although a recently washed floor may be left in a wet and slippery condition without responsibility, liability will follow when the floor, on completion of the washing, is left *unnecessarily* slippery from soap or wax.

Water, slush, and mud tracked in on the floor by reason of outdoor weather conditions that render the floor wet and slippery do not ordinarily create an actionable situation. However, if the conditions persist, the owner is required to make reasonable efforts to dry the floor.

Attractive Nuisance. A landowner who maintains what the law considers to be a dangerous instrumentality or appliance on his premises, of a character likely to attract children, or permits dangerous conditions to remain on his property with knowledge that children are in the habit of resorting to them for amusement, is responsible for a child who is injured while on his premises. Usually the owner owes no duty to a trespasser except not to wilfully or intentionally inflict injury on him. However, the exception to this rule is where children are injured by an instrumentality called an *attractive nuisance*. Of course, natural objects such as trees, no matter how attractive they may be to children, are not considered to be attractive nuisances. In order to recover for any injuries to the child, it must first be shown that some inducement led the child onto the premises, and that the landowner knew that the children were in the habit of coming on his land. If he permits any such condition to exist, he runs the risk of liability. This presents an extremely hazardous position for property-owners, because juries frequently are so sympathetic to injured children that they bring in verdicts in their favor, many of which are seemingly unjustified. There are, however, some states that do not allow recovery for injuries that result from an attractive nuisance on the owner's land; for example, New York State does not openly recognize this kind of liability. Attractive nuisance usually cannot be claimed by a child who has reached the age of discretion, which normally would be about 14 years of age. To sum up: If a dangerous instrumentality or condition lures or entices a young child upon the premises (and the child because of its youth was unable to understand the danger of the situation), and the premises are unguarded and exposed there may be responsibility. This is particularly true when the child is accustomed to playing on the premises, and the landowner knew of the child's habits in this regard.

Leaving discarded furniture, abandoned refrigerators, or the like on real property is to invite trouble, for children may be drawn to the "attractive nuisance" and become injured. They may be awarded substantial amounts of money for settlement. Besides keeping land free of such "attractions" to young children, and maintaining vigilance over the property, the only remaining protection to the owner is taking out sufficient public liability insurance.

CHAPTER 21

Neighbors

Every landowner may make any *reasonable* use of his real property provided that it is not used in such a manner as to *injure* his neighbor or his neighbor's property. However, reasonable use may be made of your real property even if, in some way, it may somehow *diminish* the value of adjoining land or prevent its being used with the full and complete comfort and pleasure that might otherwise have been anticipated. It is nevertheless true that this rule has its limitations; no one may make an *unreasonable* use of his own land that will cause a material injury to that of his neighbor. Ordinary lawful use of real property may become unreasonable, and therefore unlawful, if it harms the property of an adjacent landowner. As long as the acts of the landowner are within his legal rights, the motive that impels him to do certain things on his own land is usually regarded as immaterial. It may, on certain occasions, be done for the sole and deliberate purpose of annoying his neighbor. As an example, a landowner may erect on his land a poor-quality dwelling in close proximity to a magnificent home owned by his neighbor, for the avowed purpose of spiting and irritating the owner of the mansion. In such a case, there will be no restraint by a court. The courts have held that if the change or improvement is legitimate and lawful, it will not be considered a nuisance to be removed by court order, and the law will ordinarily not consider the motives involved.

The owner of a house usually has one or more neighbors who own land adjacent to his. It is not surprising that the relationship of one neighbor to another has been defined somewhat differently in numerous court decisions in the various states. Although a property-owner may use his land for any lawful purpose, such use may, in some instances, be limited by the consideration of the harm that may result to his neighbor.

Admittedly, this language is somewhat vague and unsatisfying, but it cannot be stated more specifically. Each act must be considered individually, and generalizations of this type are extremely difficult to put into precise words. What constitutes a "reasonable" act by a property-owner is always difficult to define; and "normal behavior" is something everyone recognizes, but has trouble describing. In the sections that follow, various problems which frequently arise between neighboring property-owners will be considered.

Light and Air.   When you buy a house, you may be impressed by the unobstructed view across your neighbor's land, and this may well be one of the considerations that influence your decision to buy. The buyer, however, should be aware that an owner of land has no legal right, in the absence of an agreement with his neighbor, to receive the benefits of such a view or the benefits of light and air that existed when he became the owner of the land. This means that your neighbor may, for example, build a five-story building immediately adjacent to your land which cuts off your view and interferes with your access to light and air. Of course, local zoning laws *may* prohibit such a building in your community. But if they do not, even though your light and view have been adversely affected, your legal rights have not been invaded. Your neighbor has exercised his right, and you have received no injury that would be recognized by law—that is, something which interferes with your full enjoyment of the property.

Therefore, the rule is well settled that an owner of land may erect on his own property a structure that shuts out the light and air from the adjoining premises without being responsible for damages. Your neighbor has the liberty to do what he wishes with his own land (subject to existing zoning laws) even though his actions may annoy others; and there is no legal remedy.

In recent years the legislatures of many states have passed statutes that prohibit the unreasonable maintenance of a structure that shuts out the light and air from the adjoining premises with a bad or evil motive for its sole purpose. (These statutes, in effect, change the general rule of law.) But these statutes do not prevent the erection of a *useful* and *valuable* structure even though, as a corollary, the structure has the effect of shutting out light and air from the adjoining land. In the absence of a special statute to the contrary, a neighbor will have no recourse and may not prevent the erection of such a structure. In one interesting and unusual case, a neighbor built a structure on adjacent land which overlooked a baseball park, so that people sitting on the roof could see the game played in the adjoining park. The courts held that no action could be maintained to prevent such use by the adjoining landowner.

The Nuisance of Noise.   Usually, routine noise will not be legally considered a nuisance even though it may be very disagreeable to you personally. A property-owner is not entitled to absolute quiet in the enjoyment of his real property, although he is entitled to a degree of quietness consistent with the standard of comfort prevailing in the particular locality or community. Many useful acts are necessarily accompanied by some degree of noise, and reasonable noises in an appropriate locality are not legally nuisances even though they are disagreeable and annoying. On the other hand, a certain type of noise may become a nuisance even though it results from the carrying on of a lawful business, industry, or trade in a town or city. To constitute a legal nuisance, a noise must be excessive and unreasonable and produce actual physical discomfort and annoyance to a person of ordinary sensibilities. The question of whether the noise constitutes a nuisance is involved; it depends on all the surrounding circumstances. A nuisance brought on solely by noise is inevitably a question of degree and must be considered in connection with the locality in which it occurs. In determining whether a noise is a nuisance, the time of the day when the noise occurs will be carefully considered. A noise that normally occurs during daylight hours may not be a nuisance; but the same noise, occurring at night, during the hours usually devoted to sleep, may be much more annoying and therefore constitute a legal nuisance.

To put this into specific terms: radio and television noise will be permitted by the courts to a reasonable degree during normal hours, say, 9 A.M. to 11 P.M. However, the same noise at 3 A.M., for example, may constitute a nuisance and produce a restraint order by the court.

Also relevant is the question of frequency. Noisy parties and loud music are not ordinarily a legal nuisance if they occur on rare occasions. If such parties are held regularly and frequently, however, they may well be regarded as a nuisance.

An unwarranted and unreasonable use of your neighbor's property in such a manner as to cause you discomfort, or to cause anyone with ordinary sensibilities to be annoyed and in a state of discomfort, will be considered to be a nuisance, especially if it arises from an unlawful act. A material discomfort or annoyance caused by an unlawful, unwarrantable, and unreasonable use of property so as to hurt another constitutes a nuisance to an adjoining landowner. Whether it arises out of a lawful business or the lawful use of property is one of the factors considered to determine whether or not the nuisance should be abated. If the act is motivated by malice or spite, the courts are much more likely to find that the act is a legal nuisance. Nuisances may be divided into types. A *private* nuisance is one that affects a single individual or a fixed number of individuals; a *public* nuisance affects many. If a nuisance exists steadily for a period of time, it is known as a *continuing* nuisance.

Atmospheric Pollution.   Although the ownership of land carries with it the normal use of air or atmosphere passing over, the pollution of the atmosphere with offensive matter may constitute a nuisance when it becomes so contaminated as to substantially impair the use of other property, or to interfere with the comfort or enjoyment of other property-owners of ordinary sensibilities. This may be true even though such contamination or pollution of the atmosphere results from the carrying on of a lawful business. It is not necessary that the corruption of the atmosphere be dangerous to health in order to amount to a nuisance. It is sufficient that ordinary senses register discomfort. For example, a bad odor may not necessarily affect health, but it may be annoying or worse.

The right to pure air is incident to the ownership of land, and a property-owner is entitled to the same protection as he has with any other legal right. However, the right to pure air refers only to a condition that is consistent with the locality and nature of the community. Pollution of the atmosphere, when indispensable to the progress of society, will not be actionable; and therefore some pollution of the atmosphere may not always constitute a nuisance. It is basically a question of degree. Once again, as in the case of noise, the court will consider the location of the land, the type of the use that has created the atmospheric pollution, the character of the neighborhood, the extent and frequency of the injury, and the effect on possible enjoyment of life, health, and property.

Dust.   Dust blown from one person's land onto a neighbor's property may be considered a nuisance if it is sufficient to cause perceptible injury to the property or it so pollutes the air as to noticeably impair enjoyment of it. However, dust is not in and of itself necessarily a nuisance. A reasonable amount of dust in manufacturing communities does not automatically constitute a nuisance even though it may cause some annoyance. Yet it might be so considered if it occurs in a purely residential community. It is, once again, a question of fact.

Fumes, Gases, and Vapors. A nuisance for which relief may be granted are noxious fumes, gases, or vapors which escape into neighboring premises to such a degree as to render persons of ordinary sensitiveness uncomfortable or even sick. Noxious gases arising in the conduct of lawful occupations are not nuisances in all situations, but they may become so if they are negligently allowed to escape.

Smells. Adjoining owners have the right to be free from the annoyance caused by obnoxious odors; and it is well established that such smells or odors may constitute a nuisance even though they are not injurious to health, but merely offensive and unpleasant to the sensibilities. However, *every* disagreeable smell is not necessarily an actionable nuisance. To determine whether unpleasant odors constitute a nuisance, all the surrounding circumstances must be considered.

Smoke, Soot, and Smudge. An actionable nuisance may be committed by causing annoyance to a neighbor by smoke, soot, and burnt particles. When pollution of the air is reasonable under the circumstances, and indispensable to the progress of society, it will not be considered as a nuisance.

The regulation of discharges of smoke and soot is within the police powers of a state; and often it is delegated to localities by statute. However, such statutes are not applicable when the discharge of smoke is *accidental* or unavoidable, on rare occasions, such as when a house or furniture catches on fire. It must be continuous or regular to become a nuisance. What has been said of other forms of air pollution is also true of ashes, cinders, burning particles, refuse, and sand.

Jarring and Vibration. The jarring of a person's premises or the causing of vibration may be a nuisance under some circumstances. However, vibration from proper acts, done in appropriate localities, is not necessarily a nuisance entitling an adjoining property-owner to relief. However, if the vibration becomes excessive and unreasonable, it may produce actual physical discomfort and annoyance to persons of ordinary sensibilities and thereby become a nuisance.

Abatement of a Nuisance. The courts have long since recognized the rights of an individual to a certain degree of self-help in order to abate a private nuisance. This means that a person may cut down the branches of a neighbor's tree overhanging his property, without the necessity of a court order. But caution and good judgment should be used in order to avoid bad feelings—and even possible litigation.

Trees on or near a Boundary. The ownership of a tree is usually determined by the position of the trunk of the tree *above the soil,* rather than by the roots below or the branches above it. This rule has been followed because it is easy to see the visible trunk and far more difficult to ascertain where the roots may lie. The product (blossoms, fruits, nuts, etc.) of a tree that stands near a boundary line belongs to the owner of the land on which the trunk of the tree stands, even though the roots and branches of the tree may partly extend over an adjoining property line. Although the adjoining owner does have the right to remove overhanging branches, this will not affect the ownership of the tree or the branches. This means that the branches of a neighbor's apple tree may overhang your land, but the apples on the branches belong to the owner of the tree. In some states, if fruit on an overhanging tree should naturally *fall* to the ground on a neighbor's land, the owner of the tree may actually enter the neighbor's land to gather the fruit. However, in most states, fruit that has naturally fallen to the ground becomes the property of the neighbor on whose land it has fallen.

Where a tree is located so close to the boundary line of an adjoining landowner that branches overhang his land and the roots encroach on his soil, such branches and roots may constitute a nuisance, and under the law, the adjoining landowner may remove them. The adjoining landowner may cut the branches and remove such roots up to the boundary, but he may not cut beyond the boundary line. He may not cut the tree down if the trunk does not lie *completely* within his land boundaries. A landowner desiring to cut off overhanging branches of trees belonging to an adjacent landowner is not required to give any notice unless he has encouraged the maintenance of the tree up to that time. Once the branches have been cut from an overhanging tree, there is ordinarily no obligation to return them to the owner of the tree.

The owner of a tree, the branches of which overhang the premises of an adjoining landowner, may also be responsible for damages caused by the overhanging branches. In some states, the right to cut off the overhanging branches is considered a sufficient remedy, and no court action is permitted. In any event, some real and serious damage must be shown to justify a court action. The mere fact that the overhanging branches make it inconvenient to sit in a back yard would be considered trivial, and the court would undoubtedly refuse to act. However, if there is a serious problem involved (especially one involving danger to life or limb), the court will almost surely take a different position.

What happens when a tree falls or threatens to fall on the adjoining premises? Usually there will be no liability on the part of the tree-owner, unless it can be shown that the tree is decayed, and is standing near the boundary line and is liable to fall during a heavy wind, and that the owner of the tree knows of the possibility. In such case, it will be deemed a nuisance which the landowner will be required to remove at the request of the adjoining owner. A property-owner has no right to keep an unsound and potentially dangerous tree near the property of his neighbor. It is his duty to maintain his premises, by the use of normal common prudence, so that they do not become a probable cause of injury to his neighbor.

A tree standing on the division line between adjoining proprietors, so that the boundary line passes through the trunk or body of a tree above the soil, is the *common* property of both landowners as tenants in common. Neither one is the absolute owner of the tree, and neither can destroy it. Each owns the portion standing on his land, and it is subject to the restriction that he shall not injure or destroy the whole.

A landowner who cuts or destroys a tree standing on the boundary line without the consent of the adjoining owner is responsible in damages for trespass. An injunction may also be granted preventing any threatened destruction. Although a co-owner cannot injure the trunk of the tree in any way, as previously stated, he may remove the branches or roots or fruit that extend over the boundary line onto his land.

The same principle applies to bushes and hedges; in the absence of a local statute regulating the width of hedges as a division fence on boundary lines, the rules with reference to a tree standing on a boundary line are applicable. However, there is one modification. So long as the hedge stands substantially on the boundary line, it is treated as one unit, and the fact that some of the individual shrubs stand wholly on one landowner's land will not justify a neighbor treating them as he would a tree. He may cut off only so much of the bushes and hedges as extend over his boundary line so as to leave a sufficient fence (should the whole be trimmed), ordinarily down to a height of about 4½ feet, and provided that he can do so without destroying or unreasonably injuring the main stalks of the shrubs that compose it. That part of the hedge which is on the land of the adjoining landowner may not be interfered with. The landowner has no right to step on his neighbor's land to cut or trim the hedges; to do so would constitute trespass.

Fences. Generally, an owner may build a fence on his land in such manner and fashion as he wishes. However, local ordinances usually regulate the height of fences built at or near the boundary line. Fences built on the boundary line may, on occasion, have to be erected, as much as possible, equally on the land of both neighbors; and each neighbor is required to contribute to the maintenance of the fence. What has come to be known as a "spite fence" is usually prohibited by statute (this is any fence deliberately erected to an unnecessary height for the purpose of annoying one's neighbor or shutting off his light). Fence heights are usually limited by statute or ordinance so that they cannot interfere with a neighbor's enjoyment of his property. What constitutes a spite fence varies from state to state; as a very general rule, however, any fence over 10 feet in height is automatically regarded as a nuisance. A spite fence may be considered as a nuisance; and court action may be taken, under certain circumstances, to eliminate it. However, if the owner has acted in good faith and for *useful* and *worthwhile* purposes, and not in spite, it will sometimes be allowed, even though the fence or other structure may be more than 10 feet in height and may obstruct the view of the neighbor. But the burden is on the owner of the fence to show the necessity for its excessive height.

Animals. Your neighbor may not permit his domestic animals to trespass on your land; and should his dog or cat stray on your land, he will normally be responsible for any damage caused to your property. If a dog or cat uproots flower beds or damages shrubbery, the animal's owner is responsible for the damage. The owner of an animal has an absolute and indisputable obligation to keep it off the land of his neighbors, and he is responsible for any damage caused by the animal.

Party Walls. A dividing wall erected on the boundary line separating two adjoining properties is known as a party wall. Each neighbor owns the part of the wall that stands on his land, but his ownership is subject to an easement or right of use by the other owner, and to the support of the wall, and sometimes (if a building is built against it) to equal use as an exterior wall. Therefore, ownership of the party wall is regarded as qualified as long as it stands. The wall need not be solid, and, furthermore, it need not actually stand on both properties, providing that it supports a structure on both lands.

Neither owner has the right to cut openings or windows in a party wall unless both agree. Nor can either owner use the party wall for his own individual advantage, such as painting a sign on either side of the exterior wall. The height and thickness of a party wall may be increased if the change is completely within the owner's land, and providing that it does not cause a weakness in the wall or prevent the use of the wall by the adjoining landowner.

Neither of the adjoining landowners has the right to tear down a party wall, unless it becomes structurally weakened and insufficient for its purpose—and then it must be rebuilt. A party wall is not an encumbrance or an encroachment on the property of either owner; and it does not render title unmarketable, unless there is an agreement in writing requiring contribution of each toward repair or the rebuilding of the wall. A party-wall agreement does not bind succeeding owners, unless it is specified in the deed and filed in the local record office by a *recorded* written agreement. If a party wall is destroyed accidentally, or the building which it supports is destroyed, the incidents of ownership of a party wall cease and the adjoining landowners once again obtain full ownership and use of their land, free of the party-wall obligations.

Right to Support of Adjacent Land (Excavations). The soil of your neighbor's land must continue to support your land, and your neighbor may not remove an amount of earth from his land to such an extent as to withdraw the natural support your land requires. This is known legally as the *right to lateral support*. It is called a *servitude*. But regardless of its precise legal name, it is a natural right which each owner enjoys.

This right of lateral support of your land, by the land of an adjoining owner, applies only to land in its natural condition. It does not extend so as to give you, as the owner of a building erected on your land, the right to have support for the increased burden caused by the weight of your building that increases lateral pressure on the soil. However, a landowner cannot, by altering the natural earth or soil condition of his land, deprive the adjoining owner of the privilege of using his land as he might have done before. As an example, if you build a house near the margin of your land, it does not prevent your neighbor from excavating his own adjacent soil merely because it may endanger your house. He may still build on his land as he might have done before the construction of your house. It is the view of the courts that the right of lateral support of buildings that are erected on land cannot be acquired by use or prescription. Of course, when a house is built by the owner of the land, and a portion of the land with the house on it is sold to another, there is an implied right of support. However, if increased burdens are thereafter placed on the soil by erecting new buildings, or adding to those already erected, and damage to the building is caused by excavations in the adjoining soil, there would be no responsibility.

If the boundary line runs through a portion of a building, the earth remaining on your neighbor's property must remain in such a manner as to support the portion of the building on your property.

If a neighboring owner removes the natural support of the soil in such a manner that your soil is disturbed or falls away, the neighboring owner is responsible for the damages caused thereby. The care that the neighboring owner must exercise in making an excavation on his soil includes reasonably foreseeing potential dangers that may be caused by the elements.

It is interesting to note that the right of lateral support does not apply between owners of adjoining mining claims or where oil wells are being dug on the property. If it is necessary to separate minerals from the soil by washing down the soil or digging into it, there is no right of lateral support. (This matter, of course, is only of interest to those living in certain parts of the country, where oil and mineral rights are important.)

In building a house near the house of another, a landowner may lawfully sink the foundation of his new house below the foundation of his neighbor's, and he is not responsible for any damage to the house of the other provided he has used *due care* and diligence to prevent injury. An excavator, however, need not guarantee that the adjoining property will not be damaged. He is not ordinarily obliged to support the building on adjoining premises while an excavation is being dug (unless there is a local law to that effect). As a rule, it is the duty of the owner of the adjoining property to shore up or prop up his own building so as to render it secure during the progress of the nearby work. Experienced contractors and builders who are acquainted with the land can best inform an owner as to what should be done under the circumstances. The condition of the weather at the time of excavation is important, because what would be a reasonable and proper operation during dry weather might be reckless and negligent in wet or stormy weather, which softens and weakens the soil.

However, if you intend to make an excavation you should, in the exercise of due care, notify the adjoining landowner *in writing* of the intended improvement so that he may take the necessary precautions to protect his own building. This obligation to give notice must be fulfilled far enough in advance to give the neighboring landowner as much time as possible to protect his property. The notice should inform the adjoining owner of the nature and extent of the excavation. But should the excavator undertake to protect the building on the adjoining owner's land, and he does so improperly, you and the excavator may be responsible for any damages. Ordinarily, however, the landowner and the excavator are under no obligation to do so unless there is a local law that requires such protection of adjacent property. *This point should be checked carefully before commencing any excavation.*

Many state legislatures have now undertaken to change the existing laws. Where a statute or ordinance requires a person making an excavation on his own land to protect the buildings on his neighbor's land, the failure to do so will render him liable for any resulting damages to the building. The statute may specifically require the party making an excavation to shore up the building on the adjoining property, as well as on his own, and in such a case implied permission is given to enter upon the neighbor's land to perform such work. Of course, if he is not given such permission by statute or by his neighbor, he may not enter upon the neighbor's premises to make such repairs or he will be liable in trespass. Further, ordinances in some municipalities provide that a landowner may not excavate to a depth greater than a specified statutory limit below the curb of the street on which his lot abuts. If such improper excavations cause damage to any wall or house on the lot of an adjoining landowner, he will be held responsible for damages, whether or not there has been any negligence in making the excavation. For injury to a neighboring building, unavoidably incident to the depression or sliding of the soil caused by your excavation on adjoining land, action may be taken only if *negligence* may have caused it. Such action may only be maintained when the land actually slides or falls, but not before it occurs.

One who causes the work to be done (the landowner) is not liable ordinarily for any injuries that result from careless performance of the work by employees of the excavating firm, who is ordinarily an independent contractor. However, if the landowner reserves a degree of control over the execution of the work, he may himself become responsible for damages. But even when injury results from the negligent act of the employees alone, but is one that might have been *anticipated* by the person ordering the work to be done, he may be held responsible. This is a very technical matter; and it may not be readily understood except by lawyers. Insurance may be the only practical solution, with coverage that is adequate to cover all possible damage and potential lawsuits.

Surface Waters.   So long as the owner of land leaves his property in its natural condition, he is not required to take any steps to prevent the flowing of surface waters from his premises onto adjoining land. However, the owner cannot collect surface water and then intentionally discharge it in greatly increased or unnatural quantities onto his neighbor's land, as by damming it up and suddenly releasing it.

There is some difference of opinion in the courts as to liability when snow or ice is precipitated from a building onto the premises of an adjoining owner. In California, Kansas, and Michigan, for example, the owner is liable under these circumstances to the adjoining owner only if he has acted unreasonably. In other jurisdictions (including Massachusetts and New York), the adjacent property-owner is ordinarily entitled to immunity from water, snow, or ice cast upon his premises from the adjoining building of his neighbor. Therefore, should such damage occur, the landowner whose building was responsible for such a flow would be responsible in damages.

Of course, if you construct an addition to your house in such a way that it will obviously and manifestly collect water and discharge it on the adjoining land, you will be guilty of trespass and liable for damages. This is true if the water is discharged directly from your building onto the adjoining land, or if it falls on your premises and accumulates, and then flows onto the adjoining premises. The owner of a building is required to have gutters of sufficient capacity to carry off the water that falls on the roof of his building in all *ordinary* storms and to prevent such rain from being discharged onto the land of an adjoining owner. Of course, if a storm is so extraordinary that no one could have reasonably guarded against it (as by erecting an additional barrier), then there would be no liability. This, again, is the court's test of "reasonableness."

The neighbor whose land has been injured by such a flow of water may also obtain a court injunction ordering the adjoining landowner to repair or maintain his building in such a manner that the water or ice will not again fall on the adjoining land to its damage.

Of course, if water has been permitted to run onto your neighbor's land for a very long period of time, you may, in many states, claim that you have a right by *prescription* to leave things the way they have been, and that your neighbor's land may continue to be used to carry off the water as it has been doing over the years. (Prescription is described on page 293.) Rights obtained by prescription vary greatly from state to state, and generalizations are not possible.

Although your neighbor has no right, ordinarily, to erect an obstruction to prevent surface water from draining over his land to the detriment of your property, nevertheless if *foul or filthy water* is willfully cast on his land from yours, he may erect an obstruction to divert the foul water, even though he thereby prevents the surface water from leaving your land.

Even though a landowner has, over the years, discharged surface waters onto the land of a neighbor, and claims the right to continue such practice, there is no equivalent right of a landowner to discharge any other liquid matter (such as oil pumped from oil wells on his land) onto the land of his neighbor. A neighbor would have a right to enjoin a landowner from such misuse of his land on the ground that it is a nuisance, and he would have the right to recover damages.

Dangerous Material Stored on Premises. A property-owner who stores any dangerous or explosive substance on his premises is responsible for any injuries to adjoining and surrounding property even though they are the natural and proximate results of an explosion, regardless of negligence or lack of it. For all practical purposes, anyone who keeps explosive or inflammable material on his property does so at his own risk, for storing such material is obviously dangerous.

Noxious Vegetation. The spread of vegetation, roots, weeds, poisonous vines, and the like may be regarded as a nuisance. The person who plants or permits such unwarranted growth will be responsible for any resulting injury to an adjoining owner. For example, a landowner who plants poisonous trees so near a boundary line that they grow over the line, and are eaten by livestock of the adjoining landowner, would be responsible for injuries caused thereby. Obviously, poisonous trees or vines are not often encountered in highly developed suburban communities. But in rural areas they are a frequent occurrence.

Streets and Highways. A street or highway is open to the public for travel and transportation. A sidewalk is generally recognized as part of the street and may also be used by the public, even though wholly on a landowner's property. The public use of a highway or street is an easement that permits the municipality to install sewers, water pipes, and gas mains under the surface, and to erect poles to light the highway and to carry electric wires. The easement does not permit the maintenance of telephone poles, which constitute a *nonstreet* use for which the owner of the land must be compensated. The right to maintain such telephone poles is usually reserved by a provision in the deed (also discussed under "Utilities," page 389). The landowner has the right to use the street or highway along with the general public, and he also has the right of access onto the street. Municipal authorities may make any reasonable use of the street, such as resurfacing, widening the road, or changing the grade. Usually, the landowner has no right to be compensated, providing that the change has been made with reasonable care and that it does not deprive him of any land. However, should the municipality take any of his property, or erect an elevated roadway, for example, the landowner would be entitled to compensation for interference with the full use of his land.

Shade Trees. Shade trees along a highway or street are considered more or less as part of the street. But the removal of branches that overhang the street, or any part of a shade tree that may have to be removed for highway safety, may be done by public authorities without payment to the homeowner.

Parking. The homeowner has no greater right than any other member of the public to park his car in front of his own premises. Nor does he, as a general rule, have the right to restrict parking in front of his home for any reason. Thus, "No Parking" signs erected by a landowner are invalid. Local regulations that require vehicles to be parked in the driveway and not in the street are within the power of the local authorities.

Obstructions. Obstructions, such as building and construction materials, interfere with public use of the street. However, temporary encroachments of this kind for the purpose of actual construction is usually held to be a reasonable use, although in some cases a municipal permit may have to be obtained. Some communities limit the dimensions of any such obstructions into the street.

Name and Number.   The name of a street or the number of a house along a street is determined by the municipality and not by the homeowner. Usually, the homeowner has no right to change the street number of his dwelling without municipal approval.

CHAPTER 22

Zoning and Restrictions on the Use of Land

A restriction, zoning ordinance, or building code may limit the use of the land you own. The owner of a parcel of land may not be permitted to build the kind of house he desires because of such limitations. A consideration of such restrictions is important to the owner of unimproved land and to the prospective purchaser of unimproved land or an existing house.

Restrictions

A restriction is anything that limits the complete freedom of use of land or buildings. It may consist of a requirement that houses cost a specified amount of money, have only one family in residence, occupy a certain minimum amount of land, or other such provisions. Restrictions are frequently encountered; and unrestricted land or property, except for some farmland, is quite rare. Usually the restrictions do not unreasonably interfere with the proposed use of an existing house or unimproved land, but this is not always the case.

Restrictions are commonly found in the deed to the land; and they are sometimes recited, word for word, in the contract of sale which the buyer and seller sign. Occasionally a restriction will be found in a recorded, written agreement or in a will that transfers ownership of the property to a named beneficiary. In most cases, however, restrictions are a matter of public record and may be verified in the land office of the county in which the real estate is located, and in which prior deeds are filed and recorded. Restrictions that have existed for long periods of time may appear ridiculous, outmoded, or unreasonable, and their lawfulness may be open to question. For example, an outmoded limitation may require that any private dwelling erected on the property be of the value of $3,000 or more. The purpose of this restriction, many years ago, may have been to preserve the high standards of the structures erected in the particular development. However, today, such a restriction has no effect, since any substantial building would cost a minimum of several times this amount. Nevertheless, this restriction appears as a public record and affects the ownership of the land.

Obviously, the problem of restrictions is a complicated one, raising problems that only an attorney can decide for you. The title company search will reveal any and all restrictions of record, and these will be reported to the prospective purchaser on an "exception sheet." At that time, these restrictions or exceptions should be carefully considered by the prospective purchaser and his attorney.

Individual Restrictions.   In recent years developers and builders have habitually incorporated restrictions into individual deeds when selling the land under development to individual owners. The builders have found that restrictions are the most effective method of compelling lot-owners to comply with reasonable limitations affecting the use of their land, and that such restrictions help preserve the character of the new community which has been created. Each landowner may look to the developer to enforce the restrictions, and in this way legal action against a violator is probable. In the past, some restrictions violated by a landowner have not been enforced, because individuals who own adjoining land may not wish to litigate in order to compel compliance with the restriction. There is, then, some security for adjoining landowners to know that the light, air, open space, residential character, and general harmony of the community will be retained in future years, and that the builder will enforce the restrictions for them.

Any landowner may insert a restriction in the deed to land when he sells it, assuming that the purchaser will agree to accept it. A group of landowners may band together and sign an agreement restricting the use of all land owned by the group for any agreed reasonable purposes. However, as previously stated, most restrictions are placed in the deed by the builder or developer of the land. It is the developer who assembles the land, plans the buildings, and who files a *plat,* or map, of the area in the land office of the county in which the land is located. This map may contain a building line drawn on each subdivided lot, showing how close to the boundary line a structure may be built. In many states, this building line will be considered a restriction which must be observed by all those who buy lots within the tract of land. The developer may also file and record a declaration of restrictions, which becomes a public record and will affect the land purchased by anyone thereafter. Usually, as sales of the subdivided lots are made, the developer will insert the restrictions as clauses in the deed. The buyer must then recognize that the use of the land is limited by these restrictions.

A more complex problem arises when you buy a home that was built many years ago, and may have had several succeeding owners. At the time of signing the contract of sale with the seller, the prospective purchaser may not know the precise nature of the restrictions that might affect the property. To protect his client, the seller's attorney may set forth in the contract of sale the usual "catch-all" phrase: ". . . subject to any covenants, restrictions, and easements, if any, contained in prior instruments of record."

The prospective purchaser may not have any knowledge of the nature of these restrictions (and it is only after a careful search of the records that his attorney or the title company will be able to advise him of their nature). In order to prevent complications at the closing, it is advisable that the clause set forth above contains the following language: ". . . provided the covenants, restrictions, or easements do not prohibit the present structure on the premises or the continued use thereof for the purposes for which the same is presently being used."

This clause provides the prospective buyer with some protection, because if a search of the records of the county land office discloses a restriction, and the house is in violation of the restriction, the buyer may refuse to complete the sale and is entitled to a return of his down payment.

Conditions and Covenants. The restriction may take the form of a *covenant* or a *condition.* This differentiation depends solely on what occurs if the owner violates the restriction. For example, let us assume an existing restriction that the land may be used only for residential purposes, one of the most frequently used restrictions. The owner of the land attempts to build a bowling alley on the premises, an obvious violation of the restriction. However, what will happen on discovery of this violation? Sometimes (although rarely) the clause is so severely worded that the ownership of the land will be transferred to another person on such a violation, and this is known as a *condition.* Usually the prior owner states that title to the property will "revert" (be transferred) to him (or his heirs), when such a violation occurs.

On the other hand, most restrictions do not specify any penalty for a violation. If no penalty is provided, the restriction is known as a *covenant* and not a condition. Nothing happens automatically, as occurs in a condition, and affirmative steps must be taken by the aggrieved parties. In most states, covenants restricting the use of property are the rule, rather than the more drastic conditions. If a covenant is violated by a landowner, court action must be taken to compel compliance with the restriction, and the court will restrain the party violating the covenant. A court order of this type is known as an *injunction,* and it orders the landowner to cease such violation. It may also order the landowner to remove any structure that has been erected, or repair any damage committed, in violation of the covenant. Occasionally, the failure to obey a covenant affecting the land will result in a lawsuit to recover damages, but this is not the usual procedure.

Whether the restriction is in the form of a covenant or a condition may be an important consideration to a prospective mortgage lender. A mortgage-lending institution will not be anxious to lend money to a prospective borrower when there is a restriction in the drastic form of a condition affecting the property. If the homeowner violates the condition, he may lose his land and his home, and this would leave the mortgage-lending institution without security for the mortgage loan. In such a situation, the mortgage lender may ask a title company to insure it against loss of the property because of any possible future violation of the condition by the homeowner. If this insurance is given to the mortgage lender, there will be no title risk to the lender because he will be protected. A title company may insure against this kind of loss if a violation is not likely to occur (and provided an extra premium is paid).

Another way of solving this problem is to approach the interested party (who would obtain ownership of the land if the condition is violated) and ask him to release the condition by signing a written agreement to that effect. This may be accomplished with or without payment, although usually something is paid. However, if the party refuses, there is still one recourse open to the prospective landowner. He may ask the party to sign an agreement with the mortgage lender to the effect that the condition will not affect the right of the mortgage lender to foreclose on the property (if the mortgage loan is not repaid) and to take possession. In other words, the right of the mortgage lender to foreclose would then come prior to the right of anyone else to take title to the house on a violation of the condition. Such an agreement is known as a *subordination* agreement. If a foreclosure of the mortgage does take place, the condition then becomes effective; and the mortgage lender who is in possession will then be sure that the condition will not be violated.

The Use of Restrictions. Restrictions may affect the position of a building on the land or the cost or character of the building itself. A common form of restriction that affects the positioning of the building on the land is as follows: "No house or any projecting part of it, such as porches, chimneys, bay windows, and stair landings, shall be placed closer to any side or nearer a lot line than twenty feet, except that projecting cornices may be placed as close to the lot line as seventeen feet."

This form of restriction does not basically impair the usefulness of the property to the owner. However, a building lot is seldom a square piece of property. It is usually a rectangle which is deeper than it is wide along its frontage. If the owner is prohibited from building within twenty feet from the side line of his property line, it may possibly limit the usefulness of the building lot to him. The affect of such a restriction should be fully understood by a prospective buyer before signing a contract, so that he is completely familiar with the limitation of use placed on the property.

Another common restriction that may also affect the actual site where the building may be erected on the land is often worded as follows: "The main body of any residence including the attached garage . . . shall not occupy more than 70% of the width of the lot on which it is erected."

This form of restriction may be typical of an over-all plan by the developer of a tract of land, in order to preserve as much open space around the dwellings as is deemed necessary to retain the basic residential character of the community. Again, the buyer should understand this type of restriction before he signs a contract.

There may be a limitation on the number of stories or the height of any building to be erected, or on the structure's use by more than one family. A common form of restriction may provide as follows: "No building of any kind may be erected thereon except a private dwelling house designed for occupancy by a single family."

This restriction specifically prohibits any structure on the land except a dwelling house. A detached garage erected on the land would actually violate this restriction. On the other hand, a restriction that limits the use of the land to "residential purposes" would not necessarily prohibit the building of a detached garage on the premises. Of course, there is an infinite variety of restrictions which may be inserted in the deed. The exact form is usually determined by the owner of the land, who imposes the restriction before, or at the time of selling the land. The owner or developer may limit the use of the land to single-family residences, or he may require that no rooms be rented in any building erected on the premises. The latter restriction would be an attempt to preserve the residential character of the neighborhood and prevent the use of a house as a rooming or boarding house. Another common restriction is one that provides for the number of square (or cubic) feet which any structure erected on the land may occupy. This will secure to the adjoining landowners the light, air, and vision from adjacent land to which they have become accustomed. It should be borne in mind that restrictions of this type will also protect the prospective purchaser if he buys property there.

A restriction which requires that the land be used only for residential purposes excludes the use of such land for schools, boarding houses, sanitoriums, or tourist homes. However, there is usually some question as to whether an apartment house may be built on such restricted land. An apartment house is used for residential purposes and would generally appear to comply with the restriction. Normally, the community has a local law, commonly known as a "zoning ordinance," which may allow apartment buildings to be erected in certain districts of the community regardless of the terms of any restriction in a deed. On the other hand, even if a restriction does not limit the use of the land for such a purpose, a zoning ordinance may still prevent such use of the land.

Occasionally, landowners form an association to protect property values in their community and agree, in writing, to common restrictions they all desire, and which are intended to preserve land values within the community. An example of a restriction that might be used in such an instance is the following:

> No buildings, fences, walls, or other structures shall be erected or maintained, nor shall any addition to, or change or alteration therein be made, until the plans and specifications, in duplicate, showing the nature, kind, shape, height, materials, location, and approximate cost of such structure have been submitted to and approved in writing by the association.

It may be that such a limitation of use may prove to be cumbersome to enforce and would be effective only if the association of landowners has the power to purchase the land from an owner who violated the restriction. Of course the association might, if it wished, institute a lawsuit to enforce its rights.

After an owner agrees to a restriction, or accepts a deed with a restriction, it will affect the land until the time specified expires, or until a release of the restriction is obtained by agreement or a court order. It may prove to be of considerable importance to understand what happens when a restriction is violated by a landowner.

Enforcement of a Covenant. We have already considered what occurs when a restriction in the form of a *condition* is violated, that is, when the land reverts, or is transferred, to another. Usually neighboring landowners may not enforce a condition. However, there is an exception: If the condition has been imposed on the land by the builder as part of a general plan of development, most states will allow any other resident of the development to enforce the condition by court action.

Where there is a violation of a *covenant,* adjoining landowners may demand that the violation of the restriction cease and that any structure which has been erected in violation of the restriction be demolished. If the landowner does not agree, a court order enjoining such use may be obtained.

However, it is important to understand that a community may change its character over the years and that the courts tend to take notice of such changes. The "change of neighborhood" rule has been recognized in most states; and courts have been slow to curb violations of restrictions, if the restrictions no longer make good sense or seem reasonable. For example, a certain community may have been completely residential a half century ago. Gradually the neighborhood has changed, with many rooming houses, small businesses being conducted in basements, and a general encroachment of commerce. An attempt at the present time (after a half century of disregarding the covenants restricting the residential nature of the community), asking the court to enjoin any violation of the restrictions would probably be rejected. Courts will act, as a rule, only if *prompt* relief is requested.

It may be dangerous for a landowner to use the property in violation of a covenant, and take a chance that a court will not enforce the restriction. In such case, an application might well be made to the court requesting a decision as to whether the restriction still affects the property. With a court ruling in favor of the landowner, the restriction will no longer limit the use of the land.

A court will also take notice of whether other landowners in the community have observed the restrictions which are a part of the builder's general plan for an entire tract of land. If violations of the restriction are so general as to be widespread and it is obvious that the restrictions have not been observed by other landowners, the court will seldom require the landowner accused of violating the restriction to obey it. The value of restrictions may be lost by repeated violations.

Some states require that a restriction specify the number of years during which it affects the land; however, most states do not.

Unlawful Restrictions. Frequently there will be a restriction in the deed worded along the following lines:

It is an express condition of this conveyance that the premises herein described shall not be conveyed or leased to any person who is not a Caucasian and the premises herein conveyed shall not be occupied by anyone who is not a Caucasian, except servants in the employ of the owner, and that this restriction shall run with the land.

In the past, race restrictions appearing in deeds to real property were common. However, restrictions that deprive other races of equal protections under the law have been ruled unconstitutional by the Supreme Court of the United States. Such restrictions are unlawful and ineffective today, and will not be enforced by the courts. Even when they still appear, they may be disregarded.

Zoning Ordinances

Originally, zoning laws were first enacted to prevent congestion in crowded city areas, and to limit the danger of fire or explosion in populated areas. The first zoning ordinances prohibited the use of land for businesses that might cause fires or explosions. These businesses were allowed to operate only in outlying districts in the less-populated areas of the city.

Gradually, zoning ordinances became more comprehensive, and today they regulate the character of structures built within the city as well as uses of the land. The modern zoning ordinances of a large city are a complex series of local laws consisting of several hundred pages, or even more. Other limitations on the use of land within a city are contained in separate volumes known as *codes,* and these include electricity, health, and building requirements. To a lesser degree, suburban communities have also passed local laws to regulate uses of land in the community. Almost every village, town, or city has a zoning ordinance and a building code that affects the landowner. For example, building codes may regulate many standards of home construction, such as the minimum cubic foot content of sleeping rooms, the minimum height of rooms, the type of plumbing to be installed, and the ventilation and electrical requirements. Other local ordinances may limit the total height of the buildings and their uses in various sections of the community. In certain sections, only residential structures may be permitted by the zoning ordinance. In other areas, commercial or industrial uses may be allowed. If a home lies within the commercial or industrial area of a municipality, the prospective buyer should be aware that a factory, bowling alley, or store may possibly be erected near his land in the future. This will not happen if the land is zoned for residential purposes only. Other ordinances will prohibit certain uses of land in residential areas, such as for funeral parlors, garages, or gasoline stations. Such occupations are regarded as injurious to the residential character of the community and to property values. As previously mentioned, most towns, villages, and cities have enacted comprehensive zoning ordinances and building codes that affect and limit the use of land in the community. It should be understood, however, that such zoning ordinances and building codes equally act to protect the homeowner.

Although a nonconforming use may be continued (if in existence at the time the zoning law was passed), no alterations will be permitted that would change the structure of the building or add materially to it. In some states, a landowner is not even permitted to repair a structure on his land if the repairs amount to a rebuilding of the structure. The theory is that nonconforming uses of property should be gradually eliminated. However, in most states, repairs of the structure will be allowed, but no changes in the structure that would alter its purpose will be permitted.

Once a nonconforming use is discontinued, any rights terminate, and the owner may not again restore the structure to its original condition.

Effect of Zoning Ordinances. A restriction in a deed to land is not nullified or superseded by a zoning ordinance; it still remains effective. If the restriction provides that the land may be used only for a dwelling house, and an ordinance is thereafter passed by the municipality that allows commercial uses in the same area, ordinarily the landowner may still not violate the restriction in the deed and argue that the zoning ordinance has nullified or superseded the restriction. This matter can become extremely complicated.

A zoning ordinance that forbids certain specified uses of land is not regarded as a legal defect, thus permitting a buyer to refuse to take title to land. A buyer who intends to build a gas station on land which he contemplates purchasing, and discovers (after signing the contract of sale) that a zoning ordinance forbids such use of the land, may not reject title and refuse to complete the sale. Everyone who deals in real property is assumed to have investigated the local ordinances that may affect his property. In the case of a homeowner, the title company will sometimes report any important zoning restrictions. However, the most direct manner of determining whether your land is affected by any ordinances is to obtain a copy of the local zoning ordinance from the municipality. The town clerk or village attorney may advise you whether the proposed use of the land is prohibited by any local ordinance. The broker who sells the land also has a knowledge of the local zoning ordinances, although this source may not be too reliable because of his natural interest in making a sale.

A mortgage lender will carefully examine the zoning ordinances to determine whether the proposed use to be made of the land is in conformity with local ordinances. The attorney for the mortgage lender may also be helpful to you if you have any question concerning the zoning ordinances in the community. The mortgage lender will require you to observe the local zoning ordinances, because any use of the land that violates a zoning ordinance may result in a lawsuit. The mortgage lender, naturally, does not wish to endanger his security for the mortgage loan.

Zoning ordinances vary greatly from community to community. Although there have been model, standardized zoning ordinances proposed from time to time, zoning ordinances are the creatures of the municipalities which enact them. Some are quite reasonable; others border on the ridiculous. This power is almost always delegated by the state legislature to the municipality, which is presumably in a better position to analyze the needs of its community. As long as the municipality or township acts in the interest of public welfare, and in a reasonable manner, the zoning ordinance is considered enforceable. This means that if the limitations placed on the use of land bear a reasonable relationship to the welfare of the community, the homeowner must obey these limitations. Some of the more common ordinances seek to prevent the congestion of population in a particular area, expedite transportation within the community, or enforce fire regulations. In so doing, the municipality attempts to reduce the risk of fire, injuries, and the like, and in consequence the safety and health of the community is promoted. Zoning ordinances have grown increasingly important in recent years as community planning has become more prevalent. The courts generally hold that any zoning ordinances that promote public health, morals, and safety are a valid use of the police powers as delegated to the municipality. Increasingly, we find that reasonable zoning ordinances will be enforced by the courts, and the homeowner must make his decisions on that basis.

In some cases, a zoning ordinance may cause an unnecessary hardship, and the literal enforcement of the ordinance may not be fair or reasonable to the landowner. In such circumstances, a board, usually composed of the building inspectors and other municipal authorities, is set up to hear complaints from individual property-owners who feel that strict compliance with the zoning laws would be unfair to them and cause great hardship. These property-owners usually request a "variance," or modification of the ordinance as it may affect them. If their request is reasonable, the variance or modification may be granted. However, the enforcement of zoning ordinances by municipalities is often fraught with political problems, and securing a variance or modification may prove to be difficult and expensive, unless only a very minor variation is sought. In communities that have an involved series of zoning ordinances, it is usually provided that a landowner may not build on his land unless he makes application for a building permit to the municipal building inspector or commissioner. The application is usually prepared by the landowner's architect, who submits the plans and specifications for the building to the municipality for approval. The municipal official then inspects the plans and specifications to make sure that they comply with the local zoning ordinances. If such use of the land is permitted, a building permit will be issued. Should this permit be issued improperly, any other property-owner may object, and the city or town attorney may commence an action to prevent such use. If he does not do so, other interested property-owners in the community may band together and commence an action to compel the local officials to carry out their official duties in accordance with the ordinance.

The courts of the various states differ on whether an improper use may be prevented *after* the landowner has expended considerable sums of money to build, in conformity with the building permit issued to him by a city official. The landowner will claim, with obvious truth and merit, that he had the right to rely on the city official performing his duties properly. If the expenditure has been large, some courts will not compel the landowner to spend substantial additional sums to return the land to another use in order to comply with the local zoning ordinance. However, other courts have held that, regardless of the cost, the landowner must conform to the zoning ordinance, even though a building permit has been issued, and the new building may have to be torn down or drastically altered.

Building Codes. Many municipalities have adopted *building codes,* which specify in great detail the many structural requirements of any building proposed to be erected on land within the community. These requirements include the size and location of rooms, types of fireproof construction, location of windows, ventilation, electrical installations, chimneys, heating plants, plumbing requirements, etc., and even the number of windows and doors.

Before proceeding with the construction of a building on land that you own or plan to purchase, be sure to review carefully these requirements with a local architect who has a working knowledge of the municipal or township regulations. Building codes of this kind are part and parcel of the new comprehensive zoning ordinances, which are becoming increasingly complex, especially in the larger municipalities. Sometimes these codes will be divided into, for example, a building code, an electrical code, and a plumbing code. It may surprise you to learn the extent to which many aspects of the construction of a house are regulated by your municipality or township. What happens to the older houses in the community which were built before these codes became effective? Older homes of this type are examples of the "nonconforming" uses previously discussed. But any material *alteration* of an older house will also have to conform to the new ordinances, particularly when new plumbing and electric wiring are installed.

The local officials responsible for the enforcement of zoning ordinances and building codes are usually authorized to make inspections at frequent intervals while the structure is under construction to determine whether there are any violations. If violations are found by the inspector, the landowner is usually given notice of the violation and time in which to correct it. If he does not correct the violation within a certain specified time, he faces possible action by local town or city authorities to enforce compliance. If such violations exist, there is usually a time lag before any municipal action may be expected. This means that a buyer of a home should *always* request a search of the municipal records to determine whether there are any violations of record at the time that title is closed. If there is a violation, the seller should be notified and required to correct the violation at his expense before the closing. Some corrections of violations, such as rewiring the home or providing a fireproof stairway in a two-family home, require the expenditure of a considerable sum of money. This means that the closing of title may be delayed for weeks, possibly even months, unless the seller is willing to deposit a substantial amount of money in escrow to insure the faithful performance of the work required to be done.

CHAPTER 23

Utilities

There is a statutory provision in almost every state setting forth that a telegraph or telephone company, or a gas or electric corporation, may acquire such real estate as may be necessary for its purposes. This property is acquired by means of a form of condemnation proceeding, or by means of an agreement.

The method used is incidental and may vary from region to region. All of these companies are regarded by the courts as public service corporations. Inasmuch as the electric, telegraph, and telephone companies are given the use of the streets and public ways for the erection of appliances that may be necessary for carrying out their services, they are also regarded as semipublic corporations which have some of the sovereign powers of the state, including the right to acquire legally the land owned by a private individual where necessary for their public purpose.

However, unless there has been a legal *condemnation* and payment to the landowner, it has long been the law that an owner may compel the removal of a telephone wire, for example, strung above his land without proper authority, even though the actual soil has not been touched or interfered with. The owner of real property, as previously stated, owns the air space above the surface of his land and has the same right to a free and uninterrupted use and enjoyment of the space above his land as the space below. The smallness of the wire in question does not affect the case in any way, because even a small wire can be large enough to prevent the owner from building to a reasonable height on his lot. If the wire were a huge cable, several inches thick, and only a foot above the ground, there would only be a difference in degree, but not in the legal principle. Even if the wire is completely supported by posts standing on abutting lots, without touching the surface of the owner's land, the difference would still be only a matter of degree. A sheriff or city marshal will usually be empowered by the court to remove such encroachments on your land.

In most states, no matter how long a wire may be strung across your land, no rights of ownership of that space will pass to a telephone or telegraph company. There is no right of prescription. There is also no right to adverse possession against the owner of the land.

In most cases, however, it will be found that an easement has been granted by a former owner of the land or by the local government to the public corporation involved. The easement is a permanent right conferred by a landowner on the public corporation to maintain something on his land. If the easement right is granted by the local government, it is said to be a *franchise;* however, if it is a right that may be taken away at the will of the owner of the land, it is called a *license.*

A written license to erect and maintain a telephone pole, string wire, and trim trees creates an easement, and the existence of telephone poles and wires on the land has been held to be notice that the company has rights in the premises that may render the easement binding on any subsequent purchaser of the property. Usually, the laws of the various states give the telephone company the right to construct, erect, and maintain any necessary fixture for its line over or under the public roads, streets, and highways in the state. This franchise is given directly by the state to the public corporation. The exact manner of its exercise, including the location of its poles and stringing of wires, is in the control of the local municipal body and is one of the police powers given to the municipality by the state. (However, the local municipality must be reasonable in its rules and restrictions.)

In the absence of an agreement or condemnation, the permission and acquiescence of a landowner in the construction and maintenance of a telephone line across his land is a license which he may cancel at any time, and the running of time does not create a perpetual right on the part of the telephone company. If a landowner purchased his premises with an existing telephone wire passing across the newly-acquired premises (assuming no agreement), and thereafter removed it after a brief notice had been given to the telephone company, he would be within his rights. Although the acts of the landowner might be open to severe criticism, the example stresses the fact that this license may be cancelled. However, the cutting of telephone wires is a drastic action to take without proper legal guidance.

As a rule, a conference with the telephone company is a better method of procedure, and in any event, all normal efforts to have undesirable telephone wires removed by the telephone company voluntarily are far better (and safer) than drastic action by the property-owner. Taking the law into one's hands is not recommended; be sure to confer with the utility and find out what they have to say on the subject.

The telephone company is also given the right, as a rule, to cut branches of trees that belong to landowners where it is required by an existing necessity, especially when it cannot be avoided by insulating the wires or employing other practical means that may be more expensive and less convenient. In every case, the right to prune, clip, or cut a tree of a landowner must be justified by an unavoidable and existing necessity; but if the desired purpose can be accomplished without extraordinary means, no right exists in any manner to interfere with the trees. Any unnecessary mutilation of the trees will constitute a trespass for which the landowner can recover.

Telephone (or telegraph) poles and wires in and over the street in *front* of the premises are not an excuse for a purchaser to refuse title and will not make a title unmarketable. However, if a wire actually crosses the premises to be conveyed, a different rule is applied. The existence of a public highway over land that is being conveyed has never been considered to be an encumbrance of which the buyer can complain; neither is the existence in the highway of sewers, water mains, and gas pipes which are regarded as incidental to the use of the land for highway purposes. However, telegraph and telephone wires and poles that are not on the highway, and used for highway purposes, may be considered a burden on the land and their presence may render the title unmarketable. The rule varies somewhat from state to state, however.

It is usually provided by statute that a gas and electric company has the power to erect and construct suitable wires or other conductors, necessary poles, pipes, or other fixtures over and under the streets, and also through public parks and places in cities, towns, and villages, under reasonable regulations set forth by the local municipality. Such utilities may acquire the necessary real estate, even though owned by private individuals, for its corporate purposes, in a manner prescribed by the condemnation laws of the state. The construction and use of surface pipes, conduits, ducts, or other fixtures in, over, and under any trees, highways, or public places necessary for its corporate purposes are considered to be public uses and purposes.

Furnishing light to a municipality is for the public use and benefit, and municipal authorities usually grant a franchise to a local company for such purpose. Lighting has been held to be an important aid to promoting the convenience, as well as the safety, of the traveling public; and the private landowner who owns land to the center of the street is not entitled to be paid for such use. However, the electric light and power companies have no rights in privately owned walks.

Usually, the statutes of your state will provide that any officer or agent of a gas or electric corporation, duly authorized by the corporation, may, at reasonable times, upon exhibiting written authority signed by an officer of the corporation, enter any house supplied with gas, electricity, or water by the corporation, for the purpose of inspecting the meters, pipes, or fittings, and for supplying, repairing, or regulating the supply of gas, electricity, or water and of ascertaining the quantity of gas, electricity, or water used.

Water Supply. In various states, local municipalities have provided for the creation of water districts and for the construction and maintenance of water works, wells, reservoirs, or basins for the purpose of supplying residents of certain water districts with water for domestic and commercial uses, and also for protection against fire. For the landowner, water bills that are in arrears for 30 days or longer are often subject to a penalty, usually amounting to about 10% of the amount due. If water charges are not paid, the water supply may be cut off approximately 60 days after the date when due. When a water main is constructed along or under the street, an assessment is often made in which each landowner abutting (touching or facing the street) must pay his proportionate share of the cost of building the water main.

Water meters are usually installed to measure the quantity of water used by the landowner, and he is charged accordingly (unless it can be shown that the meter is not correctly registering the flow). A water rate as determined by a meter is neither a tax nor an assessment, but is an obligation to pay based on a contract between the landowner and the water company. For this reason, a tenant living on the premises and using water must pay for it as he would for the gas and electricity. However, charges made by private water companies for furnishing water are not liens on real estate, and water may not be shut off for nonpayment of charges unless it is against the owner in possession for water furnished to him. Therefore, a new owner of property who accepts conveyance of land on which the water charges have not been paid cannot have his water supply cut off for nonpayment. Water rents which are due to a private water company or to a municipality may, however, by statute, become a lien on real property. Even though the lien is not equal or superior to tax lien, it will still take precedence over a prior recorded mortgage.

CHAPTER 24

Home Improvements

Every year twice as many American families buy older or previously occupied houses than they do new houses. Before buying an older house, make sure that the house you choose is a good buy. Too often the buyer of an older house finds that what originally appeared to be exactly what he wants and needs is nothing more than a millstone around his neck. Hidden costs of repair may abound and should be thoroughly checked. Inspection services (today becoming more and more widespread) may be your best protection against costly blunders. A house riddled with termites may cost you thousands of dollars in repairs, especially where damage has extended to the main beams of the house. Such damage may not be recognized in a cursory inspection, and very often not even on careful inspection. Only an expert can obtain the necessary information for you.

Not every old house is a bad risk. There are advantages in purchasing an old house. They contain nearly twice as much space as a new house in the same price range, and there are at least twice as many older houses than new houses for sale, which gives you a wider choice and a greater opportunity to make a good buy. Further, it may even be cheaper to maintain an old house than to maintain a new one. An example of the saving involved is the tax rate. In a new neighborhood the tax rate in the community will probably increase as more buildings are completed in the neighborhood. In an older community, the tax rate will probably be relatively stable and will not show any marked increase over the years. Because older houses are more difficult to sell than new ones, you may be able to make a better bargain. And older homes frequently have a charm and graciousness lacking in new, efficient streamlined houses.

Of course, there may be differences between certain sections within the same town or village. If the neighborhood seems to be changing into two-family houses, rooming houses, or other multifamily units, perhaps you should avoid buying there. The chances are that real-estate values will be on the downgrade. Remember that the location of your house is probably the most important factor in its market value, both now and in the future. With this in mind, you should check the location of schools, churches, shopping and recreational centers, and transportation facilities.

Avoid buying a house more expensive and larger or more lavish than other houses in the area. It will almost certainly prove more difficult to sell in future years, because prospective buyers will usually favor the less expensive houses in the community.

There are many things you should consider before purchasing an old house. Avoid, as a general rule, a house with only two bedrooms even though it may be ideal for your own purposes. Considering the size of the average family, you may have difficulty in reselling any house with less than three bedrooms. A big drawback is an inadequate kitchen or bathroom. These will usually account for the largest expenses of repair. The kitchen area should be at least 12' x 10', and conveniently located. A bathroom (except a guest bathroom) should be reached without having to go through another room to reach it. (The FHA will refuse a mortgage on some houses unless the main bathroom can be reached from every room without having to go through a second room.)

Although professional inspection services are not always unavailable, in many cities and towns you can hire a reliable real-estate appraiser to obtain the market value of the house. He should be a member of the Society of Residential Appraisers or the American Institute of Real Estate Appraisers. However, not all real-estate appraisers are experts in structural or mechanical details. The building officials in your county will usually be able to furnish names of reputable dealers who will provide you with a proper inspection.

Both the FHA and the VA will inspect a house from the standpoint of property value. But they do not probe deeply for structural defects other than septic tank or termite checks. The mere fact that they are willing to make a loan is not proof that the house is in satisfactory condition.

Another means of checking on your prospective home is to determine the exact year in which it was built. This may give you a general idea of the quality of a house, although admittedly many houses do not conform to the average for any particular year. For example, a house built during the 1920's may mean trouble. Many houses built in these years were inadequately wired and had a poor type of heating and plumbing installation. Extensive repairs, often of a structural nature, may be required.

After the FHA was created in 1934, houses were generally built to conform to government standards. By the late 1930's, copper and brass pipe and automatic heating were specified. The houses built in 1940 and 1941 had even higher standards. However, from 1942 throughout the war years, many inferior houses were built because of war shortages. Many of these homes were intended only for temporary housing.

Any house more than 25 years old will probably require extensive repairs at some time during the tenure of your ownership. This is the greatest potential drawback in buying an old home. The heating systems in houses more than 25 years old are always suspect. They are often in doubtful condition at best, especially when a coal furnace has been converted to oil or gas. The water tanks may last only another 5 or 10 years and have to be replaced. The pipes in houses more than 25 years old should be carefully checked. Remember also that in houses more than 15 years old, you will probably not find proper insulation. Asphalt shingle roofing, used on most of the houses in this country, has an average life of 20 years in the cooler northern climates and about 10 to 15 years in the South; these roofs may have to be replaced.

All of these possible defects should not deter you in your search for an older house if this is what you want. There are many advantages in the ownership of an older home; one of the most important is the fact that you may be able to buy it at a saving that will compensate you for any improvements you may have to make. If you are mechanically inclined and like to putter around the house, an older house may be ideal for you. The decision is yours. A rule of thumb might be: If the house is over 25 years old, set aside $5,000 for the repairs that may be required during the first few years of occupancy.

Before you decide on what repairs are required and how much you should pay for them, make yourself aware of the abuses and rackets which unfortunately abound in the home-repair field. Congressional and legislative investigations have revealed many home-improvement rackets. The fast-talking home-repair contractors who engage in fraud and deception on the unsuspecting homeowner can cause you much aggravation and excessive expense.

The fact that you may obtain a home-repair loan (with as much as 84 months to repay at low rates of interest) and the fact that the FHA sponsors this home-improvement loan will not necessarily protect you. Banks rarely make an inspection of the completed work, and they usually make only a cursory check of the contractor whose time-payment papers are submitted to the bank for discount and payment.

A few years ago the FHA tightened up its rules on inspection of home improvements, but there is still no requirement for a final inspection of the work done. This means that you are still on your own to a great degree. The FHA does have a list of firms whose work has been so poor or charges so great that they have been barred from doing any FHA-approved work. However, this will not prevent an unscrupulous contractor from operating under a different name or moving to another community. There are now more than 7,000 names on the FHA blacklist, and the list is growing every month. If you have doubts about any contractor in your community, ask the FHA to furnish you with this blacklist so that you may see whether this contractor is on the list.

The cost of home improvements in the United States is estimated to be in excess of 10 billion dollars a year. Long-term loans (up to 7 years to repay) are available to the homeowner who seeks to improve his premises. Since it is the policy of the governments, both federal and state, to encourage home ownership by private individuals, loans may be made for this purpose at your local bank at low rates of interest. Very often, contractors will suggest that the improvement may be paid for over a period of years. What is not usually mentioned is that such installment contracts carry a high rate of interest. It will usually be found that bank loans, particularly if made in conjunction with a home mortgage, are lower than those offered by the contractor.

There are of course some precautions you should take before you commit yourself to a contract for home improvement.

The most important question is whether the contractor or supplier with whom you are dealing is completely reputable and responsible. Check with your local Chamber of Commerce or Better Business Bureau (if there is one) or consult your local bank. The contractor will undoubtedly have an office in your locality; and you may obtain the names of other homeowners he has worked for, in order to find out whether they have been satisfied with the contractor's work.

It is always advisable to obtain several bids to determine the approximate cost of the improvement to your house. When a contract is submitted to you, read it carefully. Never sign a blank form, and never allow the work to begin until the specifications of the work to be performed and the exact price are agreed to *in writing*. It is always important to determine whether the contractor has liability and workmen's compensation insurance in sufficient amounts so that you will not be held responsible for any injuries to the men at work or visitors during the period while the work is being done. Make sure that the contractor agrees to hold you not liable for any claims made by persons who claim injury or property damage as the result of the improvements that are being made. An insurance certificate to this effect should be furnished to you before the work actually commences.

It is always advisable to obtain identification of any employee of a contractor before letting him come into your home; authorized employees and local building inspectors always carry such identification.

Recently, a number of instances of home-improvement rackets have been exposed in various areas. In almost every community there are responsible home-inspection consultants who, for a reasonable fee (usually less than $50) will inspect your home to determine what repairs may be necessary. Avoid the high-pressure salesman who tells you that the offer will be withdrawn if you do not agree immediately to his price.

Most important, you should avoid making any decision to sign a contract, without first reviewing it carefully. When salesmen call at your home and tell you that they have been passing by and saw the condition of your house, and that certain improvements are badly needed, don't jump at the bait. This is especially true when accompanied by statements that their workmen are employed in the vicinity and that it would be very little additional trouble for them to come over and begin work on the improvements.

Unless there is an obvious emergency, it is usually wise to call in a consultant from a responsible firm to verify that such a condition actually exists and that repairs are needed. You may then shop around with responsible contractors in your community to determine the best price. If you follow this procedure, you will not be enticed into an unfair contract with an unscrupulous contractor or salesman, and waste large sums of money for improvements of inferior quality and poor workmanship.

Remember: always get a *written, firm* price for the work to be done. It should contain a statement that there will be no extra charges unless you order it *in writing* and agree to pay an extra amount. This is most important, for in recent years many homeowners have agreed to pay a moderate and reasonable amount for certain home improvements; then, later, they have received fantastically high bills for "extras" and "finer" materials.

CHAPTER 25

Selling Your Home to Buy Another

Increasingly the United States has become a nation of home-owners. The latest Census Bureau report shows that more than 60% of all American families live in homes of their own. Before these families can buy another home, if they wish to do so, they must consider the problems involved in disposing of their old one. It would not be advisable, or in most cases possible, for them to maintain payments on the old home in addition to those on the new one.

Eventually they would receive the money paid on the principal of the mortgage, but double payments would temporarily have to be made. This would create a financial burden that most families cannot afford; and even for those who can afford it, it is undesirable.

A Question of Timing

One difficult problem in selling one house and buying another is the proper timing of giving and receiving possession. Naturally, you do not wish to move out of your old house until you can move into the new one. The person who buys your house will often have a similar problem. He will want you to provide a definite date in your contract of sale stating precisely when he is legally entitled to possession.

This problem does not always have a simple solution. If you buy your new home before you sell your old one, you will probably have two mortgages on which to make payments, a burden you may not be willing (or able) to assume. Although part of your payments on the old house are for principal, you will also have to pay interest, taxes, insurance and other expenses.

Moreover, if you sell your old house first, you will have no place to live, unless you are fortunate enough to find a buyer who is willing to wait.

What is the solution? There is no perfect way in which to protect yourself, but the best way is to avail yourself of a trade-in plan. Even the trade-in plan has its disadvantages as well as advantages, and you may not wish to use it; but it does solve the frustrating problem of proper timing.

Tax Advantages for the Homeowner

Fortunately, the tax laws give the home owner a tax advantage. If you sell your home and buy another *within a year before or after the sale,* you can—if you follow the tax rules—postpone (often indefinitely) paying tax on any profit you make on the sale. Without such a rule, it would be difficult to move to another house that better suits your needs. Because of postwar inflation, many older homes are selling for more than they cost when new. If prospective purchasers had to pay the federal government a tax on the profit and then buy another home at today's higher prices, they would find it difficult or impossible to buy a new house.

Fortunately the federal government is interested in seeing that more new houses are built, and therefore encourages new house purchases by permitting this tax advantage.

It is not necessary to know all the technicalities of the tax law in order to understand the tax advantage. If you follow the steps outlined below, it will not be necessary to pay a tax. However, if for any reason you are in doubt, consult your accountant or your attorney before you sell.

1) You must buy the new house within one year *before* or *after* the sale of the old one. This can be done only once a year, so do not plan on buying and selling more than once in one year. If you have owned your present home less than a year, be sure to consult your tax adviser before you sell. You may have to pay a tax not only on the profit from the sale of your present home, but also on any profit from the sale of a previous home (a tax you avoided by buying your present home within a year).

This tax advantage applies only to the sale of your "principal" residence. You do not receive it if you sell your summer or vacation home and replace it with another summer home or a year-round residence. If you own more than one home, be sure to consult your attorney to ascertain whether the house you are selling will be regarded as your principal residence. The problem is often difficult to decide; do not attempt to determine it by yourself without legal advice.

If you want to build a new home rather than buy one already constructed, you will receive the same tax advantage. But there are certain differences to be remembered. First, actual construction of the building must *commence* within a year after the old house is sold. If you fail to move in within 18 months, the entire tax on the profit made on the old house will have to be paid. Also if your house is not completely finished, the actual costs expended in construction during the 18-month period may be deducted for tax purposes from the gain realized on the sale of the former house.

A second important point to remember is this. If you plan to build a new house (and have just sold your old one) be sure to consult an attorney first. Have him include a penalty clause in your contract with the builder, so that you will not suffer a loss if he fails to complete the house within your 18-month deadline.

To avoid the tax entirely, the new house must cost you at least as much as you paid for the old one. If it does not, you will have to pay a tax on the difference.

In figuring what you paid for the old house, include not only the cash paid, but also the amount of the mortgage. You can also add the costs of improvements to the house (but not repairs), as well as the expenses you incurred when you bought it (attorney's fees, surveys, etc.).

In computing the amount received for the house when you sell it, selling expenses, such as a broker's commission or an attorney's fee, may be deducted. As in the case of buying, you also include any mortgage on the house as part of the sale price.

Note that if you now own a two- (or more) family house and want to buy a one-family (or another multifamily house), you get the same tax benefit on that portion of the profit attributable to the house you use as a principal residence. For example, assume that you own a two-family house originally purchased for $25,000 and occupy one of the two identical apartments. You sell the house for $35,000. The selling price for the part you used as your own apartment is $17,500 (half of $35,000) or more, and you do not pay a tax on the residential portion of the house you sold. You will, however, have to pay a tax on the profit for the other half, just as you would on the sale of any business property. If you buy a second two-family house, and occupy one of the apartments, you get the same tax treatment if the apartment you occupy costs you at least $17,500. Let us consider some problems involved in fixing the correct sales price on a house to be offered for sale, and hiring a real-estate broker.

Setting a Selling Price. Naturally, you want to get as good a price as possible for your house. But do not make the mistake so many homeowners do of setting an unreasonable price on the house. This holds true both for the asking price you set and the actual selling price you are willing to take.

Asking Price. Most buyers expect you to ask more for your house than you are actually willing to take. As a result, you will have to set a price higher than you realistically expect to receive, because if you ask the correct figure, most potential buyers will offer a lower price. But do not set the asking price too high. Most buyers are comparison shoppers, and if your asking price is too high, compared to those being asked for other homes, they will feel it is not worthwhile to undertake what may be an arduous bargaining process. While there's no set rule, your asking price should be about 10% to 12% higher than the amount you actually expect to receive.

Evaluating Your Home. The prices of older houses are not determined by any one formula. For the average homeowner, the best method is the same one used at the time of original purchase, the comparison method. Look at the houses in your area advertised for sale in the newspapers. They will generally mention an asking price; then pick out those in a comparable price range to your own. Take the time to visit them, and compare their advantages with those of your own home. Except in some subdivisions, no two homes are exactly comparable. Give yourself a plus for those features in which your home excels and a minus for those features in which the other houses are superior. After visiting three or four you can get a fair idea of what you should ask with the reasonable expectations of receiving. But be sure to be scrupulously honest and candid with yourself in evaluating your house's good and bad features.

Next pay a visit to several real-estate brokers who do business in your area. Even if you don't hire them, they can tell you the prices at which comparable houses are selling in the market. Be sure to see more than one broker. By doing so, you receive more than the benefit of their collective experience—it helps you judge them. It will also help you to find the occasional broker who will suggest an unreasonably high price for your house in order to make you think he can obtain a better price than any other broker. He does so because he anticipates that he will make you reduce your price when you find that your house cannot be sold at the inflated price. He is to be avoided. It should be emphasized that he is the exception rather than the rule. Most brokers will suggest a realistic price, not very far from the closing price.

Be sure also to visit some new houses in the course of construction in your area. They are competing with your house for prospective buyers who will inevitably draw comparisons between the new houses and yours. You cannot expect to get as much for your older house as a new house comparable in location and size will bring. The new houses, however, more or less set the upper limit on your working price. You will probably have to settle for about 15% to 20% less for your older house that offers substantially the same amount of space, and possibly even less if your home is not in first-class condition. All of these computations are based on the supposition that the old and new houses are reasonably comparable (this includes land values as well as house value). It is not necessary to discount the value of your land, as is the case with the value of the house itself. Of course, the selling price includes both; but you can easily break that down by comparing the price of vacant land in the area.

Hiring a Broker.   If you hire a broker, you will have to pay him a commission. Generally speaking, the amount of the brokerage commission will be the same regardless of whom you hire—5% to 6% of the selling price, depending on the area where your house is located. What do you get for your money?

Most of all, a good broker can help you determine what your house is actually worth. He is more familiar with the real-estate market than anyone else, and he knows the going price for comparable houses. He will point out actual comparative sales that have been made recently in your community, and thus pinpoint more closely the proper price for your house. He will know the other houses on the market (both those listed with him and those offered for sale by other brokers).

In most instances, your broker will pay for the cost of advertising your house. He bears the expense whether he ultimately sells the house or not, and thus relieves you of this burden. He, or his salesman, will always be available to show your house to prospects, which saves your time. You will also save the time you would normally waste showing the house to the curiosity-seekers who like to look at homes offered for sale even though they have not the slightest intention of buying. Your broker will also have a list of prospective purchasers. These potential buyers will ordinarily enable him to sell the home faster than you could on your own.

Your broker can also help a prospective buyer to obtain a mortgage. Unless the latter obtains a satisfactory mortgage, he probably will not be able to buy your house even if he likes it and agrees to the price. The broker is familiar with financing methods and knows the mortgage lenders in the area.

The Three Kinds of Listings. Many newspaper and magazine articles purporting to give advice to sellers and buyers mistakenly state that there are two kinds of listings: exclusive listings and open listings. Actually, there are three: the exclusive right to sell, exclusive agency, and open listing. Your rights and obligations are different under each type.

Exclusive Right to Sell. This gives the broker an *absolute* right to his commission if he actually sells the house during the listing period, or if another broker sells the house during the period or if *you sell it yourself.*

Exclusive Agency. This differs from the exclusive right to sell only in that you reserve the right to sell your house yourself without paying him a commission. You do, however, agree that you will not hire another broker during the listing period, and will pay him his commission if you sell through another broker.

Open Listing. As the name implies, this means that the listing is open to everyone. You agree to pay the broker a commission if, and only if, he sells the property, but you reserve and retain the right to hire another broker or brokers and to sell the house yourself.

Which type of listing is best for you? The broker, naturally, prefers first, the exclusive right to sell, next the exclusive agency, and last the open listing. But what the broker prefers is not always best for you. There is no hard and fast rule. The decision must be yours.

The open listing is the one under which you retain the greatest control over the sale of your property. But it also has its drawbacks. The broker who has one of the two types of exclusive listings will be willing and anxious to make an all-out effort to sell your house. He will be willing to spend more for advertising, especially under an exclusive listing. He will feel sure that his time spent on prospects and money advanced for advertisements will not be wasted, because another broker may possibly produce a buyer before he does.

Most important of all, he will not (out of fear of losing his commission) be afraid to bring the property to the attention of other brokers. As a rule, brokers are willing to cooperate and split the single commission you pay among themselves. That gives you the advantage of having several brokers, each making a determined effort to make a sale of your house.

In some areas, local real-estate boards have formed cooperative groups and created a multiple-listing service. If a broker belongs to such a group, he must bring your listing to the attention of all other brokers in the group. However, these multiple-listing services demand that the listing be an exclusive right to sell listing. So if you want the benefit of such a service, you will have to sign an exclusive right to sell listing.

Does a listing have to be in writing? The law varies from state to state, but an increasing number of states require a written agreement. Even where an oral listing is permitted, it is not desirable nor is it recommended. Your legal rights should not depend on an unwritten agreement, and may result in a misunderstanding between you and the broker. Most good brokers will urge you to sign a written agreement, and you should do so.

Warning. The prepared form agreement that you will be asked to sign will usually favor the broker, because it is prepared for him. Again, see your attorney before signing.

The usual listing agreement (and that refers to an open listing as well as an exclusive one) provides that you will pay a commission when the broker finds a buyer for you who is "ready, willing, and able" to perform, that is, to buy your house at the specified price. It reads correctly, at least on the surface. But there is a legal problem involved. In most states, if the broker brings you a buyer who is willing to pay your price and you say you are willing to sell, the courts rule that the broker has performed his contract and is automatically entitled to his commission. But suppose the buyer then goes out looking for a mortgage and is unable to obtain one large enough to finance the purchase of your house. The deal then falls through. Under the ordinary form contract, you would still have to pay the broker his commission. Your lawyer can protect you with a clause in the contract that states you are not liable in this situation. But bear in mind that this is merely one possibility, out of many that may occur.

Another common situation proves the importance of obtaining

competent legal advice. An agreement is signed with a broker which provides, "No payment shall be due until title passes."

A buyer is produced by the broker and accepted by the seller, but the buyer fails to obtain the mortgage, and the deal falls through. The broker claims his commission. You may think you are protected; title has not passed and the agreement provides that you are not liable until it does. Some courts, however, have held that you are liable. Their reasoning is to the effect that the clause refers merely to the *time* of payment of the commission and does not affect your liability. So, say these courts, you have to pay a commission. This instance shows that law can be a complex matter for the layman.

Most important, you must recognize that it is a serious problem to try to sell one house and buy another more or less simultaneously. Many homebuyers have become involved in difficulties that could easily have been avoided had they considered the problems beforehand. Often, it's enough to *know* the problems, even though you do not know all the answers.

In the contract of sale and purchase, you can protect yourself to a limited extent by computing in advance dates for possession and putting it into writing, with the advice and assistance of your attorney. You will need such a clause both in selling your house and in buying another. For instance, your attorney can protect you by including a penalty clause if you do not gain possession on the date agreed on. This will at least pay your expenses if the seller does not give you possession on the date promised.

But your attorney can only help you; he cannot solve all your problems. Here are some added pointers that may assist you in making plans.

Always assume that it will take you a minimum of 60 days to find a buyer; 90 days (or even longer) is probably a much safer margin. We are assuming that you have priced your house reasonably, at a figure which is comparable to those of similar houses in your neighborhood. Experience proves that a house so priced will *generally* sell, in a normal real estate market, within 60 days, and almost always within 90 days. But remember the word "generally"; there is no absolute assurance that you will find a buyer within that time. Recently, stock market fluctuations have become increasingly important; and it is often difficult to sell houses when the market is depressed, probably due to the fact that most stockholders dislike disposing of their stocks if they have to sell at a loss.

Trade-In Plans

To solve this vexing question of timing, some builders and brokers have worked out what are popularly called trade-in plans. You trade in your old house for another, much as you trade in an old automobile toward the price of a new one. Fundamentally, the idea is simple enough; anyone who has traded an automobile is familiar with the general procedure. But buying or selling a house is a more complicated business than trading in an automobile.

Home trade-in plans are of three types (plus some variations):

1) *The Straight Trade-In.* This greatly resembles the automobile trade-in. The builder or broker buys your home and credits you with its value toward the new one. Unfortunately, there are few such plans available. Most builders and brokers either cannot (or do not wish to) assume the financial burden of buying your house in order to sell you another. It ordinarily requires much more of an investment than they are prepared to make.

2) *The Contingent Trade-In.* The builder or broker agrees to sell you the house you want if, and only if, he can sell your house within a certain number of days. Such a plan, if the price is right, is satisfactory. But most brokers avoid this type of trade-in, because the broker cannot complete the sale of your prospective new house until they find a buyer for your old one and he cannot sell the new house to anyone else until the 60 or 90 days he has to sell your old home have expired. This is not a satisfactory situation for most sellers or builders who operate on limited capital.

3) *The Guaranteed Trade-In.* This, the most popular type, is the one generally offered by those builders or brokers who have trade-in plans. Under this plan, the broker guarantees to buy your home himself at a stated price unless he sells it within a certain number of days (generally 60 or 90 days). You agree to buy the home he wants to sell.

As you can see, any of these trade-in plans solves the question of timing. You can, by properly drawn possession clauses in your contracts, have a substantial measure of protection. However, this ready solution presents its own built-in problem: the price you have to pay for it. If a builder or broker takes your house in trade, he will have to resell it; and that, in turn, costs him money. What is more, he will have to make payments for interest, taxes, and insurance as soon as he takes it over, in addition to the cost of the money he invests in your house. As a businessman, he has to figure these costs when he offers to take your house in trade.

A study of most trade-in plans operating today shows that the costs—which you are asked to pay—run from 15% to 20% of the price you both agree the house is worth. Since a straight sale through a broker will cost you either 5% or 6%, you are paying a high price for the assurance that the timing of the sale is right. The added cost to you is at least 10% and may be as high as 15%.

The picture of trade-ins is not, however, quite as dark as it seems. Under the contingent trade-in plan, the high costs are paid only if your home is not sold within the specified time of 60 or 90 days. If it is sold before that date, you pay only the normal 5% or 6% commission. Even if it is not sold, you can provide that you do not have to sell it. It merely guarantees that you *can* sell it, if you want to, at the guaranteed, fixed price. In other words, you are assured of a *minimum* in case all other alternatives fall through.

But it is very important to bear in mind the fact that you have definitely committed yourself to *buy* another house. You must be prepared to take the minimum price if your old house is not sold within the specified time, unless you can afford to carry the financial burden of owning two houses until you sell your old one.

A final word of advice on trade-ins: Don't let a broker or builder "sell" you on the new home (and fix the price) before you establish a price on the old one. It is an old psychological selling device to make the new product so desirable that you forget about what you have to pay for it. Automobile salesmen prefer not to talk about trade-in price until they have made you want the new car they are selling. Real estate dealers use the same psychology. They "sell" you the new home before they get down to the bargaining on the price of the old one. Do not get your heart set on a new house until you've talked price on the old. For example, if your present house is valued at $15,000 the cost on a trade-in may be an *extra* $1,500, or possibly even more, on top of a normal commission of about $750.

Of course, it is always possible that an individual builder or broker will offer a better financial deal than has been outlined. This may be due to the fact that he needs cash, always a pressing problem with builders. The market for the sales of houses may be slow, which makes it important for him to make a deal. But it is extremely likely that it will cost more than if you sold your home without a trade-in, either with or without the help of a broker. In any event, pay strict attention to the costs, and compare them with a straight sale before you sign a trade-in contract.

CHAPTER 26

The Cooperative and the Condominium

Since the 1930's, the federal government has played a key role in the construction of housing. With the encouragement of the federal government (and some state governments), a remarkable increase in home-ownership has resulted since the second World War. Many former apartment dwellers have moved into their own homes as a result of the federal housing program. In recent years the federal government has attempted to bring the same benefits which it has accorded to owners of private homes to the apartment dweller. To accomplish this, Congress has extended mortgage insurance to apartment owners in cooperatives and condominiums on much the same terms as those available to the purchaser of a single-family home.

Of course, most state and federal encouragement has favored low- or medium-cost housing, but there has also been a great spread of cooperative ownership in luxury housing. There are certain important differences between a cooperative and a condominium. And these will be discussed later in this chapter. But in both cases it involves the private ownership of a particular apartment within a multiple-family dwelling.

Cooperatives

In recent years the ownership of cooperative apartments has become widespread. Existing apartment buildings have frequently been converted into cooperatives, with individual apartments sold to the tenants. Cooperative apartment buildings have been built, in addition, with FHA financing or with conventional bank financing.

The appeal to the public rests primarily on the fact that a tenant, by becoming the owner of a cooperative apartment, obtains certain deductions from federal and state income taxes for his proportionate share of taxes and interest paid by the cooperative corporation. The tax reduction substantially and effectively reduces the net yearly rent or carrying charges and often makes the cooperative apartment an economical investment in preference to conventional renting. Most cooperatives, in effect, offer a 2% or 3% net return on the required investment through the tax deductible features alone. This return is even greater when it is compared with that received from the same money invested in stocks or bonds where all dividends and interest must be reported for tax purposes.

The comparison between the tax position of the owner of a cooperative and that of a tenant is the most pertinent reason for the popularity of cooperative housing today, particularly among those people in the higher income tax brackets. The inflation in value of many cooperative apartments, together with the tax laws, constitute an incentive to middle and upper income groups. Another feature that appeals to such owners is that the price of the apartment in a cooperative development may often be partially paid by a mortgage loan exactly as in buying a private home.

Let us consider cooperative ownership in a specific case. If the owner of a cooperative apartment has an income of $25,000 per year, and pays $200 a month for the carrying charges of his cooperative apartment, he may have an offset of as much as $100 per month for his share of the taxes and interest on the mortgage paid by the cooperative corporation, as well as the interest on his own mortgage. This may be worth $50 a month to him in monies saved from taxes (assuming, for round figures, the 50% tax bracket for federal and state taxes). In this manner his rent is reduced to approximately $150 a month or a 25% reduction. Taxpayers in higher brackets usually take more expensive apartments and pay more maintenance per month, in which case the tax saving is even greater. At the same time, a part of the monthly carrying charges is used to reduce the mortgage, and the owner obtains an equity or a monetary value in his apartment.. A tenant who rents his apartment pays a monthly rental and never obtains an equity in it. At the end of his lease, he has obtained no tax advantage and has no ownership whatsoever.

Usually, the proportionate share of real estate taxes and interest paid by the cooperative corporation depends on the number of shares of stock which the tenant-owner owns in the cooperative corporation, and its relationship to the number of shares of stock of the cooperative corporation that are outstanding. For example, if there are 1,000 shares of stock issued by the cooperative corporation, and the owner of an apartment owns 50 shares of stock, he is entitled to deduct 1/20 of the taxes and interest paid by the cooperative corporation during the course of the year. This information is supplied to the owner at the end of each calendar year.

In order to take advantage of the income tax benefits there must be only one class of stock outstanding in the cooperative corporation, and the stockholders, as tenant-owners, must be the source of at least 80% of the corporation's gross income for the taxable year. As this requirement is vital, inevitably this provision is complied with.

The price you pay for the shares will depend on the relative value of your apartment compared to the other apartments in the building. For instance, if you want a 2-bedroom apartment, you will be required to buy more shares than someone who wants only a 1-bedroom apartment. The total price of all the shares will cover the value of the apartment house over and above the mortgage. In that way, it's something like the down payment you make on a home.

But there's one big difference between the mortgage you get on your home and the mortgage on a cooperative. The cooperative mortgage covers the *entire* apartment house. Since it's usually for a very large amount, you wouldn't want to buy shares if you were personally liable for its payment. That's why you are *not* personally liable on the mortgage; the lender makes the loan to the cooperative corporation, and does not require the tenant-owner to guarantee payment. The lender looks only to the value of the property for his assurance of repayment, not to the tenant-owners.

If you decide to purchase a new cooperative apartment, you will be offered a purchase agreement describing the apartment selected, the number of shares that will be issued to you in the cooperative corporation, the total purchase price, and the method of payment. A cooperative *proprietary lease* which has now become standardized, is given to the tenant. It usually provides, among other clauses, that there will be no assignment or subletting without the written consent of the cooperative management (usually a board of directors), and it may limit the tenant's liability for the principal of the mortgage to his share in the cooperative corporation. Usually very few changes (sometimes none) may be made in the proprietary lease; it is offered to the prospective owner-tenant on a take-it-or-leave-it basis.

Most important, the proprietary lease provides that the tenant-owner shall pay his proportionate share of the expenses of the corporation, based on the number of shares he holds and the number of shares of the corporation outstanding. There is usually a maintenance charge for each share owned by the tenant-owner, and the tenant-owner has the obligation of repairing, redecorating, and painting his own apartment. It is important to bear in mind that the board of directors of the cooperative may raise or lower the monthly carrying charges as it sees fit, based on the recent expenses of the cooperative corporation.

Here are some of the points that should be investigated before purchasing a cooperative apartment.

The monthly maintenance charge should be at least 40% below the rental value of each unit. This includes about 15% to cover items, usually included in rents but now paid by the tenant-owner, such as decorating, shades, venetian blinds, refrigerator and stove maintenance. It includes the 25% of the monthly rent which in a conventional building might be profit to the owner.

The next matter of interest to a prospective tenant-owner is how much of a mortgage can be obtained on the purchase of a cooperative apartment, if required. In the new FHA-financed cooperative apartments, a mortgage of as much as 80% of the value may be obtained. However, in buildings that are converted to cooperatives the amount is usually limited to ⅔ or perhaps 70%. Sometimes only 50% will be loaned, and in many expensive New York City cooperatives, no loan arrangements are made; the purchaser is expected to pay cash in full.

In some cases, the sponsor of the cooperative will take back a second mortgage at 6% interest on a buyer's individual apartment, thus reducing the amount of cash the tenant-owner will have to pay. In such cases, the tenant-owner usually deposits his stock in the cooperative corporation in escrow with the sponsor until he pays off the purchase-money mortgage. The interest paid on this mortgage may also be deducted from the tenant-owner's taxes.

Since each tenant-owner must pay his share of the carrying charges of the cooperative, the probable expenses of running this type of property must be analyzed by each prospective tenant-owner. The total carrying charges divided among all the tenant-owners should be approximately as follows (based on a nation-wide average):

The mortgage charges, including interest and amortization, should be approximately 20% of the total expense.

The real estate taxes should be approximately 20% of the total expense.

The payroll should approximate 40% of the total expenses (in a building with considerable service).

Miscellaneous expenses will probably make up the final 20%. For example, if the tenant-owner were to pay carrying charges of $400 per year a room for a 5-room apartment, or $2,000, $400 of this would be for mortgage charges, $400 for real estate taxes, $800 for the building payroll, and $400 for all other operating expenses. The payroll feature is highly variable. Some luxury cooperatives may have 20 employees on the payroll. In other cooperatives, the accent may well be on economy, and a superintendent may be the sole employee. Between these two extremes, there may be a considerable degree of variation in the total payroll.

The prospective tenant-owner should make sure that if the new cooperative is under construction, he is assured of completion and that it has the necessary mortgage commitments, together with a performance bond which will assure that any down payment made by him to the sponsor of the cooperative is protected.

Once in the apartment, it is only natural that the tenant-owner of a cooperative will take a much greater interest in the operation of the property than a tenant in a rented apartment building. The tenant-owners, being stockholders, have a right to attend all meetings of stockholders (although not necessarily of the board of directors) and to hear reports by the cooperative manager as to problems of operation. The tenant-owner is also entitled to receive periodic financial statements and copies of tax returns as filed by the cooperative sponsor. A budget of estimated income and expenses should be prepared by the cooperative manager (or board of directors) together with recommendations for improvements and modifications that will result in savings to the corporation.

As previously mentioned, a tenant-owner should be aware that the carrying charges paid each month are not the equivalent of rent. They may vary from year to year, depending on the total carrying charges incurred by the cooperative corporation. If there is less than 100% occupancy and the number of tenant-owners decreases, the proportionate share of the carrying charges of each tenant-owner will become greater. The tenant-owner should therefore seek a provision in the proprietary lease that he may terminate the proprietary lease upon notice if he cannot find a buyer for his stock. If the assessments become too high, the tenant-owner can, with this clause, move from his apartment without incurring additional charges, although he will thereby lose his ownership.

The same income tax rules that apply to selling a house also apply to selling a cooperative. If there is a gain on the sale, no tax need be paid providing that the seller purchases a new cooperative apartment or house within one year following the sale of his principal place of residence or commences building a new house within that one-year period and occupies it within 18 months following the sale. You should remember that if your share of the cooperative mortgage is allocated to you by the cooperative, this mortgage share is part of the price that you paid for the cooperative and should be included. For example, if you paid $12,000 for your cooperative apartment, and there was an existing mortgage on the building for $500,000 and the cooperative had 50 owners, your mortgage liability would be $10,000 (the mortgage liability) totals $22,000, and this is the total cost.

If a share of the cooperative mortgage has been allocated to you, there should be a provision in the proprietary lease and the mortgage that there is no personal liability on the part of the tenant-owner in the event that the cooperative mortgage is foreclosed against the building itself.

Selling Your Cooperative Apartment. In a "profit" cooperative, you can sell your shares for whatever price you can obtain on the open market. Because of rising building costs, many resales have been made at prices often twice as high as the original purchase price. The profit goes to the shareholder, not to the cooperation. However, in order to protect the other tenants, the board of directors must approve the purchaser. This provision, although it is, in effect, a restriction on the sale of your stock, also protects you against the sale by another shareholder to an undesirable tenant. You can also sublease your apartment; but again, as in the case of sale, the board of directors must approve the sublease.

In a "nonprofit" cooperative, the tenant stockholders do not have the same freedom of sale. If you want to sell your shares, you are generally required to offer them to the board of directors. If the board of directors decide to buy, the price is generally set at the price you originally paid. If prices have gone up in the meantime, you would have to pay a great deal more for another apartment or home that is comparable to the one you are selling.

Condominiums

The latest type of ownership in a multifamily dwelling, which may become as popular in the future as the cooperative is at present, is the *condominium*. The Housing Act of 1961 permits mortgage insurance for the owner of a unit in a multifamily structure. Such ownership includes the co-ownership of common areas and facilities, and commercial or community facilities, if any, that serve the apartment building in which the individual unit is located.

The whole concept of the condominium is that space occupied by the individual owner can be owned independently from the surface of the ground. The condominium owner, in effect, is the owner of a sector of space. Each proprietor owns the walls bounding his own apartment with the upper and lower occupants owning the roof and ground jointly. Coupling the ownership of the apartment with the joint ownership of all the common areas within the building eliminates the need for various easements, because any occupant of an apartment can make full use of the common facilities. A unified control is therefore possible, with an equitable sharing of the expenses and some assurance that a state of repair and maintenance will be maintained throughout the entire building.

To insure the owners of the buildings some choice as to their future neighbors, a first right of refusal is granted to the other individual owners. This right lapses, however, within a short period after the seller produces a prospective buyer. The prime motive is not financial protection as it is in a cooperative, but rather a desire to choose one's own neighbors.

Usually this first right of refusal is contained in the enabling legislation passed by the state legislatures. In general, the courts have upheld restriction on the powers of cooperative housing corporations which are more severe than those contained in the usual condominium statute. In a New York case involving a cooperative where the sale was forbidden without the consent of the board of directors or ⅔ of the stockholders, the court held that the restriction providing that "the residential nature of the enterprise included the privilege of selecting one's own neighbors and the needs of the community are not to be ignored." At present, cooperative owners have almost a complete right of selecting their prospective neighbors. How this principle of law will be applied to those who claim they have been refused on a religious or racial basis is not yet known. For the moment, the cooperative may refuse any prospective tenant without giving a reason.

The word condominium is a strange one to most Americans. It is a type of ownership which very much resembles cooperative ownership, but with certain basic differences. There is no corporation, and no shares are issued. The owners actually take title and receive a deed to a particular apartment (rather than receiving shares in the cooperative corporation), just as if they were buying a house. Together with the owners of the other apartments in the condominium, purchasers become co-owners of all the common property, the land, foundations, lobby, halls, stairways, etc.

This type of ownership, well-known in Europe for many years and now popular in South America and Puerto Rico was almost unknown in the United States until 1961, when the Housing Law of 1961 permitted the Federal Housing Administration to insure loans on condominiums.

A condominium has another outstanding advantage over a cooperative. In a cooperative, there is a blanket mortgage for a large sum covering the entire cooperative property. Shareholders must pay their proportionate share of the monthly payments of principal, interest, and maintenance. In a condominium, the owners of each individual apartment may arrange for as large or small a mortgage as they require, and thus control to some extent the monthly expenses they have to pay. This important advantage leads into another vital point. In a cooperative, if one tenant-owner fails to meet his payments, the others must take over the defaulted payments. In a condominium, an owner is responsible only for his own mortgage, not for those of other owners.

The prime advantage of the condominium over the traditional cooperative is its simplicity. Unlike the traditional cooperative, the unit owner retains the characteristic independence of a home owner; and his ownership is not dependent on his neighbor's solvency. He may pay off his mortgage or refinance, independently of his neighbors, depending on his own personal circumstances. Under a cooperative, a unit owner is restricted on resale of a share to losing money or breaking even, since the by-laws (except in luxury cooperatives) usually grant the corporation an option to purchase the stock at book value. The condominium owner, although subject to a first right of refusal, will receive, even if the right of refusal is exercised, the offering price of a willing buyer. The condominium is thus most attractive to retired couples and the newly married.

The condominium also offers advantages if the site has good commercial value. Federal regulations specifically allow part of the building to be devoted to commercial use; and if this is a part of the common area, the expenses of maintaining the building can be defrayed by income from a store. In a cooperative, if this income received is 20% or more of the gross collections, the individual shareowners lose their right to deduct the proportionate share of the interest and taxes paid by the corporation.

Index